Take the Essential Quick Refer **with you wherever you go for F**

MW01612063

THE ESSENTIAL
quick reference

VIRTUAL BOOKLET
8TH EDITION

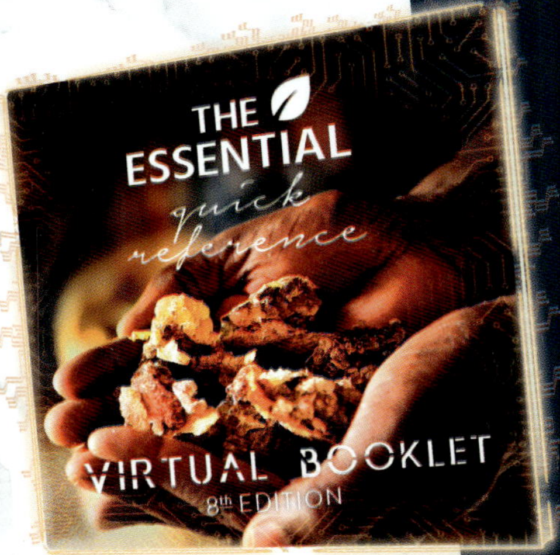

Do you love the Quick Reference guide? Sign up for a **FREE** account to our virtual book platform and receive a **complimentary virtual copy** of the Quick Reference Guide.

Scan to sign up and get your free virtual copy!

wellnessnook.life/free-veqr

ation or any
e effects of
ndorsed or
In fact, it is
otherwise
atment in
ensed and

essential
a specific

medical
om the
ntained
lication
lishing,
mation

es of
. The
ng is
...ng is a third-party
...blends, supplements, and other products produced by doTERRA, Inc.

BROUGHT TO YOU BY:

wellnessnook

OILLIFE.COM

TABLE *of* CONTENTS

Chapter 1

INTRODUCTION TO ESSENTIAL OILS

"Health is a state of complete physical, mental, and social well-being and not merely the absence of disease or infirmity."
(Constitution of the World Health Organization)

HOW TO USE THIS GUIDE

Welcome to Essential Oils Made Simple! This book serves as a basic guide to using essential oils safely and effectively—so if you're new to essential oils, you're in the right place. Here's a brief explanation of the sections of this book and how to use them.

INTRODUCTION

Learn what quality essential oils are, where they come from, and how to use them safely and effectively. Gain a basic understanding of the Wellness Pyramid, which shows how a combination of a healthy lifestyle habits and proper medical care can help you achieve and maintain health.

AILMENTS/PROTOCOLS

Quickly look up an ailment or condition and find a protocol with specific instructions for support. Discover how essential oil & wellness pyramid recommendations can work together to provide in-depth solutions along your health journey.

NATURAL SOLUTIONS

Become familiar with individual essential oils, essential oil blends, and supplementary products. Discover common uses, properties, and safety recommendations.

WELLNESS & LIFESTYLE

Learn principles that will help you establish a foundation for proper health. Discover which natural solutions can support you as you develop healthy lifestyle habits. These chapters correspond with the Eat Right, Exercise, Rest and Manage Stress, and Reduce Toxic Load steps of the Wellness Pyramid.

WELLNESS & HEALTHCARE

Learn about taking more responsibility for your overall health, become more informed about preventative health measures, and understand how to develop a relationship with medical professionals for a proactive approach to medical care. These chapters correspond with the Informed Self-Care and Proactive Medical Care steps of the Wellness Pyramid.

WHAT ARE ESSENTIAL OILS?

Essential oils are chemical compounds extracted from plants. These compounds give a plant its distinctive scent, help protect the plant, and can even play a role in pollination. They are found in the leaves, flowers, bark, stems, roots, resin, and seeds of plants. An essential oil is composed of hundreds of these chemical compounds and various concentrations of them give each essential oil distinctive qualities and healing properties.

HOW DO ESSENTIAL OILS WORK?

Because each essential oil varies in its chemical makeup, the aromas and benefits of each oil are also unique. For example, Lavender oil includes compounds that help reduce anxiety and tension, soothe irritating skin conditions, and promote more restful sleep. Frankincense oil, when taken internally, supports your immune and nervous systems, and promotes healthy cellular function. Essential oils have dozens of benefits to help you physically, mentally, and emotionally in your daily life.

VOLATILE AROMATIC COMPOUND

You may have heard the term "volatile" used when describing essential oils. Volatile simply means that these small, organic molecules tend to quickly change from a liquid to a gas at room temperature. When you first open a bottle of essential oil, you instantly notice the aroma and can typically smell it even from some distance.

WHY QUALITY MATTERS

The purity and quality of an essential oil is directly related to the benefits it can provide. Each essential oil has a specific mix of compounds, like ingredients in a recipe, that provide its unique effects. To be truly pure and therapeutic grade, we want the oil to have all the "ingredients" that are supposed to be there (with nothing that doesn't belong). A truly pure essential oil is 100% free from synthetics, additives, or harmful contaminants that can provoke adverse effects or even sickness.

Developing quality essential oils begins with cultivating the specific species of the plants that provide the most profound therapeutic benefit, nurturing them in the most favorable environment, and carefully harvesting and transporting the plant material for processing.

After the plant material is processed and the essential oils distilled or extracted, each oil should be immediately tested for its chemical composition, tested *again* at a production facility, and tested a third and final time as the oils are packaged into bottles we use as consumers. Each of these tests ensures the essential oil is free from contaminants.

Each round of testing should involve multiple tests:

- Testing involving the human senses—sight, smell, taste, and touch

- Testing for bio-hazardous microorganisms, such as fungi, bacteria, viruses, and mold

- Testing to ensure compounds are present in the proper amounts

- Testing the potency and consistent quality of a batch of essential oil

- Testing to ensure no synthetics or heavy metals are present

ARE THE BEST ESSENTIAL OILS ORGANIC?

No—they are "beyond" organic. Not only are the highest quality oils certified to be free from any foreign substances like pesticides, herbicides, or synthetics, they also have the correct chemical constituents in the proper amounts.

HOW TO USE ESSENTIAL OILS

Aromatically

APPLICATION

- *Inhale* directly from the bottle.
- *Place* 1-2 drops in your palms, rub them together, and inhale from cupped hands.
- *Wear* your favorite essential oil as a personal fragrance.
- *Use* a diffuser to continuously disperse essential oils throughout a room.

BENEFITS

- *Improves* and manages moods.
- *Provides* invigorating or uplifting effects as well as calms and soothes.

Topically

APPLICATION

- *Apply* directly to the bottoms of the feet.
- *Combine* with a carrier oil, such as fractionated coconut, and apply directly to an area of concern.
- *Massage* essential oils with a carrier oil on the back and along the spine.

BENEFITS

- *Offers* localized benefits to an area of concern.
- *Absorbs* easily and can enter the bloodstream to support the entire body.

Internally

APPLICATION

- *Place* 1-2 drops under the tongue.
- *Drink* 1-2 drops with a glass of water.
- *Add* to a gelatin or vegetable capsule.
- *Use* in your favorite recipes.

BENEFITS

- *Provides* most potent method of use.
- *Addresses* internal conditions most effectively.

SAFETY NOTE:

Some oils are not safe to ingest, such as oils from the needles of trees and some bark oils. Check the label to see if an oil is safe for internal use.

SAFETY/DILUTION

ESSENTIAL OIL *safety*

Labels

Pay attention to any warnings on essential oil packaging.

Areas to Avoid

Avoid putting oils into or near the nose, inner ear, eyes, broken skin, or other sensitive areas.

Dilution

To minimize skin sensitivity, dilute oils using a carrier oil. The suggested dilution ratio is one drop of essential oil to five drops of carrier oil. Popular carrier oils include fractionated coconut oil, avocado oil, and jojoba oil.

Strong Oils

Essential oils with a strong chemistry should always be diluted before topical application. This includes oils like Cassia, Cinnamon Bark, Clove, Oregano, Thyme, and others.

Sun Sensitivity

Some essential oils may pose a risk for sun sensitivity (particularly citrus oils). Avoid direct sunlight or UV rays for at least 12 hours after using these oils on the skin.

Safe Storage

Make sure to store essential oils out of reach of children. Keep oils away from excessive light or heat.

Supervise Young Children

Aways supervise essential oil application with your children. Always dilute oils before applying them to a child's skin.

ESSENTIAL OIL DILUTION

= drops	Adult		Child	
	Ideal Amount	24 hr Max	Ideal Amount	24 hr Max
Aromatic	—	—	—	—
Internal (capsule)	2 - 4	12 - 24	1 - 2	3 - 12
Internal (in water)	1 - 3	4 - 18	0	0
Topical	3 - 6	12 - 36	1 - 2	3 - 12

REFLEXOLOGY

Reflexology is the application of pressure to the feet and hands with specific thumb, finger, and hand techniques without the use of oil or lotion. It is based on a system of zones and reflex areas that reflect an image of the body on the feet and hands with the premise that such work creates a physical change to the body.

EAR REFLEXOLOGY

Ear Reflexology is a simple and efficient way to relieve stress and pain by applying minimal pressure to the reflex points on the ear. Each ear contains a complete map of the body, rich with nerve endings and multiple connectors to the central nervous system. For example, if the reflex point for the bladder is tender, the body may be in the beginning stages of a bladder infection. One can take preventative measures to head off the bladder infection by applying an essential oil to the reflex point on the ear followed by minimal pressure.

To begin treatment, start at the top of the right ear and slowly work your thumb and forefinger along the outer edges. Hold each point for five seconds before continuing to the end of the earlobe. For best results, repeat this procedure at least five times. Next, work the inner crevices of the ear using the pointer finger and applying minimal pressure. Repeat the procedure on left ear. If any areas in and around the crevices of the ear are sensitive, consult the ear reflexology chart to pinpoint the area of the body that may be out of balance.

This is a great technique to use personally, on family or friends, as well as with those whose hands and feet are not accessible for hand and foot reflexology. Young children are especially receptive to having their outer ears worked on, finding it calming and soothing.

Foot   Leg   Hip Thumb Hand (Palm) Finger

Sciatic Nerve
Anus
Genitals
Ureter
Prostate
Bladder
Rectum
Intestines
Pancreas
Stomach
Esophagus
Trachea
Liver
Heart
Lung
Head
Nose
Eye
Cheek

Kidneys
Abdomen
Wrist
Lower Arm
Elbow
Gall Bladder
Chest
Upper Arm
Clavicle
Shoulder
Spine
Spleen
Neck
Upper Jaw
Tongue
Lower Jaw
Mouth
Inner Ear
Tonsils

FOOT REFLEXOLOGY

Foot Reflexology is an effective method to bring the body systems into balance by applying pressure to specific places on the feet. Hand reflexology can be utilized in a similar manner. The nerves in the feet correspond with various parts of the body; thus, the entire body is mapped on the feet, telling astory of emotional and physical well-being.

One way to find imbalances in the body is to massage all the areas noted on the foot reflexology chart and feel for triggers or small knots underneath the skin. When a trigger is found, apply an essential oil to the respective location on the foot and continue to massage the trigger until it releases. Another way to use reflexology is to address a specific ailment. For instance, if a person has a headache, locate the brain on the foot chart and the corresponding point on the foot. Apply an essential oil of choice and massage the pad of the big toe to reduce tension. If a person has a tight chest induced by stress, locate the lungs/ chest on the foot chart and the corresponding point on the foot. Apply an essential oil of choice followed by a medium to light circular massage on the ball of the foot.

The autonomic nervous system is then engaged, helping toalleviate symptoms and heal the body naturally.

RIGHT PALM

LEFT PALM

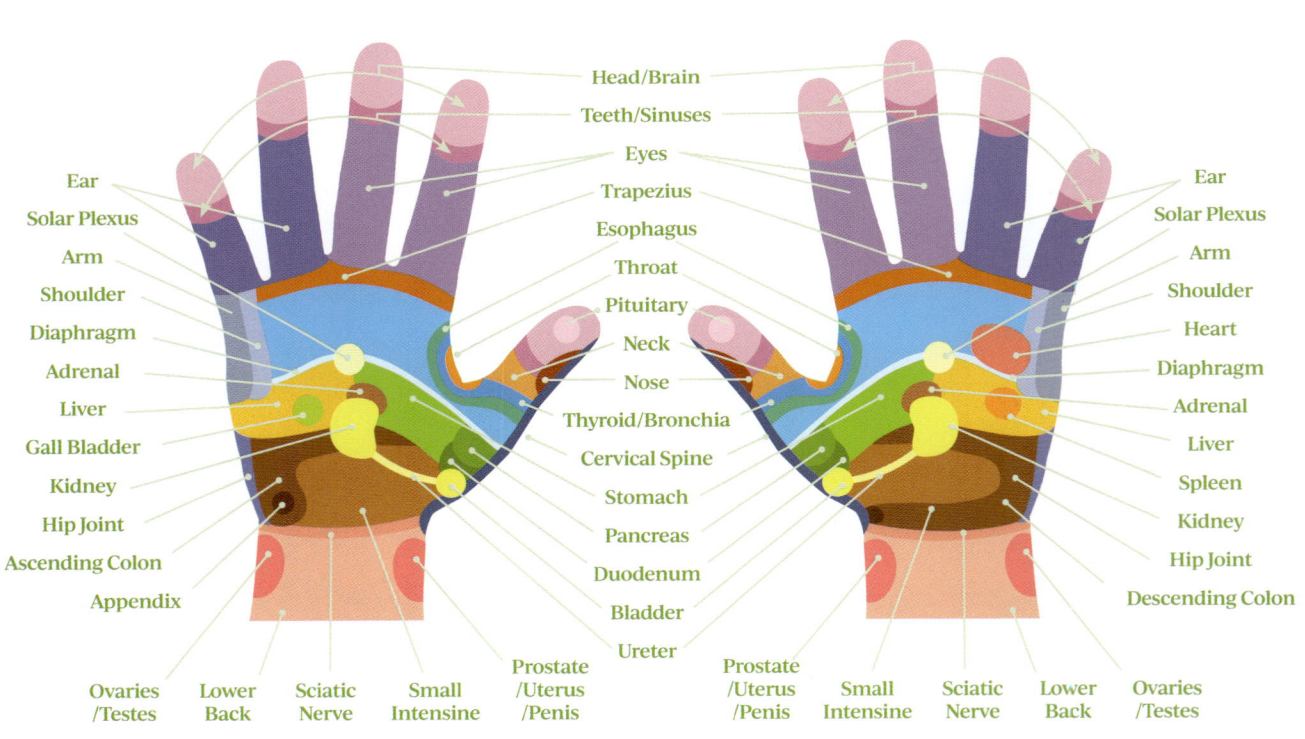

Head/Brain
Teeth/Sinuses
Eyes
Trapezius
Esophagus
Throat
Pituitary
Neck
Nose
Thyroid/Bronchia
Cervical Spine
Stomach
Pancreas
Duodenum
Bladder
Ureter

Ear
Solar Plexus
Arm
Shoulder
Diaphragm
Adrenal
Liver
Gall Bladder
Kidney
Hip Joint
Ascending Colon
Appendix

Ear
Solar Plexus
Arm
Shoulder
Heart
Diaphragm
Adrenal
Liver
Spleen
Kidney
Hip Joint
Descending Colon

Ovaries
/Testes
Lower Back
Sciatic Nerve
Small Intensine
Prostate /Uterus /Penis

Prostate /Uterus /Penis
Small Intensine
Sciatic Nerve
Lower Back
Ovaries /Testes

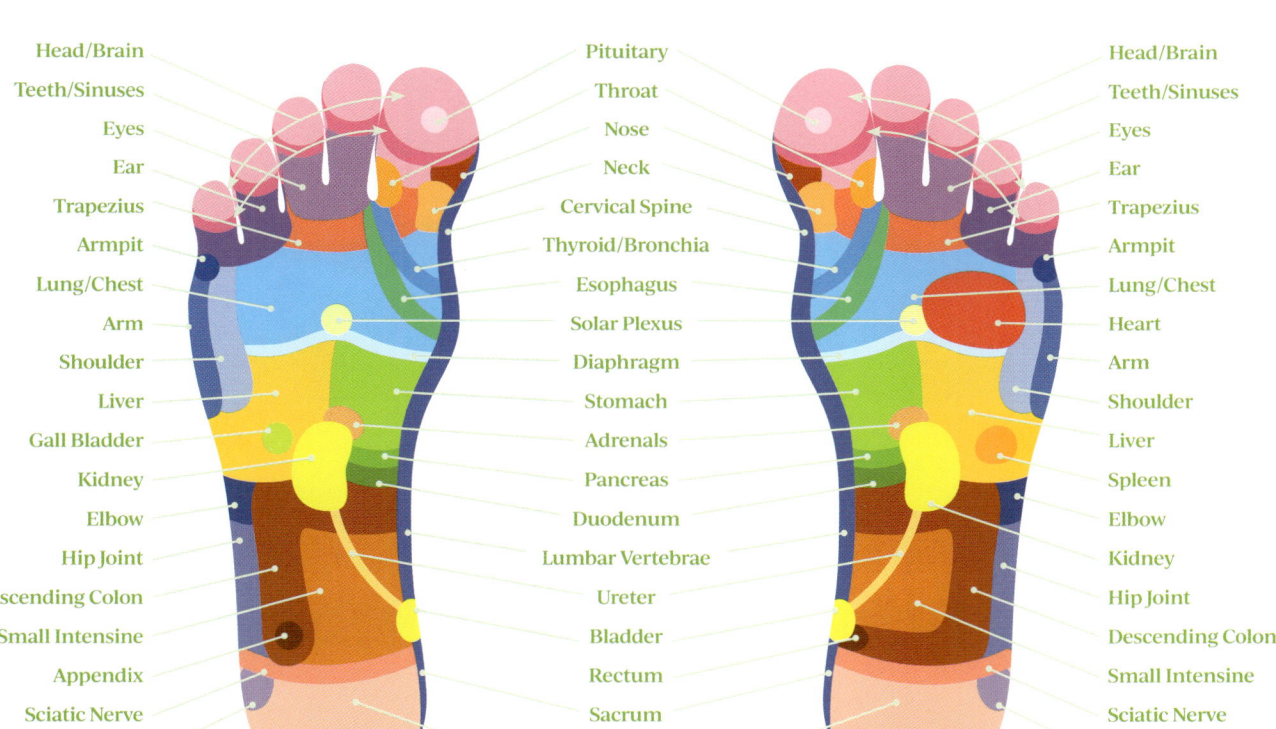

RIGHT FOOT

LEFT FOOT

Head/Brain
Teeth/Sinuses
Eyes
Ear
Trapezius
Armpit
Lung/Chest
Arm
Shoulder
Liver
Gall Bladder
Kidney
Elbow
Hip Joint
Ascending Colon
Small Intensine
Appendix
Sciatic Nerve
Knee

Pituitary
Throat
Nose
Neck
Cervical Spine
Thyroid/Bronchia
Esophagus
Solar Plexus
Diaphragm
Stomach
Adrenals
Pancreas
Duodenum
Lumbar Vertebrae
Ureter
Bladder
Rectum
Sacrum
Lower Back
/Gluteal Area

Head/Brain
Teeth/Sinuses
Eyes
Ear
Trapezius
Armpit
Lung/Chest
Heart
Arm
Shoulder
Liver
Spleen
Elbow
Kidney
Hip Joint
Descending Colon
Small Intensine
Sciatic Nerve
Knee

THE WELLNESS PYRAMID

PROACTIVE MEDICAL CARE

SELF CARE

REDUCE TOXIC LOAD/ HEALTHY HOME

REST & MANAGE STRESS

MOVEMENT & METABOLISM

EAT RIGHT/PROPER NUTRITION

Healthcare

Lifestyle

Essential oils can provide amazing benefits for your health and wellness. In order to achieve optimum wellness, essential oils should be used in combination with healthy lifestyle behaviors and proper medical care. We know many chronic diseases can be prevented by lifestyle modifications, so we can take individual responsibility to prevent chronic disease. We can choose to participate in holistic, self-directed healthcare by following the principles in the lifestyle focused Wellness Pyramid.

LIFESTYLE

Eat Right/Proper Nutrition. At the base of the Wellness Pyramid, you will find the foundation of wellness—eating right. Fueling your body with healthy, nutrient-rich foods is critical to ensure that your body's processes are operating effectively. Efficiently supports a foundation of health. Targeted supplementation can maximize your daily nutrient intake, support your digestion, and optimize your gastrointestinal tract.

Movement & Metabolism. Staying active and strong with regular exercise strengthens the muscles and supports the lymphatic, circulatory, immune, and cardiovascular systems (to name a few). Essential oils and supplementation can ease tension and promote greater energy and flexibility.

Rest and Manage Stress. Proper sleep and rest give our body the opportunity to renew and repair. Sleep is an extremely important part of our lives; however, most people either do not get the proper amount of rest or their rest lacks quality. Stress is an inevitable, unavoidable aspect of living life, and—in moderation—is good for us. However, we encounter problems when chronic perceived stress becomes a constant in our lives. Research shows 80% of health problems are estimated to be the result of persistent stress, so learning how to manage stress is pivotal. Essential oils and specific supplements provide dynamic support for getting consistent quality sleep, balancing your emotions, and managing stress.

Reduce Toxic Load/Healthy Home. From the moment we are born, we are slowly bombarded with toxic chemicals, in small doses, from various sources. These chemicals have been shown to cause damage to our bodies over a long period of time. Days, weeks, months, and years go by with the same daily habits and exposures. This can certainly add up.

Just as nature experiences cycles of cleansing, renewing, and releasing, our bodies also benefit greatly from similar seasons to counteract the constant, continual bombardment we experience as we navigate daily life. Essential oils and supplements are perfectly designed for supporting the body's natural pathways of detoxification.

MEDICAL CARE

Informed Self-Care. You can practice informed self-care by using natural solutions as the first line of defense in support of your body's various organ systems. With a trusted essential oil protocol book—such as this one—you will increase your understanding and application of the possibilities you have at your fingertips.

Proactive Medical Care. Lastly, it is vital to develop a relationship with a trusted medical professional. This allows you to be proactive instead of reactive about necessary medical care, which is one of the foundational pillars of lifelong health.

HOW TO USE THIS BOOK TO SHARE OILS

Using essential oils and natural solutions in your lifestyle naturally creates a desire to share your positive experiences with others. It's always better to help people find a solution rather than just providing it for them. Use the resources in this book to help them find solutions as you share samples, address concerns, and teach classes about essential oils.

1 *Giving someone a sample is a simple and effective way* of introducing them to essential oils. Samples you give should target a specific need or interest and should be focused on an ailment you can easily assist.

2 *After providing the sample,* show them the detailed page for that oil in the singles and blends section of this book. Share the top uses for the oil and provide instructions for use.

3 *Take a picture of the essential oil or blend* detail page, and text it to them for a reference.

4 *Remember* to follow-up!

ADDRESSING A CONCERN

1

It is always better to help people find answers to their health concerns instead of just providing it for them. Use this book to help guide them to their answers. Start by asking what concerns they or their family have.

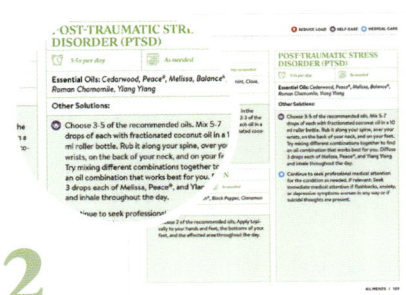

2

Look up the concern or condition in Chapter 2 Ailments/ Protocols and read through the protocols together.

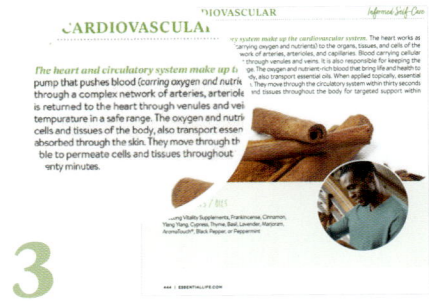

3

If the condition is not listed in the protocols, discuss what systems of the body are affected by their concern or condition. Review the relevant systems in Chapter 8 Self-Care to find recommended solutions.

4

Consider looking up each recommended essential oil or other solution in the detailed pages of Chapter 3 Natural Solutions.

5

Take a picture of the entire protocol and any desired detail pages, and text it to them as a reference.

TEACHING A CLASS

Teaching a class about essential oils can be exciting, and a little scary. Your method of teaching a class may follow a predetermined script or be unique to you. Whatever format you choose, you can use this book as a resource for the class.

USE THE *Introduction* TO TEACH:

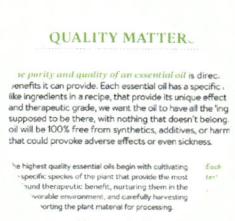
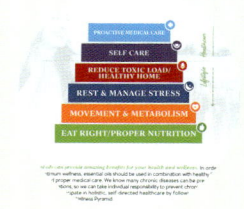

What are essential oils?

How to use them safely

Why quality matters

How essential oils work best with when combined with lifestyle changes

USE THE *Ailments & Protocols* SECTION TO:

USE THE *Singles, Blends, & Supplements* CHAPTERS TO:

Show class members how to look up a concern or interest

Find out which essential oils and natural solutions will support concerns

Look up information on any essential oils shared with class members

Discover recommended solutions for any concerns or interests of the participant

Find out additional top uses of the recommended oil and how to use them safely

AILMENTS / PROTOCOLS *Chapter* **2**

ABSCESS *(Tooth)*

3-5x per day	**While symptoms persist**

Essential Oils: *Clove, Tea Tree, Thyme, Frankincense*

Other Solutions: *On Guard® Natural Whitening Toothpaste, On Guard® Mouthwash*

 Brush your teeth morning, evening, and after meals with On Guard® toothpaste. Use On Guard® Mouthwash. Choose 2-3 of the recommended oils and apply 1 drop of each to the affected tooth throughout the day until you can visit with your dentist.

Make an appointment with your dentist right away.

ABUSE TRAUMA

3-5x per day	**While symptoms persist**

Essential Oils: *Forgive®, Frankincense, Peace®, Adaptiv™ (3-part system), Lavender, Hygge™*

Other Solutions: *Adaptiv™ Capsule, Serenity® Softgels*

 Put 1 drop of Frankincense under your tongue morning and evening. Take 1 Adaptiv™ Capsule per day. Mix 5-7 drops each of Forgive®, Peace®, and Adaptiv™ in a 10 ml roller bottle and fill the rest with fractionated coconut oil. Rub over your heart, down the back of your neck, behind your ears, and under your skull. Rub on the bottoms of your feet morning and evening.

Aim for light to moderate exercise 4-5 days per week. Adopt an exercise program that combines aerobic exercise, strength training, balance exercises, and joint flexibility exercises. Listen to your body and rest as needed. Warm up, cool down, and stretch for each exercise session.

Place 1 drop of Lavender or Serenity® on your pillow at night. Take 2 Serenity® Softgels before bed. Diffuse 3 drops of Hygge™ to create a cozy and comforting environment for yourself. Develop a good bedtime routine that feels relaxing to you. Find a hobby or meditation program. Schedule self-care rituals throughout the week that make you feel good. Seek professional attention if necessary.

ACID REFLUX

⏰ **3-4x per day as needed**	📅 *Ongoing while symptoms persist*

Essential Oils: *DigestZen®, Peppermint, Celery Seed, Ginger*

Other Solutions: *DigestZen® Chewable Tablet*

 Rub 2 drops of DigestZen® over your stomach area. Add 1 drop of Peppermint to a glass of water and drink. Take 1 drop each of Celery Seed and Ginger in a capsule 2-3 times per day.

🍏 Pay attention to your acid reflux symptoms after eating the following foods, and avoid them if they cause your symptoms to worsen: high-fat foods, tomatoes, fried foods, alcohol, citrus fruits, chocolate, onions, garlic, spicy foods, and coffee. Take smaller bites and chew your food slowly, 25-30 times per bite. Chew 1 DigestZen® Chewable Tablet as needed up to six per day to combat acid reflux.

❤️ Wait 1-2 hours after eating before you exercise. Rub DigestZen® and Peppermint over your stomach area before exercise. Maintain a healthy weight as extra pressure on your abdomen puts pressure on your stomach.

🌙 Don't lie down after a big meal. Put 1 drop of DigestZen® over your stomach and elevate the head of your bed or use a wedge pillow to prop yourself up from the waist up while sleeping.

➕ If you have difficulty swallowing or if you have pain while swallowing, especially solid food or pills, contact your doctor right away.

ACNE

⏰ **2-3x per day as needed**	📅 *Ongoing while symptoms persist*

Essential Oils: *HD Clear®, Tea Tree, Lavender, Sandalwood*

Other Solutions: *HD Clear® Foaming Face Wash, HD Clear® Facial Lotion, Sensitive skin carrier blend, Lifelong Vitality, DigestZen® TerraZyme®, PB Assist®+, DDR Prime® Softgels, Zendocrine® Complex, GX Assist®*

Wash your face or the affected area in the morning and evening with HD Clear® Foaming Face Wash, apply HD Clear® over the acne, and apply HD Clear® Facial Lotion over your face or the affected area. If you don't have HD Clear®, make a roller bottle with 7 drops each of Tea Tree, Lavender, and Sandalwood and fill the rest with sensitive skin carrier blend. Wash your face or the affected area with a toxic-free cleanser morning and evening, apply the roller bottle over the acne, and follow up with a toxic-free skin lotion.

Eat a variety of fresh fruits and vegetables. Avoid greasy foods, chocolate, refined foods, excess sugar, corn syrup, fried foods, and dairy products. Take Lifelong Vitality supplements twice per day. Take 2 DigestZen TerraZyme® with meals. Take PB Assist®+ once per day.

Wash your face or the affected area with the recommended solution before and after exercise to prevent clogged pores. Apply makeup as usual (if desired).

Avoid using toxic products on your skin. Roughly 60% of what you put on your skin gets absorbed into your body. Makeover your home by using the Abōde™ line of cleaning products, laundry pods, dishwasher pods, surface cleaner, and dish soap. Take care of your hands with Abōde™ Foaming Hand Wash and Lotion. Do a 30-day cleanse for your body 4 times each year (*you can do this each season*) to keep your skin and other organs functioning properly. For the 30-day cleanse: take 2 DDR Prime® Softgels with meals; take 1 Zendocrine® Complex with morning and evening meals; take 1 Zendocrine® Softgel with meals; take 1 GX Assist® at morning and evening meals for days 10-20; take 1 PB Assist® with meals on days 20-30. Take inventory of products you put on your skin and remove any toxic products from your home.

ADD/ADHD

⏰ *3-5x per day*	📅 *Ongoing*

Essential Oils: *Adaptiv™, InTune®, Balance®, Hygge™*

Other Solutions: *Lifelong Vitality, DigestZen TerraZyme®, PB Assist®+, Serenity® Softgels, Adaptiv™ Capsules*

♡ Rub InTune® down the back of your neck, behind your ears, over your wrists, and on the bottoms of your feet. Mix 5-7 drops each of Adaptiv™ and balance in a 10 ml roller bottle and fill with fractionated coconut oil. Apply to the back of your neck, behind your ears, over your chest, and on the bottoms of your feet morning and night.

🍎 Take Lifelong Vitality Supplements twice a day, 2-3 DigestZen TerraZyme® capsules at each meal, and PB Assist®+ once per day. Eat a variety of fresh fruits, vegetables, lean meat, healthy fats and rice. Avoid food coloring, dyes, MSG, gluten, corn, fried food, fast food, processed foods, and artificial sweeteners. Consume extra greens by incorporating smoothies into your morning routine using Greens, Greek yogurt, frozen berries, and bananas, or Greens, almond milk, frozen banana, peanut butter, flaxseed, and frozen berries.

🌙 Diffuse 3 drops of Hygge™ to create a cozy and comforting environment. Develop a structured bedtime routine. Take a shower or hot bath before bed. Take 1-2 Serenity® Softgels 30 minutes before bed. Apply 1 drop each of Serenity® and Balance® to your pillow at bedtime. Take an Adaptiv™ capsule 1-2 times per day.

⊙ Avoid the use of toxic products, and avoid putting toxic products in, on, or around your body. Don't use commerical candles or air fresheners. Makeover your home by using the Abōde™ line of cleaning products, laundry pods, dishwasher pods, surface cleaner, and dish soap. Take care of your hands with Abōde™ Foaming Hand Wash and Lotion.

ADDICTION *(Smoking)*

⏰ **3-5x per day**	📅 *Ongoing*

Essential Oils: *Black Pepper, Clove, On Guard®, Cilantro, Citronella, Hygge™*

Other Solutions: *Peppermint Beadlets*

🌸 Mix 10 drops of each recommended oil with fractionated coconut oil in a 10 ml roller bottle. Rub over your wrists, spine, the bottoms of your feet morning and evening, and the back and front of your neck. Diffuse 3-4 drops of each recommended oil throughout the day. Take Peppermint Beadlets as desired.

🌙 Diffuse 3 drops of Hygge™ to create a cozy and comforting environment.

ADRENAL FATIGUE

⏰ **3-5x per day**	📅 *Until symptoms resolve*

Essential Oils: *Peppermint, Rosemary, Basil, Black Pepper, Hygge™, Tulsi*

Other Solutions: *Peppermint Beadlets*

🌸 Choose 2-3 of the recommended oils. Diffuse 3-4 drops of each throughout the day. Mix 5-7 drops each of Peppermint, Rosemary, Basil, Black Pepper, Hygge™, and Tulsi in a 10 ml roller bottle and fill with fractionated coconut oil. Apply over your chest, temples, the back of your neck, and over your wrists throughout the day. Take Peppermint Beadlets as desired.

🌙 Diffuse 3 drops of Hygge™ to create a cozy and comforting environment.

AGITATION

🕐 **3-5x per day**	📅 *As needed*

Essential Oils: *Serenity®, Deep Blue®, Peace®, Calmer™, Balance®, Lavender, Hygge™*

Other Solutions: *Adaptiv™ Capsules*

🔽 Take 1 Adaptiv™ Capsule per day. Choose 2-3 of the recommended oils. Mix 5-7 drops of each suggested oil in a 10 ml roller bottle and fill with fractionated coconut oil. Apply down your neck and spine, behind your ears, over your heart, on your wrists, and on the bottoms of your feet. Diffuse 4-5 drops of the chosen oils throughout the day.

🍏 Avoid processed foods, fried foods, sugary treats, crackers, cookies, sugar, artificial sweeteners, MSG, food dyes, and foods with a long list of chemical ingredients.

💧 Diffuse 3 drops of Hygge™ to create a cozy and comforting environment.

AIDS/HIV

⏰ *3-4x per day*	📅 *Ongoing*

Essential Oils: *DDR Prime®, On Guard®, Melissa, Tea Tree, Cinnamon*

Other Solutions: *Lifelong Vitality, DigestZen TerraZyme®, PB Assist®+*

- ☯ Choose 3-4 recommended oils and place 1-2 drops of each in a veggie capsule. Take with water.

- 🌿 Take Lifelong Vitality Supplements twice a day, 2-3 DigestZen TerraZyme® capsules at each meal, and PB Assist®+ once per day. Drink Lemon in water (*2 drops per glass*). Eat a nutritious, balance diet full of fresh fruit and vegetables, lean proteins, healthy fats, brown rice, whole grains, grass-fed dairy, and nuts/seeds.

- ⚡ Exercise 5-6 days per week and include cardio, strength training, and flexibility exercises.

- ☾ Use oils from the emotional kit as needed. Diffuse or apply topically.

ALCOHOL ADDICTION

⏰ *Every 4 hours*	📅 *Ongoing*

Essential Oils: *Helichrysum, Cinnamon, Zendocrine®, MetaPWR™, Forgive®, Citronella, Hygge™*

Other Solutions: *Lifelong Vitality, DigestZen TerraZyme®, PB Assist®+, Serenity® Softgels*

 Mix 7-10 drops each of Helichrysum, Cinnamon, Zendocrine®, and MetaPWR™ with fractionated coconut oil in a 10 ml roller bottle and rub over your wrists, spine, feet, and the front and back of your neck every 4 hours. Rub Forgive® over your heart and wrists 3-4 times per day. Diffuse 3-4 drops of each throughout the day.

🟢 Take Lifelong Vitality Supplements twice a day, 2-3 DigestZen TerraZyme® capsules at each meal, and PB Assist®+ once per day. Add a citrus oil (*Lemon, Wild Orange, Lime, or Grapefruit*) to water (*2 drops per glass*) and drink. Eat a nutritious, balance diet full of fresh fruit and vegetables, lean proteins, healthy fats, brown rice, whole grains, grass-fed dairy, and nuts/seeds.

🟠 Exercise 5-6 days per week and include cardio, strength training, and flexibility exercises.

🔵 Diffuse 3 drops of Hygge™ to create a cozy and comforting environment. Put 1 drop each of Serenity® and Balance® on your pillow at night. Take 2 Serenity® Softgels if you have a hard time sleeping. Set healthy boundaries with your time and energy. Spend time with yourself and develop new hobbies and activities. Take a walk in nature a few times per week. Use oils from the yoga kit and do yoga or meditate a few times per week. Rub Frankincense over your forehead and journal your feelings. Celebrate your success with healthy choices, and let go of what you can't control. Find a healthy balance between home, work, social life, and recovery activities. Use oils from the emotional kit as needed. Connect with other people in recovery and attend meetings on a regular basis. Consider supporting others through their recovery. See more tips for sleeping well on page 416.

🔴 If tolerated, do a 30-day cleanse each season. See the 30-day cleanse on page 434.

A-C

ALERTNESS

| 🕐 *3-4x per day* | 📅 *As needed* |

Essential Oils: *Peppermint, InTune®, Pink Pepper*

Other Solutions: *Peppermint Beadlets*

 Apply 1 drop of Peppermint or a swipe of InTune® topically to both of your temples, over your forehead, and on the back of your skull as needed, or diffuse into the air or inhale from your hands. Apply 1 drop of Pink Pepper to your palms and inhale. Add 1 drop of Peppermint or Pink Pepper to your water and sip throughout the day. Take Peppermint beadlets as needed.

If you get oils in your eyes or on your face while inhaling from your hands, apply plain coconut oil over your eye or face to soothe the area. Repeat as needed.

ALLERGIES

| 🕐 *3-5x per day* | 📅 *During allergy season or when symptoms appear* |

Essential Oils: *Lemon, Lavender, Peppermint, DigestZen®*

Other Solutions: *Lifelong Vitality, DigestZen® TerraZyme®, PB Assist®+, TriEase® Softgels*

Diffuse 4 drops each of Lemon, Lavender, and Peppermint when at home or work. Add 5-7 drops of each oil to a 10 ml roller bottle and fill the rest with fractionated coconut oil. Rub over your temples, your forehead, behind your ears, and over your thymus. Take 1-2 TriEase® Softgels as needed. Rub DigestZen® over your sinuses and temples morning and evening.

Take Lifelong Vitality Supplements twice a day, 2-3 DigestZen TerraZyme® capsules at each meal, and PB Assist®+ once per day. Add 2 drops of Lemon to a glass of water and drink.

ALTITUDE SICKNESS

 3-5x per day   *As needed*

Essential Oils: *Ginger, Peppermint, DigestZen®, Balance®*

Other Solutions: *Ginger drops*

💜 Add 5-7 drops of Ginger, DigestZen®, and Balance® to a 10 ml roller bottle and fill the rest with fractionated coconut oil. Rub over your belly, on your wrists' pulse points, down the back of your neck, and over your chest. Rub the blend over your palms and inhale. Suck on a ginger drop throughout the day. Add 1 drop of Peppermint to your water and drink throughout the day.

If you get oils in your eyes or on your face while inhaling from your hands, apply plain coconut oil over your eye or face to soothe the area. Repeat as needed.

ALZHEIMER'S DISEASE

⏰ *4-5x per day*	📅 *Ongoing*

Essential Oils: *Frankincense, Copaiba, InTune®, Immortelle, Black Spruce, Hygge™*

Other Solutions: *Lifelong Vitality, DigestZen® TerraZyme®, PB Assist®+, Serenity® Softgels*

🌑 Place 1 drop each of Frankincense and Copaiba under your tongue morning and evening. Rub InTune® behind your ears and down your neck. Rub Immortelle down your neck and below your skull. Diffuse 3-4 drops each of Frankincense and Black Spruce throughout the day.

🍏 Take Lifelong Vitality Supplements twice a day, 2-3 DigestZen TerraZyme® capsules at each meal, and PB Assist®+ once per day. Eat a variety of fresh fruits, vegetables, lean meats, healthy fats, and brown rice. Avoid MSG, gluten, corn, fried food, fast food, and processed foods. Drink half your weight in ounces of water and add 1-2 drops of Lemon per glass.

🔸 Do aerobic exercises, strength training, and balance exercises.

🌙 Diffuse 3 drops of Hygge™ to create a cozy and comforting environment. Develop a regular sleep routine. Avoid watching TV too close to bedtime. Apply Serenity® or Lavender to your pillow at bedtime. Take 1-2 Serenity® Softgels 30 minutes before bed. Allow yourself extra time to complete your tasks. Use oils from the emotional kit to support your emotional health; diffuse or use topically as needed.

🔴 Makeover your home by using the Abōde™ line of cleaning products, laundry pods, dishwasher pods, surface cleaner, and dish soap. Take care of your hands with Abōde™ Foaming Hand Wash and Lotion. If tolerated, do a 30-day cleanse each season. See the 30-day cleanse on page 434.

AMENORRHEA

⏰ **3-5x per day**	📅 **As needed**

Essential Oils: *ClaryCalm®, Clary Sage, Whisper®, Ylang Ylang, Jasmine, Geranium, Sandalwood, Lavender, Tulsi*

Other Solutions: *Phytoestrogen Essential Complex, Bone Nutrient Essential Complex, Lifelong Vitality, DigestZen TerraZyme®, PB Assist®+, Serenity® Softgels*

 Combine 5-7 drops each of Sandalwood, Geranium, Ylang Ylang, Tulsi, and Clary Sage with fractionated coconut oil in a 10 ml roller bottle. Apply over your lower abdominal region, on your feet, and along your spine in the lower back area 2 times per day. Rotate between the ClaryCalm® roller and Jasmine roller throughout the day in-between using the homemade roller. Diffuse 5 drops of Whisper® throughout the day.

 Pre- and peri-menopausal women should take one 1-2 Phytoestrogen Essential Complex capsules daily with food. Post-menopausal women should take 2 Phytoestrogen Essential Complex capsules daily with food. Take 4 Bone Nutrient Essential Complex capsules daily with food. Take Lifelong Vitality Supplements twice a day, 2-3 DigestZen TerraZyme® capsules at each meal, and PB Assist once per day. Consume avocados, flaxseed, broccoli, pomegranate, salmon, leafy greens, nuts, organic soy, turmeric, quinoa, and brown rice. Avoid excess sugar, simple carbohydrates, trans fats, and processed foods.

🌙 Place 1 drop of Lavender or Serenity® on your pillow at night. Take 2 Serenity® Softgels before bed.

ANEMIA

⏰ *3-5x per day*	📅 *Ongoing*

Essential Oils: *Zendocrine®, Helichrysum, Geranium, Cinnamon*

Other Solutions: *Lifelong Vitality, DigestZen TerraZyme®, PB Assist®+*

🟣 Place 1 drop of each oil in a capsule and take twice per day. Mix 5-7 drops of each oil with fractionated coconut oil in a 10 ml roller bottle and rub it over your wrists, along your spine, over your abdominal region, and on the bottoms of your feet morning and night.

🍎 Take Lifelong Vitality Supplements twice a day, 2-3 DigestZen TerraZyme® capsules at each meal, and PB Assist® once per day. Eat a variety of fresh fruits, green leafy vegetables, lean meats, dark chocolate, fatty fish, oysters, beef liver, healthy fats, and rice. Include iron-fortified foods, such as fortified orange juice; fortified ready-to-eat cereals; foods made from fortified refined flour, such as white bread; fortified pasta; foods made from fortified corn-meal; and fortified white rice. Cook with a cast-iron skillet to increase iron intake. Eat foods rich in folate and vitamin B-12.

➕ Continue to seek professional medical attention for the condition as needed, especially if you find yourself bruising easily, short of breath, and constantly exhausted. There could be an underlying reason for your anemia, so it is best to work with your health care provider should you suspect anemia.

ANGER

⏰ **3-5x per day**	📅 **As needed**

Essential Oils: *Balance®, Peace®, Forgive®, Hygge™, Madagascar Vanilla*

Other Solutions: *Lifelong Vitality, DigestZen® TerraZyme®, PB Assist®+, Serenity® Softgels*

 Choose 1-2 of the recommended oils. Put 1-2 drops of each oil in your palm and dilute with 1/2 teaspoon of fractionated coconut oil. Apply over your heart, your abdomen, the back of your neck, and behind your ears. Inhale deeply from your palms 3 times. Diffuse 3-4 drops of each oil in a diffuser throughout the day.

If you get oils in your eyes or on your face while inhaling from your hands, apply plain coconut oil over your eye or face to soothe the area. Repeat as needed.

 Take Lifelong Vitality Supplements twice a day, 2-3 DigestZen TerraZyme® capsules at each meal, and PB Assist® once per day. Eat a variety of fresh fruits, vegetables, lean meats, fatty fish, healthy fats, and brown rice. Avoid MSG, gluten, corn, fried food, fast food, and processed foods. Drink half your weight in ounces of water, and add 1-2 drops of Lemon or another citrus oil to each glass of water.

⊙ Do aerobic exercises, strength training, and balance exercises. Apply Deep Blue® Rub to any sore muscles or joints following exercise.

🌙 Diffuse 3 drops of Hygge™ and 2 drops Vanilla to create a cozy and comforting environment. Apply 1 drop each of Serenity® and Balance® to your pillow at bedtime. Take 1-2 Serenity® Softgels 30 minutes before bed. Use other emotional oils to soothe your emotions as needed.

ANOREXIA

⏰ **3-4x per day**	📅 **Ongoing as needed**

Essential Oils: *Bergamot, Wild Orange, Frankincense, Patchouli*

Other Solutions: *Lifelong Vitality, DigestZen TerraZyme®, PB Assist®+, Serenity® Softgels*

🌙 Mix 5-7 drops of each recommended oil with fractionated coconut oil in a 10 ml roller bottle and rub it over your abdominal area, your pulse points on your wrists, down the back of your neck, and on the bottoms of your feet morning and night. Place 1 drop of Wild Orange or Bergamot in water or a smoothie and sip throughout the day. Place Frankincense under your tongue twice daily, morning and evening.

🌿 Take Lifelong Vitality Supplements twice a day, 2-3 DigestZen TerraZyme® capsules at each meal, and PB Assist® once per day. Eat a balance diet with a variety of fresh fruits, vegetables, lean meats, fatty fish, healthy fats, and brown rice. Avoid MSG, gluten, corn, fried food, fast food, and processed foods. Drink half your weight in ounces of water, and add 1-2 drops of Lemon or another citrus oil to each glass of water.

🔸 Take a light walk 4-5 times per week, preferably in nature, after nutritional rehabilitation is complete. Add strength training into your routine 2-3 times per week. Work at your own pace and stay hydrated. Listen to your body and rest as needed. Focus on getting stronger rather than losing weight when you exercise.

🌙 Apply 1 drop of Serenity® or Lavender to your pillow at bedtime. Take 1-2 Serenity® Softgels 30 minutes before bed. Adopt a habit of journaling your feelings, and join a support group if desired. Practice yoga or meditation a few times per week. Work with a life coach to set goals for your future. Use emotional oils as needed throughout the day.

➕ Work with health care professionals to monitor your diet and progress. Strict medical oversight is necessary to monitor levels of phosphorus, magnesium, potassium, calcium, and thiamine; it must be monitored for the first 5 days after meeting with a medical professional and every other day for several weeks. An electrocardiogram (EKG) should also be performed. Avoid the potentially fatal refeeding syndrome, caused by the rapid refeeding of someone in a state of starvation.

ANXIETY

 Daily as needed   *Ongoing while symptoms persist*

Essential Oils: *Bergamot, Serenity®, Balance®, Basil, Adaptiv™ (3-part system), Ylang Ylang, Vetiver, Roman Chamomile, Hygge™, Vanilla*

Other Solutions: *Lifelong Vitality, DigestZen TerraZyme®, PB Assist®+, Serenity® Softgels, Adaptiv™ Capsules*

🟣 Diffuse 3-4 drops each of Bergamot, Basil, Balance®, and Vetiver throughout the day. Mix 5-7 drops each of Roman Chamomile, Bergamot, Vetiver, and Ylang Ylang with fractionated coconut oil in a 10 ml roller bottle. Rub it down your neck, over your spine, over wrist pulse points, and the bottoms of your feet often throughout the day. Buy a diffuser necklace or place a combination of any of the oils on a cotton ball. When you experience the first sign of anxiety, inhale the oils from the cotton ball or necklace and take slow, deep breaths. Do this as often as needed throughout the day. Take Adaptiv™ Capsules as directed. Use Adaptiv™ roller alone or rotate its use with the homemade roller throughout the day.

🟢 Take Lifelong Vitality Supplements twice a day, 2-3 DigestZen TerraZyme® Capsules at each meal, and PB Assist® once per day. Eat a variety of fresh fruits, vegetables, lean meats, healthy fats, and rice. Avoid MSG, gluten, corn, fried food, fast food, processed foods, and artificial sweeteners.

🌙 Diffuse 3 drops of Hygge™ and 2 drops of Vanilla to create a cozy and comforting environment. Apply 1 drop of Serenity® or Lavender to your pillow at bedtime. Take 1-2 Serenity® Softgels 30 minutes before bed. Meditate frequently throughout the week. Get a meditation app or adopt some practices recommended in the Rest and Manage Stress chapter (page 410). Take a sauna or a long walk. Implement deep diaphragmatic breaths often throughout the day.

🔻 Makeover your home by using the Abōde™ line of cleaning products, laundry pods, dishwasher pods, surface cleaner, and dish soap. Take care of your hands with Abōde™ Foaming Hand Wash and Lotion. Do a 30-day cleanse each season. See the 30-day cleanse on page 434.

APATHY

⏰ **3-5x per day**	📅 *As needed*

Essential Oils: *Lemongrass, Lime, Vetiver, Patchouli*

Other Solutions: *Lifelong Vitality, DigestZen TerraZyme®, PB Assist®+, Serenity® Softgels*

🌙 Choose 2-3 of the recommended oils. Diffuse 3-5 drops in a diffuser throughout the day. Mix 5-7 drops of your chosen oils in a 10 ml roller bottle with fractionated coconut oil. Apply topically to the bottoms of your feet morning and night, as well as over your chest and down the back of your neck and temples.

🍏 Take Lifelong Vitality Supplements twice a day, 2-3 DigestZen TerraZyme® Capsules at each meal, and PB Assist® once per day. Eat a variety of fresh fruits, vegetables, lean meats, fatty fish, healthy fats, whole grains, and brown rice. Avoid MSG, gluten, corn, fried food, fast food, processed foods, and artificial sweeteners.

🍊 Do aerobic exercises, strength training, and balance exercises.

🌙 Apply 1 drop of Serenity® or Lavender to your pillow at bedtime. Take 1-2 Serenity® Softgels 30 minutes before bed. Adopt a yoga or meditation practice, work with a life coach, or take some classes in breathwork. Use oils from the emotional kit to manage emotions: either diffuse 4-5 drops of each oil, or use topically with fractionated coconut oil over your heart, the back of your neck, and the bottoms of your feet.

🔴 If tolerated, do a 30-day cleanse each season. See the 30-day cleanse on page 434.

APPETITE SUPPRESSANT

🕐 *3-5x per day*   📅 *As needed*

Essential Oils: *MetaPWR™, Grapefruit, Ginger*

Other Solutions: *Lifelong Vitality, DigestZen TerraZyme®, PB Assist®+, MetaPWR™ Softgels, MetaPWR™ Gum*

 Take 3-5 MetaPWR™ Softgels throughout the day to manage hunger. Chew MetaPWR™ gum throughout the day. Add 1 drop of MetaPWR™ or Grapefruit to your water. Mix 5-7 drops each of MetaPWR™, Grapefruit, and Ginger in a 10 ml roller bottle and fill the remainder with fractionated coconut oil. Apply topically to your stomach, inside your wrists, and to the bottoms of your feet morning and evening, or diffuse into the air and inhale as needed.

If you get oils in your eyes or on your face while inhaling from your hands, apply plain coconut oil over your eye or face to soothe the area. Repeat as needed.

🟢 Take Lifelong Vitality Supplements twice a day, 2-3 DigestZen TerraZyme® capsules at each meal, and PB Assist® once per day. Eat a variety of fresh fruits, vegetables, lean meats, fatty fish, healthy fats, and whole grains. Avoid MSG, fried food, fast food, processed foods, and artificial sweeteners. Stay hydrated throughout the day by drinking half your body weight in ounces of water.

🔴 Do aerobic exercises, strength training and balance exercises. Put 1 drop of MetaPWR™ in your water during workouts.

ARRHYTHMIA

🕐 *3-5x per day*   📅 *Ongoing as needed*

Essential Oils: *Lavender, Ylang Ylang, Basil, Rosemary, Melissa*

Other Solutions: *N/A*

 Choose 2-3 of the recommended oils. Mix 5-7 drops of each oil in a 10 ml roller bottle and fill the remainder with fractionated coconut oil. Rub over your heart, pulse points, down your spine, and on the bottoms of your feet morning and evening.

ARTERIOSCLEROSIS

⏰ **3-5x per day**	📅 **Ongoing as needed**

Essential Oils: *Black Pepper, Lemongrass, Cinnamon, Juniper Berry, On Guard®*

Other Solutions: *Lifelong Vitality*

💜 Choose 2-3 of the recommended oils. Mix 5-7 drops of each oil in a 10 ml roller bottle and fill the remainder with fractionated coconut oil. Rub over your heart, pulse points, down your spine, and on the bottoms of your feet morning and evening.

🍏 Choose high-fiber, low-sodium, and high-potassium foods such as vegetables, fruits, melons, avocados, bananas, and seeds. Choose omega-3-rich foods like grass-fed beef, wild-caught salmon, chia seeds, and flaxseed. Eat dark chocolate, garlic, spinach, sunflower seeds, tomatoes, and broccoli. Avoid high-sodium processed foods such as pickles, olives, and canned foods. Limit sugar, caffeine, and alcohol.

❤️ Exercise 45 minutes a day for 4-5 days a week. Combine cardio and strength training 3-4 times per week, starting with light weights and working your way up to heavier weights. Warm up, cool down, and stretch for each exercise session.

➕ Call your doctor if you have ongoing feelings of being sluggish or winded, have a rapid heart rate, have pain that moves down your arm, or have a rapid or irregular pulse. Seek medical attention right away if you experience any severe tightness in your chest; sudden chest pain or pressure; feeling like a belt is being tightened around your chest; pain that spreads from the center of the chest to your arms, shoulders, neck, or jaw; excessive sweating, nausea, vomiting, dizziness, or shortness of breath; a fullness, indigestion, or choking feeling; rapid or irregular heartbeat; extreme weakness or anxiety.

ARTHRITIS

⏰ 4-5x per day	📅 *Ongoing while symptoms persist*

Essential Oils: *Marjoram, Cypress, Copaiba, Lemongrass, Frankincense, Siberian Fir*

Other Solutions: *Lifelong Vitality, DigestZen TerraZyme®, PB Assist®+, Turmeric Dual Chamber Capsules, Deep Blue® Polyphenol Complex, Serenity® Softgels, Copaiba Softgels, Deep Blue® Rub, Deep Blue® Stick*

🟣 Mix 10 drops each of Marjoram, Cypress, Copaiba, Lemongrass, Frankincense, and Siberian Fir in a 10 ml roller bottle and fill the rest with fractionated coconut oil. Apply with Deep Blue® Rub over the affected joint(s). Take Copaiba Softgels twice per day for pain. Take 2 Turmeric Dual Chamber Capsules daily for inflammation.

🟢 Take Lifelong Vitality Supplements twice a day, 2-3 DigestZen TerraZyme® capsules at each meal, and PB Assist® once per day. Take 2 Turmeric Dual Chamber Capsules each day. Take 2 Deep Blue® Polyphenol Complex supplements per day. Eat a variety of fresh fruits, vegetables, lean meats, healthy fats, and rice. Avoid MSG, gluten, corn, fried food, fast food, processed foods, and artificial sweeteners.

🔴 Rub Deep Blue® Rub or Stick over affected joints before and after exercise. Do aerobic exercises, strength training, and balance exercises.

🔵 Apply 1 drop of Serenity® or Lavender to your pillow at bedtime. Take 1-2 Serenity® Softgels 30 minutes before bed. Use emotional oils as needed throughout the day.

ASPERGER SYNDROME

⏰ 3-5x per day	📅 *Ongoing*

Essential Oils: *InTune®, Balance®, Frankincense, Lavender, Vetiver, Adaptiv™ (3-part system)*

Other Solutions: *Lifelong Vitality, DigestZen TerraZyme®, PB Assist®+, Adaptiv™ Capsules*

🟣 Place 1 drop of Frankincense under your tongue morning and evening. Rub InTune® down the back of your neck and over your pulse points 3-5 times per day. Mix 5-7 drops each of Balance®, Lavender, Vetiver, and Frankincense in a 10 ml roller bottle filled with fractionated coconut oil. Apply the roller bottle to your wrists, over your heart, and down the back of your neck. Apply the roller bottle to the bottoms of your feet morning and evening. Diffuse 5 drops of Adaptiv™ and Vetiver throughout the day as needed. Take 1-2 Adaptiv™ Capsules during the day as needed.

🟢 Take Lifelong Vitality Supplements twice a day, 2-3 DigestZen TerraZyme® capsules at each meal, and PB Assist® once per day. Eat a variety of fresh fruits, vegetables, lean meats, healthy fats, and rice. Avoid MSG, gluten, corn, fried food, fast food, processed foods, and artificial sweeteners.

🔵 Take a 1-hour break from electronics 3 times per day. Use emotional oils as needed.

🔴 Makeover your home by using the Abōde™ line of cleaning products, laundry pods, dishwasher pods, surface cleaner, and dish soap. Take care of your hands with Abōde™ Foaming Hand Wash and Lotion. If tolerated, do a 30-day cleanse each season. See the 30-day cleanse on page 434.

ASTHMA

⏰ **3-5x per day**	📅 **As needed**

Essential Oils: *Breathe®, Eucalyptus, Peppermint*

Other Solutions: *Breathe® Drops, Lifelong Vitality*

- 🌙 Choose 2 of the recommended oils. Mix 3-5 drops of each in a diffuser and diffuse throughout the day. Place 1 drop each of Breathe® and Peppermint into your palms and inhale 3 slow, deep breaths to open your airways and allow clear breathing. Mix 5-7 drops of each oil in a 10 ml roller bottle with fractionated coconut oil and apply to your chest, upper- and mid-back, and the bottoms of your feet. If you get oils in your eyes or on your face while inhaling from your hands, apply plain coconut oil over your eye or face to soothe the area. Repeat as needed.

- 🍏 Take Lifelong Vitality Supplements twice a day. Eat a variety of fresh fruits, vegetables, lean meats, healthy fats, and rice to keep inflammation at bay. Avoid dairy, MSG, gluten, corn, fried food, fast food, processed foods, and artificial sweeteners.

- ➕ Watch for symptoms of severe shortness of breath, chest tightness, or coughing and wheezing. If you are unable to speak more than a few short sentences or have to strain your chest muscles to breathe, seek medical attention right away. Always carry a quick-acting inhaler with you.

ATHLETE'S FOOT

⏰ **3-5x per day**	📅 ***Ongoing, as athlete's foot can reappear over and over again.***

Essential Oils: *Tea Tree, Copaiba, Arborvitae, Citronella, HD Clear®*

Other Solutions: *HD Clear® Foaming Wash, HD Clear® Lotion*

- 🌙 Mix 5-7 drops of each oil in a 10 ml roller bottle and fill with fractionated coconut oil. Apply topically between your toes and around your toenails at least 3 times a day. Wash your feet and between your toes with HD Foaming Wash after exercise or wearing shoes or socks for long periods of time. Dry your feet and between your toes thoroughly, and apply oils once they are dry. Apply HD Clear® Lotion. Allow your feet to air out at night or at home or the office.

- 🧡 Avoid keeping your shoes and socks on after exercise. After exercising, wash your feet and in-between your toes with HD Clear® Foaming Wash. Keep your feet clean and dry. Make sure to fully dry your feet and in-between your toes after showering. Apply HD Clear® Lotion. Let your feet air out at the end of the day. Avoid cotton or wool socks and opt for socks that allow for moisture wicking. Continue to use the recommended oils after the symptoms have subsided, as athlete's foot can reappear over and over again.

AUTISM

⏰ **3-5x per day**	📅 *Ongoing*

Essential Oils: *InTune®, Balance®, Frankincense, Lavender, Vetiver, Adaptiv™ (3-part system)*

Other Solutions: *Lifelong Vitality, DigestZen TerraZyme®, PB Assist®+, Adaptiv™ Capsules*

● Place 1 drop of Frankincense under your tongue morning and evening. Rub InTune® down the back of your neck and over your pulse points 3-5 times per day. Mix 5-7 drops of Balance®, Lavender, Vetiver, and Frankincense in a 10 ml roller bottle filled with fractionated coconut oil. Apply the roller bottle to your wrists, over your heart, and down the back of your neck. Apply the roller bottle to the bottoms of your feet morning and evening. Diffuse 5 drops of Adaptiv™ and Vetiver throughout the day as needed. Take 1-2 Adaptiv™ Capsules per day as needed.

● Take Lifelong Vitality Supplements twice a day, 2-3 DigestZen TerraZyme® capsules at each meal, and PB Assist® once per day. Eat a variety of fresh fruits, vegetables, lean meats, healthy fats, and rice. Avoid MSG, gluten, corn, fried food, fast food, processed foods, and artificial sweeteners.

● Take a 1-hour break from electronics 3 times per day. Use emotional oils as needed.

● Makeover your home by using the Abōde™ line of cleaning products, laundry pods, dishwasher pods, surface cleaner, and dish soap. Take care of your hands with Abōde™ Foaming Hand Wash and Lotion. If tolerated, do a 30-day cleanse each season. See the 30-day cleanse on page 434.

AUTOIMMUNE DISORDER

⏰ *4-5x per day*	📅 *Ongoing*

Essential Oils: *On Guard®, DDR Prime®, Lavender, Turmeric, Zendocrine®, Lemongrass, Tulsi*

Other Solutions: *Lifelong Vitality, DigestZen TerraZyme®, PB Assist®+, Turmeric Dual Chamber Capsules, Serenity® Softgels, Deep Blue® Rub*

Put 1-2 drops each of On Guard®, DDR Prime®, Turmeric, Tulsi, and Zendocrine® in a capsule and take 3 times per day. Take 2 Turmeric Dual Chamber Capsules a day. Mix 5-7 drops each of On Guard®, DDR Prime®, Turmeric, and Zendocrine® in a 10 ml roller bottle filled with fractionated coconut oil and apply to your abdomen, down your spine, and on the bottoms of your feet morning and night.

Take Lifelong Vitality Supplements twice a day, 2-3 DigestZen TerraZyme® capsules at each meal, and PB Assist® once per day. Eat a variety of fresh fruits, vegetables, lean meat, healthy fats, and rice. Avoid MSG, gluten, corn, fried food, fast food, processed foods, and artificial sweeteners.

Exercise on days when you feel good. Alternate light to moderate cardio and strength training as tolerated. Listen to your body and rest when needed. Apply Lemongrass and Deep Blue® Rub to muscles and joints that are sore or inflamed.

Apply 1 drop of Serenity® or Lavender to your pillow at bedtime. Take 1-2 Serenity® Softgels 30 minutes before bed. Use emotional oils as needed.

Include meditation, prayer, and spending time in nature as part of your regular routine to rest and manage your stress. Join an online support group or reach out to friends and family for help as needed.

Makeover your home by using the Abōde™ line of cleaning products, laundry pods, dishwasher pods, surface cleaner, and dish soap. Take care of your hands with Abōde™ Foaming Hand Wash and Lotion. If tolerated, do a 30-day cleanse each season. See the 30-day cleanse on page 434.

AUTOINTOXICATION

⏰ **3-5x per day**	📅 **As needed**

Essential Oils: *Zendocrine®, Cilantro, Geranium, Thyme*

Other Solutions: *Lifelong Vitality, DigestZen TerraZyme®, PB Assist®+, Serenity® Softgels*

 Put 1-2 drops each of Zendocrine®, Cilantro, Geranium, and Thyme in a capsule and take 4 times per day. Mix 5-7 drops of each oil in a 10 ml roller bottle with fractionated coconut oil and apply topically to your abdomen, lower back, down your neck, and on the bottoms of your feet morning and night.

🟢 Take Lifelong Vitality Supplements twice a day, 2-3 DigestZen TerraZyme® capsules at each meal, and PB Assist® once per day. Eat a clean diet with a variety of fresh fruits, vegetables, lean meat, healthy fats, and rice. Avoid MSG, gluten, corn, fried food, fast food, processed foods, and artificial sweeteners. Add 1 drop of Peppermint to a glass of water and drink.

🔵 Apply 1 drop of Serenity® or Lavender to your pillow at bedtime. Take 1-2 Serenity® Softgels 30 minutes before bed. Use emotional oils as needed throughout the day.

🔻 Makeover your home by using the Abōde™ line of cleaning products, laundry pods, dishwasher pods, surface cleaner, and dish soap. Take care of your hands with Abōde™ Foaming Hand Wash and Lotion. If tolerated, do a 30-day cleanse each season. See the 30-day cleanse on page 434.

BACK PAIN

⏰ *4-5x per day*	🗓 *Until symptoms subside*

Essential Oils: *Lemongrass, Marjoram, Wintergreen, Cypress, AromaTouch®, Copaiba*

Other Solutions: *Lifelong Vitality, DigestZen TerraZyme®, PB Assist®+, Serenity® Softgels, Copaiba Softgels, Turmeric Dual Chamber Capsules, Deep Blue® Rub, Deep Blue® Stick*

🌱 Apply Deep Blue Stick or create the following ointment. Get a 4-ounce glass jar and fill 3/4 with hard coconut oil. Add 2 quarter-sized drops of Deep Blue® Rub and 15 drops each of Lemongrass, Marjoram, Wintergreen, Cypress, AromaTouch®, and Copaiba. Stir well. Apply liberally over the affected area, massaging it into the soft tissues. If you get oils in your eyes or on your face, apply plain coconut oil over your eye or face to soothe the area. Repeat as needed.

🍎 Take Lifelong Vitality Supplements twice a day; 2-3 DigestZen TerraZyme® capsules at each meal; PB Assist® once per day; and Turmeric Dual Chamber Capsules twice per day. Eat a clean diet with a variety of fresh fruits, vegetables, lean meat, healthy fats, and rice. Avoid MSG, gluten, corn, fried food, fast food, processed foods, and artificial sweeteners. Take 2 Copaiba Softgels twice a day.

⊙ Listen to your body. Do 5 days of light to moderate cardio if tolerated. Do 3 days of strength training *(making sure to support your back)* if tolerated. Warm up, cool down, and stretch after each exercise session. While exercising, make sure to tighten your core to support your lower back.

☾ Place 1 drop of Serenity® or Lavender on your pillow at night. Take Serenity® Softgels 30 minutes before bed. Use a pillow under your knees when you sleep or rest on your back, and in-between your knees when you rest or lay on your side. Avoid sitting for long periods of time. Get up every couple of hours and go for a 5-minute walk if possible. Use oils from the emotional kit to manage stress and emotions.

✚ Seek professional medical attention from your doctor or chiropractor if the problem persists, if you have pain that radiates down your thigh or leg, if you have bowel or bladder incontinence, if you lose sensation in your groin or legs, or if you do not see an improvement in your condition after a couple of weeks on this protocol. A chiropractor can help determine the type of bulging disc you are suffering from and help you pinpoint some of the underlying causes. Physical therapy and massage can also help.

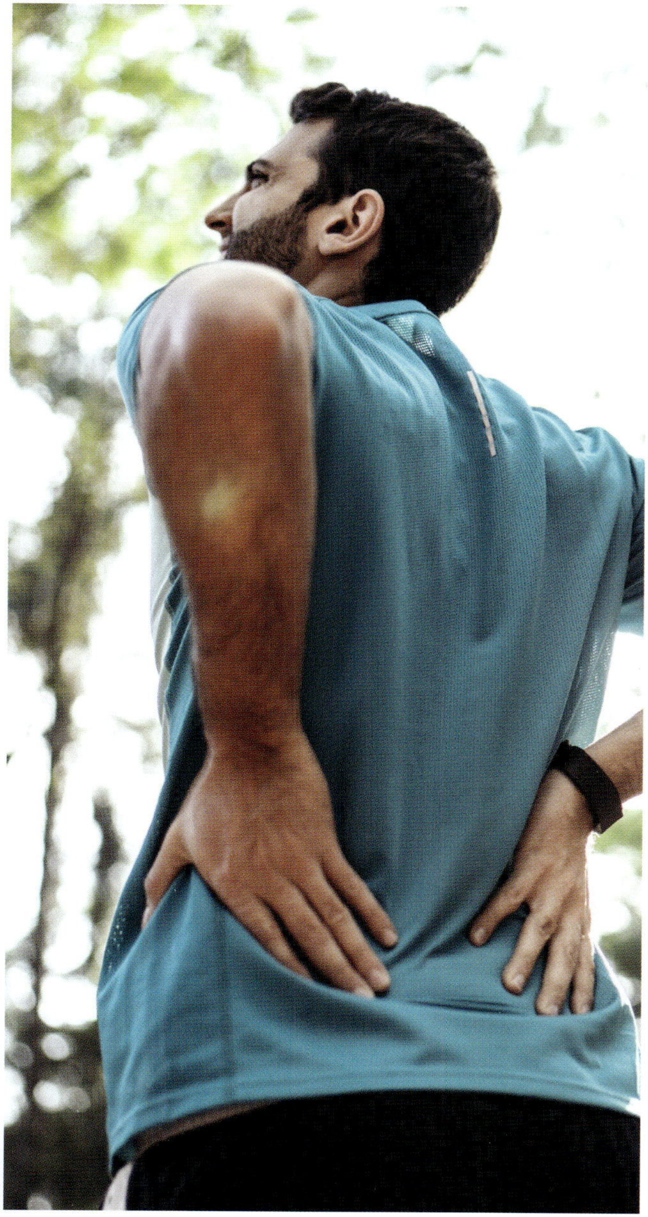

BACTERIA

⏰ *4-5x per day*	📅 *Until symptoms subside*

Essential Oils: *On Guard®, Oregano, Thyme, Peppermint*

Other Solutions: *On Guard® Beadlets, On Guard® Softgels, On Guard® Tablets*

🟣 Choose 2 of the recommended oils. Put 1-2 drops of each oil into a capsule and take with water. Mix 5-7 drops of each oil in a 10 ml roller bottle and fill with fractionated coconut oil. Apply over the affected area or on the bottoms of your feet and down your spine. Take On Guard® Beadlets, Tablets, or Softgels as needed. If you have a fever, apply 1 drop of Peppermint to the back of your neck, over your chest, down your spine, and on the bottoms of your feet morning and evening.

If you get Peppermint in your eyes or on your face, apply plain coconut oil over your eye or face to soothe the area. Repeat as needed.

🍏 Take Lifelong Vitality Supplements twice a day; 2-3 DigestZen TerraZyme® capsules at each meal; PB Assist® once per day; and Turmeric Dual Chamber Capsules twice per day. Avoid fried food, fast food, processed foods, and artificial sweeteners.

🌙 Diffuse Serenity®, Balance®, and Breathe® and rest as needed. Take 2 Serenity® Softgels before bed.

BAD BREATH

⏰ *4-5x per day*	📅 *As needed*

Essential Oils: *Peppermint, Spearmint, Zendocrine®*

Other Solutions: *On Guard® Natural Whitening Toothpaste, On Guard® Mouthwash, Peppermint Beadlets, Zendocrine® Softgels*

 Brush your teeth with On Guard® toothpaste 3 times per day. Use On Guard® Mouthwash after brushing teeth, 3 times per day. Place 1 drop of Peppermint or Spearmint on your tongue until symptoms subside. Take 1-2 drops of Zendocrine® in a capsule or take 1-2 Zendocrine® Softgels. Soak your dental floss in warm salt water for 5 minutes, adding 1 drop of Peppermint, Spearmint, or On Guard®. Floss daily. Brush your tongue each time you brush your teeth. Add 1 drop of Peppermint, Spearmint, or On Guard® to your toothbrush before brushing your tongue or teeth. Use Peppermint Beadlets during the day to combat bad breath.

 Avoid some of the key offenders of bad breath: onions, garlic, horseradish, dairy, and canned fish. Avoid starchy foods that can get stuck in your mouth (*like potato chips*). If you consume sugar, eat it with a meal.

🔴 Practice oil pulling to remove toxins and harmful bacteria from your mouth: take a tablespoon of hard coconut oil and place 1 drop of On Guard® and 1 drop of Peppermint or Spearmint on top of the coconut oil. Allow the oil to melt in your mouth, and then swish it around for 5-15 minutes. Pull the oil through your teeth and on both sides of your mouth. When you are done, spit it out in the garbage—not down the sink, as the hard coconut oil could clog the drain over time. Repeat this process a few times per week. Hint: Start off at 1 minute and work your way up, eventually finding the amount of time that feels best to you.

BALANCE PROBLEMS

⏰ *4-5x per day*	📅 *As needed*

Essential Oils: *Ginger, Cedarwood, Rosemary, Balance®*

Other Solutions: *Ginger Drops*

 Choose 2-3 of the recommended oils. Mix 5-7 drops of each oil in a 10 ml roller bottle and fill the rest with fractionated coconut oil. Apply down the back of your neck, behind your ears, down your spine, and on the bottoms of your feet morning and night. In addition, rub the blend over your palms and inhale deeply 3 times throughout the day as needed. Take Ginger Drops as needed. If you get oils in your eyes or on your face while inhaling from your hands, apply plain coconut oil over your eye or face to soothe the area. Repeat as needed.

 Practice balance exercises on a regular basis as tolerated. Alternate cardio and strength training 5-6 times per week.

BED BUGS

⏰ *Twice daily*	📅 *As needed*

Essential Oils: *TerraShield®, Arborvitae, Eucalyptus, Siberian Fir, Peppermint, Citronella*

Other Solutions: *On Guard® Laundry Detergent*

 Clean bedding, linens, curtains, and clothing with On Guard® Laundry Detergent. Apply 1-2 drops of TerraShield® on a stiff brush and scrub the mattress to remove bugs and their eggs, then vacuum the mattress. Choose 2 of the recommended oils besides TerraShield®. Combine 5-7 drops of each and 5-7 drops of TerraShield® in a 2-ounce glass bottle and fill the rest with water. Spray over the floors, mattress, pillows, and linens and allow to dry before making the bed. Spray liberally around the bed, floors, curtains, behind pictures, etc.

BED SORES

⏰ *3-5x per day*	📅 *While symptoms persist*

Essential Oils: *Lavender, Myrrh, Geranium, Frankincense, Cypress*

Other Solutions: *N/A*

 Put 2 drops of each recommended oil into a gloved hand and dilute with 1 teaspoon of fractionated coconut oil. Apply over the affected area throughout the day. Keep the area clean and dry. Try to move around frequently to prevent added pressure on the area.

BED-WETTING

⏰ 2-3x per day	📅 *An hour before bed, at bedtime, and anytime you wake up in the middle of the night*

Essential Oils: *Cypress, Copaiba, Juniper Berry, Black Pepper, Thyme, Lemongrass, Madagascar Vanilla*

Other Solutions: *Serenity® Softgel*

- Choose 2-3 of the recommended oils. Mix 5-7 drops of each oil in a 10 ml roller bottle and fill remainder with fractionated coconut oil. Apply over your lower abdomen, lower back, and the bottoms of your feet morning and night.

- Drink water throughout the day, but avoid drinking too much liquid within 2 hours of bed. Don't eat or drink caffeine, chocolate milk, or chocolate later in the day.

- Diffuse 3 drops of Vanilla and to create a cozy and comforting environment. Opt for an earlier sleep time and develop a good sleep routine. Take 1 Serenity® Softgel an hour before bed when winding down for the evening. Avoid electronics too close to bedtime.

BEE STING

⏰ **3x per day**	📅 **As needed**

Essential Oils: *Lavender, Purify, Basil, Roman Chamomile*

Other Solutions: *N/A*

- Choose 2 of the recommended oils. Apply 1-2 drops with a tablespoon of fractionated coconut oil over the bee sting as soon as possible.
- Seek immediate medical attention if you experience shortness of breath, itching, hives, dizziness, flushed face, pale skin, wheezing, or swelling in your face, throat, or tongue.

BELL'S PALSY

⏰ **3-5x per day**	📅 **Until symptoms improve**

Essential Oils: *Helichrysum, Lavender, Peppermint, Juniper Berry, Rosemary, Marjoram*

Other Solutions: *N/A*

- Add 10 drops of Helichrysum, 5 drops each of Lavender and Peppermint, and 3 drops each of Juniper Berry, Rosemary, and Marjoram to a 10 ml roller bottle with fractionated coconut oil. Apply to the affected area often throughout the day.

BENIGN PROSTATIC HYPERPLASIA

⏰ **4-5x per day**	📅 **As needed**

Essential Oils: *Frankincense, Rosemary, Myrrh, Sandalwood, Juniper Berry, Lemon*

Other Solutions: *DDR Prime® Softgels, Turmeric Dual Chamber Capsules*

- Choose 3-4 of the recommended oils. Combine 10 drops of each in a 10 ml roller bottle with fractionated coconut oil. Apply over your lower abdominal region, lower back, and feet several times per day. Take 2 Turmeric Dual Chamber Capsules daily with meals. Take 2 DDR Prime® Softgels daily.

BINGE EATING DISORDER (BED)

⏰ **3-5x per day**	📅 *As needed*

Essential Oils: *MetaPWR™, Serenity®, Console®, Patchouli*

Other Solutions: *Lifelong Vitality, DigestZen TerraZyme®, PB Assist®+, Serenity® Softgels*

- 💜 Place 2 drops of MetaPWR™ in your water 2-3 times per day. Mix 5-7 drops each of Serenity®, Console®, and Patchouli in a 10 ml roller bottle and fill remainder with fractionated coconut oil. Apply over your heart, stomach, abdomen, spine, and the bottoms of your feet morning and night.

- 🍏 Take Lifelong Vitality Supplements twice a day, 2-3 DigestZen TerraZyme® capsules at each meal, and PB Assist® once per day. Adopt the 80/20 rule when it comes to eating: eat healthily 80 percent of the time and let yourself have whatever you want 20 percent of the time.

- 🟠 Take the focus off your weight and set goals of getting stronger; building endurance; and enjoying how your mood, outlook, and energy levels increase when you adopt a regular exercise routine.

- 🗣 Apply 1 drop of Serenity® or Lavender to your pillow at bedtime. Take 1-2 Serenity® Softgels 30 minutes before bed. Use emotional oils as needed throughout the day. Include meditation, prayer, and spending time in nature as part of your regular routine to rest and manage your stress. Join an online support group or reach out to friends and family for help as needed.

- ➕ Don't struggle alone. Reach out for professional help if you feel you are out of control with your eating.

BIPOLAR DISORDER

 3-5x per day   **As needed**

Essential Oils: *Balance®, Bergamot, Peace®, Serenity®, Adaptiv™ (3-part system), InTune®*

Other Solutions: *Lifelong Vitality, DigestZen TerraZyme®, PB Assist®+, Serenity® Softgels, Adaptiv™ Capsules*

◉ Rub InTune® down the back of your neck, behind your ears, and on your wrists throughout the day when you need to focus. Mix 5-7 drops of Balance®, Bergamot, and Adaptiv™ in a 10 ml roller bottle and fill remainder with fractionated coconut oil. Rub over your heart, down the back of your neck, and on your spine. Rub the roller bottle on the bottoms of your feet morning and evening. When you feel overwhelmed, rub it over your palms and inhale deeply 3 times. Diffuse Peace® and Serenity® throughout the day in your home or workspace. Take 1-2 Adaptiv™ Capsules each day.

🍎 Take Lifelong Vitality Supplements twice a day, 2-3 DigestZen TerraZyme® capsules at each meal, and PB Assist® once per day. Eat a clean diet with a variety of fresh fruits, vegetables, lean meats, healthy fats, and rice. Avoid MSG, gluten, corn, fried food, fast food, processed foods, and artificial sweeteners.

🔆 Take a walk or hike in nature for 30-45 minutes, 5-6 times per week. Do strength training 3 times per week. Practice balance exercises 3-4 times per week.

🌙 Apply 1 drop of Serenity® or Balance® to your pillow at bedtime. Take 1-2 Serenity® Softgels 30 minutes before bed. Use emotional oils as needed throughout the day to manage stress. Join an online support group or reach out to friends and family for help as needed.

➕ Seek professional medical attention if your symptoms cause ongoing or persistent issues in your relationships, work life, or family. If you have ongoing issues with sleep, mood, energy, appetite, concentration, and motivation or if you do not see an improvement in your condition after a month on this protocol, seek medical attention. If you are feeling suicidal, contact your medical provider or call emergency services right away.

BLADDER CONTROL

⏰ **3-5x per day**	📅 **As needed**

Essential Oils: *Cypress, Thyme, Lavender, Rosemary*

Other Solutions: *Lifelong Vitality*

- 💧 Choose 2-3 of the recommended oils. Mix 5-7 drops of each oil in a 10 ml roller bottle and fill the rest with fractionated coconut oil. Rub the roller bottle over your lower abdomen and lower back throughout the day. Apply the roller bottle to the bottoms of your feet morning and evening.

- 🍎 Take Lifelong Vitality Supplements twice a day. Sip water throughout the day, and don't drink or gulp liquids in one sitting. Avoid excess caffeine.

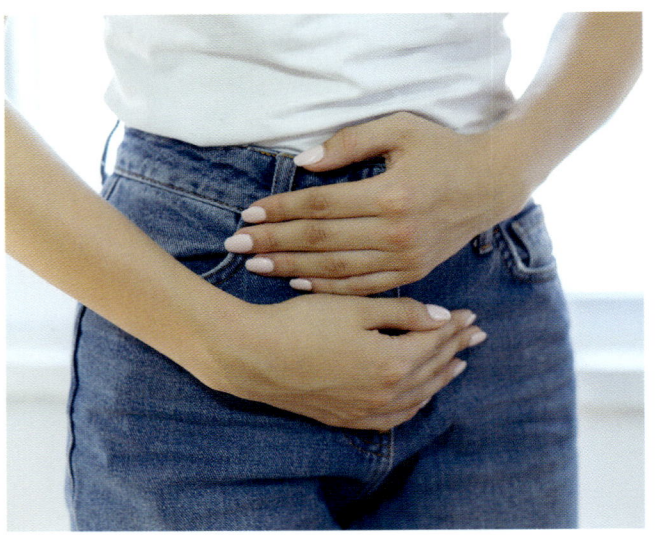

BLADDER INFECTION *(Cystitis)*

⏰ **4-5x per day**	📅 **While symptoms persist**

Essential Oils: *Juniper Berry, On Guard®, On Guard™+ Softgels, Basil, Rosemary, Frankincense, Lemon, Lemon Eucalyptus, Citronella*

Other Solutions: *On Guard™+ Softgels, On Guard® Tablets*

- 💧 Choose 3-4 of the recommended oils. Mix 10 drops of each with fractionated coconut oil in a 10 ml roller bottle. Rub over your abdominal area and on your lower back over your spine every 2-3 hours or until symptoms diminish. Take 1 On Guard® Softgel or Tablet 3 times per day. Add 1 drop of Lemon to warm water or tea and sip throughout day. Drink at least half your body weight in ounces of water per day.

- 🍎 Avoid sugary foods.

- ✚ Make an appointment with your doctor right away if symptoms last more than 5 days or get worse and are accompanied by lower back pain under the ribs.

BLEEDING

⏰ *3-5x per day*	📅 *As needed*

Essential Oils: *Helichrysum, Yarrow|Pom, Geranium, Myrrh*

Other Solutions: *Correct-X*

- ☺ Choose 2-3 of the recommended oils. Apply 1-2 drops of each oil to the affected area. Put a small amount of Correct-X over the affected area, and apply an adhesive bandage or gauze. Change the bandage as needed.

- ⊕ Seek medical attention if the cut does not stop bleeding, is bleeding excessively, or if you need stitches.

BLEEDING GUMS

⏰	*2x per day and after meals*	📅	*Ongoing*

Essential Oils: *Helichrysum, Cinnamon Bark, Spearmint, Myrrh, Clove, Tea Tree, On Guard®*

Other Solutions: *On Guard® Natural Whitening Toothpaste, On Guard® Mouthwash, Peppermint Beadlet*

💜 Combine 1 drop of Helichrysum in 2 ounces of water, shake well, and gargle twice daily, morning and evening. Place 1 drop of Helichrysum onto a soft toothbrush once daily and gently brush your teeth. Use On Guard® Toothpaste and On Guard® Mouthwash every morning and evening. Soak your dental floss in warm salt water with 1 drop of Tea Tree or Spearmint or 1 drop of On Guard® for 5 minutes. Floss daily. Brush your tongue each time you brush your teeth. Place 1 drop of Clove, Cinnamon Bark, or On Guard® on your toothbrush prior to brushing your tongue or teeth. Use Peppermint Beadlets during the day to combat bad breath. Practice oil pulling.

🍎 Eliminate sugar and refined carbohydrates. Avoid sticky candies and sweets like lollipops, caramels, and sugary cough drops. Avoid starchy foods that can get stuck in your mouth, like potato chips. If you eat sugar, eat it with a meal. Eat nuts; seeds; salmon and other fatty fish; grass-fed beef; red and green bell peppers; broccoli; sweet potatoes; and probiotic-containing foods, such as kefir, sauerkraut, fermented yogurt, and kimchi.

🔻 Practice oil pulling to remove toxins and harmful bacteria from your mouth: take a tablespoon of hard coconut oil and place 1 drop of On Guard® and 1 drop of Peppermint or Spearmint on top of the coconut oil. Allow the oil to melt in your mouth, and then swish it around for 5-15 minutes. Pull the oil through your teeth and on both sides of your mouth. When you are done, spit it out in the garbage—not down the sink, as the hard coconut oil could clog the drain over time. Repeat this process a few times per week. Hint: Start off at 1 minute and work your way up, eventually finding the amount of time that feels best to you.

➕ Schedule regular appointments with your dentist to monitor oral health.

BLISTERS *(Foot)*

⏰ **3-5x per day**	📅 *Until symptoms subside*

Essential Oils: *Frankincense, Myrrh, Lavender, Tea Tree*

Other Solutions: *N/A*

 Choose 2-3 of the recommended oils. Mix 5-7 drops of each oil in a 10 ml roller bottle and fill the remainder with fractionated coconut oil. Apply the roller bottle over the blister throughout the day. Place an adhesive bandage over the blister to protect it.

BLOATING

⏰ **3-5x per day**	📅 *Until symptoms subside*

Essential Oils: *DigestZen®, Fennel, Ginger*

Other Solutions: *Ginger Drops, Peppermint Softgels, Peppermint Beadlets, Lifelong Vitality, DigestZen TerraZyme®, PB Assist®+*

 Take up to 2 Peppermint Softgels an hour before meals. Choose 2-3 of the recommended oils. Mix 5-7 drops of each in a 10 ml roller bottle and fill the rest with fractionated coconut oil. Rub the roller bottle over your entire abdomen and your lower back throughout the day. Put 1 drop of Fennel and Peppermint under your tongue and drink some water. Use Ginger Drops as needed. Take Peppermint Beadlets as desired.

⊕ Take Lifelong Vitality Supplements twice a day, 2-3 DigestZen TerraZyme® capsules at each meal, and PB Assist® once per day. Avoid foods that may causes bloating: beans, carbonated beverages, wheat, broccoli, cauliflower, cabbage, Brussels sprouts, onions, dairy products, apples, garlic, sugar alcohols, and beer. Take smaller bites and chew your food slowly (25-30 times).

 Give yourself at least an hour or two after eating before exercising to prevent acid reflux. Rub DigestZen® and Peppermint over your stomach area before exercise.

 If tolerated, do a 30-day cleanse each season. See the 30-day cleanse on page 434.

A-C

BLOOD CLOT

⏰ **3-5x per day**	📅 *Until symptoms subside*

Essential Oils: *Helichrysum, Clove, Copaiba, Fennel*

Other Solutions: *Serenity® Softgels*

🌸 Choose 2-3 of the recommended oils. Place 1-2 drops of each oil in a capsule and take twice a day. Mix 5-7 drops of each oil in a 10 ml roller bottle and fill remainder with fractionated coconut oil. Apply over affected area and on the bottoms of your feet morning and night.

🟢 Include a variety of red-colored foods to your daily diet to support cardiovascular health.

🔴 Do aerobic exercises, strength training, and balance exercises.

🌙 Apply 1 drop of Serenity® or Balance® to your pillow at bedtime. Take 1-2 Serenity® Softgels about 30 minutes before bed. Use emotional oils as needed throughout the day.

🔻 Avoid sitting for long periods of time. Get up and walk around for 5 minutes each hour. Drink plenty of water throughout the day. Don't smoke or drink excess alcohol.

➕ If you experience any of the following symptoms, seek medical attention right away: swelling, redness, pain, or hotness in an area of your arm or leg; lightheadedness; difficult or painful breathing; chest pain or tightness; pain extending down your shoulder, arm, back, or jaw; sudden weakness or numbness of your face, arm, or leg; sudden difficulty speaking or understanding your speech; sudden changes in your vision.

BLOOD TOXICITY

🕐 **4-5x per day**	📅 *While symptoms persist*

Essential Oils: *Geranium, Zendocrine®, DDR Prime®, Frankincense*

Other Solutions: *Turmeric Dual Chamber Capsules*

 Take 2 Turmeric Dual Chamber Capsules per day. Place 1 drop of Frankincense under your tongue morning and evening. Choose 2-3 of the recommended oils. Mix 5-7 drops of each oil in a 10 ml roller bottle and fill remainder with fractionated coconut oil. Apply over your chest, down your neck and spine, and on the bottoms of your feet in the morning and evening.

➕ Call your doctor right away if you experience chills; fever; weakness; rapid breathing; increased heart rate or heart palpitations; or pale skin.

BLURRED VISION

🕐 **3-5x per day**	📅 *Ongoing as needed*

Essential Oils: *DDR Prime®, Copaiba, Helichrysum, Lemongrass*

Other Solutions: *DDR Prime® Capsules, Copaiba Softgels*

➿ Take 1 drop each of DDR Prime® and Copaiba in a capsule 3 times per day. If you don't want to make your own capsules, you can purchase DDR Prime® Softgels and Copaiba Softgels and take 1 of each, 3 times per day. Mix 5-7 drops each of Copaiba, Helichrysum, and Lemongrass in a 10 ml roller bottle and fill remainder with fractionated coconut oil. Apply topically to your forehead, temples, the base of your skull, and behind your ears.

➕ If you experience ongoing and extended blurred vision, seek advice from an eye doctor and your primary care physician.

BODY ODOR

 3-5x per day   *Ongoing as needed*

Essential Oils: *Zendocrine®, Arborvitae, Petitgrain*

Other Solutions: *Natural Deodorant with Balance®, Zendocrine® Softgels*

 Place 1 drop of Zendocrine® in a capsule or take 1 Zendocrine® Softgel, 3 times per day. Mix 5-7 drops each of Arborvitae and Petitgrain in a 10 ml roller bottle and fill remainder with fractionated coconut oil. Apply to areas where you sweat and on the bottoms of your feet morning and evening. Use Natural Deodorant with Balance® in the morning
or after working out.

 Eliminate these foods and see if there is an improvement: broccoli, cauliflower, cabbage, kale, Brussels sprouts, asparagus, garlic, onions, cumin, curry, seafood, and alcohol.

 Take a shower after each exercise session. Apply the oil blend as needed. Use Natural Deodorant with Balance® after showering.

BOILS

⏰ *3-5x per day*	📅 *Until symptoms subside*

Essential Oils: *Tea Tree, Purify, Lavender*

Other Solutions: *N/A*

 Choose 2 of the recommended oils. Mix 5-7 drops of each oil in a 10 ml roller bottle and fill remainder with fractionated coconut oil. Apply the roller bottle to the affected area throughout the day.

BONE PAIN

⏰ *4-5x per day*	📅 *Ongoing as needed*

Essential Oils: *Helichrysum, Wintergreen, Birch*

Other Solutions: *Bone Nutrient Essential Complex, Turmeric Dual Chamber Capsules, Deep Blue® Polyphenol Complex Capsules, Deep Blue® Rub, Deep Blue® Stick*

 Mix 5-7 drops each of Helichrysum, Wintergreen, and Birch in a 10 ml roller bottle and fill with fractionated coconut oil. Apply to affected area throughout the day. Apply Deep Blue® Rub over affected area after applying the roller bottle blend. Take 4 Bone Nutrient capsules daily with food. If you get oils in your eyes or on your face, apply plain coconut oil over your eye or face to soothe the area. Repeat as needed.

 Take 2 Turmeric Dual Chamber Capsules each day. Take 2 Deep Blue® Polyphenol Complex capsules per day.

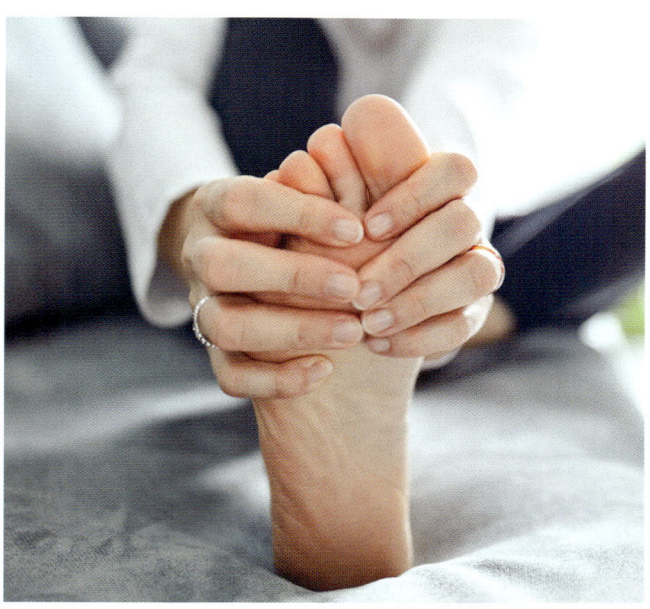

BONE SPURS

⏰ *3-5x per day*	📅 *As needed*

Essential Oils: *Cypress, Eucalyptus, Basil, Lemongrass, Wintergreen*

Other Solutions: *Turmeric Dual Chamber Capsules, Copaiba Softgels, Deep Blue® Stick*

 Take 2 Turmeric Dual Chamber Capsules per day. Take 2 Copaiba Softgels per day. Choose 3 of the recommended oils. Mix 5-7 drops of each oil in a 10 ml roller bottle and fill the rest with fractionated coconut oil. Apply over the affected area throughout the day. Rub on the bottoms of your feet morning and evening.

BRAIN FOG

⏰ *4-5x per day*	📅 *Ongoing as needed*

Essential Oils: *Peppermint, Motivate®, InTune®*

Other Solutions: *Peppermint Beadlets, Mito2Max®, Lifelong Vitality, DigestZen TerraZyme®, PB Assist®+*

🌙 Apply InTune® down the back of your neck, under your skull, and over your forehead. Put 1 drop of Peppermint in your water and drink throughout the day. Diffuse 4-5 drops each of Peppermint and Motivate® in the room you are in. Place 1 drop each of Peppermint and Motivate® in your palms and rub them together. Inhale deeply 3 times and repeat as needed. Take Peppermint Beadlets throughout the day as needed. Take 2 Mito2Max® per day with food.

If you get oils in your eyes or on your face while inhaling from your hands, apply plain coconut oil over your eye or face to soothe the area. Repeat as needed.

🌿 Take Lifelong Vitality Supplements twice a day, 2-3 DigestZen TerraZyme® Capsules at each meal, and PB Assist® once per day. Eat a variety of fresh fruits, vegetables, lean meats, healthy fats, and rice. Avoid artificial dyes and colorings, MSG, gluten, corn, fried food, fast food, processed foods, and artificial sweeteners.

🔶 Combine 1 drop each of Peppermint and Motivate® with 1 tablespoon of fractionated coconut oil. Rub over your chest and behind your neck before exercise. Add 1 drop of Peppermint to your water bottle *(glass or stainless steel)*. Do aerobic exercises, strength training, and balance exercises.

🔴 Makeover your home by using the Abōde™ line of cleaning products, laundry pods, dishwasher pods, surface cleaner, and dish soap. Take care of your hands with Abōde™ Foaming Hand Wash and Lotion. If tolerated, do a 30-day cleanse each season. See the 30-day cleanse on page 434.

BRAIN INJURY

4-5x per day	🗓 Ongoing

Essential Oils: *Frankincense, Copaiba, DDR Prime®, Balance®, Celery Seed*

Other Solutions: *Turmeric Dual Chamber Capsules, DDR Prime® Softgel*

 Put 1 drop each of Frankincense and Copaiba under your tongue morning and evening. Mix 5-7 drops of each recommended oil in a 10 ml roller bottle and mix with fractionated coconut oil. Apply down the back of your neck, below your skull, behind your ears, down your spine, and on the bottoms of your feet, morning and evening. Take 1 DDR Prime® Softgel 3 times per day. Take 2 Turmeric Dual Chamber Capsules per day with meals.

BREASTFEEDING *(Milk Supply)*

⏰ 4-5x per day	🗓 As needed

Essential Oils: *Fennel, Lavender, Clary Sage, Basil*

Other Solutions:

 Choose 2 of the recommended oils. Mix 5-7 drops of each oil in a 10 ml roller bottle and fill remainder with fractionated coconut oil. Massage into your breasts throughout the day. Apply the roller bottle to the bottoms of your feet morning and evening.

🌀 Avoid taking Peppermint (or any blends that have Peppermint in them) internally, as it can decrease milk supply.

🌙 Try to rest when the baby rests. Aim to get 7-9 hours of sleep per night. Place 1 drop of Lavender or Serenity® on your pillow at bedtime.

BREATHING PROBLEMS

⏰ *4-5x per day*	📅 *As needed*

Essential Oils: *Breathe®, Eucalyptus, Peppermint, Serenity®*

Other Solutions: *Breathe® Drops, Breathe® Vapor Stick, Correct-X, Serenity® Softgels*

🌙 Choose 2 of the recommended oils. Put 1-2 drops of each oil in your palm and mix with a tablespoon of fractionated coconut oil. Rub over your chest, your mid/upper back, and on the bottoms of your feet morning and night. After applying the oils, inhale from your hands slowly and deeply, taking 3 full belly breaths. Repeat often throughout the day. Use Breathe® Drops and the Breathe® Vapor Stick as needed. If you get oils in your eyes or on your face while inhaling from your hands, apply plain coconut oil over your eye or face to soothe the area. Repeat as needed. Use a cotton swab to apply a dab of Correct-X into your nose for added immune support.

🌱 Avoid dairy if you are experiencing breathing issues, as it can cause excess mucus.

🌙 Diffuse 4-5 drops each of Serenity® and Breathe® at bedtime, or put 1 drop of each on your pillow. Take Serenity® Softgels before bed.

➕ Watch for symptoms of severe shortness of breath, chest tightness, or coughing and wheezing. If you are unable to speak more than a few short sentences or have to strain your chest muscles to breathe, seek medical attention right away.

BRITTLE NAILS

⏰ *3-5x per day*	📅 *Until symptoms subside*

Essential Oils: *Arborvitae, Frankincense, Myrrh*

Other Solutions: *Lifelong Vitality, DigestZen TerraZyme®, PB Assist®+, Bone Nutrient Essential Complex*

🌙 Choose 2 of the recommended oils. Rub 1-2 drops of each with 1 tablespoon of fractionated coconut oil over your nails throughout the day. Apply 1-2 drops of each oil to the bottoms of your feet morning and evening.

🌱 Take Lifelong Vitality Supplements twice a day; 2-3 DigestZen TerraZyme® capsules at each meal; PB Assist® once per day; and 4 Bone Nutrient Essential Complex capsules a day. Add Lemon to your water (*2 drops per glass*) and drink half your body weight in ounces of water per day.

🌙 Avoid too much exposure to water. Avoid using gel or acrylic nails. Give your nails a break from polish. Keep your nails short. Don't use your nails to do things (like opening soda cans); opt for a paperclip or other tool instead. Use a shampoo and handwash that won't dry your hands out.

BROKEN HEART SYNDROME

⏰ **3-5x per day**	📅 **As needed**

Essential Oils: *Console®, Adaptiv™ (3-part system), Ylang Ylang, Peace®*

Other Solutions: *Adaptiv™ Capsules*

 Diffuse 3-5 drops each of Console®, Ylang Ylang, and Peace® throughout the day. Take 1 Adaptiv™ Capsule per day. Rub 1 drop each of Adaptiv™, Console®, and Peace® with 1 tablespoon of fractionated coconut oil over your heart, on the back of your neck, and on the bottoms of your feet morning and evening.

BRONCHITIS

⏰ **3-5x per day**	📅 **As needed**

Essential Oils: *Breathe®, Eucalyptus, Cardamom, Serenity®*

Other Solutions: *Breathe® Drops, Breathe® Vapor Stick, Serenity® Softgels*

 Choose 2 of the recommended oils. Mix 5-7 drops of each in a 10 ml roller bottle and fill remainder with fractionated coconut oil. Apply over your chest, your mid/upper back, and the bottoms of your feet morning and evening. Put 1 drop each of Breathe® and Eucalyptus in your palms, rub them together, and inhale from your palms slowly and deeply 3 times or as needed. Use Breathe® Drops and the Breathe® Vapor Stick as needed.

If you get oils in your eyes or on your face while inhaling from your hands, apply plain coconut oil over your eye or face to soothe the area. Repeat as needed.

🍎 Avoid dairy products. Add 1-2 drops of Lemon to your water, and drink half your body weight in ounces of water.

🌙 Diffuse 4-5 drops each of Serenity® and Breathe® at bedtime, or put 1 drop of each on your pillow. Use Serenity® Softgels before bed.

➕ Watch for symptoms of severe shortness of breath, chest tightness, or coughing and wheezing. If you are unable to speak more than a few short sentences or have to strain your chest muscles to breathe, seek medical attention right away.

BRUISE

⏰ *3-5x per day*	📅 *Until bruising is gone*

Essential Oils: *Helichrysum, Geranium, Deep Blue®*

Other Solutions: *Deep Blue® Stick*

- 💜 Choose 2 of the recommended oils. Apply 1-2 drops of each oil with a tablespoon of fractionated coconut oil over the bruise throughout the day. You can alternatively apply Deep Blue® Stick.

- ➕ Talk to your doctor if you get frequent bruising, as it could be caused by an underlying medical condition.

BRUISED MUSCLES

⏰ *3-5x per day*	📅 *Until bruising is gone and pain subsides*

Essential Oils: *Helichrysum, Geranium, Deep Blue®*

Other Solutions: *Deep Blue® Stick*

- 💜 Choose 2 of the recommended oils. Apply 1-2 drops of each oil with a tablespoon of fractionated coconut oil over the bruise throughout the day. You can alternatively apply Deep Blue® Stick.

- ➕ Talk to your doctor if you frequently bruise, as it could be caused by an underlying medical condition.

BULIMIA

⏰ **3-5x per day**	📅 **As needed**

Essential Oils: *Melissa, Cinnamon, Grapefruit, Forgive®, Patchouli*

Other Solutions: *Peppermint Beadlets, Ginger Drops, Lifelong Vitality, DigestZen TerraZyme®, PB Assist®+, Serenity® Softgels*

 Diffuse 4-5 drops each of Forgive®, Grapefruit, and Patchouli throughout the day. Put 1-2 drops of Grapefruit in your water and drink. Choose 3 of the recommended oils. Mix 5-7 drops of each in a 10 ml roller bottle and fill with fractionated coconut oil. Rub over your abdomen and lower back, down the back of your neck, and over your pulse points. Take Peppermint Beadlets as desired. Take Ginger Drops as needed.

🌿 Take Lifelong Vitality Supplements twice a day, 2-3 DigestZen TerraZyme® capsules at each meal, and PB Assist® once per day. Seek professional attention for ongoing support.

❤ Take the focus off your weight and set goals of getting stronger; building endurance; and enjoying how your mood, outlook, and energy levels increase when you adopt a regular exercise routine.

🌙 Apply 1 drop of Serenity® or Lavender to your pillow at bedtime. Take 1-2 Serenity® Softgels 30 minutes before bed. Use emotional oils as needed throughout the day. Include meditation, prayer,

and spending time in nature as part of your regular routine to rest and manage your stress. Join an online support group or reach out to friends and family for help as needed.

➕ Don't struggle alone. Reach out for professional help if you feel you are out of control with your eating.

BUNIONS

⏰ **3-5x per day**	📅 **As needed**

Essential Oils: *Copaiba, Eucalyptus, Cypress*

Other Solutions: *N/A*

 Choose 2 of the recommended oils. Apply 1-2 drops of each oil with a tablespoon of fractionated coconut oil to the affected joint throughout the day.

BURNS

⏰ **4-5x per day**	📅 **Until symptoms resolve**

Essential Oils: *Lavender, Tea Tree, Helichrysum*

Other Solutions: *Yarrow|Pom Body Renewal Serum, Yarrow|Pom Botanical Nutritive Duo*

Apply 1 drop of Lavender with 1 drop of Tea Tree or Helichrysum over the burn throughout the day. Apply Yarrow|Pom Body Renewal Serum around burn twice daily. Take 2 Yarrow|Pom Botanical Nutritive Duo capsules per day.

If you experience oozing, increased pain, redness, blistering, or swelling or notice the burn is not getting better, seek medical attention right away.

BURSITIS

4-5x per day	**While symptoms persist**

Essential Oils: *Copaiba, Frankincense, AromaTouch®, Cypress, Wintergreen, Siberian Fir*

Other Solutions: *Lifelong Vitality, DigestZen TerraZyme®, PB Assist®+, Serenity® Softgels, Turmeric Dual Chamber Capsules, Deep Blue® Polyphenol Complex, Deep Blue® Rub, Deep Blue® Stick*

⊙ Put 1 drop each of Frankincense and Copaiba under your tongue morning and evening. Mix 5-7 drops each of AromaTouch®, Cypress, Wintergreen, and Siberian Fir in a 10 ml roller bottle and fill with fractionated coconut oil. Apply over affected joint(s), and then massage Deep Blue® Rub or Deep Blue® Stick over affected joints. If you get oils in your eyes or on your face, apply plain coconut oil over your eye or face to soothe the area. Repeat as needed.

⊙ Take Lifelong Vitality Supplements twice a day, 2-3 DigestZen TerraZyme® Capsules at each meal, and PB Assist® once per day. Take 2 Turmeric Dual Chamber Capsules each day. Take 2 Deep Blue® Polyphenol Complex capsules per day. Eat a variety of fresh fruits, vegetables, lean meats, healthy fats, and rice. Avoid MSG, gluten, corn, fried food, fast food, processed foods, and artificial sweeteners.

⊙ Rub Deep Blue® Rub or Deep Blue® Stick over affected joints before and after exercise. Do 35-45 minutes of low-impact aerobic activity, 5 times per week do moderate strength training 3-4 times per week. Do joint flexibility exercises on affected joints. Warm up, cool down, and stretch for each exercise session.

⊙ Apply 1 drop of Serenity® or Lavender to your pillow at bedtime. Take 1-2 Serenity® Softgels 30 minutes before bed. Rub the roller blend and Deep Blue® rub to the affected area at bedtime. Use oils from the emotional kit to manage emotional health.

CALLUSES

3-4x per day	**While symptoms persist**

Essential Oils: *Tea Tree, Peppermint, Roman Chamomile, Copaiba*

Other Solutions: *Yarrow|Pom Body Renewal Serum, Yarrow|Pom Botanical Nutritive Duo*

 Choose 2-3 of the recommended oils. Apply 1 drop each oil with a tbsp of fractionated coconut oil over the callus throughout the day. Apply Yarrow|Pom Body Renewal Serum to the affected area twice daily and take 2 Yarrow|Pom Botanical Nutritive Duo capsules per day.

CANCER

4-5x per day	**Ongoing**

Essential Oils: *DDR Prime®, Frankincense, Thyme, Arborvitae*

Other Solutions: *Ginger Drops, Lifelong Vitality, DigestZen TerraZyme®, PB Assist®+, Turmeric Dual Chamber Capsules*

 Take 2-3 Turmeric Dual Chamber Capsules per day. Put 1 drop of Frankincense under your tongue 3 times per day. Mix 5-7 drops each of DDR Prime®, Frankincense, Thyme, and Arborvitae in a 10 ml roller bottle and fill remainder with fractionated coconut oil. Apply over the organ or tissue that has cancer throughout the day. Apply the roller blend to the bottoms of your feet morning and evening. Take Ginger Drops as desired.

 Take Lifelong Vitality Supplements twice a day, 2-3 DigestZen TerraZyme® capsules at each meal, and PB Assist® once per day. Eat a variety of fresh fruits, vegetables, lean meats, healthy fats, and rice. Avoid MSG, gluten, corn, fried food, fast food, processed foods, and artificial sweeteners.

CANDIDIASIS

4-5x per day	While symptoms persist

Essential Oils: *Tea Tree, Lemon Eucalyptus, Siberian Fir, DDR Prime®, Thyme, Oregano, Pink Pepper, Geranium, Clove, Citronella*

Other Solutions: *Lifelong Vitality, DigestZen TerraZyme®, PB Assist®+, GX Assist®*

- Mix 7 drops each of Lemon Eucalyptus, Tea Tree, Thyme, Oregano, and Geranium with fractionated coconut oil in a 10 ml roller bottle. Rub along your spine, over your abdominal region, on your wrists, and on your feet every 2-3 hours or until symptoms diminish. Take 1 drop each of Siberian Fir, Clove, DDR Prime®, and Pink Pepper in a capsule with a carrier oil twice daily with meals.

- Take Lifelong Vitality Supplements twice a day and 2-3 DigestZen TerraZyme® capsules at each meal. Take 1-2 GX Assist® for 10 days and follow it up with PB Assist® once per day for 20 days. Eat a variety of fresh fruits, vegetables, lean meats, healthy fats, and rice. Avoid MSG, gluten, corn, fried food, fast food, processed foods, and artificial sweeteners.

- If tolerated, do a 30-day cleanse each season. See the 30-day cleanse on page 434.

CANKER SORES

4-5x per day	While symptoms persist

Essential Oils: *Tea Tree, On Guard®, Myrrh*

Other Solutions: *N/A*

- Apply 1 drop of each recommended oil directly on your canker sore. Gargle a few drops of each oil mixed with water several times daily, apply topically to gums, or take internally as needed.

CARDIOVASCULAR DISEASE

⏰ *3-5x per day*	📅 *Ongoing*

Essential Oils: *Copaiba, Marjoram, Ylang Ylang, Petitgrain*

Other Solutions: *Turmeric Dual Chamber Capsules, Lifelong Vitality, DigestZen TerraZyme®, PB Assist®+, Serenity® Softgels*

💧 Mix 5-7 drops of each oil in a 10 ml roller bottle and fill remainder with fractionated coconut oil. Apply over your heart, over the pulse points on your wrists, down your spine, and on the bottoms of your feet morning and night. Take 2 Dual Chamber Turmeric Capsules daily.

🍎 Take Lifelong Vitality Supplements twice a day, 2-3 DigestZen TerraZyme® Capsules at each meal, and PB Assist® once per day. Eat a variety of fresh fruits, vegetables, lean meats, healthy fats, and rice. Include red foods in your daily diet. Avoid MSG, gluten, corn, fried food, fast food, processed foods, and artificial sweeteners.

🔄 Do aerobic exercises, strength training, and balance exercises.

☾ Apply 1 drop of Serenity® or Lavender to your pillow at bedtime. Take 1-2 Serenity® Softgels 30 minutes before bed. Adopt a meditation or yoga practice for stress relief. Use oils from the emotional kit to manage emotional health.

➕ If you experience any of the following symptoms, seek medical attention right away: swelling, redness, pain, or hotness in an area of your arm or leg; lightheadedness; difficult or painful breathing; chest pain or tightness; pain extending down your shoulder, arm, back, or jaw; sudden weakness or numbness of your face, arm, or leg; sudden difficulty speaking or understanding your speech; sudden changes in your vision.

CARPAL TUNNEL SYNDROME

⏰ 3-5x per day	📅 While symptoms persist

Essential Oils: *Wintergreen, Copaiba, Lemongrass, Deep Blue® Rub, Siberian Fir*

Other Solutions: *Lifelong Vitality, DigestZen TerraZyme®, PB Assist®+, Turmeric Dual Chamber Capsules, Deep Blue® Polyphenol Complex, Deep Blue® Stick*

 Mix 5-7 drops of Wintergreen, Copaiba, Lemongrass, and Siberian Fir in a 10 ml roller bottle and fill remainder with fractionated coconut oil. Apply over the affected wrist(s) throughout the day. Follow it up by applying Deep Blue® Rub or Deep Blue Stick® over the affected wrist(s). Take 1 Deep Blue® Polyphenol Complex morning and evening. If you get oils in your eyes or on your face, apply plain coconut oil over the eye or face to soothe the area. Repeat as needed.

🌱 Take Lifelong Vitality Supplements twice a day, 2-3 DigestZen TerraZyme® capsules at each meal, and PB Assist® once per day. Take 2 Turmeric Dual Chamber Capsules each day. Take 2 Deep Blue® Polyphenol Complex capsules per day. Eat a variety of fresh fruits, vegetables, lean meats, fatty fish, healthy fats, and rice. Avoid MSG, gluten, corn, fried food, fast food, processed foods, and artificial sweeteners.

CARTILAGE INJURY

⏰ 4-5x per day	📅 As needed

Essential Oils: *Helichrysum, Wintergreen, Marjoram, Copaiba, Lemongrass, Frankincense, Siberian Fir, Deep Blue® Rub, Deep Blue® Stick*

Other Solutions: *Deep Blue® Polyphenol Complex*

 Choose 2-3 of the recommended oils. Mix 5-7 drops of each with fractionated coconut oil in a 10 ml roller bottle. Apply over the affected joint(s). Take 2 Deep Blue® Polyphenol Complex capsules per day with food. Use Deep Blue® Rub or Deep Blue® Stick over the affected area as needed.

CAVITIES

⏰ 3-5x per day	📅 While symptoms persist

Essential Oils: *Clove, On Guard®, Tea Tree*

Other Solutions: *On Guard® Natural Whitening Toothpaste, On Guard® Mouthwash*

 Brush your teeth with On Guard® toothpaste 3 times per day. Use On Guard® Mouthwash after brushing your teeth, 3 times per day. Place 1 drop each of Clove, On Guard®, and Tea Tree over the cavity throughout the day.

🌱 Eliminate sugar and refined carbohydrates. Avoid sticky candies and sweets like lollipops, caramels, and sugary cough drops. Avoid starchy foods that can get stuck in your mouth, like potato chips. If you eat sugar, eat it with a meal.

CELIAC DISEASE

⏰ **4-5x per day**	📅 *While symptoms persist*

Essential Oils: *DigestZen®, Petitgrain, Copaiba, Celery Seed, On Guard®*

Other Solutions: *Turmeric Dual Chamber Capsules, Lifelong Vitality, DigestZen TerraZyme®, PB Assist®+*

 Place 1 drop each of Copaiba, DigestZen®, Celery Seed, and On Guard® in a capsule and take 3 times per day. Rub 1 drop each of DigestZen®, Petitgrain, and On Guard® with a tablespoon of fractionated coconut oil over your abdomen and your mid/lower back throughout the day. Take 2 Turmeric Dual Chamber Capsules per day.

 Avoid wheat or any gluten-containing foods or products. Take Lifelong Vitality Supplements twice a day, 2-3 DigestZen TerraZyme® capsules at each meal, and PB Assist® once per day. Eat a variety of fresh fruits, vegetables, lean meats, healthy fats, and rice. Avoid MSG, gluten, corn, fried food, fast food, processed foods, and artificial sweeteners.

CELLULITE

 Morning and evening   *While symptoms persist*

Essential Oils: *MetaPWR™, Grapefruit, Eucalyptus, Lemongrass, Green Mandarin*

Other Solutions: *MetaPWR™ Softgels, Yarrow|Pom Body Renewal Serum, Yarrow|Pom Botanical Nutritive Duo capsules*

- Fill a 4-ounce glass Mason jar with hard coconut oil. Add 10 drops of each recommended oil to the jar and mix slowly with the end of a spoon (*make sure you mix it well and don't spill the oils*). Apply the mixture to cellulite morning and evening, massaging it into the tissues. Apply Yarrow|Pom Body Renewal Serum on the affected area. Take 2 Yarrow|Pom Botanical Nutritive Duo capsules per day. Take 1 MetaPWR™ Softgel with meals.

- Add 1-2 drops of MetaPWR™, Lemon, Grapefruit, or Green Mandarin to your water and drink. Eat a healthy diet full of green leafy vegetables, fresh fruit, healthy fats, sweet potatoes, and lean protein. Avoid processed foods, junk foods, fried foods, sugar, artificial sweeteners, and trans fats.

- Exercise 5-6 times per week. Choose from cardio, yoga, strength, balance exercises, and flexibility exercises.

- Do a dry skin brush before showering 3 times per week. After showering, apply the essential oil mixture. Get a good night's rest each night.

- If tolerated, do a 30-day cleanse each season. See the 30-day cleanse on page 434.

CHAPPED SKIN

🕐 *3-5x per day*	📅 *While symptoms persist*

Essential Oils: *Myrrh, Roman Chamomile, Immortelle*

Other Solutions: *Yarrow|Pom Body Renewal Serum, Yarrow|Pom Botanical Nutritive Duo*

🟣 Choose 2-3 of the recommended oils. Apply 1-2 drops of each oil topically to the affected area as often as needed. Roll Immortelle over the affected area throughout the day. Apply Yarrow|Pom Body Renewal Serum on the affected area twice daily. Take 2 Yarrow|Pom Botanical Nutritive Duo capsules per day.

CHEST INFECTION

🕐 *3-5x per day*	📅 *As needed*

Essential Oils: *Breathe®, Eucalyptus, Tea Tree, On Guard®, Zendocrine®*

Other Solutions: *Breathe® Drops, Breathe® Vapor Stick, On Guard® Beadlets, On Guard™+ Softgels, On Guard® Tablets*

🟣 Choose 3 of the recommended oils. Mix 5-7 drops of each in a 10 ml roller bottle and fill with fractionated coconut oil. Apply over your chest, your mid/upper back, and the bottoms of your feet morning and evening. Put 1 drop each of Breathe® and Eucalyptus in your palms, rub them together, and inhale slowly and deeply 3 times as needed. If you get oils in your eyes or on your face while inhaling from your hands, apply plain coconut oil over your eye or face to soothe the area. Repeat as needed. Take Breathe® Drops as needed. Rub a Breathe® Vapor Stick over your chest and upper back throughout the day. Take On Guard® Beadlets as desired. Take On Guard™+ Softgels 3-4 times per day.

🟢 Avoid dairy products. Add 1-2 drops of Lemon to your water and drink. Drink half your body weight in ounces of water.

🔵 Watch for severe shortness of breath, chest tightness, or coughing and wheezing. If you are unable to speak more than a few short sentences or have to strain your chest muscles to breathe, seek medical attention right away.

CHEST PAIN

| ⏰ *3-5x per day* | 📅 *While symptoms persist* |

Essential Oils: *On Guard®, Douglas Fir, DDR Prime®, AromaTouch®*

Other Solutions: *Breathe® Drops, Breathe® Vapor Stick*

 Apply 1-2 drops each of AromaTouch®, Douglas Fir, and On Guard® topically with a tablespoon of fractionated coconut oil to your chest. Put 1-2 drops of DDR Prime® and On Guard® in a capsule and take twice daily. Use Breathe® Drops and the Breathe® Vapor Stick as needed.

 Watch for symptoms of severe shortness of breath, chest tightness, or coughing and wheezing. If you are unable to speak more than a few short sentences or have to strain your chest muscles to breathe, seek medical attention right away.

CHICKEN POX

| ⏰ *3-5x per day* | 📅 *While symptoms persist* |

Essential Oils: *DDR Prime®, Thyme, Tea Tree, On Guard®*

Other Solutions: *On Guard® Beadlets, On Guard® Tablets*

 Put 1-2 drops each of DDR Prime®, Thyme, and On Guard® in a capsule and take 3 times daily. Mix 5-7 drops each of DDR Prime®, Thyme, Tea Tree, and On Guard® in a 10 ml roller bottle and fill remainder with fractionated coconut oil. Apply the roller bottle over the chicken pox throughout the day. Take 3 On Guard® Beadlets or Tablets.

CHIGGERS

| ⏰ *3-5x per day* | 📅 *While symptoms persist* |

Essential Oils: *Lemongrass, TerraShield®, Purify, Zendocrine®*

Other Solutions: *Zendocrine® Softgels*

 Put 1-2 drops of Zendocrine® in a capsule and take 3 times per day, or purchase Zendocrine® Softgels and take 3 per day. Choose 2-3 of the recommended oils. Mix 5-7 drops of each in a 10 ml roller bottle and fill with fractionated coconut oil. Apply to the bottoms of your feet morning and evening and rub over the chigger bites throughout the day.

CHRONIC FATIGUE

| ⏰ *3-5x per day* | 📅 *Ongoing as needed* |

Essential Oils: *Peppermint, Rosemary, Basil, Black Pepper*

Other Solutions: *Peppermint Beadlets*

 Choose 2-3 of the recommended oils. Diffuse 3-4 drops of each oil in a diffuser throughout the day. Mix 5-7 drops each of Peppermint, Rosemary, Basil, and Black Pepper in a 10 ml roller bottle and fill with fractionated coconut oil. Apply over your chest, temples, the back of your neck, and over your wrists throughout the day. Use Peppermint Beadlets as needed.

CHRONIC MIGRAINES

⏰ **3-5x per day**	📅 *While symptoms persist*

Essential Oils: *Peppermint, Copaiba, Frankincense*

Other Solutions: *Peppermint Beadlets, Lifelong Vitality, DigestZen TerraZyme®, PB Assist®+, Serenity® Softgels*

◉ Choose 2 of the recommended oils. Apply a few drops of each oil topically to your forehead, temples, the base of your skull, the back of your neck, and the bottoms of your feet, or diffuse into the air and inhale as needed. Use Peppermint Beadlets as needed. Use Deep Blue® Rub or Deep Blue® Stick on affected areas when possible.

● Take Lifelong Vitality Supplements twice a day, 2-3 DigestZen TerraZyme® capsules at each meal, and PB Assist® once per day. Eat a variety of fresh fruits, vegetables, lean meats, healthy fats, and rice. Avoid trigger foods: lunch meats, sulphites, tyramine, nitrates, nitrites, bananas, excessive caffeine, aged cheese, yeast-based products (*like bread and pizza*), soy sauce, milk, beans, alcohol, MSG, gluten, corn, fried food, fast food, processed foods, and artificial sweeteners.

◉ Apply the blend to back of your neck and under your skull before exercise. Do aerobic exercises, strength training, and balance exercises.

◉ Place 1 drop of Lavender or Serenity® on your pillow at night. Turn off electronic devices an hour or two before bed.

◉ Makeover your home by using the Abōde™ line of cleaning products, laundry pods, dishwasher pods, surface cleaner, and dish soap. Take care of your hands with Abōde™ Foaming Hand Wash and Lotion. If tolerated, do a 30-day cleanse each season. See the 30-day cleanse on page 434.

CHRONIC PAIN

⏰ 4-5x per day	📅 As needed

Essential Oils: *Copaiba, Wintergreen*

Other Solutions: *Lifelong Vitality, DigestZen TerraZyme®, PB Assist®+, Serenity® Softgels, Deep Blue® Rub, Deep Blue® Stick*

- Choose 2 of the recommended oils. Apply 1-2 drops of each oil with a tablespoon of fractionated coconut oil over the affected area throughout the day. Use Deep Blue® Rub or Deep Blue® Stick on affected areas when possible.

- Take Lifelong Vitality Supplements twice a day, 2-3 DigestZen TerraZyme® capsules at each meal, and PB Assist® once per day. Eat a variety of fresh fruits, vegetables, lean meats, healthy fats, and rice. Avoid MSG, gluten, corn, fried food, fast food, processed foods, and artificial sweeteners.

- Do aerobic exercises, strength training, and balance exercises.

- Place 1 drop of Lavender or Serenity® on your pillow at night. Turn off electronic devices an hour or two before bed. Apply the recommended oils to the affected area before bed or during the night if the pain wakes you.

- If tolerated, do a 30-day cleanse each season. See the 30-day cleanse on page 434.

CIRRHOSIS

⏰ 4-5x per day	📅 As needed

Essential Oils: *Geranium, Myrrh, Cypress, Marjoram, Celery Seed*

Other Solutions: *Ginger Drops, Zendocrine® Softgels*

- Place 1 drop of Celery Seed in a glass of water and drink, twice per day. Combine 5 drops each of Geranium, Marjoram, Cypress, Myrrh, and Celery Seed in a 10 ml roller bottle with fractionated coconut oil. Apply over your kidney area, to the left and right of your spine just under your rib cage, and to the right side of your abdominal area. Prior to applying the blend, apply a warm compress to increase blood flow to the area and enhance absorption. Take 2 Zendocrine® Softgels daily, one each with morning and evening meals. Take Ginger Drops as needed.

- Seek medical attention right away if you experience yellowing of the eyes or skin or tenderness in the upper abdominal area.

CLOGGED PORES

⏰ **2-3x per day as needed**	📅 *Ongoing while symptoms persist*

Essential Oils: *HD Clear®, Tea Tree, Lavender, Sandalwood*

Other Solutions: *HD Clear® Foaming Face Wash, HD Clear® Facial Lotion, Lifelong Vitality, DigestZen Terra-Zyme®, PB Assist®+, DDR Prime® Softgels, Zendocrine® Complex, Zendocrine® Softgels, GX Assist®*

💜 Wash your face or the affected area in the morning and evening with HD Clear® Foaming Face Wash, apply HD Clear® over the acne, and apply HD Clear® Facial Lotion over your face or the affected area. If you don't have HD Clear®, make a roller bottle with 7 drops each of Tea Tree, Lavender, and Sandalwood and fill the rest with fractionated coconut oil. Wash your face or the affected area with a toxic-free cleanser morning and evening, apply the roller bottle over the acne, and follow up with a toxic-free skin lotion.

🌿 Eat a variety of fresh fruits and vegetables. Avoid greasy foods, chocolate, refined foods, excess sugar, corn syrup, fried foods, and dairy products. Take Lifelong Vitality supplements twice per day. Take 2 DigestZen TerraZyme® with meals. Take PB Assist®+ once per day.

🔶 Wash your face or the affected area with the recommended solution before and after exercise to prevent clogged pores. Apply makeup as usual if desired.

🔻 Avoid using toxic products on your skin. Sixty percent of what you put on your skin gets absorbed into your body. Take inventory of products you put on your skin and remove any toxic products from your home. Read labels and make sure that you research the safety of ingredients before using anything topically. Do a 30-day cleanse for your body 4 times each year *(you can do this each season)* to keep your skin and other organs functioning properly. Suggested 30-day cleanse: Take 2 DDR Prime® Softgels with meals; take 1 Zendocrine® Complex with morning and evening meals; take 1 Zendocrine® Softgel with meals; take 1 GX Assist® at morning and evening meals for days 10-20; take 1 PB Assist® with meals on days 20-30.

COLD BODY TEMPERATURE

 3x per day | *As needed*

Essential Oils: *AromaTouch®, Black Pepper, Cinnamon*

Other Solutions: *N/A*

 Choose 2 of the recommended oils. Apply topically to your chest, the bottoms of your feet, and inside of your wrists as needed.

COLD SORES

 3-5x per day | *While symptoms persist*

Essential Oils: *Clove, On Guard®, Tea Tree*

Other Solutions: *N/A*

Choose 2 of the recommended oils. Apply 1 drop of each oil topically to the affected area with fractionated coconut oil as needed.

COLIC

 3-4x per day | *While symptoms persist*

Essential Oils: *Fennel, Tamer™, DigestZen®, Serenity®*

Other Solutions: *N/A*

 Choose 2 of the recommended oils. Mix 1 drop of each in a 10 ml roller bottle and fill with fractionated coconut oil. Apply topically to the baby's stomach and back before the baby goes to sleep or as needed.

 If you are breastfeeding, consider eliminating foods from your diet that may cause gas and bloating for the baby: dairy products, broccoli, cauliflower, cabbage, beans, Brussels sprouts, fermented foods, spicy foods, peppermint, parsley, sage, nuts, seeds, eggs, artificial sweeteners, chocolate, and caffeine.

A-C

COMMON COLD

⏰ *3-5x per day*	📅 *While symptoms persist*

Essential Oils: *On Guard®, Thyme, Black Pepper, Tea Tree*

Other Solutions: *On Guard™+ Softgels, On Guard® Beadlets, On Guard® Protecting Throat Drops, Correct-X, On Guard® Tablets*

 Choose 2-3 of the recommended oils. Mix 5-7 drops of each in a 10 ml roller bottle and fill with fractionated coconut oil. Apply down the back of your neck, behind your ears, over your chest, and on the bottoms of your feet morning and evening. Take 3 On Guard™+ Softgels per day. Use On Guard® Beadlets, On Guard® Tablets, and On Guard® Protecting Throat Drops as needed. Use a cotton swab to apply a dab of Correct-X into your nose for added immune support.

🍎 Drink plenty of water with 1-2 drops of Lemon.

CONCENTRATION

⏰ *3-5x per day*	📅 *While symptoms persist*

Essential Oils: *InTune®, Adaptiv™, Vetiver, Rosemary*

Other Solutions: *Peppermint Beadlets*

 Apply InTune® down the back of your neck, behind your ears, and over your temples. Choose 2 of the other recommended oils. Mix 1-2 drops of each with a tablespoon of fractionated coconut oil and apply to your forehead, temples, the base of your skull, and behind your ears, or diffuse in the air and inhale. Take Peppermint Beadlets as needed.

CONCUSSION

 3-5x per day   *While symptoms persist*

Essential Oils: *Frankincense, Copaiba, Bergamot, Cedarwood, Cypress*

Other Solutions: *Ginger Drops, Turmeric Dual Chamber Capsules*

⊙ Take 3 Turmeric Dual Chamber Capsules per day. Place 1 drop each of Frankincense and Copaiba under your tongue morning and evening. Diffuse 3-4 drops of Frankincense, Bergamot, and Cedarwood in a diffuser throughout the day. Mix 5-7 drops of Copaiba, Frankincense, Bergamot, Cedarwood, and Cypress in a 10 ml roller bottle and fill with fractionated coconut oil. Apply down the back of your neck, under your skull, over your temples, and on the bottoms of your feet morning and evening. Use Ginger Drops as needed.

CONGENITAL HEART DISEASE

 3x per day   *Ongoing*

Essential Oils: *Geranium, Ylang Ylang, Helichrysum, Basil, Passion®*

Other Solutions: *N/A*

⊙ Mix 5-7 drops of each recommended oil with fractionated coconut oil in a 10 ml roller bottle. Apply to your chest, feet, and the back of your neck.

CONGESTION

 3-5x per day   *As needed*

Essential Oils: *Peppermint, Lemon, Eucalyptus*

Other Solutions: *Peppermint Beadlets, Breathe® Drops, Breathe® Vapor Stick, Correct-X*

 Add 2-3 drops of Lemon to your water and drink throughout the day. Put 2 drops of Peppermint and Eucalyptus in your palms and add a tablespoon of fractionated coconut oil. Rub over your chest, over your mid/upper back, and under your nose, and then inhale from cupped hands. Take Peppermint Beadlets as needed. Use Breathe® Drops. Rub the Breathe® Vapor Stick over your chest and forehead or below your nose when needed. If you get oils in your eyes or on your face while inhaling from your hands, apply plain coconut oil over your eye or face to soothe the area. Repeat as needed. Use a cotton swab to apply a dab of Correct-X into your nose for added immune support.

⊙ Avoid dairy products.

CONJUNCTIVITIS *(Pink Eye)*

 3-5x per day   *As needed*

Essential Oils: *Tea Tree, Rosemary, Lavender*

Other Solutions: *N/A*

⊙ Choose 2 of the recommended oils. Apply 1-2 drops around *(but not in)* your eyes, or apply to the bottoms of your feet several times a day.

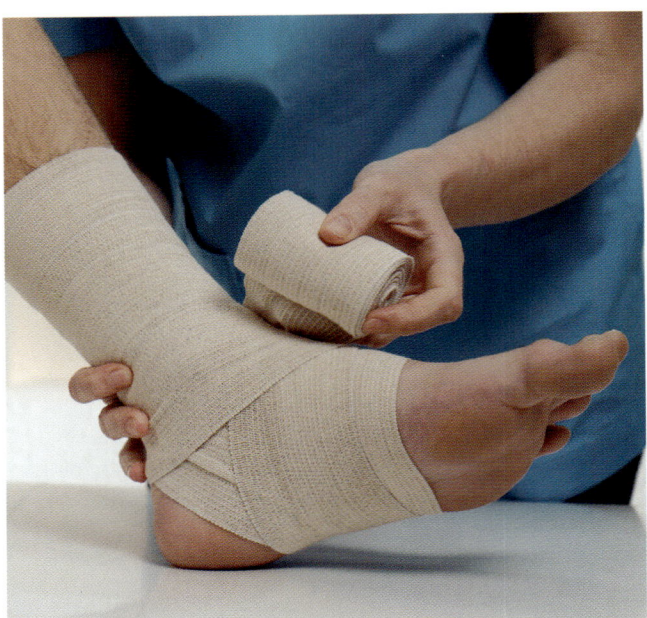

CONNECTIVE TISSUE INJURY

⏰ **4-5x per day**	📅 **As needed**

Essential Oils: *Helichrysum, Wintergreen, Marjoram, Copaiba, Lemongrass, Frankincense, Siberian Fir*

Other Solutions: *Deep Blue® Polyphenol Complex, Deep Blue® Rub, Deep Blue® Stick*

 Choose 2-3 of the recommended oils. Mix 5-7 drops of each with fractionated coconut oil in a 10 ml roller bottle. Apply over the affected joint(s). Take 2 Deep Blue® Polyphenol Complex capsules per day with food. Use Deep Blue® Rub or Deep Blue® Stick over the affected area as needed.

CONSTIPATION

⏰ **3-5x per day**	📅 **As needed**

Essential Oils: *DigestZen®, Green Mandarin, Ginger, Peppermint*

Other Solutions: *Peppermint Softgels*

 Add 1 drop of Peppermint to your water and drink throughout the day. Take a Peppermint Softgel 1 hour before meals. Choose 2 of the recommended oils. Apply a few drops of each topically with a tablespoon of fractionated coconut oil to your lower abdomen and lower back as needed.

🍃 Drink half your body weight in ounces of water. Add 2 drops of Lemon or 1 drop of Peppermint to your water. Add prunes, apples, pears, kiwi, figs, citrus fruits, leafy greens, Jerusalem artichokes, chicory, sweet potato, chia seeds, oat bran, kefir, and dates to your diet.

🔸 Avoid sitting for long periods of time. Go for a hike or walk in nature. Aim to exercise 5-6 days per week, alternating between cardio and strength training.

🔻 If tolerated, do a 30-day cleanse each season. See the 30-day cleanse on page 434.

CONVALESCENCE

🕐 *3-5x per day*	📅 *As needed*

Essential Oils: *Petitgrain, Frankincense, Spikenard, Console®, Myrrh, Copaiba*

Other Solutions: *Serenity® Softgels*

 Put 1 drop each of Frankincense and Copaiba under your tongue morning and evening. Choose 2-3 of the recommended oils. Mix 5-7 drops of each in a 10 ml roller bottle and fill the rest with fractionated coconut oil. Apply topically over your heart, the back of your neck, your temples, and under the ridge of your skull. Diffuse 4 drops of Console® throughout the day.

 Place 1 drop of Lavender or Serenity® on your pillow at night. Take 2 Serenity® Softgels before bed. Use oils from the emotional kit to manage emotions throughout the day.

CORNS

🕐 *3-5x per day*	📅 *As needed*

Essential Oils: *Arborvitae, Lemon, DDR Prime®, Clove, Ylang Ylang*

Other Solutions: *Turmeric Dual Chamber Capsules*

 Take 2 Turmeric Dual Chamber Capsules per day. Choose 3 of the recommended oils. Mix 5-7 drops of each in a 10 ml roller bottle and fill remainder with fractionated coconut oil. Apply over the affected area throughout the day. Rub on the bottoms of your feet morning and evening.

CORTISOL IMBALANCE

⏰ *3-5x per day*	📅 *Ongoing*

Essential Oils: *Adaptiv™ (3-part system), Black Spruce, Ylang Ylang, Petitgrain, Tulsi*

Other Solutions: *Lifelong Vitality, DigestZen TerraZyme®, PB Assist®+, Serenity® Softgels, Adaptiv™ Capsule, Mito2Max®*

🌙 Choose 2-3 of the recommended oils. Mix 5-7 drops of each in a 10 ml roller bottle and fill remainder with fractionated coconut oil. Apply to the back of your neck, behind your ears, down your spine, and on the bottoms of your feet morning and evening. Take 1 Adaptiv™ Capsule per day.

🍏 Take Lifelong Vitality Supplements twice a day, 2-3 DigestZen TerraZyme® capsules at each meal, and PB Assist® once per day. Eat a variety of fresh fruits, vegetables, lean meats, healthy fats, and rice. Avoid MSG, gluten, corn, fried food, fast food, processed foods, and artificial sweeteners. Avoid caffeine close to bedtime.

🔶 Aim for light to moderate exercise 4-5 days per week. Adopt an exercise program that combines aerobic exercise, strength training, balance exercises, and joint flexibility exercises. Listen to your body and rest as needed. Warm up, cool down, and stretch for each exercise session.

🌙 Place 1 drop of Lavender or Serenity® on your pillow at night. Take 2 Serenity® Softgels before bed. Turn off electronic devices an hour or two before bed. Avoid stressful conversations or television before meals or bed. Develop a good bedtime routine that feels relaxing to you. Find a hobby or meditation program. Increase the laughter in your life by watching a comedy or hanging with friends and family members who make you laugh. Take 2 Mito2Max® supplements throughout the day if you need energy without a stimulant effect.

COUGH

| 🕐 **4-5x per day** | 📅 *While symptoms persist* |

Essential Oils: *Breathe®, Lemon, Rosemary*

Other Solutions: *Breathe® Drops, Breathe® Vapor Stick, Peppermint Beadlets, Correct-X*

 Place 1 drop of Breathe® and 1 drop of Rosemary in your palms with 1 tablespoon of fractionated coconut oil. Rub over your chest and mid/upper back throughout the day. Cup your hands and inhale 3 deep breaths. Put 2 drops of Lemon in your water to act as a decongestant and for immune support. Take Breathe® Drops as needed. Rub the Breathe® Vapor Stick over your chest 3 times daily. Take Peppermint Beadlets as needed. If you get oils in your eyes or on your face while inhaling from your hands, apply plain coconut oil over your eye or face to soothe the area. Repeat as needed. Use a cotton swab to apply a dab of Correct-X into your nose for added immune support.

🌱 Avoid dairy while symptoms persist.

CRADLE CAP

| 🕐 **3-5x per day** | 📅 *While symptoms persist* |

Essential Oils: *Lavender, Tea Tree, Sandalwood, Frankincense, Immortelle*

Other Solutions: *N/A*

 Choose 2-3 of the recommended oils. Mix 2-3 drops of each oil in a 10 ml roller bottle and fill 3/4 of the bottle with fractionated coconut oil. Apply to affected area throughout the day.

CRAMPS *(Abdominal)*

| 🕐 **4-5x per day** | 📅 *While symptoms persist* |

Essential Oils: *AromaTouch®, Marjoram, Arborvitae*

Other Solutions: *Deep Blue® Rub, Deep Blue® Stick*

 Choose 2-3 of the recommended oils. Put 1 drop of each oil in your palm with 1 tablespoon of fractionated coconut oil and rub over your abdomen and mid to low back throughout the day. Apply Deep Blue® Rub or Deep Blue® Stick to the affected area.

CRAMPS *(Intestinal)*

3-4x per day	*While symptoms persist*

Essential Oils: *DigestZen®, Marjoram, Ginger, Turmeric, Cardamom, Citronella*

Other Solutions: *Ginger Drops, DigestZen® Softgels*

- Choose 2-3 of the recommended oils. Mix 5-7 drops of each oil in a 10 ml roller bottle and fill remainder with fractionated coconut oil. Apply to your abdomen and lower back and on the bottoms of your feet morning and evening. Take 1 DigestZen® Softgel each morning and afternoon. Take Ginger Drops as needed.

CRAMPS *(Menstrual)*

4-5x per day	*While symptoms persist*

Essential Oils: *AromaTouch®, Marjoram, Arborvitae, ClaryCalm®, Clary Sage*

Other Solutions: *Deep Blue® Rub, Deep Blue® Stick*

- Choose 3-4 of the recommended oils. Put 1 drop of each oil in your palm with 1 tablespoon of fractionated coconut oil. Rub over your lower abdomen and lower back throughout the day. Rub a ClaryCalm® roller over your abdomen morning and evening. Apply Deep Blue® Rub or Deep Blue® Stick to the affected area.

CRAMPS *(Muscular)*

3-5x per day	*As needed*

Essential Oils: *Marjoram, AromaTouch®, PastTense®, Siberian Fir*

Other Solutions: *Deep Blue® Rub, Lifelong Vitality, Deep Blue® Polyphenol Complex*

- Choose 2-3 of the recommended oils. Mix 5-7 drops of each oil in a 10 ml roller bottle and fill with fractionated coconut oil. Apply over the affected area. Apply warm compresses over the area to relax the muscles, and then apply Deep Blue® Rub or Deep Blue® Stick over the affected area. Take 2 Deep Blue® Polyphenol Complex capsules a day with meals in the morning and evening.

- Take Lifelong Vitality Supplements twice daily. Drink half your body weight in ounces of water.

- Take a 5-10 minute walk to warm up muscles. Do stretching or joint flexibility exercises.

CROHN'S DISEASE

⏰ 3-5x per day	📅 Until symptoms improve

Essential Oils: *Peppermint, DigestZen®, Ginger, Fennel, Celery Seed, Lemon, Pink Pepper, Lavender, Citronella*

Other Solutions: *Ginger Drops, Peppermint Softgels, DigestZen TerraZyme®*

 Choose 3-4 of the recommended oils. Mix 5 drops of each oil with fractionated coconut oil in a 10 ml roller bottle. Rub it over your abdominal area, your spine in the lower back area, and the bottoms of your feet. In addition, diffuse 3-4 drops of each chosen oil in a diffuser throughout the day. For adults, take up to 2 Peppermint Softgels before meals. For children 8 years and older, take 1 Peppermint Softgel before meals. For best results, take the Peppermint Softgels 30-60 minutes before meals. Take 1-3 DigestZen TerraZyme® capsules daily with meals. Take DigestZen® Softgels 1 or more times daily as needed. Experiment with Peppermint Softgels and DigestZen® Softgels to see which one works best for your body chemistry. Take Ginger Drops as needed.

CROUP

⏰ 4-5x per day	📅 Until symptoms improve

Essential Oils: *Eucalyptus, Lemon, Breathe®*

Other Solutions: *Breathe® Drops, Breathe® Vapor Stick, Peppermint Beadlets*

 Place 1 drop of Eucalyptus and 1 drop of Breathe® in your palms with 1 tablespoon of fractionated coconut oil. Rub over your chest, mid/upper back, under your nose, and behind your ears. Cup your hands and inhale 3 deep breaths. Rub Breathe® and Eucalyptus on the bottoms of your feet morning and evening. Put 2 drops of Lemon in your water to act as a decongestant and for immune support. Take Breathe® Drops as needed. Rub the Breathe® Vapor Stick over your chest 3 times daily. Take Peppermint Beadlets as needed. If you get oils in your eyes or on your face while inhaling from your hands, apply plain coconut oil over your eye or face to soothe the area. Repeat as needed.

🍎 Avoid dairy while symptoms persist.

CUSHING'S SYNDROME

⏰ *3-5x per day*	📅 *Ongoing*

Essential Oils: *Clove, Black Pepper, Basil, DDR Prime®, Geranium, Citrus Bliss®, Tulsi*

Other Solutions: *Lifelong Vitality, DigestZen TerraZyme®, PB Assist®+, Serenity® Softgels*

🌸 Choose 2-3 of the recommended oils. Mix 5-7 drops of each in a 10 ml roller bottle and fill with fractionated coconut oil. Apply to the back of your neck, behind your ears, down your spine, and on the bottoms of your feet morning and evening. Put 1 drop each of Basil, Clove, DDR Prime®, and Black Pepper in a capsule and take twice daily, morning and evening.

🍏 Take Lifelong Vitality Supplements twice a day, 2-3 DigestZen TerraZyme® capsules at each meal, and PB Assist® once per day. Eat a variety of fresh fruits, vegetables, lean meats, healthy fats, and rice. Avoid MSG, gluten, corn, fried food, fast food, processed foods, and artificial sweeteners. Avoid caffeine close to bedtime.

🔶 Aim for light to moderate exercise 4-5 days per week. Adopt an exercise program that combines aerobic exercise, strength training, balance exercises, and joint flexibility exercises. Listen to your body and rest as needed. Warm up, cool down, and stretch for each exercise session.

🌙 Place 1 drop of Lavender or Serenity® on your pillow at night. Take 2 Serenity® Softgels before bed. Turn off electronic devices an hour or two before bed. Develop a good bedtime routine that feels relaxing to you. Find a hobby or meditation program. Increase the laughter in your life by watching a comedy or hanging with friends and family members who make you laugh.

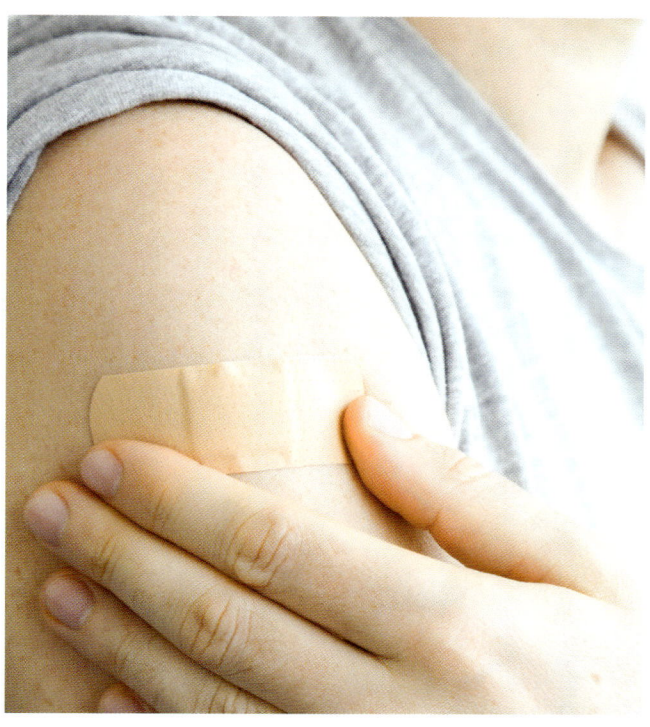

CYST

⏰ **3-5x per day**	📅 **Until resolved**

Essential Oils: *Lemongrass, Thyme, On Guard®, DDR Prime®*

Other Solutions: *N/A*

 Choose 2 of the recommended oils. Dilute 1-2 drops of each oil with 1/2 teaspoon of fractionated coconut oil. Apply to the affected area throughout the day.

CYSTIC FIBROSIS

⏰ **4-5x per day**	📅 **As needed**

Essential Oils: *Eucalyptus, Douglas Fir, Lemon, Breathe®, Frankincense*

Other Solutions: *Breathe® Drops, Breathe® Vapor Stick*

 Choose 2-3 of the recommended oils. Diffuse 3 drops of each and inhale throughout the day. Mix 5 drops of each chosen oil in a 10 ml roller bottle with fractionated coconut oil. Apply to your chest, feet, and the back of your neck down over to your shoulder area *(on the top of the lung field)*. Use Breathe® drops and a Breathe® Vapor Stick as needed.

CUTS

⏰ **2-3x per day**	📅 **Until cut is sealed and healing**

Essential Oils: *Lavender, Myrrh, Tea Tree*

Other Solutions: *Correct-X*

 Choose 2 of the recommended oils. Dilute 1 drop of each oil with 1/2 teaspoon of fractionated coconut oil and apply to cut. If the cut requires protection, add a bit of Correct-X over the cut and cover with a bandage.

D-F

DANDRUFF

⏰ *2-3x per week*	📅 *Until resolved*

Essential Oils: *Cedarwood, Rosemary, Tea Tree*

Other Solutions: *N/A*

 Choose 2 of the recommended oils. Dilute 1-2 drops of each with 1/2 teaspoon of fractionated coconut oil. Massage into your scalp. Rinse after 60-90 minutes.

DEHYDRATED SKIN

⏰ *3-5x per day*	📅 *While symptoms persist*

Essential Oils: *Rose, Myrrh, Sandalwood, Immortelle*

Other Solutions: *Yarrow|Pom Body Renewal Serum, Yarrow|Pom Botanical Nutritive Duo*

 Choose 2 of the recommended oils. Dilute 1-2 drops of each with 1/2 teaspoon of fractionated coconut oil. Apply to dehydrated skin throughout the day. Apply Yarrow|Pom Body Renewal Serum on the affected area twice daily. Take 2 Yarrow|Pom Botanical Nutritive Duo capsules per day.

🍏 Make sure to hydrate often. Put 1-2 drops of a citrus oil in your water and drink throughout the day. Drink half your body weight in ounces per day.

DEMENTIA

| *3-5x per day* | *Ongoing* |

Essential Oils: *Frankincense, DDR Prime®, Green Mandarin*

Other Solutions: *N/A*

 Put 1 drop of Frankincense under your tongue morning and evening. Mix 5-7 drops of each recommended oil in a 10 ml roller bottle and fill the rest with fractionated coconut oil. Apply over your forehead, temples, the base of your skull, down your neck, and behind your ears throughout the day.

DENGUE FEVER

| *3-5x per day* | *While symptoms persist* |

Essential Oils: *Lemon Eucalyptus, Eucalyptus, Tea Tree, On Guard®, Thyme, TerraShield®, Citronella, Peppermint*

Other Solutions: *N/A*

 Choose 2-3 of the recommended oils. Mix 5-7 drops of each oil in a 10 ml roller bottle and fill with fractionated coconut oil. Roll down your spine, over the rash, and on the bottoms of your feet morning and evening. Use TerraShield® when in a tropical or humid environment where mosquitoes are located. Place 2 drops of Peppermint in a small bowl of cold water. Place a clean washcloth in the water and then put the washcloth over your forehead or upper back to take down fever.

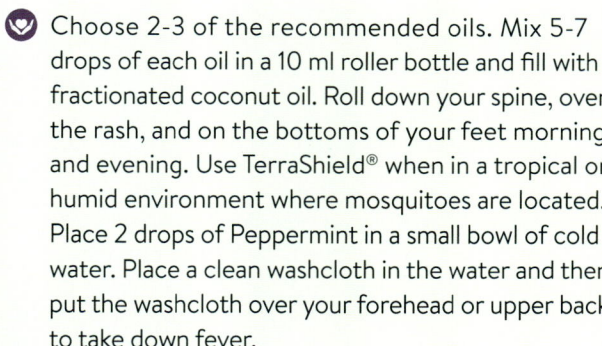 Seek medical attention right away if you have a high fever, a rash, or muscle and joint pain after being bit by a mosquito.

DENTAL INFECTION

| *4-5x per day* | *While symptoms persist* |

Essential Oils: *On Guard®, Clove, Cinnamon*

Other Solutions: *N/A*

 Choose 2 of the recommended oils. Dilute 1 drop of each with 1 teaspoon of fractionated coconut oil. Apply to your gums and around your teeth throughout the day.

D-F

DEPRESSION

3-5x per day	*Ongoing as needed*

Essential Oils: *Melissa, Elevation, Cheer®, Frankincense, Adaptiv™ (3-part system), Neroli Touch*

Other Solutions: *Lifelong Vitality, DigestZen TerraZyme®, PB Assist®+, Serenity® Softgels, Adaptiv™ Capsule*

- Choose 2-3 of the recommended oils. Mix 5-7 drops of each in a 10 ml roller bottle and fill remainder with fractionated coconut oil. Apply to the back of your neck, behind your ears, over your heart, and on the bottoms of your feet morning and evening. You can also use the Neroli Touch roller as well. Take 1 Adaptiv™ Capsule per day. Diffuse 5 drops of Adaptiv™ in a diffuser daily and inhale. Rotate between using the Adaptiv™ roller and the recommended roller blend throughout the day.

- Take Lifelong Vitality Supplements twice a day, 2-3 DigestZen TerraZyme® capsules at each meal, and PB Assist® once per day. Eat a variety of fresh fruits, vegetables, lean meats, healthy fats, and rice. Avoid MSG, gluten, corn, fried food, fast food, processed foods, and artificial sweeteners.

- Dilute 1 drop of Peppermint with 1 teaspoon of fractionated coconut oil and apply it to your chest and upper back before exercise. Do aerobic exercises, strength training, and balance exercises.

- Place 1 drop of Lavender or Serenity® on your pillow at night. Take 2 Serenity® Softgels before bed. Turn off electronic devices an hour or two before bed. Avoid stressful conversations or television before meals or bed. Develop a good bedtime routine that feels relaxing to you. Find a hobby or meditation program. Listen to music, go for a walk in nature, or go out with friends. Increase the laughter in your life by watching a comedy or hanging with friends and family members who make you laugh. Schedule self-care rituals throughout the week that make you feel good.

- If tolerated, do a 30-day cleanse each season. See the 30-day cleanse on page 434.

DERMATITIS

3-5x per day	**Ongoing as needed**

Essential Oils: *Helichrysum, Rose, Blue Tansy, Patchouli, Siberian Fir, Cedarwood*

Other Solutions: *Yarrow|Pom Body Renewal Serum, Yarrow|Pom Botanical Nutritive Duo, Lifelong Vitality, DigestZen TerraZyme®, PB Assist®+*

 Choose 2-3 of the recommended oils. Mix 5-7 drops of each oil in a 10 ml roller bottle and fill with fractionated coconut oil. Apply over the affected skin. Apply Yarrow|Pom Body Renewal Serum on the affected area twice daily. Take 2 Yarrow|Pom Botanical Nutritive Duo capsules per day.

Take Lifelong Vitality Supplements twice a day, 2-3 DigestZen TerraZyme® capsules at each meal, and PB Assist® once per day. Eat a variety of fresh fruits, vegetables, lean meats, healthy fats, and rice. Pay attention to how your skin reacts when you consume MSG, gluten, corn, fried food, fast food, processed foods, and artificial sweeteners.

If tolerated, do a 30-day cleanse each season. See the 30-day cleanse on page 434.

DETOXIFICATION

3x per day	**Ongoing as needed**

Essential Oils: *Zendocrine®, Clove, Celery Seed*

Other Solutions: *Peppermint Beadlets, Lifelong Vitality*

 Put 1 drop of each recommended oil in a capsule and take 3 times per day. Rub 1 drop of Zendocrine® diluted with 1/2 teaspoon of fractionated coconut oil under your ribcage on the right side of your body, over your abdomen, and over your lower back throughout the day. Rub 1 drop each of Zendocrine® and Clove diluted with 1 teaspoon of fractionated coconut oil on the bottoms of your feet morning and evening. Take Peppermint Beadlets as needed.

Take Lifelong Vitality Supplements twice a day. Eat a variety of fresh fruits, vegetables, lean meats, healthy fats, and rice. Avoid MSG, gluten, corn, fried food, fast food, processed foods, and artificial sweeteners. Pay attention to how your body reacts when you reintroduce these foods.

If tolerated, do a 30-day cleanse each season. See the 30-day cleanse on page 434.

D-F

DIABETES

⏰	*3-5x per day*	📅	*Ongoing*

Essential Oils: *Cinnamon, Coriander, Juniper Berry, MetaPWR™, Cassia, Celery Seed, Zendocrine®*

Other Solutions: *MetaPWR™ Softgels, MetaPWR™ Metabolic Gum, Zendocrine® Softgels, Lifelong Vitality, DigestZen TerraZyme®, PB Assist®+*

- 🌙 Choose 2-3 of the recommended oils. Mix 5-7 drops of each oil with fractionated coconut oil in a 10 ml roller bottle and apply beneath your breastbone and to your upper abdomen area. Apply the blend to the bottoms of your feet morning and evening. Put 2-3 drops of MetaPWR™ in your water and drink. Take 2 Zendocrine® Softgels, or put 1-2 drops of Zendocrine® in a capsule and take 2 times per day. Chew MetaPWR™ Metabolic Gum between meals. Take 2 MetaPWR™ Softgels with breakfast and lunch.

- 🍎 Take Lifelong Vitality Supplements twice a day, 2-3 DigestZen TerraZyme® capsules at each meal, and PB Assist® once per day. Eat a variety of fresh fruits, vegetables, lean meats, healthy fats, and rice. Pay attention to how your skin reacts when you consume MSG, gluten, corn, fried food, fast food, processed foods, and artificial sweeteners.

- 🔶 Put 2 drops of MetaPWR™ in your water before exercising. Do aerobic exercises, strength training, and balance exercises.

DIABETIC SORES

⏰	*3x per day*	📅	*As needed until condition improves*

Essential Oils: *Myrrh, Lavender, Patchouli, Sandalwood, Geranium*

Other Solutions: *N/A*

- 🌙 Combine 5-7 drops of each oil in a 10 ml roller bottle with fractionated coconut oil. Apply topically to the affected area.

D-F

DIAPER RASH

 *After each diaper change*   *While symptoms persist*

Essential Oils: *Lavender, Roman Chamomile, Patchouli*

Other Solutions: *Sensitive Skin Carrier Oil*

 Choose 2 of the recommended oils. Dilute 1-2 drops of each with 1/2 teaspoon Sensitive Skin Carrier Oil and apply topically to the affected area several times daily until the rash disappears.

DIARRHEA

 3-4x per day   *While symptoms persist*

Essential Oils: *DigestZen®, Coriander, Ginger*

Other Solutions: *Peppermint Softgels, Peppermint Beadlets, Ginger Drops*

 Put 1 drop of each recommended oil in a capsule and take 3 times per day. Dilute 1 drop of DigestZen® with 1 teaspoon of fractionated coconut oil and apply over your abdomen and to your mid/lower back throughout the day. Take 1 Peppermint Softgel before meals. Take Peppermint Beadlets as desired. Take Ginger Drops as needed.

Drink plenty of clear liquids throughout the day. Avoid caffeine and alcohol. Add semi-solid and low-fiber foods back to your diet gradually as your bowel movements return to normal. Start with rice, chicken, eggs, and crackers if tolerated.

DIPHTHERIA

 3-5x per day   *While symptoms persist*

Essential Oils: *Eucalyptus, Breathe®, On Guard®, DigestZen®, Thyme, Peppermint*

Other Solutions: *N/A*

 Choose 2-3 of the recommended oils. Mix 5-7 drops of each oil in a 10 ml roller bottle and fill with fractionated coconut oil. Roll down your spine, over your throat and glands, and on the bottoms of your feet morning and evening. Place 2 drops of Peppermint in a small bowl of cold water. Place a clean washcloth in the water and then put the washcloth over your forehead or upper back to take down fever.

Seek medical attention right away if you experience a sore throat, fever, swollen glands, swollen lymph nodes, and weakness.

DIVERTICULITIS

⏰ *3-5x per day*	📅 *While symptoms persist*

Essential Oils: *DigestZen®, Ginger, Basil, MetaPWR™, AromaTouch®, Celery Seed, DDR Prime®, Cardamom*

Other Solutions: *Lifelong Vitality, DigestZen TerraZyme®, PB Assist®+*

 Choose 2-3 of the recommended oils. Mix 5-7 drops of each oil in a 10 ml roller bottle and fill the rest with fractionated coconut oil. Apply to your abdomen, lower back, and on the bottoms of your feet morning and evening. Put 2 drops each of Celery Seed, Basil, and Cardamom in a capsule and take 3 times per day. Rub AromaTouch® over your abdomen throughout the day.

🌿 Consume bone broth, collagen, eggs, fatty fish, free-range chicken, rice, cooked leafy greens, fennel, and carrots. Take Lifelong Vitality Supplements twice a day, 2-3 DigestZen TerraZyme® capsules at each meal, and PB Assist® once per day. Add MetaPWR™ to water (*2 drops per glass*) and drink.

➕ Seek medical attention right away if you experience severe abdominal pain, excessive nausea, vomiting, fever (*with or without chills*), or a sudden change in appetite.

DIZZINESS

⏰ *3-5x per day*	📅 *While symptoms persist*

Essential Oils: *Basil, Balance®, Ginger, Cedarwood*

Other Solutions: *Ginger Drops*

 Choose 2-3 of the recommended oils. Dilute 1-2 drops of each with 1 teaspoon of fractionated coconut oil. Apply behind your ears, down the back of your neck, under your skull, under your nose, and on your wrists throughout the day. Take Ginger Drops as needed.

DOWN SYNDROME

⏰ *3-5x per day*	📅 *Ongoing*

Essential Oils: *DDR Prime®, Balance®, Frankincense*

Other Solutions: *N/A*

🌙 Choose 2 of the recommended oils. Dilute 2 drops of each oil with 1 teaspoon of fractionated coconut oil. Apply to your chest, temples, and the bottoms of your feet morning and evening. Put 1 drop of Frankincense under your tongue morning and evening.

D-F

D-F

DRUG ADDICTION

3-4x per day	*Ongoing*

Essential Oils: *Pink Pepper, Zendocrine®, Patchouli, Purify, Citronella*

Other Solutions: *Peppermint Beadlets, Ginger Drops*

 Choose 2-3 of the recommended oils. Mix 5-7 drops of each oil in a 10 ml roller bottle and fill with fractionated coconut oil. Rub the blend on the bottoms of your feet morning and evening. Roll down the back of your neck, under your skull, behind your ears, and over your temples throughout the day. Put 1-2 drops of Pink Pepper in your water and sip throughout the day. Take Peppermint Beadlets as desired and Ginger Drops as needed.

DRY HAIR

Daily or 3x per week	*Ongoing until symptoms improve*

Essential Oils: *Sandalwood, Patchouli, Geranium, Copaiba, Rosemary*

Other Solutions: *Salon Essentials Protecting Shampoo, Salon Essentials Smoothing Conditioner, Healthy Hold Glaze, Root to Tip Serum, Yarrow|Pom Body Renewal Serum, Yarrow|Pom Botanical Nutritive Duo capsules, Lifelong Vitality, DigestZen TerraZyme®, PB Assist®+*

Use Protecting Shampoo and Smoothing Conditioner to clean your hair. Apply Healthy Hold Glaze and Root to Tip Serum on damp hair. Choose 3-4 of the recommended oils. Put 10 drops of each oil into a glass jar with a lid. Add 1.5 ounces of jojoba oil and 1.5 ounces of grapeseed oil to the jar. Place the lid on the jar and shake well. Apply the mixture generously to your hair and scalp *(dry or wet)* daily or 3 times per week. Leave it in your hair for at least 20 minutes. You can leave it in overnight; use a shower cap or towel to prevent staining linens. Shampoo, rinse, and style as usual. Massage Yarrow|Pom Body Renewal Serum on your scalp after washing. Take 2 Yarrow|Pom Botanical Nutritive Duo capsules per day.

Take Lifelong Vitality Supplements twice a day, 2-3 DigestZen TerraZyme® capsules at each meal, and PB Assist® once per day. Eat a variety of fresh fruits *(like blueberries, kiwi, and guava)*, carrots, almond butter, lentils, oysters, lean meat, healthy fats, barley, and rice. Avoid MSG, high amounts of sugar, and swordfish *(high amounts of mercury may be linked to hair health)*. Avoid processed foods, artificial sweeteners, and starchy foods.

D-F

DRY LIPS

⏰ **4-5x per day**	📅 **As needed**

Essential Oils: *Myrrh, Geranium, Sandalwood, Lavender, Frankincense*

Other Solutions: *Spa Lip Balm*

 Choose 2-3 of the recommended oils. Mix 5-7 drops of each oil in a 10 ml roller bottle and fill remainder with fractionated coconut oil. Roll over your lips throughout the day. Use Spa Lip Balm as needed.

DRY SKIN

⏰ **3-5x per day**	📅 **While symptoms persist**

Essential Oils: *Myrrh, Petitgrain, Patchouli, Sandalwood, Immortelle*

Other Solutions: *Yarrow|Pom Body Renewal Serum, Yarrow|Pom Botanical Nutritive Duo*

 Choose 2-3 recommended oils. Dilute 1-2 drops of each with 1 teaspoon of fractionated coconut oil. Apply to dry skin throughout the day. Apply Yarrow|Pom Body Renewal Serum on the affected area twice daily. Take 2 Yarrow|Pom Botanical Nutritive Duo capsules per day.

● Hydrate often. Put 1-2 drops of a citrus oil in your water and drink throughout the day. Drink half your body weight in ounces of water per day.

DYSENTERY

⏰ **3-4x per day**	📅 **While symptoms persist**

Essential Oils: *Ginger, DigestZen®, Myrrh, Siberian Fir*

Other Solutions: *Peppermint Beadlets, Ginger Drops*

 Choose 2 of the recommended oils. Mix 5-7 drops of each oil in a 10 ml roller bottle and fill with fractionated coconut oil. Apply to your abdomen, lower back, and on the bottoms of your feet morning and evening. Take Peppermint Beadlets as desired. Take Ginger Drops as needed.

 Drink plenty of clear liquids throughout the day. Avoid caffeine and alcohol. Add semi-solid and low-fiber foods back to your diet gradually as your bowel movements return to normal. Start with rice, chicken, eggs, and crackers if tolerated.

D-F

DYSMENORRHEA

⏰ **3-5x per day**	📅 **As needed**

Essential Oils: *ClaryCalm®, Clary Sage, Whisper®, Ylang Ylang, Jasmine, Geranium, Sandalwood, Lavender*

Other Solutions: *Yarrow|Pom Body Renewal Serum, Yarrow|Pom Botanical Nutritive Duo capsules, Lifelong Vitality, DigestZen TerraZyme®, PB Assist®+, Serenity® Softgels, Bone Nutrient Essential Complex, Phytoestrogen Essential Complex*

- Combine 5-7 drops each of Sandalwood, Geranium, Ylang Ylang, and Clary Sage with fractionated coconut oil in a 10 ml roller bottle. Apply over your lower abdominal region, on your feet, and along your spine in the lower back area 2 times per day. Rotate between using this roller, a ClaryCalm® roller, and a Jasmine roller throughout the day. Diffuse 5 drops of Whisper® throughout the day. Apply Yarrow|Pom Body Renewal Serum over your lower abdomen. Take 2 Yarrow|Pom Botanical Nutritive Duo capsules per day.

- Pre- and peri-menopausal women, take one 1-2 Phytoestrogen Essential Complex capsules daily with food. Take 4 Bone Nutrient Essential Complex capsules daily with food. Take Lifelong Vitality Supplements twice a day, 2-3 DigestZen TerraZyme® capsules at each meal, and PB Assist® once per day. Consume avocados, flaxseed, broccoli, pomegranate, salmon, leafy greens, nuts, organic soy, turmeric, quinoa, and brown rice. Avoid excess sugar, simple carbohydrates, trans fats, and processed foods.

- Place 1 drop of Lavender or Serenity® on your pillow at night. Take 2 Serenity® Softgels at bedtime.

DYSPHAGIA

⏰ **3-5x per day**	📅 **While symptoms persist**

Essential Oils: *Ginger, Black Pepper, Peppermint*

Other Solutions: *N/A*

- Choose 2 of the recommended oils. Mix 7-10 drops of each oil in a 10 ml roller bottle and fill with fractionated coconut oil. Apply on the front and back of your neck throughout the day.

D-F

E. COLI

 4-5x per day | *While symptoms persist*

Essential Oils: *Cinnamon, On Guard®, Oregano, Clove*

Other Solutions: *Ginger Drops, Peppermint Beadlets, On Guard® Beadlets, On Guard™+ Softgels, Serenity® Softgels, On Guard® Tablets*

- Choose 2-3 of the recommended oils. Put 2 drops of each in a capsule and take 3 times per day. Mix 5-7 drops of each chosen oil in a 10 ml roller bottle and fill remainder with fractionated coconut oil. Apply to your stomach, the bottoms of your feet, and down your spine throughout the day. Take On Guard® Beadlets and On Guard® Tablets as needed. Take 3-4 On Guard™+ Softgels throughout the day.

- If tolerated, eat or drink Lemon/Ginger tea, chicken broth, bone broth, cooked carrots, crackers, chicken, and coconut oil.

- Place 1 drop of Lavender or Serenity® on your pillow at night. Take 2 Serenity® Softgels before bed.

- If symptoms persist, seek medical attention right away.

EAR INFECTION

 3-5x per day | *While symptoms persist*

Essential Oils: *Tea Tree, Basil, Helichrysum, Rosemary*

Other Solutions: *On Guard™+ Softgels, On Guard® Beadlets, On Guard® Tablets*

- Choose 2-3 of the recommended oils. Mix 5-7 drops of each oil in a 10 ml roller bottle and fill with remainder fractionated coconut oil. Rub on the bottoms of your feet morning and evening. Roll the blend down the back of your neck, under your skull, and behind your ears throughout the day. Take 3 On Guard™+ Softgels throughout the day. Take On Guard® Beadlets and On Guard® Tablets as needed.

EARACHE

 3-5x per day | *While symptoms persist*

Essential Oils: *Tea Tree, Basil, Helichrysum, Rosemary*

Other Solutions: *On Guard™+ Softgels, On Guard® Beadlets, On Guard® Tablets*

- Choose 2-3 of the recommended oils. Mix 5-7 drops of each oil in a 10 ml roller bottle and fill the rest with fractionated coconut oil. Roll down the back of your neck, under your skull, and behind your ears throughout the day. Take 3 On Guard™+ Softgels throughout the day. Take On Guard® Beadlets and On Guard® Tablets as needed.

ECZEMA

| ⏰ *3-5x per day* | 📅 *While symptoms persist* |

Essential Oils: *HD Clear®, Helichrysum, Cedarwood*

Other Solutions: *Yarrow|Pom Body Renewal Serum, Yarrow|Pom Botanical Nutritive Duo*

 Choose 2 of the recommended oils. Dilute 1-2 drops of each with 1 teaspoon of fractionated coconut oil. Apply to dehydrated skin throughout the day. If using HD Clear®, apply over the affected area throughout the day. Apply Yarrow|Pom Body Renewal Serum on the affected area twice daily. Take 2 Yarrow|Pom Botanical Nutritive Duo capsules per day.

 Hydrate often. Put 1-2 drops of a citrus oil in your water and drink throughout the day. Drink half your body weight in ounces of water per day.

EDEMA

| ⏰ *3-5x per day* | 📅 *While symptoms persist* |

Essential Oils: *Cypress, Lemon, Grapefruit*

Other Solutions: *N/A*

 Choose 2 of the recommended oils. Put 2 drops of each oil in your palm and dilute with 1 teaspoon of fractionated coconut oil. Rub over the affected area throughout the day. Rub on the bottoms of your feet morning and evening. Put 2 drops of Lemon in water and sip throughout the day.

EMOTIONAL TRAUMA

| ⏰ *3-5x per day* | 📅 *While symptoms persist* |

Essential Oils: *Forgive®, Frankincense, Peace®, Adaptiv™ (3-part system)*

Other Solutions: *Adaptiv™ Capsules, Serenity® Softgels*

 Put 1 drop of Frankincense under your tongue morning and evening. Take 1 Adaptiv™ Capsule per day. Mix 5-7 drops each of Forgive®, Peace®, and Adaptiv™ in a 10 ml roller bottle and fill the rest with fractionated coconut oil. Rub over your heart, down the back of your neck, behind your ears, and under your skull. Rub on the bottoms of your feet morning and evening.

 Aim for light to moderate exercise 4-5 days per week. Adopt an exercise program that combines aerobic exercise, strength training, and balance and joint flexibility exercises. Listen to your body and rest as needed. Warm up, cool down, and stretch for each exercise session.

🌙 Place 1 drop of Lavender or Serenity® on your pillow at night. Take 2 Serenity® Softgels before bed. Avoid stressful conversations or television before meals or bed. Develop a good bedtime routine that feels relaxing to you. Find a hobby or meditation program. Listen to music, go for a walk in nature, or go out with friends. Increase the laughter in your life by watching a comedy or hanging with friends and family members who make you laugh. Schedule self-care rituals throughout the week that make you feel good.

D-F

EMPHYSEMA

⏰ **4-5x per day**	📅 **As needed**

Essential Oils: *Black Pepper, Eucalyptus, Douglas Fir, Breathe®*

Other Solutions: *Breathe® Drops, Breathe® Vapor Stick, Peppermint Beadlets*

 Choose 2-3 of the recommended oils. Mix 5-7 drops of each oil in a 10 ml roller bottle and fill with fractionated coconut oil. Apply over your chest, your mid/upper back, and down your spine throughout the day. Rub on the bottoms of your feet morning and evening. Rub the mixture on your palms and inhale 3 deep breaths as needed. Take Breathe® Drops as desired. Rub the Breathe® Vapor Stick over your chest throughout the day. Take Peppermint Beadlets as needed. If you get oils in your eyes or on your face while inhaling from your hands, apply plain coconut oil over your eye or face to soothe the area. Repeat as needed.

🍏 Avoid dairy products if you notice that they make your phlegm thicker. Avoid foods that cause gas and bloating: beans, fried foods, onions, cauliflower, broccoli, cabbage, Brussels sprouts. Avoid any foods that you know cause you excess gas. Put 2 drops of Lemon in your water to thin the mucus and boost your immune system. Drink half your body weight in ounces of water per day.

ENDOMETRIOSIS

⏰ **3-5x per day**	📅 **As needed**

Essential Oils: *Clary Sage, Geranium, Petitgrain, Thyme, Rosemary, DDR Prime®, Copaiba, Tulsi*

Other Solutions: *Deep Blue® Rub*

 Choose 3-4 of the recommended oils. Mix 5-7 drops of each oil in a 10 ml roller bottle and fill with fractionated coconut oil. Apply over your lower abdomen, lower back area, and on the bottoms of your feet morning and evening. Massage Deep Blue® Rub over your lower abdomen throughout the day for pain relief.

D-F

ENGORGEMENT

4-5x per day		*While symptoms persist*

Essential Oils: *Peppermint, AromaTouch®, Deep Blue®, PastTense®, Ginger*

Other Solutions: *N/A*

 Choose 3-4 of the recommended oils. Place 2 drops of each oil in a small bowl of cold water. Dip a clean washcloth into the water. Apply the washcloth over the affected breasts for 10 minutes. Apply PastTense® over the affected breasts morning and evening.

EPILEPSY

3-5x per day		*While symptoms persist*

Essential Oils: *Frankincense, DDR Prime®, Cedarwood, Clary Sage, Spikenard*

Other Solutions: *N/A*

 Put 1 drop each of Frankincense and DDR Prime® in a capsule and take 3 times per day. Choose 2-3 of the recommended oils. Mix 5-7 drops of each oil in a 10 ml roller bottle and fill with fractionated coconut oil. Apply down the back of your neck, under your skull, behind your ears, and down your spine. Apply to the bottoms of your feet morning and evening.

ERECTILE DYSFUNCTION

3-5x per day		*As needed*

Essential Oils: *Neroli Touch, Cypress, Ylang Ylang, Sandalwood*

Other Solutions: *N/A*

 Choose 2-3 of the recommended oils. Mix 5-7 drops of each oil in a 10 ml roller bottle and fill with fractionated coconut oil. Apply over your temples, down the back of your neck, over your wrists, and over your lower abdomen.

Consume cocoa, dark chocolate, watermelon, tomatoes, grapefruit, red peppers, pistachios, tea, and wine.

Keep your weight in a healthy range. Do a combination of strength training and cardio 5-7 times per week.

D-F

ESTROGEN IMBALANCE

⏰ *3-5x per day*	📅 *Ongoing as needed*

Essential Oils: *Whisper®, Clary Sage, Zendocrine®, Clary Calm®, Citronella, Tulsi*

Other Solutions: *N/A*

- 💜 Choose 2-3 of the recommended oils. Mix 5-7 drops of each oil in a 10 ml roller bottle and fill with fractionated coconut oil. Apply over your lower abdomen, lower back, down the back of your neck, and on the bottoms of your feet morning and evening.

- 🍏 Consume avocados, flaxseed, broccoli, pomegranate, salmon, leafy greens, nuts, organic soy, turmeric, quinoa, and brown rice. Avoid excess sugar, simple carbohydrates, trans fats, and processed foods.

EXHAUSTION

⏰ *3-5x per day*	📅 *As needed*

Essential Oils: *Citrus Bliss®, Passion®, Wild Orange, Tulsi*

Other Solutions: *Peppermint Beadlets, Lifelong Vitality, Serenity® Softgels*

- 💜 Choose 2-3 of the recommended oils. Diffuse 4-5 drops of each in a diffuser throughout the day. Mix 5-7 drops of each oil in a 10 ml roller bottle and fill the rest with fractionated coconut oil. Apply over your temples, down the back of your neck, behind your ears, and over the pulse points on your wrist. Take Peppermint Beadlets as needed.

- 🍏 Take Lifelong Vitality Supplements twice a day. Consume fresh fruits and vegetables, whole unprocessed foods, lean protein, whole grains, complex carbohydrates, nuts, and seeds. Drink half your body weight in ounces of water.

- 🟠 Get out into the fresh air for aerobic exercise 5-6 times per week. Add yoga and stretching 2-3 times per week.

- 🌙 Put 1 drop of Lavender or Serenity® on your pillow at night. Take 2 Serenity® Softgels at bedtime. Develop a sleep routine. Keep your room cool and dark.

D·F

FAINTING

3-5x per day	**As needed**

Essential Oils: *Peppermint, Rosemary, Frankincense, Citrus Bliss®*

Other Solutions: *N/A*

 Choose 2-3 of the recommended oils. Diffuse 4-5 drops of each in a diffuser throughout the day. Mix 5-7 drops of each chosen oil in a 10 ml roller bottle and fill the rest with fractionated coconut oil. Apply over your temples, down the back of your neck, behind your ears, and over the pulse points on your wrist.

FATIGUE

3-5x per day	**As needed**

Essential Oils: *Motivate®, Passion®, Basil, Citrus Bliss®, Wild Orange, Peppermint, Tulsi*

Other Solutions: *Peppermint Beadlets, Lifelong Vitality, Serenity® Softgels*

 Choose 2-3 of the recommended oils. Diffuse 4-5 drops of each throughout the day. Mix 5-7 drops each of your chosen oils in a 10 ml roller bottle and fill remainder with fractionated coconut oil. Apply over your temples, down the back of your neck, behind your ears, and over your pulse points on your wrists. Dilute 1 drop of Peppermint with 10 drops of fractionated coconut oil in your palm. Apply to the back of your neck and under your nose. Inhale from your palms 3 times in deep breaths. Take Peppermint Beadlets as needed. If you get oils in your eyes or on your face while inhaling from your hands, apply plain coconut oil over your eye or face to soothe the area. Repeat as needed.

Take Lifelong Vitality Supplements twice a day. Consume fresh fruits and vegetables, whole unprocessed foods, lean protein, whole grains, complex carbohydrates, nuts, and seeds. Drink half your body weight in ounces of water.

Do aerobic exercise in fresh air 5-6 times per week. Add in yoga and stretching 2-3 times per week.

Place 1 drop of Lavender or Serenity® on your pillow at night. Take 2 Serenity® Softgels at bedtime. Develop a sleep routine. Keep your room cool and dark.

D-F

FEAR

 3-5x per day | *As needed*

Essential Oils: *Juniper Berry, Wild Orange, Peace®, Balance®*

Other Solutions: *N/A*

 Choose 2-3 recommended oils. Diffuse 4-5 drops of each in a diffuser throughout the day. Mix 5-7 drops of each oil in a 10 ml roller bottle and fill remainder with fractionated coconut oil. Apply over your temples, down the back of your neck, behind your ears, and over the pulse points on your wrist.

FEVER

 3-5x per day | *As needed*

Essential Oils: *Peppermint, Eucalyptus, Pink Pepper*

Other Solutions: *Peppermint Beadlets*

 Choose 2-3 of the recommended oils. Dilute 1-2 drops of each with 1 teaspoon of fractionated coconut oil. Apply topically to the back of your neck, over your chest, and on your temples. Diffuse 4-5 drops of each oil throughout the day. Take Peppermint Beadlets as needed.

D-F

FEVER BLISTERS

 3-5x per day | *While symptoms persist*

Essential Oils: *Clove, On Guard®, Tea Tree*

Other Solutions: *N/A*

 Choose 2 of the recommended oils. Mix 1 drop of each with 20 drops of fractionated coconut oil in your palm. Apply topically to the affected area as needed.

FIBROCYSTIC BREASTS

 3-5x per day | *Ongoing as needed*

Essential Oils: *Clary Sage, Sandalwood, Geranium, Tulsi*

Other Solutions: *N/A*

 Choose 2-3 of the recommended oils. Mix 5-7 drops of each oil in a 10 ml roller bottle and fill remainder with fractionated coconut oil. Apply over your breasts throughout the day.

FIBROIDS

 3-5x per day | *Ongoing as needed*

Essential Oils: *Sandalwood, Frankincense, Lemongrass, Tulsi*

Other Solutions: *N/A*

 Choose 2-3 of the recommended oils. Mix 5-7 drops of each oil in a 10 ml roller bottle and fill remainder with fractionated coconut oil. Apply over your lower abdomen and lower back throughout the day.

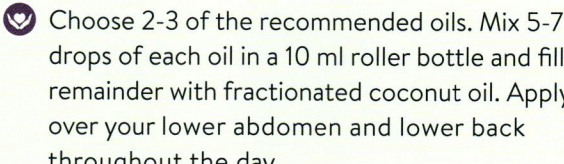

FIBROMYALGIA

3-5x per day	**Ongoing as needed**

Essential Oils: *AromaTouch®, Ginger, Copaiba*

Other Solutions: *Deep Blue® Polyphenol Complex, DDR Prime® Softgels, Turmeric Dual Chamber Capsules, DDR Prime®, Lifelong Vitality, DigestZen TerraZyme®, PB Assist®+, Serenity® Softgels, Deep Blue® Rub*

 Mix 5-7 drops each of AromaTouch®, Ginger, and Copaiba in a 10 ml roller bottle and fill the rest with fractionated coconut oil. Rub a dime-sized amount of Deep Blue® Rub plus the roller bottle over sore muscles and joints as needed throughout the day. Take 2 Turmeric Dual Chamber Capsules per day. Take 2 DDR Prime® Capsules per day. Take 1 Deep Blue® Polyphenol Complex with meals.

 Take Lifelong Vitality Supplements twice a day, 2-3 DigestZen TerraZyme® capsules at each meal, and PB Assist® once per day. Eat a variety of fresh fruits, vegetables, lean meats, healthy fats, and rice. Avoid MSG, gluten, corn, fried food, fast food, processed foods, and artificial sweeteners.

 Do 30-45 minutes of aerobic exercise per day, preferably out in nature/fresh air. Listen to your body and don't push it.

 Apply 1 drop of Serenity® or Lavender to your pillow at bedtime. Take 1-2 Serenity® Softgels 30 minutes before bed. Use emotional oils as needed. Include meditation, prayer, and spending time in nature as part of your regular routine to rest and manage your stress. Join an online support group or reach out to friends and family for help as needed.

 Makeover your home by using the Abōde™ line of cleaning products, laundry pods, dishwasher pods, surface cleaner, and dish soap. Take care of your hands with Abōde™ Foaming Hand Wash and Lotion. If tolerated, do a 30-day cleanse each season. See the 30-day cleanse on page 434.

D-F

FLEAS

3-4x per day	**As needed**

Essential Oils: *Citronella, Lemon Eucalyptus, Arborvitae, Cedarwood, TerraShield®, Lavender*

Other Solutions: *N/A*

🖤 Choose 4 of the recommended oils. Put 10 drops of each oil in a 2-ounce glass spray bottle. Fill with 3/4 water and 1/4 witch hazel. Shake the bottle well to mix the oils. Spray over your animal's collar, clothes, mat, or anywhere else you need to repel fleas.

D-F

FLU

	Hourly at first signs of symptoms, then 4-5x per day until symptoms resolve.		*While symptoms persist*

Essential Oils: *Frankincense, On Guard®, Oregano, Tea Tree, Lemon, Eucalyptus, Breathe®*

Other Solutions: *Ginger Drops, Breathe® Drops, Breathe® Vapor Stick, Peppermint Beadlets, On Guard™+ Softgels, On Guard® Beadlets, Correct-X, Lifelong Vitality, DigestZen TerraZyme®, PB Assist®+, Serenity® Softgels, On Guard® Tablets*

Mix 7 drops of each recommended oil in a 10 ml roller bottle and fill with fractionated coconut oil. Rub over your chest, neck, upper/mid back, and on the bottoms of your feet morning and evening. Put 2 drops each of Frankincense, Lemon, Tea Tree, Oregano, and On Guard® in a capsule and take 3 times per day. Take Ginger Drops as needed. Take Breathe® Drops as needed. Rub the Breathe® Vapor Stick over your chest and forehead and under your nose. Take Peppermint Beadlets as needed. Take 1 On Guard® Softgel 3 times per day. Take On Guard® Beadlets and On Guard® Tablets as needed. Put a small amount of Correct-X on a cotton swab and swab the inside of your nose for extra immune support.

Eat or drink Lemon/Ginger tea, chicken broth, bone broth, cooked carrots, crackers, chicken, and co-conut oil. Take Lifelong Vitality Supplements twice a day, 2-3 DigestZen TerraZyme® capsules at each meal, and PB Assist® once per day. Drink Lemon in water (*2 drops per glass*). Listen to your body. Eat when you can.

Rest as much as possible. Apply 1 drop of Serenity® or Lavender to your pillow while resting. Take 1-2 Serenity® Softgels 30 minutes before bed. Use emotional oils as needed.

D-F

FOCUS

⏰ *3-4x per day*	📅 *As needed*

Essential Oils: *Peppermint, InTune®, Pink Pepper, Vetiver, Cedarwood*

Other Solutions: *Peppermint Beadlets*

 Choose 2 of the recommended oils. Diffuse 4 -5 drops of each oil. Apply 1 drop of Peppermint or a swipe of InTune® topically on both of your temples, over your forehead, and on the back of your skull as needed. Diffuse 5 drops of Peppermint into the air or swipe InTune® on your palm and inhale. Apply 1 drop of Pink Pepper to palms and inhale. Add 1 drop of Peppermint or Pink Pepper to your water and sip throughout the day. Take Peppermint Beadlets an needed. If you get oils in your eyes or on your face while inhaling from your hands, apply plain coconut oil over the eye or face to soothe the area. Repeat as needed.

D-F

FOOD ADDICTION

3-4x per day | *As needed*

Essential Oils: *Grapefruit, MetaPWR™, Peppermint, Ginger, Basil*

Other Solutions: *Peppermint Beadlets, MetaPWR™ Softgels, MetaPWR™ Gum, Lifelong Vitality, DigestZen TerraZyme®, PB Assist®+, Serenity® Softgels*

- Put 2 drops of Grapefruit or MetaPWR™ in water and drink throughout the day. Put 1 drop of Peppermint on your tongue for sugar cravings. Take 1 MetaPWR™ Softgel before meals. Chew MetaPWR™ gum in between meals. Take Peppermint Beadlets as needed for sugar cravings.
- Take Lifelong Vitality Supplements twice a day, 2-3 DigestZen TerraZyme® capsules at each meal, and PB Assist® once per day. Adopt the 80/20 rule when it comes to eating: eat healthily 80 percent of the time and let yourself have whatever you want 20 percent of the time.
- Take the focus off your weight and set goals of getting stronger; building endurance; and enjoying how your mood, outlook, and energy levels increase when you adopt a regular exercise routine.
- Apply 1 drop of Serenity® or Lavender to your pillow at bedtime. Take 1-2 Serenity® Softgels 30 minutes before bed. Use emotional oils as needed throughout the day. Include meditation, prayer, and spending time in nature as part of your regular routine to rest and manage your stress. Join an online support group or reach out to friends and family for help as needed.
- Don't struggle alone. Reach out for professional help if you feel you are out of control with your eating.

FOOD POISONING

4-5x per day	*While symptoms persist*

Essential Oils: *Petitgrain, DigestZen®, Zendocrine®, Tea Tree*

Other Solutions: *Ginger Drops, Breathe® Drops, Peppermint Beadlets, On Guard™+ Softgels, On Guard® Beadlets*

⊘ Choose 2-3 of the recommended oils. Put 2 drops of each in a capsule and take 3 times per day. Mix 5-7 drops of each oil in a 10 ml roller bottle and fill the rest with fractionated coconut oil. Apply to your stomach, the bottoms of your feet, and down your spine throughout the day. Take Ginger Drops as needed. Take Breathe® Drops as needed. Take Peppermint Beadlets as needed. Take 1 On Guard® Softgel 3 times per day. Take On Guard® Beadlets as needed.

⊘ If tolerated, eat or drink Lemon/Ginger tea, chicken broth, bone broth, cooked carrots, crackers, chicken, and coconut oil.

D-F

D-F

FRAGILE HAIR

Daily or 3x per week	*Ongoing until symptoms improve*

Essential Oils: *Rosemary, DDR Prime®, Thyme, Cedarwood, Geranium*

Other Solutions: *Salon Essentials Protecting Shampoo, Salon Essentials Smoothing Conditioner, Healthy Hold Glaze, Root to Tip Serum, Yarrow|Pom Body Renewal Serum, Yarrow|Pom Botanical Nutritive Duo capsules, Lifelong Vitality, DigestZen TerraZyme®, PB Assist®+*

Use Protecting Shampoo and Smoothing Conditioner to clean your hair. Apply Healthy Hold Glaze and Root to Tip Serum on damp hair. Combine 1.5 ounces of jojoba oil and 1.5 ounces of grapeseed oil in a glass jar with a lid. Add 20 drops each of Cedarwood, DDR Prime®, Rosemary, and Geranium. Place the lid on the jar, shake well, and apply generously to your hair and scalp *(dry or wet)* daily or 3 times per week. Leave in your hair for at least 20 minutes. You can leave it in overnight; use a shower cap or towel to prevent staining linens. Shampoo, rinse, and style as usual. Massage Yarrow|Pom Body Renewal Serum on your scalp after washing. Take 2 Yarrow|Pom Botanical Nutritive Duo capsules per day.

Take Lifelong Vitality Supplements twice a day, 2-3 DigestZen TerraZyme® capsules at each meal, and PB Assist® once per day. Eat a variety of fresh fruits *(like blueberries, kiwi, and guava)*, carrots, almond butter, lentils, oysters, lean meat, healthy fats, barley, and rice. Avoid MSG, high amounts of sugar, and swordfish *(high amounts of mercury may be linked to hair loss)*. Avoid processed foods and artificial sweeteners along with starchy foods.

Take proactive steps in reducing stress and getting an adequate quality and quantity of rest by following the recommendations in the Rest and Manage Stress chapter (page 410).

FROZEN SHOULDER

 3-5x per day | *Until symptoms improve*

Essential Oils: *Wintergreen, Siberian Fir, Lemongrass, Lavender, PastTense®*

Other Solutions: *Turmeric Dual Chamber Capsules, Deep Blue® Rub*

 Combine 5-7 drops of each recommended oil in a 10 ml roller bottle with fractionated coconut oil. Rub over the affected shoulder. Use Deep Blue® Rub as needed. Take 2 Turmeric Dual Chamber Capsules daily with meals. Use a PastTense® roller over the affected shoulder as needed. Immediately ice the affected shoulder right after injury occurs. Avoid activities that cause shoulder pain to keep inflammation down.

FUNGAL SKIN

 3-5x per day | *While symptoms persist*

Essential Oils: *Tea Tree, Arborvitae, Cedarwood, Citronella, Lemon Eucalyptus, HD Clear®*

Other Solutions: *HD Clear® Foaming Face Wash, HD Clear® Facial Lotion*

 Wash the affected area with HD Clear® Foaming Face Wash and allow to dry. Choose 2 of the recommended oils and apply 1-2 drops to the affected area throughout the day. After applying the oils, apply HD Clear® Facial Lotion.

GALLBLADDER DISEASE

⏰ *3-5x per day*	📅 *Ongoing as needed*

Essential Oils: *MetaPWR™, Turmeric, Grapefruit, Zendocrine®, Geranium, Green Mandarin*

Other Solutions: *Ginger Drops, Peppermint Beadlets*

💜 Choose 2-3 of the recommended oils. Mix 5-7 drops of each in a 10 ml roller bottle and fill with fractionated coconut oil. Apply under your middle and right rib cage throughout the day. Put 2 drops of each in a capsule and take 2 times per day. Take Ginger Drops as needed. Take Peppermint Beadlets as desired.

🍏 While symptoms persist, avoid high-fat dairy and meat, fried foods, cookies, cakes, processed foods, refined white flour, creamy soups and sauces, pizza, soda, and alcohol.

✚ Seek professional medical attention if you experience persistent abdominal pain, severe nausea or vomiting, shoulder pain, yellowing of the skin, or frequent diarrhea.

G-I

GALLBLADDER STONES

3-5x per day	*Ongoing as needed*

Essential Oils: *Lemon, Cilantro, Juniper Berry*

Other Solutions: *Ginger Drops, Peppermint Beadlets*

 Choose 2 -3 of the recommended oils. Mix 5-7 drops of each in a 10 ml roller bottle and fill the rest with fractionated coconut oil. Apply under your middle and right rib cage throughout the day. Put 2 drops of each in a capsule and take 2 times per day. Take Ginger Drops as needed. Take Peppermint Beadlets as desired.

Seek professional medical attention if you experience persistent abdominal pain, severe nausea or vomiting, shoulder pain, yellowing of the skin, or frequent diarrhea.

GAS *(Flatulence)*

3-5x per day	*While symptoms persist*

Essential Oils: *Black Pepper, DigestZen®, Peppermint*

Other Solutions: *Ginger Drops, Peppermint Beadlets, Peppermint Softgels*

 Choose 2-3 of the recommended oils. Mix 5-7 drops of each in a 10 ml roller bottle and fill remainder with fractionated coconut oil. Apply over your abdomen throughout the day. Put 2 drops of each chosen oil in a capsule and take 2 times per day. Take 2 Peppermint Softgels for lower bowel gas. Take Ginger Drops as needed. Take Peppermint Beadlets as desired.

GANGLION CYST

3-5x per day	*Until resolved*

Essential Oils: *Lemongrass, Thyme, On Guard®, DDR Prime®*

Other Solutions: *N/A*

 Choose 2 of the recommended oils. Dilute 1-2 drops of each with 1/2 teaspoon of fractionated coconut oil. Apply to the affected area throughout the day.

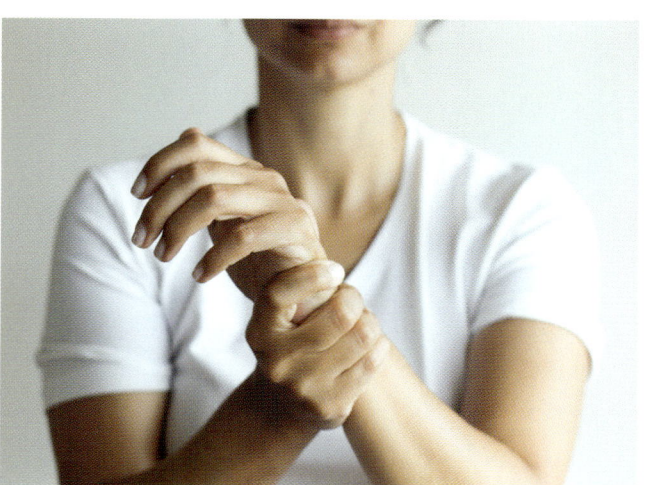

G-I

GASTRITIS

🕐 **3-5x per day**	📅 **Ongoing as needed**

Essential Oils: *Petitgrain, Fennel, Peppermint, Ginger*

Other Solutions: *Peppermint Beadlets, Ginger Drops*

 Choose 2-3 of the recommended oils. Mix 5-7 drops of each oil in a 10 ml roller bottle and fill with fractionated coconut oil. Apply over your stomach and on your upper/mid back area throughout the day as needed. Put 1 drop of each oil in a capsule and take 3 times per day. Take Ginger Drops as needed. Take Peppermint Beadlets as desired.

 Avoid alcohol, coffee, acidic foods, fruit juices, fatty foods, fried foods, carbonated drinks, and spicy foods.

GASTROENTERITIS
(Stomach Flu)

🕐 **3-4x per day**	📅 **While symptoms persist**

Essential Oils: *Cardamom, Peppermint, Ginger, DigestZen®, Thyme*

Other Solutions: *Ginger Drops, Peppermint Beadlets, On Guard® Protecting Throat Drops, On Guard® Beadlets, On Guard® Tablets*

 Choose 2-3 of the recommended oils. Mix 5-7 drops of each oil in a 10 ml roller bottle and fill with fractionated coconut oil. Apply to your abdomen and lower back and on the bottoms of your feet morning and evening. Put 1 drop of Peppermint in your water and sip throughout the day. Take Ginger Drops as needed. Take Peppermint Beadlets as needed. Take On Guard® Protecting Throat Drops as needed. Take On Guard® Beadlets and On Guard® Tablets as needed.

 Drink plenty of clear liquids throughout the day. Avoid caffeine and alcohol. Add semi-solid and low-fiber foods back into your diet gradually as your bowel movements return to normal. Start with rice, chicken, eggs, and crackers if tolerated.

GASTROESOPHAGEAL REFLUX (GERD)

3-5x per day	*Ongoing as needed*

Essential Oils: *DigestZen®, Zendocrine®, Coriander, Ginger, Green Mandarin, Celery Seed*

Other Solutions: *Peppermint Beadlets, Ginger Drops*

- Choose 3 of the recommended oils. Mix 5-7 drops of each oil in a 10 ml roller bottle and fill with fractionated coconut oil. Put 1 drop each of the following oils in a capsule and take 3 times per day: Lemon, Ginger, Zendocrine®, DigestZen®, Coriander. Take Ginger Drops as needed. Take Peppermint Beadlets as desired.

- Avoid high-fat foods, fried foods, full-fat dairy products, high-fat deli meats, creamy sauces, oily and greasy foods, refined sugar, high-fructose corn syrup, trans fats, processed foods, baked goods, artificial sweeteners, and chips.

GENITAL WARTS

3-5x per day	*Ongoing as needed*

Essential Oils: *Arborvitae, Frankincense, Thyme*

Other Solutions:

- Choose 2-3 of the recommended oils. Mix 5-7 drops of each oil in a 10 ml roller bottle and fill with fractionated coconut oil. Apply over the affected area throughout the day as needed.

GIARDIA

3-5x per day	*While symptoms persist*

Essential Oils: *Rosemary, Oregano, Spearmint*

Other Solutions:

- Choose 2-3 of the recommended oils. Mix 5-7 drops of each oil in a 10 ml roller bottle and fill with fractionated coconut oil. Apply over your stomach and on your upper/mid back area throughout the day as needed. Put 1 drop of each oil in a capsule and take 3 times per day.

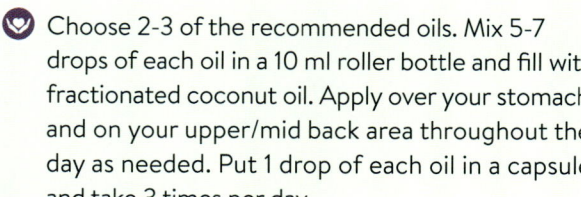

G-I

GINGIVITIS

⏰ **3x per day**	📅 **Ongoing**

Essential Oils: *On Guard®, Clove*

Other Solutions: *On Guard® Natural Whitening Toothpaste, On Guard® Mouthwash, Peppermint Beadlets*

 Brush your teeth 3 times per day with On Guard® toothpaste and follow it up with On Guard® Mouthwash. Take Peppermint Beadlets as desired. Practice oil pulling.

🔻 Practice oil pulling to remove toxins and harmful bacteria from your mouth: Take a tablespoon of hard coconut oil and place 1 drop of On Guard® and 1 drop of Peppermint or Spearmint on top of the coconut oil. Allow the oil to melt in your mouth, and then swish it around for 5-15 minutes. Pull the oil through your teeth and on both sides of your mouth. When you are done, spit it out in the garbage—not down the sink, as the hard coconut oil could clog the drain over time. Repeat this process a few times per week. Hint: start off at 1 minute and work your way up, eventually finding the amount of time that feels best to you.

GOITER

⏰ **3-5x per day**	📅 **Ongoing**

Essential Oils: *Myrrh, Lemongrass, DDR Prime®, Frankincense, Patchouli*

Other Solutions: *N/A*

 Combine 5-7 drops each of Lemongrass, Myrrh, Frankincense, and Patchouli with fractionated coconut oil in a 10 ml roller bottle. Apply over your throat area and the back of your neck. Put 1 drop of DDR Prime® in a capsule and take 3 times per day.

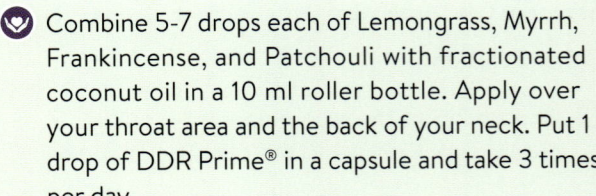

G-I

GONORRHEA

⏰ **4-5x per day**	📅 *Ongoing as needed until condition resolves*

Essential Oils: *Tea Tree, Frankincense, Oregano, Copaiba, Basil, On Guard®*

Other Solutions: *Lifelong Vitality, DigestZen TerraZyme®, PB Assist®+*

 Choose 3-4 of the recommended oils. Mix 5-7 drops of each with fractionated coconut oil in a 10 ml roller bottle. Rub it over your lower abdomen. Make a veggie capsule using 1 drop of each oil. Take 3 times per day until the condition resolves. If you choose to use Oregano in the veggie capsule, do not take it more than 10 days in a row. After 10 days, eliminate Oregano from your veggie capsule for a week, then add it back in if necessary. Diffuse 3-4 drops of each chosen oil throughout the day.

 If the condition has affected your throat, combine 1 tablespoon of raw honey with 1 drop of Lemon and On Guard® and take 3 times per day. Eat sunflower seeds, pumpkin seeds, kefir, cage-free eggs, wild-caught fish, broccoli, spinach, bell peppers, sauerkraut, and citrus fruits. Add garlic to meals regularly. Take Lifelong Vitality Supplements twice a day, 2-3 DigestZen TerraZyme® capsules at each meal, and PB Assist® once per day.

🌙 Rest often to encourage healing. Opt for an earlier bedtime and develop a good sleep routine. Try to get 7-9 hours of quality sleep per night. Diffuse Lavender or Serenity® an hour before bed when winding down for the evening. Avoid electronics too close to bedtime.

✚ If left untreated, this condition can cause infertility in both men and women along with other serious health problems. Often it is asymptomatic. Seek medical care immediately if you experience any of the following symptoms: vaginal discharge *(watery, creamy, or slightly green)*; fever; pain or a burning sensation while urinating; frequent urination; heavier periods or spotting; sore throat; pain during sexual intercourse; sharp pain in the lower abdomen.

G-I

G-I

GOUT

  3-5x per day	 *Ongoing as needed until condition resolves*

Essential Oils: *Celery Seed, Wintergreen, Deep Blue®, Siberian Fir, Lemongrass, Copaiba, Lavender*

Other Solutions: *Turmeric Dual Chamber Capsules, Lifelong Vitality, PB Assist®+, Greens, Protein*

 Choose 3-4 of the recommended oils. Mix 5-7 drops of each oil with fractionated coconut oil in a 10 ml roller bottle and rub it over the affected area. Diffuse 3-4 drops each of Lavender and Copaiba throughout the day to help ease stress and pain. Stay off your feet, if possible, when flare-ups occur. Rest. Keep any weight or clothes off the area with gout. Ice the inflamed area while elevating it to reduce inflammation. Take 1 Turmeric Capsule at each meal.

Drink at least half your body weight in ounces of water. Eat leafy green vegetables (*like spinach*), nuts, berries, whole grains, avocado, bananas, olive oil, omega-3 fatty acids, and tart cherry juice. Take Lifelong Vitality Supplements twice a day; PB Assist® once per day; and 1 scoop of Greens in a morning smoothie that includes berries, tart cherry juice, baby spinach, 1 scoop of vanilla Protein, and 1 cup almond milk. Avoid inflammatory or processed foods, beer, grain liquors, excessive amounts of red meat, refined grains, baked goods, and artificial sweeteners.

Seek medical attention right away if you experience redness, pain, swelling, or hotness in your affected joint or if you can't walk or ambulate.

GRIEF

  3-5x per day	 *While symptoms persist*

Essential Oils: *Console®, Melissa, Magnolia, Adaptiv™ (3-part system), Neroli Touch*

Other Solutions: *Adaptiv™ Capsules, Lifelong Vitality, DigestZen TerraZyme®, PB Assist®+*

Place 10 drops of Console® or 5 drops of Console® and 5 drops of Melissa in a diffuser and diffuse throughout the day, or place 1-2 drops of Console® and 1-2 drops of Melissa in an aromatherapy diffuser necklace, bracelet, or inhaler. You can also use Adaptiv™: Add 10 drops to the diffuser or 2-4 drops to aromatherapy jewelry or an inhaler. Use consistently throughout day as feelings of grief become apparent. Combine 5-7 drops each of Console® and Melissa in a 10 ml roller bottle with fractionated coconut oil. Apply to the back of your neck, your wrist pulse points, and your chest. Use the Magnolia, Adaptiv™, or Neroli Touch roller to provide on-the-go relief. Apply the roller to the back of your neck, your wrist pulse points, and your heart. Take 1 Adaptiv™ Capsule in the morning with food.

Take Lifelong Vitality Supplements twice a day, 2-3 DigestZen TerraZyme® capsules at each meal, and PB Assist® once per day. Eat a variety of fresh fruits, vegetables, lean meat, fatty fish, healthy fats, and brown rice. Avoid MSG, gluten, corn, fried food, fast food, and processed foods. Drink half your weight in ounces of water.

Do 30-45 minutes of aerobic exercise per day, preferably out in nature/fresh air.

GROWING PAINS

 3x per day and 1x prior to bed   *While symptoms persist*

Essential Oils: *Lemongrass, Marjoram, Cypress, Lavender*

Other Solutions: *Greens, PB Assist® Jr, IQ Mega®, Deep Blue® Stick*

🟣 Place 3 drops each of Lemongrass, Marjoram, Cypress, and Lavender in a 10 ml roller bottle with fractionated coconut oil, or combine 5-7 drops of each oil with fractionated coconut oil in a 2-ounce glass spray bottle. Apply to the affected area. Alternatively, apply Deep Blue® Stick to the impacted area. Diffuse 5 drops of Lavender in a diffuser throughout the day, or use a diffuser bracelet to help promote calm feelings. Use a heat pack prior to applying oils to encourage blood flow and increase absorption.

🟢 Eat green leafy vegetables (such as salad greens, kale, broccoli, and spinach) and nuts *(such as almonds and cashews)*. For fussy eaters, mix 1 scoop of Greens with 8 ounces of liquid, or add 1 scoop of Greens to a smoothie with 8 ounces or more of coconut milk *(depending on consistency preference)*, 1 cup of frozen mixed berries, 1 cup of Greek yogurt, and organic maple syrup or honey to sweeten, if needed. Take PB Assist® Jr in the morning on an empty stomach *(2 tablets per day with a meal for children and 3 tablets per day with a meal for adults)*. Take 1 teaspoon of IQ Mega® per day.

🔴 Stretch gently after strenuous activity.

G-I

G-I

GUM DISEASE

⏰	**2x per day and after meals**	📅	*Ongoing*

Essential Oils: *Clove, Cinnamon Bark, Myrrh, Tea Tree, Spearmint, On Guard®*

Other Solutions: *On Guard® Natural Whitening Toothpaste, On Guard® Mouthwash, Peppermint Beadlets*

💜 Combine 1 drop of Cinnamon Bark, Spearmint, or Myrrh in 2 ounces of water, shake well, and gargle twice daily. Use On Guard® toothpaste and On Guard® Mouthwash every morning and evening. Soak your dental floss in warm salt water with 1 drop of Tea Tree or On Guard® for 5 minutes. Floss after each meal, prior to bed, and upon waking. Brush your tongue each time you brush your teeth. Add 1 drop of Clove, Cinnamon Bark, or On Guard® to your toothbrush prior to brushing your tongue or teeth. Use Peppermint Beadlets during the day to combat bad breath.

🍏 Eliminate sugar and refined carbohydrates. Avoid sticky candies and sweets like lollipops, caramels, and sugary cough drops. Avoid starchy foods that can get stuck in your mouth, like potato chips. If you eat sugar, eat it with a meal. Eat nuts, seeds, salmon and other fatty fish, grass-fed beef, red and green bell peppers, broccoli, sweet potatoes, and probiotic-containing foods (such as kefir, sauerkraut, fermented yogurt, and kimchi).

➕ Schedule regular appointments with your dentist to monitor oral health.

H. PYLORI

⏰	**3-5x per day**	📅	*While symptoms persist*

Essential Oils: *Cassia, Black Pepper, Oregano, Ginger, Thyme*

Other Solutions: *N/A*

💜 Choose 2-3 of the recommended oils. Mix 5-7 drops of each oil in a 10 ml roller bottle and fill the rest with fractionated coconut oil. Apply under the front of your ribs, down your spine, and on the bottoms of your feet morning and evening. Put 1 drop each of Oregano, Cassia, Black Pepper, and Thyme in a capsule with 2 drops of fractionated coconut oil and take twice daily.

HAIR LOSS

⏰ *Daily or 3x per week*	📅 *Ongoing until hair growth improves*

Essential Oils: *DDR Prime®, Cedarwood, Rosemary, Clary Sage*

Other Solutions: *Salon Essentials Protecting Shampoo, Salon Essentials Smoothing Conditioner, Healthy Hold Glaze, Root to Tip Serum, Yarrow|Pom Serum, Yarrow|Pom Botanical Nutritive Duo Capsules, Lifelong Vitality, DigestZen TerraZyme®, PB Assist®+*

Use Protecting Shampoo and Smoothing Conditioner to clean your hair. Apply Healthy Hold Glaze and Root to Tip Serum on damp hair. Combine 1.5 ounces of jojoba oil and 1.5 ounces of grapeseed oil in a glass jar with a lid. Add 20 drops each of Cedarwood, DDR Prime®, Rosemary, and Clary Sage. Place the lid on the jar, shake well, and apply generously to your hair and scalp *(dry or wet)* daily or 3 times per week. Leave in your hair for at least 20 minutes. You can leave it in overnight; use a shower cap or towel to prevent staining linens. Shampoo, rinse, and style as usual. Massage Yarrow|Pom Serum into cleanly washed hair and take 2 Yarrow|Pom Botanical Nutritive Duo Capsules per day.

Take Lifelong Vitality Supplements twice a day; 2-3 DigestZen TerraZyme® Capsules at each meal; PB Assist® once per day. Eat a variety of fresh fruits like blueberries, kiwi, and guava, carrots, almond butter, lentils, oysters, lean meat, healthy fats, barley, and rice. Avoid MSG, high amounts of sugar, and swordfish due to the high amount of mercury present which may be linked to hair loss. Avoid processed foods and artificial sweeteners along with starchy foods.

Take proactive steps to reduce stress. Get an adequate quality and quantity of rest by following the recommendations in the Rest and Manage Stress chapter (page 410).

G-I

HALITOSIS

4-5x per day	**As needed**

Essential Oils: *Peppermint, On Guard®, Spearmint, Zendocrine®*

Other Solutions: *Peppermint Beadlets, Zendocrine® Softgels, On Guard® Natural Whitening Toothpaste, On Guard® Mouthwash*

- Brush your teeth with On Guard® toothpaste 3 times per day. Use On Guard® Mouthwash after brushing your teeth, 3 times per day. Place 1 drop of Peppermint or Spearmint on your tongue until symptoms subside. Take 1-2 drops of Zendocrine® in a capsule or take 1-2 Zendocrine® Softgels. Soak your dental floss in warm salt water with 1 drop of Peppermint or Spearmint or 1 drop of On Guard® for 5 minutes. Floss daily. Brush your tongue each time you brush your teeth. Include 1 drop of Peppermint, Spearmint, or On Guard® on your toothbrush prior to brushing your tongue or teeth. Use Peppermint Beadlets during the day to combat bad breath. Practice oil pulling.

- Avoid some of the key offenders of bad breath: onions, garlic, horseradish, dairy and canned fish. Avoid starchy foods that can get stuck in your mouth like potato chips. If eating sugar, eat it with a meal due to the increased saliva production.

- Practice oil pulling to remove toxins and harmful bacteria from your mouth: Take a tablespoon of hard coconut oil and place 1 drop of On Guard® and 1 drop of Peppermint or Spearmint on top of the coconut oil. Allow the oil to melt in your mouth, and then swish it around for 5-15 minutes. Pull the oil through your teeth and on both sides of your mouth. When you are done, spit it out in the garbage—not down the sink, as the hard coconut oil could clog the drain over time. Repeat this process a few times per week. Hint: start off at 1 minute and work your way up, eventually finding the amount of time that feels best to you.

G-I

HALLUCINATIONS

3-5x per day	*While symptoms persist*

Essential Oils: *Balance®, Frankincense, Cedarwood, Peace®, Serenity®*

Other Solutions: *N/A*

- Put 1 drop of Frankincense under your tongue morning and evening. Choose 3 of the recommended oils. Mix 5-7 drops of each oil in a 10 ml roller bottle and fill with fractionated coconut oil. Roll down your neck, over your temples, on your wrists, and on the bottoms of your feet. Diffuse 4 drops of each chosen oil throughout the day.

- Call your doctor if symptoms persist.

HAND, FOOT, & MOUTH DISEASE

3-5x per day	*Ongoing until symptoms resolve*

Essential Oils: *Children over 5 years old and adults: Clove, Tea Tree, On Guard®. Children under 5 years old: Tea Tree, On Guard®, Lavender, Frankincense, Roman Chamomile, Lemon*

Other Solutions: *N/A*

- Children over 5 years old and adults: make a salve using 4 tablespoons of fractionated coconut oil, 10 drops of On Guard®, 10 drops of Tea Tree, and 5 drops of Clove. Swirl together in an amber glass container. Apply a thin layer to the affected area as recommended. Children under 5 years old: make a salve using 4 tablespoons of fractionated coconut oil, 3 drops of Frankincense, 3 drops of Tea Tree, and 2 drops each of On Guard®, Lavender, Roman Chamomile, and Lemon. Swirl together in an amber glass container and apply to the affected area as recommended. If the blisters are on your feet, use socks after application. You can also create a paste with 1 teaspoon of baking soda, a dash of water, 1 drop of Tea Tree, and 1 drop of Lavender. Apply the paste directly over the itchy area to relieve itching.

- Eat foods that do not require a lot of chewing. Drink cold beverages, such as ice water or milk. Suck on ice pops or ice chips, or enjoy ice cream in moderation. Avoid acidic foods and beverages, such as citrus fruits, fruit drinks, and soda. Avoid salty or spicy foods.

G-I

HANGOVER

🕐 **3-5x per day**	📅 *As needed*

Essential Oils: *Zendocrine®, PastTense®, Grapefruit, Peppermint, Lemon*

Other Solutions: *Ginger Drops, Peppermint Beadlets, Zendocrine® Softgels*

💜 Lay in a quiet room. Take 1 Zendocrine® Capsule in the morning. Stay hydrated by drinking at least half your body weight in ounces of water. Add 1 drop of Lemon, Grapefruit, or Zendocrine® to your water and drink throughout the day. Diffuse 5 drops of Peppermint in a nearby diffuser. Apply a PastTense® roller to your temples and the back of your neck 3-5 times per day or more if needed. Take Ginger Drops as needed. Take Peppermint Beadlets as desired.

G-I

HARDENING OF ARTERIES

 3-5x per day   *Ongoing*

Essential Oils: *Black Pepper, Lemongrass, Cinnamon, Grapefruit, Lemon*

Other Solutions: *Turmeric Dual Chamber Capsules, Lifelong Vitality, DigestZen TerraZyme®, PB Assist®+, Serenity® Softgels*

◉ Choose 3 of the recommended oils. Mix 5-7 drops of each oil in a 10 ml roller bottle and fill the rest with fractionated coconut oil. Apply over your heart, over your pulse points, down your spine, and on the bottoms of your feet morning and night. Take 2 Turmeric Dual Chamber Capsules daily.

◉ Take Lifelong Vitality Supplements twice a day, 2-3 DigestZen TerraZyme® capsules at each meal, and PB Assist® once per day. Eat a variety of fresh fruits, vegetables, lean meats, healthy fats, and rice. Include red foods as part of your diet on a daily basis. Avoid MSG, gluten, corn, fried food, fast food, processed foods, and artificial sweeteners.

◉ Do a combination of aerobic exercises, strength training, and balance exercises.

◉ Apply 1 drop of Serenity® or Lavender to your pillow at bedtime. Take 1-2 Serenity® Softgels 30 minutes before bed. Adopt a meditation or yoga practice for stress relief. Use oils from the emotional kit to manage emotional health.

◉ If you experience any of the following symptoms, seek medical attention right away: swelling, redness, pain, or hotness in an area of your arm or leg; light-headedness; difficult or painful breathing; chest pain or tightness; pain extending down your shoulder, arm, back, or jaw; sudden weakness or numbness of your face, arm, or leg; sudden difficulty speaking or understanding your speech; sudden changes in your vision.

G-I

HASHIMOTO'S DISEASE

⏰ *3-5x per day*	📅 *Ongoing*

Essential Oils: *DDR Prime®, Myrrh, Zendocrine®, Lemongrass, Peppermint, On Guard®, Tulsi*

Other Solutions: *Salon Essentials Protecting Shampoo, Salon Essentials Smoothing Conditioner, Healthy Hold Glaze, Root to Tip Serum, Lifelong Vitality, DigestZen TerraZyme®, PB Assist®+, Serenity® Softgels*

- Combine 5-7 drops each of Lemongrass, Myrrh, Tulsi, and Zendocrine® with fractionated coconut oil in a 10 ml roller bottle. Apply over your throat area and the back of your neck. Put 1 drop of DDR Prime® in a capsule and take 3 times per day. Put 1 drop of Peppermint in your water and sip throughout the day. Rub 1 drop of On Guard® over your abdomen morning and evening. Use Protecting Shampoo and Smoothing Conditioner to clean your hair. Apply Healthy Hold Glaze and Root to Tip Serum to damp hair.

- Take Lifelong Vitality Supplements twice a day, 2-3 DigestZen TerraZyme® capsules at each meal, and PB Assist® once per day. Eat a variety of fresh fruits, vegetables, lean meats, healthy fats, and rice. Avoid MSG, gluten, corn, fried food, fast food, processed foods, and artificial sweeteners.

- Place 1 drop of Lavender or Serenity® on your pillow at night. Take 1-2 Serenity® Softgels at bedtime. Develop a sleep routine. Avoid electronics an hour before bed.

- Makeover your home by using the Abōde™ line of cleaning products, laundry pods, dishwasher pods, surface cleaner, and dish soap. Take care of your hands with Abōde™ Foaming Hand Wash and Lotion. If tolerated, do a 30-day cleanse each season. See the 30-day cleanse on page 434.

HAY FEVER

 3-5x per day

 As needed

Essential Oils: *Lemon, Lavender, Peppermint, DigestZen®*

Other Solutions: *TriEase® Softgels, Lifelong Vitality, DigestZen TerraZyme®, PB Assist®+, Greens, Protein*

● Diffuse 4 drops each of Lemon, Lavender, and Peppermint when at home or at work. Add 10 drops each of Lemon, Lavender, and Peppermint to a 10 ml roller bottle and fill the rest with fractionated coconut oil. Rub over your temples and forehead, behind your ears, and over your thymus. Take 1-2 TriEase® Softgels as needed. Rub DigestZen® over your sinuses and temples morning and evening.

● Eat celery, limes, green apples, olive oil, broccoli, beets, grass-fed beef, collagen, fatty fish, free-range chicken, eggs, bone broth, spinach, lemon, green vegetables, coconut oil, avocado, berries, green tea, ripe fruit, garlic, potatoes, sweet potatoes, and brown rice. Take Lifelong Vitality Supplements twice a day; 2-3 DigestZen TerraZyme® capsules at each meal; PB Assist® once per day; Lemon in water (*2 drops per glass*); and 1 scoop of Greens in a morning smoothie that includes berries, baby spinach, 1 scoop of vanilla Protein, and 1 cup almond milk.

G-I

HEAD LICE

 Every 5-10 days with daily use of coconut oil | *At least 2 weeks*

Essential Oils: *Tea Tree, Lavender, Ylang Ylang, Eucalyptus, Citronella*

Other Solutions: *Salon Essentials® Protecting Shampoo, Salon Essentials® Smoothing Conditioner, Healthy Hold Glaze, Root to Tip Serum*

Combine 3 tablespoons of fractionated coconut oil with 25 drops of each recommended oil in a small bowl or small spray bottle. Apply the mixture all over your scalp, massage it in well, and pull it through the ends of your hair. Comb your hair with a fine-tooth comb. Cover your head with a shower cap and let it sit for 2 hours. If possible, sit in the sun or use a hair dryer to periodically to warm up the cap. Carefully remove the cap and place it in a sealable plastic bag for disposal. Comb your hair again, and then wash and rinse it thoroughly using Protecting Shampoo and Smoothing Conditioner. Combine 2 cups of apple cider vinegar and 1 cup of water in a small spray bottle, and spray half of the bottle on your wet scalp and hair, making sure you saturate your hair. Pour the remainder of the bottle over your hair while leaning over a sink or tub. Massage it into your hair. Rinse your hair thoroughly and comb it again. Follow with a light application of coconut oil to smother lice. Keep the coconut oil on your hair until your next washing. Repeat this process every 5-10 days for at least 2 weeks to eradicate all lice and eggs. Between treatments, comb your hair morning and night with a fine-tooth comb and use regular coconut oil as a leave-in conditioner. Coconut oil both repels and kills lice, so at the first notification of a lice outbreak, start using coconut oil as a leave-in conditioner. Apply Healthy Hold Glaze and Root to Tip Serum to damp hair.

G-I

HEADACHE

| *3-5x per day* | *Ongoing as needed until symptoms resolve* |

Essential Oils: *Frankincense, Peppermint, Lavender, Wintergreen, PastTense® roller, Copaiba, Copaiba Softgels, Dual Chamber Turmeric Capsules, Deep Blue® Polyphenol Complex*

Other Solutions: *Peppermint Beadlets, Turmeric Dual Chamber Capsules, Deep Blue® Polyphenol Complex, Copaiba Softgels, Lifelong Vitality, DigestZen TerraZyme®, PB Assist®+*

Combine 10 drops each of Lavender, Peppermint, and Wintergreen in a 10 ml roller bottle with fractionated coconut oil. Use on your forehead and temples, the back of your neck, and along your spine 4-5 times per day. Take 1 Turmeric Capsule with a meal twice per day. Take 1 Deep Blue® Polyphenol Complex with a meal per day. Take 1 Copaiba Softgel with a meal. Place 1 drop each of Frankincense and Copaiba under your tongue morning and evening. Place 1 drop of Frankincense on your thumb and place it on the roof of your mouth up to 3 times per day. Use a PastTense® roller 4-5 times per day or more if needed. Take Peppermint Beadlets as desired.

Eat leafy greens, dark chocolate, tomatoes, flaxseed, red peppers, yellow peppers, red grapes, pomegranates, cherries, sardines, fatty fish, salmon, berries, carrots, broccoli rabe, figs, sweet potatoes, kale, beets, omega-3 fatty acids, coconut oil, grass-fed beef, farm-raised chicken, and eggs.

Take Lifelong Vitality Supplements twice a day, 2-3 DigestZen TerraZyme® capsules at each meal, and PB Assist® once per day.

Rest or lay down in a dark, quiet room. Avoid electronics.

G-I

HEADACHE *(Blood Sugar)*

⏰ **3-5x per day**	📅 **As needed**

Essential Oils: *Cassia, Zendocrine®, Sim & Sassy, On Guard®, Coriander*

Other Solutions: *N/A*

 Choose 2-3 of the recommended oils. Add 5-7 drops of each oil to a 10 ml roller bottle and fill the rest with fractionated coconut oil. Rub over your temples and forehead, behind your ears, and over your thymus. Put 2-3 drops of MetaPWR™ in your water and sip throughout the day.

 If you experience low blood sugar, make sure to eat every 3 hours. Combine lean protein, healthy fats, and complex carbs at each meal.

HEADACHE *(Sinus)*

⏰ **3-5x per day**	📅 **As needed**

Essential Oils: *Basil, Cedarwood, Rosemary, Peppermint, Eucalyptus, DigestZen®*

Other Solutions: *TriEase® Softgels*

 Choose 2-3 of the recommended oils. Add 5-7 drops of each oil to a 10 ml roller bottle and fill the rest with fractionated coconut oil. Rub over your temples and forehead, behind your ears, and over your thymus. Take 1-2 TriEase® Softgels as needed. Mix 1 drop of DigestZen® with 10 drops of fractionated coconut oil in your palm. Rub over your sinuses and temples morning and evening.

HEADACHE *(Tension)*

⏰ **3-5x per day**	📅 **As needed**

Essential Oils: *PastTense®, Peppermint, Deep Blue®, AromaTouch®, Frankincense*

Other Solutions: *Peppermint Beadlets*

 Put 1 drop of Frankincense under your tongue morning and evening. Roll PastTense® over your forehead and temples and down the back of your neck. Choose 2 other oils and apply 1 drop of each over the PastTense®. Take Peppermint Beadlets as needed.

HEARING PROBLEMS

| ⏰ *3-5x per day and overnight* | 📅 *Ongoing as needed* |

Essential Oils: *Frankincense, Helichrysum, Basil*

Other Solutions: *N/A*

 Combine 10 drops of each recommended oil in a 10 ml roller bottle with fractionated coconut oil. Apply topically to your temples, forehead, and around the opening of your ear. Put 5 drops of each recommended oil on a cotton ball and place it over your ear opening overnight. Do not apply into your ear.

G-I

G-I

HEARTBURN

⏰ *3-5x per day*	📅 *Ongoing as needed*

Essential Oils: *DigestZen®, Fennel, Ginger, Peppermint, Celery Seed, Lemon*

Other Solutions: *Peppermint Beadlets, Peppermint Softgels, Ginger Drops, DigestZen® Softgels, DigestTab*

● Dilute 1 drop of Celery Seed or DigestZen® in 4 ounces of liquid and swallow. Take DigestZen® Softgels 1-3 times per day. Chew DigestTabs up to 6 times per day as needed. Add 30 drops of DigestZen® to a 10 ml roller bottle with fractionated coconut oil, or place 5 drops of DigestZen® in your palm. Rub the roller bottle or your palm directly over your abdomen for about a minute. Combine 5 drops each of Peppermint, Celery Seed, Ginger, Fennel, and Lemon with fractionated coconut oil in a 10 ml roller bottle and apply it to your abdomen before and after meals. Wear loose clothing. Stand up straight, especially after eating, and elevate your upper body. Chew gum to help dilute acid. Take Peppermint Beadlets as desired and Ginger Drops and Peppermint Softgels as needed.

● Avoid spicy, acidic, or fried/fatty foods; caffeine; alcohol; chocolate; onions; and tomato-based sauces. Avoid eating 2-3 hours before bed.

HEAT EXHAUSTION

⏰ *3-5x per day*	📅 *As needed*

Essential Oils: *Peppermint, Lavender, Lemon*

Other Solutions: *N/A*

 Apply 2 drops each of Peppermint and Lavender topically to your forehead, the back of your neck, inside of your wrists, and the bottoms of your feet. Add 1-2 drops of Lemon to your water and sip slowly. In a 2-ounce spray bottle, combine 15 drops of Peppermint and 10 drops of Lavender and fill the rest of the bottle with water. Spritz over your chest and on the back of your neck as needed. Move to an air-conditioned place immediately if you experience early warning signs such as nausea, lightheadedness, fatigue, muscle cramping, or dizziness. Take a cold shower or use a cold compress. Remove tight or extra clothing layers immediately.

 Be sure to drink at least half your body weight in ounces of water on a daily basis; if temperatures are high, drink more. Drink natural electrolyte-containing drinks, such as coconut water.

G-I

G-I

HEATSTROKE

4-5x per day	*As needed*

Essential Oils: *Peppermint, Lavender, Lemon*

Other Solutions: *N/A*

- Apply 2 drops each of Peppermint and Lavender topically to your forehead, the back of your neck, inside of your wrists, and the bottoms of your feet. Add 1 drop of Lemon to water and sip slowly. In a 2-ounce spray bottle, combine 15 drops of Peppermint and 10 drops of Lavender and fill the rest of the bottle with water. Spritz over your chest and the back of your neck as needed.

- Drink at least half your body weight in ounces of water on a daily basis; if temperatures are high, drink more. Drink natural electrolyte-containing drinks, such as coconut water. Do not wait until you are thirsty to start hydrating.

- Stay hydrated on a regular basis, preferably days before a high-intensity exercise event in high temperatures occurs.

- Heatstroke requires immediate medical attention, unlike heat exhaustion. Call emergency services immediately if someone shows the following symptoms: headache; confusion; no sweating; rapid heart rate; nausea or vomiting; or loss of consciousness. Move the person to a cooler place and use cold compresses to get their temperature down. Do not give them fluids.

HEAVY METAL TOXICITY

3-5x per day	*As needed*

Essential Oils: *Cilantro, Zendocrine®, Black Pepper, Citronella, Thyme*

Other Solutions: *N/A*

- Put 1-2 drops each of Cilantro, Zendocrine®, and Black Pepper in a capsule and take 2 times per day. Choose 3 of the recommended oils. Mix 5-7 drops of each in a 10 ml roller bottle and fill with fractionated coconut oil. Rub over your liver, down the back of your neck, behind your ears, and on the bottoms of your feet morning and evening.

- See the heavy metal cleanse on page 442 of the Reduce Toxic Load chapter.

HEMATOMA

4-5x per day	*As needed until discoloration improves*

Essential Oils: *AromaTouch®, Helichrysum, Myrrh, Cypress, Frankincense*

Other Solutions: *N/A*

- Add 5-7 drops each of AromaTouch®, Helichrysum, Myrrh, Cypress, and Frankincense to a 10 ml roller bottle topped off with fractionated coconut oil. Massage gently over the affected area frequently until discoloration resolves. If possible, keep the affected part of the body elevated to prevent blood pooling. Wrap ice in a cloth and apply to the affected area for about 20 minutes.

HEMOPHILIA

 2x per day, morning and evening   *Ongoing as needed*

Essential Oils: *Geranium, Helichrysum, Lavender, Roman Chamomile, Vetiver*

Other Solutions: *N/A*

◐ Choose 3-4 of the recommended oils. Mix 5-7 drops of each oil in a 10 ml roller bottle and fill with fractionated coconut oil. Apply down your spine, over your heart, and on bottoms of your feet morning and evening.

✚ Seek medical care right away if you experience any of the following symptoms: deep bruises; pain; swelling and tightness of your joints; blood in your urine or stool; sudden weakness; convulsions or seizures; double vision; nosebleeds without a cause; or painful, prolonged headaches.

HEMORRHOIDS

 3-5x per day   *Until symptoms lessen*

Essential Oils: *Cypress, Helichrysum, Yarrow|Pom, Myrrh, Roman Chamomile, Celery Seed, Tea Tree*

Other Solutions: *N/A*

◐ Combine 5 drops each of Cypress, Helichrysum, Yarrow|Pom, Myrrh, Roman Chamomile, and Celery Seed in a 10 ml roller bottle and top it off with fractionated coconut oil. Apply to the affected area several times per day. Saturate a cotton ball with witch hazel and add 2 drops of Tea Tree. Apply to the affected area daily.

● Refrain from heavy lifting or exercises that increase abdominal pressure or straining.

✚ Call your doctor for an appointment if you experience any of the following symptoms: rectal bleeding; pain or discomfort in your rectum or anus; no relief from symptoms with natural solutions; or bowel movements that are maroon, black, or tarry in color.

G-I

HEPATITIS

🕐 **4-5x per day**	📅 **As needed**

Essential Oils: *Geranium, Zendocrine®, Cypress, Celery Seed, Myrrh*

Other Solutions: *Ginger Drops, Zendocrine® Softgels*

 Place 1 drop each of Celery Seed and Zendocrine® under your tongue twice per day, or add 1 drop of each oil to a 4-ounce glass of water and swallow. Combine 5 drops each of Geranium, Zendocrine®, Cypress, Myrrh, and Celery Seed in a 10 ml roller bottle with fractionated coconut oil. Apply this blend topically over your kidney area (*to the left and right of your spine just under your rib cage*) and to the right side of your abdominal area. Before applying the blend, apply a warm compress to the area to increase blood flow and enhance absorption. Take 2 capsules of Zendocrine® daily, one each with morning and evening meals. Take Ginger Drops as needed.

➕ If you experience yellowing of the eyes or skin or tenderness in the upper abdominal area, seek medical attention right away.

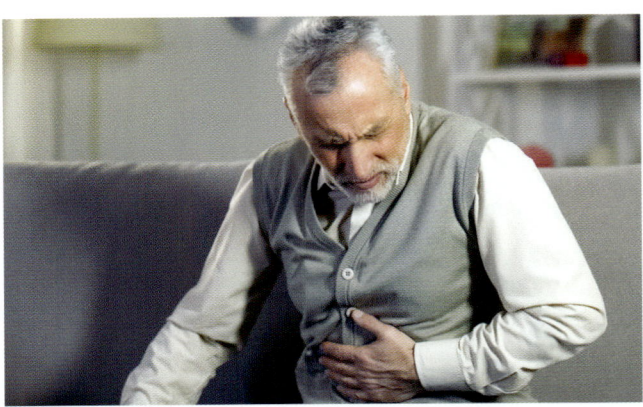

HERNIA *(Hiatal)*

🕐 **3-5x per day**	📅 **Until symptoms lessen**

Essential Oils: *Peppermint, Fennel, Cypress, DigestZen®*

Other Solutions: *Ginger Drops*

 Combine 5-7 drops each of Peppermint, Fennel, Cypress, and DigestZen® in a 10 ml roller bottle with fractionated coconut oil. Rub over your abdominal region daily. Add 1 drop of DigestZen® to 4 ounces of water and swallow. Take Ginger Drops as needed.

🌱 Eat several smaller meals throughout the day rather than a few large meals. Avoid foods that trigger heartburn, such as fatty/fried foods, tomato sauce, alcohol, chocolate, mint, garlic, onion, and caffeine. Avoid lying down after a meal or eating late in the day. Eat at least two to three hours before bedtime.

➕ If the hernia becomes red, swollen, and painful, contact your doctor immediately.

G-I

HERNIATED DISC

⏰ *4-5x per day*	📅 *Ongoing as needed*

Essential Oils: *Black Pepper, Siberian Fir, Frankincense, Marjoram, Wintergreen, PastTense®*

Other Solutions: *Deep Blue® Polyphenol Complex, Turmeric Dual Chamber Capsules, Lifelong Vitality, DigestZen TerraZyme®, PB Assist®+*

 Combine 5-7 drops each of Black Pepper, Siberian Fir, Frankincense, Marjoram, and Wintergreen in a 10 ml roller bottle with fractionated coconut oil. Apply over the affected area several times per day. Take 2 Dual Chamber Turmeric Capsules per day with meals. Take 2 Deep Blue® Polyphenol Complex supplements a day with meals (*morning and evening*).

 Avoid inflammatory foods. Take Lifelong Vitality Supplements twice a day, 2-3 DigestZen Terra-Zyme® capsules at each meal, and PB Assist® once per day. Eat a variety of fresh fruits, vegetables, lean meat, fatty fish, healthy fats, and brown rice. Avoid MSG, gluten, corn, fried food, fast food, and processed foods. Drink half your weight in ounces of water.

Stay active by engaging in moderate activity daily, such as walking. Avoid sitting for prolonged periods of time. If you must sit for long stretches, be sure to take a break and stand up or walk around every 20-30 minutes. Get a supportive ergonomic chair. Stretch regularly. Alternate hot and cold therapy throughout the day. Incorporate posture exercises into your daily routine.

Seek professional medical attention from your doctor or chiropractor if the problem persists, if you have pain that radiates down your thigh or leg, if you have bowel or bladder incontinence, if you lose sensation in your groin or legs, or if you do not see an improvement in your condition after a couple of weeks on this protocol. A chiropractor can help determine the type of bulging disc you are suffering from and help you pinpoint some of the underlying causes. Physical therapy and massage can also help.

G-I

HERPES SIMPLEX

🕐 **3-5x per day**	📅 **Ongoing as needed**

Essential Oils: *Tea Tree, Peppermint, On Guard®, Basil, Helichrysum, Melissa*

Other Solutions: *N/A*

Choose 3-4 of the recommended oils. Mix 5-7 drops of each with fractionated coconut oil in a 10 ml roller bottle and roll around the area of the breakout. Make a veggie capsule with 1 drop of each oil and take 3-4 times per day.

HICCUPS

🕐 **3x per day**	📅 **As needed**

Essential Oils: *Fennel, Ginger, Peppermint, Serenity®, Lavender*

Other Solutions: *Ginger Drops, Peppermint Beadlets*

Combine 5-7 drops of Fennel, Ginger, and Peppermint in a 10 ml roller bottle with fractionated coconut oil. Massage topically into your chest and stomach area. Make a veggie capsule with 2 drops each of Fennel, Ginger, and Peppermint and take at the onset of hiccups. Place 1 drop of Peppermint on your thumb and press it onto the roof of your mouth. Put 2 Peppermint Beadlets into your mouth when hiccups start. If hiccups are induced by stress, diffuse 5 drops of Serenity® or Lavender. Take Ginger Drops if needed.

G-I

HIGH BLOOD PRESSURE

 3-5x per day   *Ongoing*

Essential Oils: *Copaiba, Marjoram, Ylang Ylang, Petitgrain, Hygge*

Other Solutions: *Lifelong Vitality, DigestZen TerraZyme®, PB Assist®+, Serenity® Softgels*

⊻ Choose 2-3 of the recommended oils. Mix 5-7 drops of each oil in a 10 ml roller bottle and fill with fractionated coconut oil. Apply over your heart, over your pulse points on your wrists, down your spine, and on the bottoms of your feet morning and night.

🍏 Take Lifelong Vitality Supplements twice a day, 2-3 DigestZen TerraZyme® capsules at each meal, and PB Assist® once per day. Eat a variety of fresh fruits, vegetables, lean meats, healthy fats, and rice. Include red foods in your diet on a daily basis. Avoid MSG, gluten, corn, fried food, fast food, processed foods, and artificial sweeteners.

🔶 Do aerobic exercises, strength training, and balance exercises.

🌙 Apply 1 drop of Serenity® or Lavender to your pillow at bedtime. Take 1-2 Serenity® Softgels 30 minutes before bed. Adopt a meditation or yoga practice for stress relief. Use oils from the emotional kit to manage emotional health.

⊕ If you experience any of the following symptoms, seek medical attention right away: swelling, redness, pain, or hotness in an area of your arm or leg; lightheadedness; difficult or painful breathing; chest pain or tightness; pain extending down your shoulder, arm, back, or jaw; sudden weakness or numbness of your face, arm, or leg; sudden difficulty speaking or understanding your speech; sudden changes in your vision.

G-I

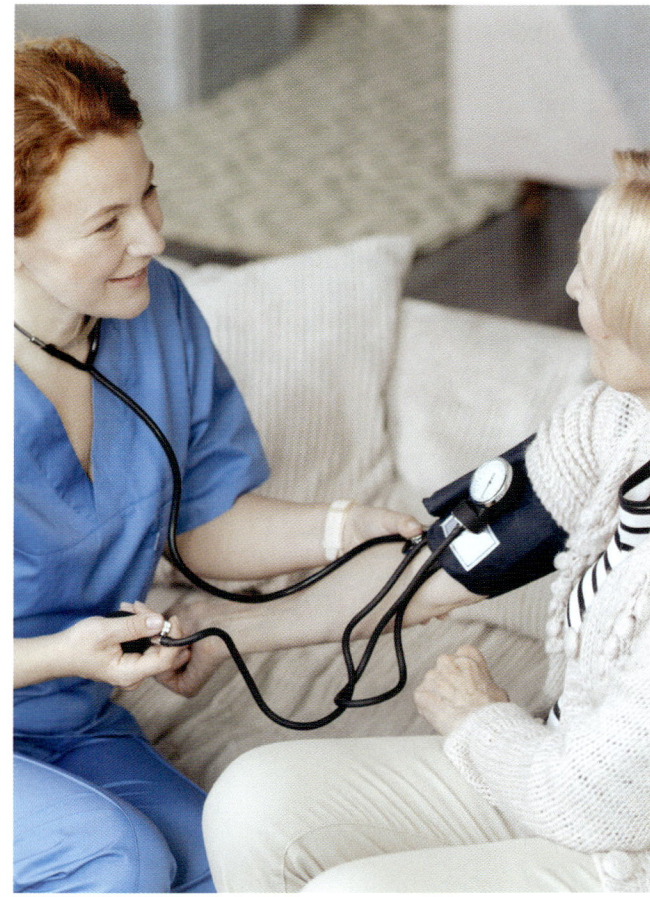

HIGH CHOLESTEROL

⏰ **3-5x per day**	📅 *Ongoing*

Essential Oils: *MetaPWR™, Lemon, Lemongrass, Cinnamon, Ylang Ylang*

Other Solutions: *MetaPWR™ Softgels, Turmeric Dual Chamber Capsules, Lifelong Vitality, DigestZen TerraZyme®, PB Assist®+*

 Put 3 drops of MetaPWR™ in your water 2 times per day. Take 2 Turmeric Dual Chamber Capsules per day. Put 1-2 drops each of Lemon, Lemongrass, Cinnamon, and Ylang Ylang in a capsule and take 3 times per day. Take MetaPWR™ Softgels with meals.

🍏 Take Lifelong Vitality Supplements twice a day, 2-3 DigestZen TerraZyme® capsules at each meal, and PB Assist® once per day. Eat a variety of fresh fruits, vegetables, lean meats, healthy fats, and rice. Avoid MSG, gluten, corn, fried food, fast food, processed foods, and artificial sweeteners.

 Do aerobic exercises, strength training, and balance exercises.

G-I

HIVES

 4-5x per day | *Ongoing until symptoms subside*

Essential Oils: *Tea Tree, Frankincense, Peppermint, Adaptiv™, Adaptiv™ roller*

Other Solutions: *N/A*

Combine 5-7 drops each of Tea Tree, Frankincense, and Peppermint in a 10 ml roller bottle with fractionated coconut oil. Gently apply to the area of concern. If hives are brought on by stress, use the Adaptiv™ roller on the back of your neck, your wrist pulse points, and on your feet prior to bed. Saturate a cotton ball with witch hazel. Place 2 drops of Tea Tree on a cotton ball and apply to the area of concern. You can also combine a teaspoon of baking soda, a splash of water, and 2 drops of Tea Tree; apply to your hives, let it dry, and then gently rinse it off. Diffuse 5 drops of Adaptiv™ during stressful times. Avoid hot baths or showers while you have hives. Wear loose-fitting clothing. For children with hives, avoid bathing them in water that is too hot, and keep clothing loose-fitting and breathable. Place a cool compress on the hives to decrease inflammation.

Keep a food diary to pinpoint potential food allergies.

HOARSE VOICE

 4-5x per day | *Until symptoms lessen*

Essential Oils: *Lemon, Ginger, Peppermint, Frankincense*

Other Solutions: *Peppermint Beadlets*

Combine 1-2 drops of either Lemon, Peppermint, Ginger, or Frankincense with warm water or tea. Sip it slowly. Choose 1-2 of the recommended oils, mix 1 drop of each with 1 teaspoon raw honey, and swallow. Combine 5 drops of each recommended oil in a 10 ml roller bottle with fractionated coconut oil. Apply over your throat area several times a day to reduce inflammation. Take Peppermint Beadlets as needed.

G-I

HORMONE IMBALANCE
(Female)

⏰	**3-5x per day**	📅	**As needed**

Essential Oils: *ClaryCalm®, Clary Sage, Whisper®, Tulsi, Ylang Ylang, Jasmine, Geranium, Sandalwood, Lavender, Madagascar Vanilla*

Other Solutions: *Phytoestrogen Essential Complex, Bone Nutrient Essential Complex, Lifelong Vitality, DigestZen TerraZyme®, PB Assist®+, Serenity® Softgels*

🟣 Combine 5-7 drops each of Tulsi, Sandalwood, Geranium, Ylang Ylang, and Clary Sage with fractionated coconut oil in a 10 ml roller bottle. Apply over your lower abdominal region, on your feet, and along your spine in the lower back area 2 times per day. Alternate between using the ClaryCalm® roller and Jasmine roller throughout the day in-between application of the blend. Diffuse 5 drops of Whisper® throughout the day.

🟢 Pre- and peri-menopausal women should take one 1-2 Phytoestrogen Essential Complex capsules daily with food. Post-menopausal women should take 2 Phytoestrogen Essential Complex capsules daily with food. Take 4 Bone Nutrient Essential Complex capsules daily with food. Take Lifelong Vitality Supplements twice a day, 2-3 DigestZen TerraZyme® capsules at each meal, and PB Assist® once per day. Eat avocados, flaxseed, broccoli, pomegranate, salmon, leafy greens, nuts, organic soy, turmeric, quinoa, and brown rice. Avoid excess sugar, simple carbohydrates, trans fats, and processed foods.

🔵 Place 1 drop of Lavender or Serenity® on your pillow at night. Take 2 Serenity® Softgels before bedtime.

🔴 Makeover your home by using the Abōde™ line of cleaning products, laundry pods, dishwasher pods, surface cleaner, and dish soap.

HORMONE IMBALANCE *(Male)*

⏰ *3-5x per day*   📅 *Until symptoms resolve*

Essential Oils: *Sandalwood, Patchouli, Ylang Ylang, Cinnamon, Ginger, Lavender, Madagascar Vanilla*

Other Solutions: *Serenity® Softgels*

 Choose 4-5 of the recommended oils. Mix 5-7 drops of each oil with fractionated coconut oil in a 10 ml roller bottle. Rub it over your lower abdominal region, on your feet, and along your spine in the lower back area every 4 hours.

⊙ Consume cocoa, dark chocolate, watermelon, tomatoes, grapefruit, red peppers, pistachios, tea, and wine.

🌙 Place 1 drop of Lavender on your pillow at night. Take 2 Serenity® Softgels before bed. Avoid stressful conversations or television before bed. Develop a good bedtime routine. Increase the laughter in your life by watching a comedy or hanging with friends and family members who make you laugh.

 Makeover your home by using the Abōde™ line of cleaning products, laundry pods, dishwasher pods, surface cleaner, and dish soap.

HOT FLASHES

⏰ *3-5x per day*   📅 *As needed*

Essential Oils: *Clary Calm, Tulsi, Whisper®, Clary Sage, Madagascar Vanilla, Peppermint, Lavender*

Other Solutions: *N/A*

 Apply a ClaryCalm® roller to your abdominal region, wrist pulse points, and chest morning and evening. Diffuse 3 drops each of Whisper®, Tulsi, Madagascar Vanilla, and Clary Sage throughout the day. Combine 15 drops of Peppermint (*or 7 drops each of Lavender and Peppermint*) and 2 tablespoons of witch hazel in a 2-ounce glass spray bottle and fill the rest of the bottle with water. Shake well before each use and spritz on your face and neck.

 Makeover your home by using the Abōde™ line of cleaning products, laundry pods, dishwasher pods, surface cleaner, and dish soap.

G-I

HYPERACTIVITY

4-5x per day	*Ongoing*

Essential Oils: *Hygge™, Adaptiv™, InTune®, Balance®, Vetiver*

Other Solutions: *N/A*

 Combine 5-7 drops each of Adaptiv™, Vetiver, and Balance® in a 10 ml roller with fractionated coconut oil. Apply to the back of your neck, behind your ears, over your chest, and on the bottoms of your feet. Alternate between using this roller and an InTune® roller. Diffuse 3-5 drops each of Hygge™, Adaptiv™, Vetiver, and Balance® throughout the day, or place 3 drops of each oil on aromatherapy jewelry and inhale as needed.

G-I

HYPERGLYCEMIA

⏰ *3-5x per day*	📅 *Ongoing*

Essential Oils: *Cinnamon, Coriander, Cassia, MetaPWR™, Fennel*

Other Solutions: *Lifelong Vitality, DigestZen TerraZyme®, PB Assist®+, Greens, Protein*

 Combine 5 drops each of Cinnamon, Coriander, Cassia, and Fennel in a 10 ml roller with fractionated coconut oil. Apply to your chest, the bottoms of your feet, and inside of your wrists/wrist pulse points 3 times per day. Place 1-2 drops each of the same oils in a veggie capsule. Take twice daily. Drink at least half your body weight in ounces of water daily, and add 1 drop of MetaPWR™ to your water. Diffuse 5 drops of MetaPWR™ throughout the day.

🍏 Eat blueberries, leafy greens, Greek yogurt, cherries, red grapes, broccoli, tomatoes, garlic, spinach, sweet potatoes, grass-fed beef, digestive enzymes, free-range chicken, eggs, avocado, onions, peppers, omega-3 fatty acids, coconut oil, brown rice, and fatty fish. Take Lifelong Vitality Supplements twice a day; 2-3 DigestZen TerraZyme® capsules at each meal; PB Assist® once per day; and 1 scoop of Greens in a morning smoothie that includes berries, baby spinach, 1 scoop of vanilla Protein, and 1 cup almond milk. Eat something that balances protein/carbohydrate/fat every 3 hours to maintain blood sugar levels.

HYPERSOMNIA

⏰ *3-5x per day*	📅 *As needed*

Essential Oils: *Wild Orange, DDR Prime®, Spearmint*

Other Solutions: *N/A*

 Combine 10 drops each of Wild Orange, DDR Prime®, and Spearmint in a 10 ml roller bottle with fractionated coconut oil. Apply to your forehead, temples, the base of your skull, and behind your ears, or diffuse 3-5 drops of each oil into the air and inhale. Place 1 drop of Spearmint on your thumb and press to the roof of your mouth. Place 1 drop of Wild Orange and/or Spearmint in the palm of your hand and inhale deeply for 1 minute.

HYPERTENSION

⏰ **3-5x per day**	📅 *Ongoing while symptoms persist*

Essential Oils: *Petitgrain, Marjoram, Clove, Helichrysum, Ylang Ylang, Celery Seed*

Other Solutions: *N/A*

🌸 Combine 5 drops each of Petitgrain, Marjoram, Clove, Helichrysum, and Ylang Ylang with fractionated coconut oil in a 10 ml roller bottle. Apply over your chest, the front of your neck, your pulse points, and on the bottoms of your feet. Place 1 drop of Celery Seed under your tongue twice daily, morning and evening.

🍏 Choose high-fiber, low-sodium, and high-potassium foods such as vegetables, fruits, melons, avocados, bananas, and seeds. Choose omega-3-rich foods such as grass-fed beef, wild-caught salmon, chia seeds, and flaxseed. Consume dark chocolate, garlic, spinach, sunflower seeds, tomatoes, and broccoli. Avoid high-sodium processed foods such as pickles, olives, and canned foods. Limit sugar, caffeine, and alcohol.

🔵 Aim to get 7-9 hours of sleep per night for rest and recovery. Apply 1-2 drops of Serenity® and Lavender to your pillow at bedtime. Take 1-2 Serenity® Softgels 30 minutes before bed.

➕ Call your doctor if you have ongoing feelings of being sluggish or winded, have a rapid heart rate, have pain that moves down your arm, or have a rapid or irregular pulse. Seek medical attention right away if you experience any severe or persistent episodes of the following symptoms: tightness in your chest; sudden chest pain or pressure; feeling like a belt is being tightened around your chest; pain that spreads from the center of your chest to your arms, shoulders, neck, or jaw; excessive sweating, nausea, vomiting, dizziness, or shortness of breath; a fullness, indigestion, or choking feeling; rapid or irregular heartbeat; extreme weakness or anxiety.

G-I

HYPERTHYROIDISM

 3-5x per day   *Ongoing*

Essential Oils: *Frankincense, Lemongrass, Myrrh, Clove, Lavender, Peppermint*

Other Solutions: *N/A*

Combine 5 drops each of Frankincense, Lemongrass, Myrrh, Clove, Lavender, and Peppermint with fractionated coconut oil in a 10 ml roller bottle. Apply over your throat area and the back of your neck. Make a veggie capsule with 1 drop of each recommended oil and take 3 times per day.

HYPOGLYCEMIA

 3-5x per day   *As needed*

Essential Oils: *MetaPWR™, Coriander, Cassia*

Other Solutions: *MetaPWR™ Softgels*

Combine 5-7 drops each of MetaPWR™, Coriander, and Cassia in a 10 ml roller bottle with fractionated coconut oil. Apply topically to your chest, the bottoms of your feet, and inside of your wrists. Place 1-2 drops of each recommended oil in a veggie capsule and take twice daily. Add 1 drop of MetaPWR™ to warm or cold water or tea and sip throughout the day. Drink at least half your body weight in ounces of water each day. Take 1 MetaPWR™ Softgel with meals.

HYPOTHYROIDISM

⏰ *3-5x per day*	📅 *Ongoing*

Essential Oils: *Lemongrass, Myrrh, Frankincense, Clove*

Other Solutions: *N/A*

 Combine 10 drops each of Lemongrass, Myrrh, Frankincense, and Clove with fractionated coconut oil in a 10 ml roller bottle. Apply over your throat area and the back of your neck. Make a veggie capsule with 1 drop each of the recommended oils and take 3 times per day.

IMMUNE SYSTEM

⏰ *3-5x per day*	📅 *While symptoms persist*

Essential Oils: *On Guard®, Thyme, Black Pepper, Tea Tree*

Other Solutions: *On Guard® beadlets, On Guard® Softgels, On Guard® Tablets*

 Choose 2-3 of the recommended oils. Mix 5-7 drops of each in a 10 ml roller bottle and fill with fractionated coconut oil. Apply down the back of your neck, behind your ears, over your chest, and on the bottoms of your feet morning and evening. Take 3-4 On Guard™+ Softgels throughout the day. Use On Guard® Beadlets as desired along with On Guard® Tablets.

🍏 Drink plenty of water with 1-2 drops of Lemon.

G-I

IMPOTENCE

 4-5x per day   *Ongoing as needed*

Essential Oils: *Sandalwood, Rose, Ylang Ylang, Cypress, Cinnamon, Basil, Lavender, Ginger, Clove*

Other Solutions: *N/A*

 Combine 10 drops of Sandalwood, 5 drops each of Ylang Ylang, Cypress, and Lavender, and 3 drops each of Cinnamon, Basil, Ginger, and Clove in a 10 ml roller bottle. Apply over your lower abdominal region, on your feet, and along your spine in the lower back area. If possible, apply within the hour before intercourse. Use a Rose roller over your lower back and lower abdominal area twice daily, morning and evening.

Drink a lot of water to flush out the kidneys. Eat high-fiber foods such as nuts, seeds, fruits, and vegetables. Eat wheat germ, green leafy vegetables, pumpkin seeds, sunflower seeds, chia seeds, beef, lamb, spinach, watercress seeds, sesame seeds, and Brazil nuts.

Follow the guidelines in Chapter 5 Exercise (page 385).

Don't smoke; smoking makes it difficult to attain an erection during sexual intercourse.

INCONTINENCE

 2-3x per day (an hour before bed, at bedtime, and if you awake in the middle of the night)   *Ongoing as needed*

Essential Oils: *Cypress, Copaiba, Juniper Berry, Black Pepper, Lemongrass*

Other Solutions: *N/A*

 Choose 2-3 of the recommended oils. Mix 5-7 drops of each oil in a 10 ml roller bottle and fill with fractionated coconut oil. Apply over your lower abdomen and lower back and the bottoms of your feet morning and night.

Drink water throughout the day, but avoid drinking too much liquid within 2 hours of bed. Eliminate caffeine, chocolate milk, and chocolate later in the day.

Opt for an earlier sleep time and develop a good sleep routine. Diffuse 4-5 drops of Lavender or Serenity® an hour before bed when winding down for the evening. Avoid electronics too close to bedtime.

G-I

INDIGESTION

⏰ **3-5x per day**	📅 **Ongoing as needed**

Essential Oils: *DigestZen®, Fennel, Ginger, Peppermint, Celery Seed, Lemon*

Other Solutions: *Ginger Drops, Peppermint Beadlets, Peppermint Softgels, DigestZen® Softgels, DigestTab®*

 Dilute 1 drop of Celery Seed or DigestZen® in 4 ounces of liquid and swallow. Take DigestZen® Softgels 1-3 times per day. Chew DigestTabs® up to 6 times per day as needed. Take up to two Peppermint Softgels before meals as needed. Add 30 drops of DigestZen® to a 10 ml roller bottle with fractionated coconut oil, or place 5 drops of DigestZen® in your palm. Rub the roller bottle or your palm directly over your abdomen for about a minute. Combine 5 drops of the other oils listed *(every oil except DigestZen® and Celery Seed)* with fractionated coconut oil in a 10 ml roller bottle and apply to your abdomen before and after meals. Wear loose clothing. Stand up straight, especially after eating, and elevate your upper body. Chew gum to help dilute acid. Take Ginger Drops as needed. Take Peppermint Beadlets as desired.

🍏 Avoid spicy, acidic, or fried/fatty foods; caffeine; alcohol; chocolate; onions; and tomato-based sauces. Avoid eating 2-3 hours before bed.

INFANT REFLUX

⏰ **3x per day**	📅 **As needed**

Essential Oils: *DigestZen®, Roman Chamomile, Lavender*

Other Solutions: *N/A*

 Add 1 drop of DigestZen® and 1 drop of either Lavender or Roman Chamomile in a 10 ml roller bottle with fractionated coconut oil. Apply to the baby's abdominal region, gently massaging in a clockwise motion. After applying the roller over the baby's abdominal region, apply it along the baby's spine in the mid-back area and on the baby's feet.

INFECTED WOUNDS

⏰ **3-5x per day**	📅 **Until symptoms improve**

Essential Oils: *Tea Tree, Myrrh, Helichrysum*

Other Solutions: *Correct-X*

🟣 Combine 10 drops each of Tea Tree, Myrrh, and Helichrysum in a 10 ml roller bottle with fractionated coconut oil. Apply to the affected area. Put a small amount of Correct-X on a cotton swab and apply to the affected area a few times per day.

G-I

INFECTION

4-5x per day	*Until symptoms subside*

Essential Oils: *On Guard®, Oregano, Thyme*

Other Solutions: *On Guard® Beadlets, On Guard® Softgels, On Guard® Tablets, Lifelong Vitality, Digest-Zen TerraZyme®, PB Assist®+, Turmeric Dual Chamber Capsules*

Choose 2 of the recommended oils. Put 1-2 drops of each oil into a capsule and take with water twice a day. Mix 5-7 drops of each oil in a 10 ml roller bottle and fill with fractionated coconut oil. Apply over the affected area or on the bottoms of your feet and down your spine. Take On Guard® Beadlets, On Guard™+ Softgels, and On Guard® Tablets as needed. If you have a fever, apply 1 drop of Peppermint to the back of your neck, over your chest, down the spine, and at the bottoms of your feet morning and evening. If you get oils in your eyes or on your face, apply plain coconut oil over your eye or face to soothe the area. Repeat as needed.

Take Lifelong Vitality Supplements twice a day, 2-3 DigestZen TerraZyme® capsules at each meal, PB Assist® once per day, and Turmeric Dual Chamber Capsules 2 times per day. Avoid fried food, fast food, processed foods, and artificial sweeteners.

Diffuse 3-4 drops each of Serenity®, Balance®, and Breathe® and rest as needed.

G-I

INFERTILITY *(Female)*

⏰ *4-5x per day*	📅 *Ongoing as needed*

Essential Oils: *Clary Sage, Tulsi, DDR Prime®, Geranium, Ylang Ylang, Rose roller*

Other Solutions: *DDR Prime® Softgels, Phytoestrogen Essential Complex, Bone Nutrient Essential Complex, Lifelong Vitality, DigestZen TerraZyme®, PB Assist®+, Serenity® Softgels*

 Add 10 drops each of Clary Sage, Tulsi, DDR Prime®, Geranium, and Ylang Ylang in a 10 ml roller bottle with fractionated coconut oil. Apply to your abdominal region 3 times per day. After applying the roller over your abdominal region, apply it along your spine in the lower-back area and on your feet. Use a Rose roller 2 times daily, morning and evening. Take 2 DDR Prime® Softgels, one in the morning and evening.

 Pre- and peri-menopausal women should take one 1-2 Phytoestrogen Essential Complex capsules daily with food. Take 4 Bone Nutrient Essential Complex capsules daily with food. Take Lifelong Vitality Supplements twice a day, 2-3 DigestZen TerraZyme® capsules at each meal, and PB Assist® once per day. Consume avocados, flaxseed, broccoli, pomegranate, salmon, leafy greens, nuts, organic soy, turmeric, quinoa, and brown rice. Avoid excess sugar, simple carbohydrates, trans fats, and processed foods.

🌙 Add 1 drop of Lavender or Serenity® to your pillow at night. Take 2 Serenity® Softgels at bedtime.

Avoid stressful conversations or television before meals or bed. Develop a good bedtime routine that feels relaxing to you. Find a hobby or meditation program. Listen to music, go for a walk in nature, or go out with friends. Increase the laughter in your life by watching a comedy or hanging with friends and family members who make you laugh. Schedule self-care rituals throughout the week that make you feel good.

🔻 Don't smoke; smoking makes it difficult to attain an erection during sexual intercourse.

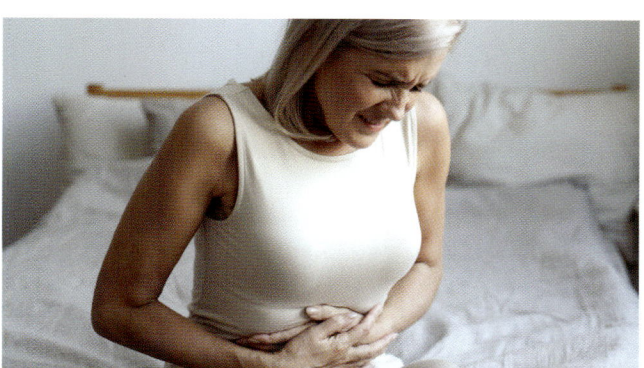

INFLAMMATORY BOWEL DISEASE

3-5x per day	Ongoing until symptoms subside

Essential Oils: *Peppermint, DigestZen®, Ginger, Fennel, Celery Seed, Lemon, Zendocrine®, Rosemary*

Other Solutions: *Ginger Drops, Peppermint Beadlets, Peppermint Softgel, DigestZen TerraZyme®, DigestZen® Softgels*

 Choose 3-4 of the recommended oils. Mix 5 drops of each oil with fractionated coconut oil in a 10 ml roller bottle. Rub it over your abdominal area, your spine in the lower back area, and the bottoms of your feet. In addition, diffuse 3-4 drops of each in a diffuser throughout the day. For adults, take up to 2 Peppermint Softgels before meals. For children 8 years and older, take 1 Peppermint Softgel before meals. For best results, take the Peppermint Softgels 30-60 minutes before meals. Take 1-3 DigestZen TerraZyme® capsules daily with meals. Take DigestZen® Softgels 1 or more times daily as needed. Experiment with Peppermint Softgels and DigestZen® Softgels to see which one works best for your body chemistry. Take Ginger Drops as needed. Take Peppermint beadlets as desired.

INFLAMMATION

4-5x per day	While symptoms persist

Essential Oils: *AromaTouch®, Frankincense, Turmeric, Ginger, Copaiba*

Other Solutions: *Turmeric Dual Chamber Capsules, Deep Blue® Polyphenol Complex, Deep Blue® Rub, Deep Blue® Stick, DDR Prime® Softgels*

Combine 5 drops each of AromaTouch®, Frankincense, Turmeric, Ginger, and Copaiba in a 10 ml roller bottle and apply to sore joints and muscles. Choose 3 of the recommended oils and diffuse 3-4 drops of each throughout the day. Take 2 Dual Chamber Turmeric Capsules, one each with a meal. Take 2 DDR Prime® Softgels with meals. Take 2 Deep Blue® Polyphenol Complex a day with meals, morning and evening. Use Deep Blue® Stick over affected area as needed.

G-I

INGROWN TOENAIL

⏰ **3-5x per day**	📅 *While symptoms persist*

Essential Oils: *Ylang Ylang, DDR Prime®, Tea Tree*

Other Solutions: *N/A*

 Combine 10 drops each of Ylang Ylang, DDR Prime®, and Tea Tree in a 10 ml roller bottle with fractionated coconut oil. Apply to the affected area 3-5 times per day.

INSECT REPELLENT

⏰ **4-5x per day**	📅 *Ongoing when pests are prevalent*

Essential Oils: *TerraShield®, Citronella, Lemon Eucalyptus*

Other Solutions: *N/A*

 Combine 10 drops each of TerraShield®, Citronella, and Lemon Eucalyptus in a 10 ml roller bottle with fractionated coconut oil. Apply topically to exposed skin before going outdoors. Repeat as needed.

INSECT BITES

⏰ **3x per day**	📅 *As needed*

Essential Oils: *Lavender, Purify, Basil, Roman Chamomile, Blue Tansy*

Other Solutions: *N/A*

Choose 2-3 of the recommended oils. Apply 1-2 drops of each with 1 tablespoon of fractionated coconut oil over the bite as soon as possible.

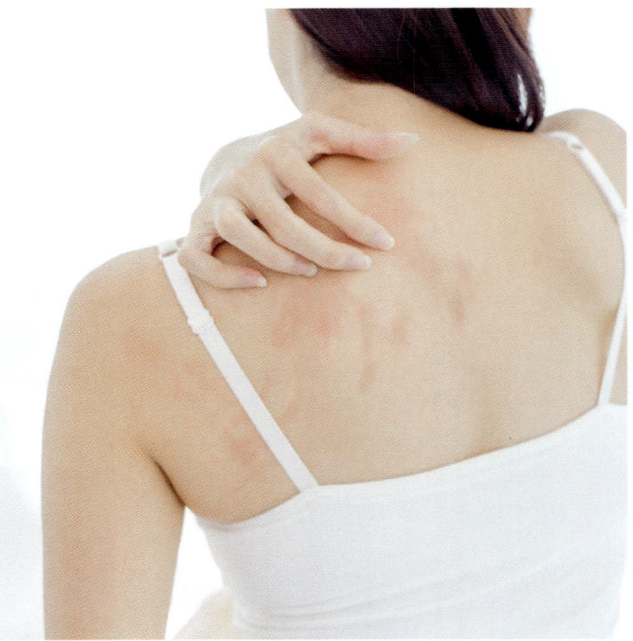

INSOMNIA

3-5x per day	*Until symptoms improve*

Essential Oils: *Lavender, Magnolia, Serenity®, Vetiver, Roman Chamomile, Breathe®, Madagascar Vanilla*

Other Solutions: *Adaptiv™ Capsules, Copaiba Softgels, Lifelong Vitality, DigestZen TerraZyme®, PB Assist®+, Serenity® Softgels*

Take 1-2 Serenity® Softgels before going to sleep. Choose 3-4 of the recommended oils *(if you have trouble staying asleep, be sure to include Vetiver)*. Start diffusing these oils at least 2 hours before bedtime. Meditate before bed to calm your thoughts. During meditation, either diffuse your chosen oils *(3-4 drops of each)* or mix 5-7 drops of 4-5 recommended oils with fractionated coconut oil in a 10 ml roller bottle and rub deeply into your feet for about 3 minutes. Rub the same roller on your wrists, the back of your neck, your chest, and along your spine. Rub a Magnolia roller along your neck prior to bed, and swirl some in your hand and inhale deeply 5 times. Take 1 Adaptiv™ Capsule daily to reduce potential stress. Take 1 Copaiba Softgel prior to bed.

Take Lifelong Vitality Supplements twice a day; 2-3 DigestZen TerraZyme® capsules at each meal; PB Assist® once per day. Try not to eat within 2-3 hours of bedtime.

Refrain from exercising right before bed.

Do not use electronics within 1-2 hours of bedtime.

G-I

G-I

INSULIN IMBALANCES

⏰ *3-5x per day*	📅 *Ongoing*

Essential Oils: *Oregano, MetaPWR™, Coriander*

Other Solutions: *MetaPWR™ Softgels, Lifelong Vitality, DigestZen TerraZyme®, PB Assist®+, Greens, Protein*

💜 Combine 10 drops each of Oregano, MetaPWR™, and Coriander in a 10 ml roller bottle with fractionated coconut oil. Apply to your wrists, chest, the back of your neck, and your feet. Take 1 MetaPWR™ Softgel with meals.

🌱 Eat blueberries, leafy greens, Greek yogurt, cherries, red grapes, broccoli, tomatoes, garlic, spinach, sweet potatoes, grass-fed beef, digestive enzymes, free-range chicken, eggs, avocado, onions, peppers, omega-3 fatty acids, coconut oil, brown rice, and fatty fish. Take Lifelong Vitality Supplements twice a day; 2-3 DigestZen TerraZyme® capsules at each meal; PB Assist® once per day; and 1 scoop of Greens in a morning smoothie that includes berries, baby spinach, 1 scoop of vanilla Protein, and 1 cup almond milk. Eat something that balances protein/carbohydrate/fat every 3 hours to maintain blood sugar levels.

INSULIN RESISTANCE

⏰ *3-5x per day*	📅 *Ongoing*

Essential Oils: *Cinnamon, Coriander, Zendocrine®, MetaPWR™, Cassia, Celery Seed*

Other Solutions: *MetaPWR™ Softgels, MetaPWR™ Metabolic Gum, Zendocrine® Softgels, Lifelong Vitality, DigestZen TerraZyme®, PB Assist®+*

💜 Choose 3-4 of the recommended oils. Mix 5-7 drops of each oil with fractionated coconut oil in a 10 ml roller bottle. Apply beneath your breastbone and upper abdomen area. Apply to the bottoms of your feet morning and evening. Put 2-3 drops of MetaPWR™ in your water and drink. Take 2 Zendocrine® Softgels a day, or put 1-2 drops of Zendocrine® in a capsule and take 2 times per day. Chew MetaPWR™ gum between meals. Take 1 MetaPWR™ Softgel with meals.

🌱 Take Lifelong Vitality Supplements twice a day, 2-3 DigestZen TerraZyme® capsules at each meal, and PB Assist® once per day. Eat a variety of fresh fruits, vegetables, lean meats, healthy fats, sweet potatoes, and brown rice. Avoid refined sugar, MSG, gluten, corn, fried food, fast food, processed foods, and artificial sweeteners.

🔶 Put 2 drops of MetaPWR™ in your water and drink while exercising. Do a combination of aerobic exercises, strength training, and balance exercises.

IRRITABLE BOWEL SYNDROME

⏰ *3-5x per day*　　📅 *Until symptoms improve*

Essential Oils: *Peppermint, DigestZen®, Ginger, Fennel, Celery Seed, Lemon, Oregano, Rosemary*

Other Solutions: *Ginger Drops, Peppermint Beadlets, DigestZen® Softgels, Peppermint Softgels, Lifelong Vitality, DigestZen TerraZyme®, PB Assist®+*

 Choose 3-4 of the recommended oils. Mix 5 drops of each oil with fractionated coconut oil in a 10 ml roller bottle. Rub it over your abdominal area, your spine in the lower back area, and the bottoms of your feet. In addition, diffuse 3-4 drops of each in a diffuser throughout the day. For adults, take up to 2 Peppermint Softgels before meals. For children 8 years and older, take 1 Peppermint Softgel before meals. For best results, take Peppermint Softgels 30-60 minutes before meals. Take 1-3 DigestZen TerraZyme® capsules daily with meals. Take DigestZen® Softgels 1 or more times daily as needed. Experiment with Peppermint Softgels and DigestZen® Softgels to see which one works best for your body chemistry. Take Ginger Drops as needed. Take Peppermint Beadlets as desired.

🌱 Take Lifelong Vitality Supplements twice a day, 2-3 DigestZen TerraZyme® capsules at each meal, and PB Assist® once per day. Eat a variety of fresh fruits, vegetables, lean meats, healthy fats, sweet potatoes, and brown rice. Avoid refined sugar, MSG, gluten, corn, fried food, fast food, processed foods, and artificial sweeteners.

ITCHING

⏰ *4-5x per day*　　📅 *Until itching improves*

Essential Oils: *Tea Tree, Zendocrine®, Lemon Eucalyptus, Lavender*

Other Solutions: *N/A*

 Combine 5-7 drops each of Tea Tree, Zendocrine®, Lemon Eucalyptus, and Lavender in a 10 ml roller bottle with fractionated coconut oil. Apply to the affected area as recommended.

JAUNDICE

⏰ *3-5x per day*　　📅 *Until symptoms improve*

Essential Oils: *Zendocrine®, Geranium, Rosemary*

Other Solutions: *Zendocrine® Softgels*

 If the condition is affecting your eyes, combine 10 drops of each recommended oil in a 10 ml roller bottle with fractionated coconut oil and apply around (*not in*) the opening of your eyes. Add 1 drop of each recommended oil to a cotton ball and place over your closed eyes overnight (*do not apply into your eyes*). Place 1 drop each of Zendocrine®, Geranium, and Rosemary in a veggie cap and take as needed; or take 1 Zendocrine® Softgel 1-3 times daily.

➕ Seek medical attention to rule out pathology. Be aware of the symptoms of liver damage or failure, which include jaundiced skin or eyes, abdominal pain, discolored or bloody waste secretions, tiredness, nausea, and anorexia.

G-J

JET LAG

🕐 **3x per day**	📅 *Until symptoms lessen*

Essential Oils: *Lavender, Lemon, Eucalyptus, Peppermint, Rosemary*

Other Solutions: *Peppermint Beadlets*

 Combine 8 drops each of Lavender and Eucalyptus, 10 drops of Lemon, and 5 drops each of Peppermint and Rosemary in a 2-ounce spray bottle and top it off with water. Shake well and spritz over the back of your neck, the front of your neck, and in the air. Spray the blend into your palm and inhale deeply. You can also use the same oils in the same amounts in a 10 ml roller bottle with fractionated coconut oil. Take Peppermint Beadlets as needed.

JOINT PAIN

🕐 **4-5x per day**	📅 *As needed*

Essential Oils: *Deep Blue®, Marjoram, Cypress, Copaiba, Lemongrass, Frankincense, Siberian Fir*

Other Solutions: *Deep Blue® Polyphenol Complex, Deep Blue® Rub, Deep Blue® Stick*

 Choose 2-3 of the recommended oils. Mix 5-7 drops of each oil with fractionated coconut oil in a 10 ml roller bottle and apply over the affected joint(s). Take 2 Deep Blue® Polyphenol capsules per day with food. Uses Deep Blue® Rub over the affected area as needed. Use Deep Blue® Rub or Deep Blue® Stick over the affected area as needed.

JOCK ITCH

🕐 **4-5x per day**	📅 *Until symptoms lessen*

Essential Oils: *Tea Tree, Thyme, Patchouli, Citronella, HD Clear®*

Other Solutions: *HD Clear® Foaming Face Wash*

 Wash the affected area with HD Clear® Foaming Face Wash. Allow to dry. Combine 5-7 drops each of Tea Tree, Thyme, Citronella, and Patchouli in a 10 ml roller bottle with fractionated coconut oil. Apply to the affected area.

J-L

KIDNEY INFECTION

 3-5x per day | *As needed until symptoms resolve*

Essential Oils: *Cinnamon, Juniper Berry, Lemongrass, On Guard®, Lemon*

Other Solutions: *On Guard™+ Softgels, On Guard® Tablets*

● Take 1-3 On Guard™+ Softgels per day. Take up to 3 On Guard® Tablets per day. Drink at least half your body weight in ounces of water per day, and add 1 drop of Lemon to your water. Combine 5-7 drops each of Cinnamon, Juniper Berry, Lemongrass, and On Guard® in a 10 ml roller bottle with fractionated coconut oil. Use over your abdominal region, on your back over your kidney area, and on your feet.

KIDNEY STONES

 4-5x per day | *Until symptoms lessen*

Essential Oils: *Lemon, Sandalwood, Wintergreen*

Other Solutions: *N/A*

● Drink at least half your body weight in ounces of water per day. Add 1 drop of Lemon to each cup of water. Add 15 drops of Wintergreen and 10 drops each of Lemon and Sandalwood in a 10 ml roller bottle with fractionated coconut oil. Apply over your abdominal region, on your feet, and on your back over your kidneys.

J-L

KNEE CARTILAGE INJURY

⏰ *4-5x per day*	📅 *As needed*

Essential Oils: *Helichrysum, Wintergreen, Marjoram, Copaiba, Lemongrass, Frankincense, Siberian Fir*

Other Solutions: *Deep Blue® Polyphenol Complex, Deep Blue® Rub, Deep Blue® Stick*

 Choose 2-3 of the recommended oils. Mix 5-7 drops of each oil with fractionated coconut oil in a 10 ml roller bottle. Apply over the affected joint(s). Take 2 Deep Blue® Polyphenol Complex capsules per day with food. Use Deep Blue® Rub or Deep Blue® Stick over the affected area as needed.

LABOR

⏰ *While in labor*	📅 *Until baby is born*

Essential Oils: *Ylang Ylang, ClaryCalm®, Clary Sage, Frankincense, Serenity®, Lavender, Madagascar Vanilla*

Other Solutions: *Deep Blue® Rub*

 Diffuse 3 drops each of Ylang Ylang, Clary Sage, Madagascar Vanilla and Lavender near the laboring mother. Use a ClaryCalm® roller bottle frequently over your abdominal region. Combine 5 drops each of Clary Sage, Frankincense, Ylang Ylang, and Serenity® in a 10 ml roller bottle with fractionated coconut oil. Apply to your lower back, abdominal region, and feet. Use Deep Blue® Rub over your lower back if back labor is prevalent.

LACTATION PROBLEMS

⏰ *4-5x per day*	📅 *As needed*

Essential Oils: *Fennel, Lavender, Clary Sage, Basil*

Other Solutions: *N/A*

 Choose 2-3 of the recommended oils. Mix 5-7 drops of each oil in a 10 ml roller bottle and fill with fractionated coconut oil. Massage into your breasts throughout the day. Apply to the bottoms of your feet morning and evening.

🍏 Avoid taking Peppermint (or any blends that have Peppermint in them) internally, as it can decrease milk supply.

🌙 Try to rest when the baby rests. Aim to get 7-9 hours of sleep per night. Place 1 drop of Lavender or Serenity® on your pillow at bedtime.

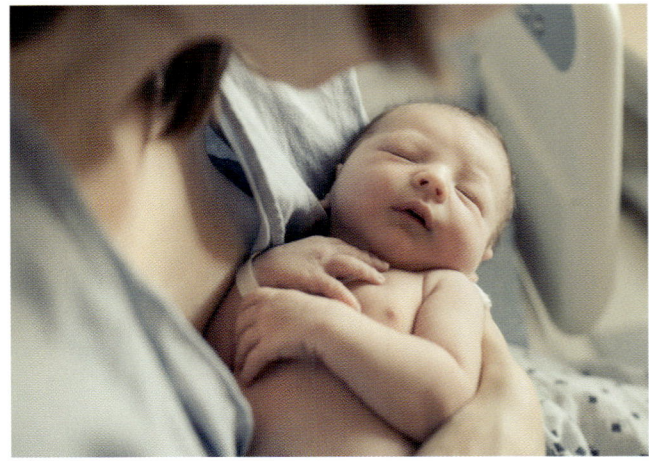

J-L

LACTOSE INTOLERANCE

🕐 *3-5x per day*	📅 *As needed until symptoms resolve*

Essential Oils: *DigestZen®, Coriander, Cardamom, Ginger*

Other Solutions: *Ginger Drops, Peppermint Beadlets, DigestZen® Softgels, DigestZen TerraZyme®*

 Combine 5-7 drops each of DigestZen®, Ginger, Coriander, and Cardamom in a 10 ml roller bottle with fractionated coconut oil. Apply to your abdominal region and on your mid-to-lower-back region. Take DigestZen® Softgels 1 or more times daily as needed. Combine 1 drop of each recommended oil in a veggie capsule and take 2 times per day. Take Ginger Drops as needed. Take Peppermint Beadlets as desired.

🍏 Avoid foods containing lactose. Avoid cheese, especially soft cheeses like cream cheese, cottage cheese, ricotta, and mozzarella. Avoid all types of milk. Avoid buttermilk, butter, whipped cream, sour cream, frozen yogurt, and ice cream. Be sure to read labels carefully for added dairy, because lactose can be found in many prepared food products, such as convenience meals, baked goods and desserts, instant potato mixes, waffle and pancake mix, breakfast cereals, and cream-based or cheesy sauces.

LARYNGITIS

🕐 *3-5x per day*	📅 *As needed*

Essential Oils: *On Guard®, Myrrh, Lemon, Frankincense*

Other Solutions: *On Guard® Protecting Throat Drops, Peppermint Beadlets*

 Combine 5 drops each of On Guard®, Myrrh, Lemon, and Frankincense in a 10 ml roller bottle with fractionated coconut oil. Apply topically over your throat area. Add 1 drop of any of the recommended oils to warm water or tea. Add 1 drop of each recommended oil to 1 teaspoon of honey and swallow 2 times per day. Take On Guard® Protecting Throat Drops as needed. Take Peppermint Beadlets as desired.

J-L

 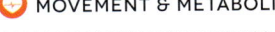
LEAKY GUT SYNDROME

3-5x per day	*Until symptoms improve*

Essential Oils: *Myrrh, Lemongrass, Cardamom, Peppermint, DigestZen®, Fennel, Celery Seed*

Other Solutions: *Ginger Drops, Peppermint Beadlets, DigestZen® Softgels, Peppermint Softgels, Lifelong Vitality, DigestZen TerraZyme®, PB Assist®+*

Choose 3-4 of the recommended oils. Mix 5 drops of each oil with fractionated coconut oil in a 10 ml roller bottle. Rub it over your abdominal area, your spine in the lower back area, and the bottoms of your feet. In addition, diffuse 3-4 drops of each chosen oil in a diffuser throughout the day. For adults, take up to 2 Peppermint Softgels before meals. For children 8 years and older, take 1 Peppermint Softgel before meals. For best results, take Peppermint Softgels 30-60 minutes before meals. Take 1-3 DigestZen TerraZyme® capsules daily with meals. Take DigestZen® Softgels 1 or more times daily as needed. Experiment with Peppermint Softgels and DigestZen® Softgels to see which one works best for your body chemistry. Take Ginger Drops as needed. Take Peppermint Beadlets as desired.

Take Lifelong Vitality Supplements twice a day, 2-3 DigestZen TerraZyme® capsules at each meal, and PB Assist® once per day. Eat a variety of fresh fruits, vegetables, lean meats, healthy fats, sweet potatoes, and brown rice. Avoid refined sugar, MSG, gluten, corn, fried food, fast food, processed foods, and artificial sweeteners.

If tolerated, do a 30-day cleanse each season. See the 30-day cleanse on page 434.

LEARNING DIFFICULTIES

 4-5x per day | While symptoms persist

Essential Oils: *Peppermint, InTune®, Vetiver, Lavender*

Other Solutions: *Peppermint Beadlets*

◉ Apply InTune® down the back of your neck, behind your ears, and over your temples. Mix 5-7 drops each of Peppermint, Lavender, and Vetiver with fractionated coconut oil and apply to your forehead, temples, the base of your skull, and behind your ears, or diffuse the same oils, 3-5 drops each, in the air and inhale. Take Peppermint Beadlets as needed.

LEG CRAMPS/CHARLEY HORSE

 3-5x per day | As needed

Essential Oils: *PastTense® roller, AromaTouch®, Copaiba*

Other Solutions: *Deep Blue® Polyphenol Complex, Deep Blue® Rub*

◉ Apply a Past Tense roller to the affected area. Place 1 drop of Copaiba under your tongue 2 times per day. Combine 10 drops each of AromaTouch® and Copaiba in a 10 ml roller bottle with fractionated coconut oil. Rub over the affected area as directed. Take 2 Deep Blue® Polyphenol Complex a day with meals, in the morning and evening.

LIBIDO (Low)

 3-5x per day | Ongoing until symptoms lessen

Essential Oils: *Ylang Ylang, Neroli Touch, Passion®*

Other Solutions: *N/A*

◉ Diffuse 3-5 drops each of Ylang Ylang and Passion® throughout the day and especially prior to desired activity. Combine 10 drops each of Ylang Ylang and Passion® in a 10 ml roller bottle with fractionated coconut oil. Apply to your chest, the back of your neck, your abdomen, and your wrists and feet. Use a Neroli Touch roller over same areas.

J-L

LIVER DISEASE

4-5x per day	*As needed*

Essential Oils: *Geranium, Myrrh, Cypress, Marjoram, Celery Seed*

Other Solutions: *Ginger Drops, Zendocrine® Softgels*

● Take a 1 drop of Celery Seed internally in a glass of water, twice per day. Combine 5 drops each of Geranium, Marjoram, Cypress, Myrrh, and Celery Seed in a 10 ml roller bottle with fractionated coconut oil. Apply over your kidney area, to the left and right of your spine just under your rib cage, and to the right side of your abdominal area. Prior to applying the blend, apply a warm compress to the area to increase blood flow and enhance absorption. Take 2 Zendocrine® Softgels daily, one each with morning and evening meals. Take Ginger Drops as needed.

● Seek medical attention right away if you experience yellowing of the eyes or skin or tenderness in the upper abdominal area.

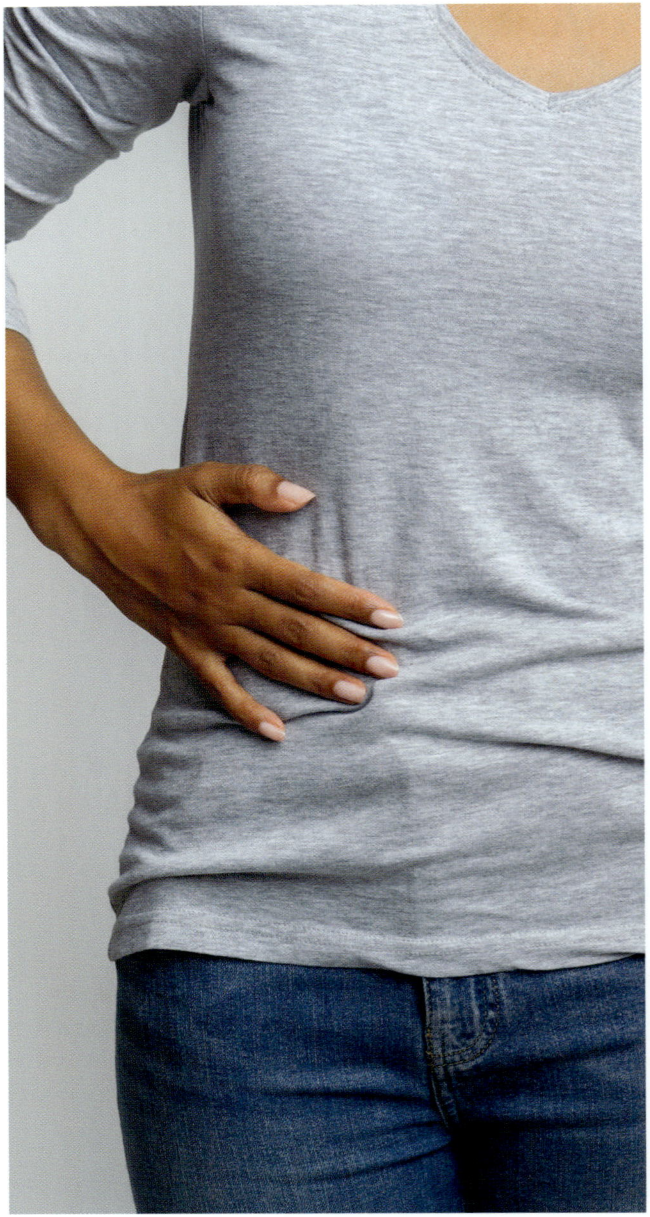

J-L

LOW BLOOD PRESSURE

 3-5x per day   *Ongoing*

Essential Oils: *Basil, Helichrysum, Thyme*

Other Solutions: *Lifelong Vitality, DigestZen TerraZyme®, PB Assist®+, Serenity® Softgels*

- Choose 2 of the recommended oils. Mix 5-7 drops of each oil in a 10 ml roller bottle and fill with fractionated coconut oil. Apply over your heart, over your pulse points on your wrists, down your spine, and on the bottoms of your feet morning and night.

- Take Lifelong Vitality Supplements twice a day, 2-3 DigestZen TerraZyme® capsules at each meal, and PB Assist® once per day. Eat a variety of fresh fruits, vegetables, lean meats, healthy fats, and rice. Include red foods in your daily diet. Avoid MSG, gluten, corn, fried food, fast food, processed foods, and artificial sweeteners.

- Do aerobic exercises, strength training, and balance exercises. If you experience any dizziness or lightheadedness, stop exercising immediately.

- Apply 1 drop of Serenity® or Lavender to your pillow at bedtime. Take 1-2 Serenity® Softgels 30 minutes before bed. Adopt a meditation or yoga practice for stress relief. Use oils from the emotional kit to manage emotional health.

- If you experience any of the following symptoms, seek medical attention right away: swelling, redness, pain, or hotness in an area of your arm or leg; light-headedness; difficult or painful breathing; chest pain or tightness; pain extending down your shoulder, arm, back, or jaw; sudden weakness or numbness of your face, arm, or leg; sudden difficulty speaking or understanding your speech; sudden changes in your vision.

J-L

LOW BLOOD SUGAR

⏰ **3-5x per day**	📅 **Ongoing as needed**

Essential Oils: *Cypress, Cassia, Geranium, Fennel, MetaPWR™*

Other Solutions: *Lifelong Vitality, DigestZen TerraZyme®, PB Assist®+*

 Choose 2-3 of the recommended oils. Mix 5-7 drops of each oil in a 10 ml roller bottle and fill with fractionated coconut oil. Rub the roller bottle over your abdomen, down your spine, over your pulse points on your wrists, and on the bottoms of your feet morning and evening. Add 2-3 drops of MetaPWR™ to your water and drink throughout the day.

 Eat small amounts of food every 3 hours to keep your blood sugar balance. Consume some protein, fat, and carbohydrates at each meal. Take Lifelong Vitality Supplements twice a day, 2-3 DigestZen TerraZyme® capsules at each meal, and PB Assist® once per day. Eat a variety of fresh fruits, vegetables, lean meats, healthy fats, and rice. Avoid MSG, gluten, corn, fried food, fast food, processed foods, refined carbohydrates, sweets, and artificial sweeteners *(these cause fluctuations in blood sugar)*. Carry around small snacks *(like power bars and fruit)* for times when your blood sugar drops and you can't sit down for a meal.

LOW CONFIDENCE

⏰ **3-5x per day**	📅 **As needed**

Essential Oils: *Adaptiv™, Bergamot, Neroli Touch, Motivate®*

Other Solutions: *Peppermint Beadlets*

 Choose 2-3 of the recommended oils. Dilute 1 drop of each oil with 1 tablespoon of fractionated coconut oil. Apply a few drops topically to your forehead, temples, the base of your skull, and behind your ears, or diffuse in the air and inhale. Take Peppermint Beadlets as needed.

J-L

LOW ENDURANCE

3-5x per day	*As needed*

Essential Oils: *Peppermint, Basil, MetaPWR™, Breathe®, Motivate®*

Other Solutions: *Peppermint Beadlets, Serenity® Softgels*

- Put 1 drop of Peppermint in your water and drink. Diffuse 4-5 drops of each recommended oil throughout the day. Rub 1 drop of Peppermint diluted with 10 drops of fractionated coconut oil down the back of your neck, under your skull, and behind your ears. Put 1 drop of each recommended oil in your palms and inhale deeply 3 times as needed. If you get oils in your eyes or on your face while inhaling from your hands, apply plain coconut oil over your eye or face to soothe the area. Repeat as needed. Take Peppermint Beadlets as desired.

- Apply 1 drop of Peppermint diluted with 10 drops of fractionated coconut oil over your chest before exercise. Do aerobic exercises, strength training, and balance exercises.

- Place 1 drop of Lavender or Serenity® on your pillow at night. Take 2 Serenity® Softgels before bedtime.

J-L

LOW METABOLISM

3-5x per day	*Ongoing as needed*

Essential Oils: *Grapefruit, MetaPWR™, Cinnamon, Clove, DDR Prime®*

Other Solutions: *MetaPWR™ Softgels, Mito2Max®, Lifelong Vitality, DigestZen TerraZyme®, PB Assist®+*

- Put 1-2 drops of MetaPWR™ or Grapefruit in your water and drink. Take 1 MetaPWR™ Softgel with meals. Choose 3 of the recommended oils. Mix 5-7 drops of each in a 10 ml roller bottle and fill with fractionated coconut oil. Apply blend to your abdomen, over your wrists, and on the bottoms of your feet morning and evening. Take 2 Mito2Max® daily with food; avoid taking it before bed.

- Take Lifelong Vitality Supplements twice a day, 2-3 DigestZen TerraZyme® capsules at each meal, and PB Assist® once per day. Eat a variety of fresh fruits, vegetables, lean meats, healthy fats, and rice. Avoid MSG, gluten, corn, fried food, fast food, processed foods, and artificial sweeteners.

- Put 2 drops of MetaPWR™ in your water and drink while exercising. Do a combination of aerobic exercises, strength training, and balance exercises.

- If tolerated, do a 30-day cleanse each season. See the 30-day cleanse on page 434.

LOW ENERGY

3-5x per day	*As needed*

Essential Oils: *Peppermint, Wild Orange, Siberian Fir*

Other Solutions: *Peppermint Beadlets*

- Put 1 drop of Peppermint in your water and drink. Diffuse 4-5 drops of each recommended oil in a diffuser and diffuse throughout the day. Rub 1 drop of Peppermint diluted with 1 teaspoon of fractionated coconut oil down the back of your neck, under your skull, and behind your ears. Put 1 drop of each oil in your palms and inhale deeply 3 times as needed. Take Peppermint Beadlets as needed. If you get oils in your eyes or on your face while inhaling from your hands, apply plain coconut oil over your eye or face to soothe the area. Repeat as needed.

- Apply 1 drop of Peppermint diluted with 1 teaspoon of fractionated coconut oil over your chest before exercise. Do aerobic exercises, strength training, and balance exercises.

J-L

LOW MILK SUPPLY

🕐 *4-5x per day*	📅 *As needed*

Essential Oils: *Fennel, Lavender, Clary Sage, Basil*

Other Solutions: *N/A*

- Choose 2-3 of the recommended oils. Mix 5-7 drops of each oil in a 10 ml roller bottle and fill with fractionated coconut oil. Massage into your breasts throughout the day. Apply to the bottoms of your feet morning and evening.

- Avoid taking Peppermint (*or any blends that have Peppermint in them*) internally, as it can decrease milk supply.

- Try to rest when the baby rests. Aim to get 7-9 hours of sleep per night. Place 1 drop of Lavender or Serenity® on your pillow at bedtime.

LOW TESTOSTERONE

🕐 *3-5x per day*	📅 *Until symptoms resolve*

Essential Oils: *Sandalwood, Patchouli, Ylang Ylang, Cinnamon, Ginger, Lavender*

Other Solutions: *Serenity® Softgels*

- Choose 4-5 of the recommended oils. Mix 5-7 drops of each oil with fractionated coconut oil in a 10 ml roller bottle. Rub it over your lower abdominal region, on your feet, and along your spine in the lower back area every 4 hours.

- Eat cocoa, dark chocolate, watermelon, tomatoes, grapefruit, red peppers, pistachios, tea, and wine.

- Place 1 drop of Lavender on your pillow at night. Take 2 Serenity® Softgels at bedtime. Avoid stressful conversations or television before bed. Develop a good bedtime routine. Increase the laughter in your life by watching a comedy or hanging with friends and family members who make you laugh.

LUMBAGO

⏰ **4-5x per day**	📅 *Ongoing until symptoms lessen*

Essential Oils: *Lemongrass, Marjoram, Wintergreen, Cypress, AromaTouch®, Copaiba*

Other Solutions: *Deep Blue® Rub, Deep Blue® Stick, Lifelong Vitality, DigestZen TerraZyme®, PB Assist®+, Serenity® Softgels, Turmeric Dual Chamber Capsules, Deep Blue® Polyphenol Complex, Copaiba Softgels*

 Use a 4-ounce glass jar and fill 3/4 with hard coconut oil. Add 2 quarter-sized drops of Deep Blue® Rub and 15 drops each of Lemongrass, Marjoram, Wintergreen, Cypress, AromaTouch®, and Copaiba. Stir well. Apply liberally over the affected area, massaging it into the soft tissues. Take 2 Deep Blue® Polyphenol Complex capsules a day with meals, in the morning and evening. Take 2 Turmeric Dual Chamber Capsules per day. Use Deep Blue® Rub or Deep Blue® Stick over lower back area.

🍏 Take Lifelong Vitality Supplements twice a day, 2-3 DigestZen TerraZyme® capsules at each meal, PB Assist® once per day, and Turmeric Dual Chamber Capsules 2 times per day. Eat a clean diet with a variety of fresh fruits, vegetables, lean meats, healthy fats, and rice. Avoid MSG, gluten, corn, fried food, fast food, processed foods, and artificial sweeteners. Take 2 Copaiba Softgels twice a day.

🔸 Listen to your body. Do 5 days of light to moderate cardio if tolerated. Do 3 days of strength training *(making sure to support your back)* if tolerated. Warm up, cool down, and stretch for each exercise session.

While exercising, tighten your core to support your lower back.

🌙 Place 1 drop of Serenity® or Lavender on your pillow at night. Take 2 Serenity® Softgels 30 minutes before bed. Place a pillow under your knees when you sleep or rest on your back, and in-between your knees when you rest or lay on your side. Avoid sitting for long periods of time. Get up every couple of hours and go for a 5-minute walk if possible. Use oils from the emotional kit to manage stress and emotions.

➕ Seek professional medical attention if the problem persists, if you have pain that radiates down your thigh or leg, you have bowel or bladder incontinence, loss of sensation in the groin or legs or if you do not see an improvement in your condition after a couple of weeks on this protocol.

LYME DISEASE

⏰ *3-5x per day*	📅 *Ongoing*

Essential Oils: *Oregano, Thyme, Clove, Cassia, Frankincense, On Guard®, DDR Prime®, Lemongrass, Lavender, Serenity®*

Other Solutions: *Deep Blue® Rub, On Guard™+ Softgels, DDR Prime® Softgels, Cleanse & Restore Kit, Lifelong Vitality, DigestZen TerraZyme®, PB Assist®+, Serenity® Softgels*

 Put 1-2 drops each of Oregano, Thyme, Clove, Cassia, Frankincense, and DDR Prime® in a capsule with fractionated coconut oil. Take twice daily for 10 days and then stop taking the capsule for 14-21 days, depending on how your body feels. Repeat the 10 and 14-21 day cycle until symptoms improve. Mix 5-7 drops each of Oregano, Thyme, Clove, Cassia, Frankincense, and DDR Prime® in a 10 ml roller bottle and fill with fractionated coconut oil. Apply to your abdomen, down your spine, and on the bottoms of your feet morning and night in the same 10/14-21 day cycle. If you have a new tick bite, take 2 On Guard™+ Softgels and 2 DDR Prime® Softgels per day for 14 days and use the roller blend for 10 days.

 Take Lifelong Vitality Supplements twice a day, 2-3 DigestZen TerraZyme® capsules at each meal, and PB Assist® once per day. Eat a variety of fresh fruits, vegetables, lean meats, healthy fats, and rice. Avoid MSG, gluten, corn, fried food, fast food, processed foods, and artificial sweeteners.

Exercise on days when you feel good. Alternate light to moderate cardio and strength training as tolerated. Listen to your body and rest when needed. Apply 1-2 drops of Lemongrass and Deep Blue® Rub to muscles and joints that are sore or inflamed.

Apply 1 drop of Serenity® or Lavender to your pillow at bedtime. Take 1-2 Serenity® Softgels 30 minutes before bed. Use emotional oils as needed. Include meditation, prayer, and spending time in nature as part of your regular routine to rest and manage your stress. Join an online support group or reach out to friends and family for help as needed.

Makeover your home by using the Abōde™ line of cleaning products, laundry pods, dishwasher pods, surface cleaner, and dish soap. Take care of your hands with Abōde™ Foaming Hand Wash and Lotion. If tolerated, do a 30-day cleanse each season. See the 30-day cleanse on page 434.

J-L

M-O

MALARIA

🕐 **3-5x per day**	📅 **Until symptoms lessen**

Essential Oils: *Copaiba, Melissa, Frankincense, DDR Prime®, Oregano, Cinnamon, Turmeric, Grapefruit, Ginger, Black Pepper, TerraShield®, Lemon Eucalyptus*

Other Solutions: *DDR Prime® Softgels, Turmeric Dual Chamber Capsules, Lifelong Vitality*

 Mix 5 drops each of Copaiba, Melissa, Frankincense, DDR Prime®, and Oregano with fractionated coconut oil in a 10 ml roller bottle. Rub it over your abdominal area, your spine in the lower back area, and the bottoms of your feet. Diffuse 3-4 drops each of Grapefruit and Copaiba throughout the day. Place 1-2 drops of Cinnamon, Black Pepper, Ginger, and Oregano in a veggie capsule with a carrier oil and take daily; after day 10, stop adding Oregano, and wait 10 days until adding it again. Place 1 drop of Copaiba under your tongue in the morning and 1 drop of Frankincense under your tongue at night. Take 2 DDR Prime® Softgels and 2 Turmeric Dual Chamber Capsules daily along with Lifelong Vitality daily. Mix 15 drops of TerraShield® and 10 drops Lemon Eucalyptus in a 10 ml roller bottle to repel pests. Apply topically over your pulse points prior to going outdoors, and frequently reapply throughout the day (*every 2 hours minimum*). Diffuse 4-5 drops each of TerraShield® and Lemon Eucalyptus daily to repel pests.

MASTITIS

🕐 **4-5x per day**	📅 **While symptoms persist**

Essential Oils: *Lavender, DDR Prime®, Thyme, Peppermint, Oregano, PastTense®*

Other Solutions: *Yarrow|Pom Body Renewal Serum*

🌀 Choose 3-4 of the recommended oils. Put 2 drops of each oil and 2 tablespoons of fractionated coconut oil in a small bowl filled with cold water. Dip a clean washcloth into the water. Wring out the cloth and apply it over the affected breasts for 10 minutes. Apply PastTense® over the affected breasts morning and evening. Apply Yarrow|Pom Body Renewal Serum on the affected breast twice daily.

➕ Seek medical attention if you have a fever or chills or if your breasts become too uncomfortable and are red or hot to the touch.

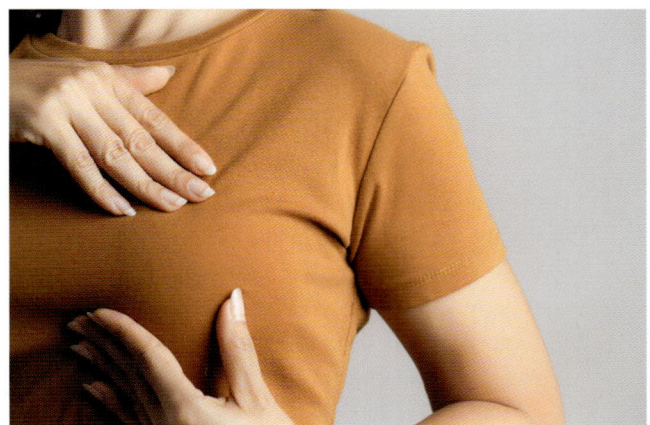

MEASLES

| ⏰ *3-5x per day* | 📅 *Until symptoms resolve* |

Essential Oils: *Eucalyptus, Blue Tansy, Tea Tree*

Other Solutions: *N/A*

 Combine 10 drops each of Eucalyptus, Blue Tansy, and Tea Tree in a 10 ml roller bottle with fractionated coconut oil. Apply to the affected area. You can also saturate a cotton ball with witch hazel and add 3 drops of each recommended oil. Dab the cotton ball on your spots topically several times daily.

MENIERE'S DISEASE

| ⏰ *3-5x per day* | 📅 *As needed* |

Essential Oils: *Basil, Balance®, Ginger, Cedarwood*

Other Solutions: *Ginger Drops*

 Choose 2-3 of the recommended oils. Dilute 1 drop of each with 1/2-3/4 teaspoons fractionated coconut oil. Apply behind your ears, down the back of your neck, under your skull, under your nose, and on your wrists throughout the day. Take Ginger Drops as needed.

M-O

MENINGITIS

⏰ *4-5x per day*	📅 *Until condition improves*

Essential Oils: *Frankincense, Copaiba, Tea Tree, On Guard®, Clove, Basil*

Other Solutions: *DDR Prime® Softgels*

🌸 Place 2 drops each of Frankincense and Copaiba under your tongue, twice per day. Combine 5 drops each of Tea Tree, On Guard®, Copaiba, Clove, and Basil in a 10 ml roller bottle with fractionated coconut oil. Apply to your neck, feet, under your skull, and the front of your neck often throughout the day. Take 2 DDR Prime® Softgels twice daily.

MENOPAUSE

⏰ *4-5x per day*	📅 *Ongoing until symptoms lessen*

Essential Oils: *ClaryCalm® roller, Clary Sage, Passion®, Tulsi*

Other Solutions: *N/A*

🌸 Use a ClaryCalm® roller 3 times a day by applying it to your wrists, over your heart/chest area, on your feet, and on the back of your neck. Combine 10 drops each of Clary Sage, Tulsi, and Passion® in a 10 ml roller bottle with fractionated coconut oil. Apply to the same areas. Diffuse 3-5 drops each of Clary Sage and Passion® and inhale throughout the day.

🔄 Makeover your home by using the Abōde™ line of cleaning products, laundry pods, dishwasher pods, surface cleaner, and dish soap. Take care of your hands with Abōde™ Foaming Hand Wash and Lotion. If tolerated, do a 30-day cleanse each season. See the 30-day cleanse on page 434.

M-O

MENORRHAGIA
(Excessive Menstrual Bleeding)

4-5x per day	*Until symptoms improve*

Essential Oils: *Helichrysum, Clary Sage, Geranium, Rose*

Other Solutions: *N/A*

 Combine 10 drops each of Helichrysum, Rose, Clary Sage, and Geranium in a 10 ml roller bottle with fractionated coconut oil. Massage into your abdomen, lower back, and shoulders. Apply a warm compress over your uterus area, or take 1 drop each recommended oil in a veggie capsule as needed.

● Makeover your home by using the Abōde™ line of cleaning products, laundry pods, dishwasher pods, surface cleaner, and dish soap. Take care of your hands with Abōde™ Foaming Hand Wash and Lotion. If tolerated, do a 30-day cleanse each season. See the 30-day cleanse on page 434.

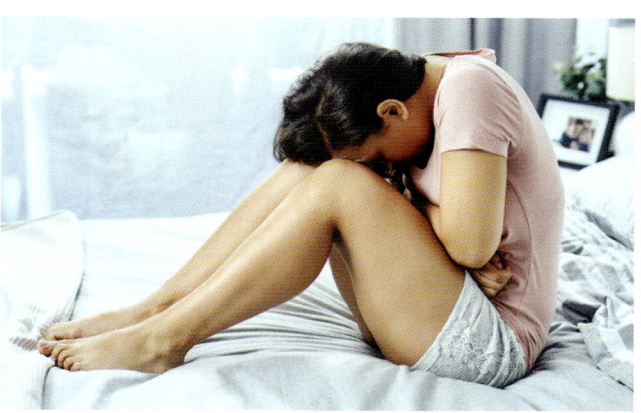

MENSTRUAL BLEEDING
(Excessive)

4-5x per day	*Until symptoms improve*

Essential Oils: *Helichrysum, Clary Sage, Geranium, Rose*

Other Solutions: *N/A*

● Combine 10 drops each of Helichrysum, Rose, Clary Sage, and Geranium in a 10 ml roller bottle with fractionated coconut oil. Massage into your abdomen, lower back, and shoulders. Apply a warm compress over your uterus area, or take 1 drop each recommended oil in a veggie capsule as needed.

● Makeover your home by using the Abōde™ line of cleaning products, laundry pods, dishwasher pods, surface cleaner, and dish soap. Take care of your hands with Abōde™ Foaming Hand Wash and Lotion. If tolerated, do a 30-day cleanse each season. See the 30-day cleanse on page 434.

M-O

MENSTRUAL CYCLE
(Irregular/Scanty)

 3-5x per day | *As needed*

Essential Oils: *ClaryCalm®, Clary Sage, Whisper®, Ylang Ylang, Jasmine, Tulsi, Geranium, Sandalwood, Lavender*

Other Solutions: *Phytoestrogen Essential Complex, Bone Nutrient Essential Complex, Lifelong Vitality, DigestZen TerraZyme®, PB Assist®+, Serenity® Softgels*

⬤ Combine 5-7 drops each of Sandalwood, Geranium, Ylang Ylang, Tulsi, and Clary Sage with fractionated coconut oil in a 10 ml roller bottle. Apply over your lower abdominal region, on your feet, and along your spine in the lower back area 2 times per day. Rotate between using a ClaryCalm® roller and a Jasmine roller throughout the day in-between using the homemade roller. Diffuse 5 drops of Whisper® throughout the day.

⬤ Pre- and peri-menopausal women should take one 1-2 Phytoestrogen Essential Complex capsules daily with food. Take 4 Bone Nutrient Essential Complex capsules daily with food. Take Lifelong Vitality Supplements twice a day, 2-3 DigestZen TerraZyme® capsules at each meal, and PB Assist® once per day. Consume avocados, flaxseed, broccoli, pomegranate, salmon, leafy greens, nuts, organic soy, turmeric, quinoa, and brown rice. Avoid excess sugar, simple carbohydrates, trans fats, and processed foods.

⬤ Place 1 drop of Lavender or Serenity® on your pillow at night. Take 1-2 Serenity® Softgels at bedtime.

⬤ Makeover your home by using the Abōde™ line of cleaning products, laundry pods, dishwasher pods, surface cleaner, and dish soap. Take care of your hands with Abōde™ Foaming Hand Wash and Lotion. If tolerated, do a 30-day cleanse each season. See the 30-day cleanse on page 434.

MENSTRUAL PAIN

 3-5x per day | *Until symptoms resolve*

Essential Oils: *ClaryCalm®, Clary Sage, PastTense®*

Other Solutions: *Deep Blue® Rub, Deep Blue® Stick*

⬤ Apply a warm compress to your lower abdominal region and apply Deep Blue® Stick a dime-sized amount of Deep Blue® Rub over the area. Alternate between using Deep Blue® Rub and PastTense® over the area. Use a ClaryCalm® roller over your wrists, chest, lower back, and abdomen 3 times per day. Diffuse 5 drops of Clary Sage throughout the day.

M-O

MENTAL FATIGUE

🕐 *3-5x per day*	📅 *As needed*

Essential Oils: *Wild Orange, Peppermint, Spearmint, Rosemary*

Other Solutions: *Peppermint Beadlets*

 Combine 5 drops each of Wild Orange and Peppermint with 3 drops each of Spearmint and Rosemary in a diffuser. Diffuse and inhale the air throughout the day. Combine 5 drops of each recommended oil in a 10 ml roller bottle with fractionated coconut oil. Take Peppermint Beadlets as needed.

MENTAL FOCUS

🕐 *3x per day*	📅 *Until symptoms lessen*

Essential Oils: *InTune®, Vetiver, Peace®, Cedarwood, Motivate®, Peppermint*

Other Solutions: *Peppermint Beadlets*

 Rub InTune® down the back of your neck, over your temples, and under your skull throughout the day. Diffuse 5 drops each of Peppermint, Peace®, Motivate®, and Cedarwood throughout the day. Rub Vetiver down the back of your neck, over your temples, and on the bottoms of your feet morning and evening. Take Peppermint Beadlets as desired.

M-O

MIGRAINES

⏰ *3-5x per day*	📅 *While symptoms persist*

Essential Oils: *Peppermint, Copaiba, Frankincense*

Other Solutions: *Lifelong Vitality, DigestZen TerraZyme®, PB Assist®+, Serenity® Softgels, Peppermint Beadlets*

 Choose 2 of the recommended oils. Mix 1-2 drops of each with 15 drops of fractionated coconut oil in your palms. Apply to your forehead, temples, the base of your skull, the back of your neck, and the bottoms of your feet. You can also diffuse 4-5 drops each of the chosen oils and inhale as needed. Place 1 drop of Frankincense on your thumb and put it on the roof of your mouth. Take Peppermint Beadlets as needed.

🌱 Take Lifelong Vitality Supplements twice a day, 2-3 DigestZen TerraZyme® capsules at each meal, and PB Assist® once per day. Eat a variety of fresh fruits, vegetables, lean meats, healthy fats, and rice. Avoid trigger foods: lunch meats, sulphites, tyramine, nitrates, nitrites, bananas, excessive caffeine, aged cheese, yeast-based products (*like bread and pizza*), soy sauce, milk, beans, alcohol, MSG, gluten, corn, fried food, fast food, processed foods, and artificial sweeteners.

 Apply the suggested blend to the back of your neck and under your skull before exercise. Do aerobic exercises, strength training, and balance exercises.

🌙 Place 1 drop of Lavender or Serenity® on your pillow at night. Turn off electronic devices an hour or two before bed.

🔴 Makeover your home by using the Abōde™ line of cleaning products, laundry pods, dishwasher pods, surface cleaner, and dish soap. Take care of your hands with Abōde™ Foaming Hand Wash and Lotion. If tolerated, do a 30-day cleanse each season. See the 30-day cleanse on page 434.

M-O

MOLD/MILDEW

 Set diffuser on intermittent setting and run throughout the day

 As needed

Essential Oils: *Tea Tree, Purify, Oregano, On Guard®*

Other Solutions: *On Guard® Cleaner Concentrate*

Combine 1 teaspoon of On Guard® Cleaner Concentrate, 10 drops of Purify, 10 drops of Tea Tree, 10 drops of On Guard®, and 1/4 cup of white vinegar in a 16-ounce glass spray bottle. Fill the rest of the bottle with water. Spray over the area of concern and allow to dry. Diffuse 4-5 drops each of Tea Tree, Purify, Oregano, and On Guard® into the air where mold is present several times daily until no longer needed.

MOLES

 3-5x per day

 Until symptoms resolve

Essential Oils: *HD Clear®, Frankincense, Sandalwood*

Other Solutions: *N/A*

Apply an HD Clear® roller to the mole several times per day. Apply 1 drop of Frankincense and 1 drop of Cedarwood to the mole 2 times per day.

MONONUCLEOSIS

 3-5x per day

 Ongoing as needed

Essential Oils: *Melissa, Thyme, Cinnamon, Eucalyptus, On Guard®, Lavender*

Other Solutions: *DDR Prime® Softgels, Lifelong Vitality, DigestZen TerraZyme®, PB Assist®+, Mito2Max®, Deep Blue® Rub, On Guard™+ Softgels, On Guard® Tablets*

Choose 2-3 recommended oils. Mix 5-7 drops of each oil in a 10 ml roller bottle and fill with fractionated coconut oil. Apply down your spine, under ridge of your skull, under your right rib cage in the front of your body, and on the bottoms of your feet morning and evening. Take 2 DDR Prime® Softgels per day. Take 2 Mito2Max® during the day. Put 2 drops of On Guard® in a capsule and take twice daily or take 1 On Guard® Softgel twice daily. Take up to 3 On Guard® Tablets per day.

Take Lifelong Vitality Supplements twice a day, 2-3 DigestZen TerraZyme® capsules at each meal, and PB Assist® once per day. Eat a variety of fresh fruits, vegetables, lean meats, healthy fats, and rice. Avoid MSG, gluten, corn, fried food, fast food, processed foods, and artificial sweeteners.

Exercise on days when you feel good. Alternate light to moderate cardio and strength training as tolerated. Listen to your body and rest when needed. Apply Deep Blue® Rub to muscles and joints that are sore or inflamed.

Place 1 drop of Lavender on your pillow at night.

M-O

MOOD SWINGS

⏰ *3-5x per day*	📅 *Until symptoms resolve*

Essential Oils: *ClaryCalm®, Clary Sage, Whisper®, Ylang Ylang, Tulsi, Jasmine, Geranium, Sandalwood*

Other Solutions: *Phytoestrogen Essential Complex, Bone Nutrient Essential Complex, Lifelong Vitality, DigestZen TerraZyme®, PB Assist®+, Serenity® Softgels*

💜 Combine 5-7 drops each of Sandalwood, Geranium, Tulsi, Ylang Ylang, and Clary Sage with fractionated coconut oil in a 10 ml roller bottle. Apply over your lower abdominal region, on your feet, and along your spine in the lower back area 2 times per day. Rotate using a ClaryCalm® roller and a Jasmine roller throughout the day in-between using the homemade roller. Diffuse 5 drops of Whisper® throughout the day.

🍎 Pre- and peri-menopausal women should take one 1-2 Phytoestrogen Essential Complex capsules daily with food. Take 4 Bone Nutrient Essential Complex capsules daily with food. Take Lifelong Vitality Supplements twice a day, 2-3 DigestZen TerraZyme® capsules at each meal, and PB Assist® once per day. Consume avocados, flaxseed, broccoli, pomegranate, salmon, leafy greens, nuts, organic soy, turmeric, quinoa, and brown rice. Avoid excess sugar, simple carbohydrates, trans fats, and processed foods.

🌙 Place 1 drop of Lavender or Serenity® on your pillow at night. Take 2 Serenity® Softgels at bedtime. Avoid stressful conversations or television before meals or bed. Develop a good bedtime routine that feels relaxing to you. Find a hobby or meditation program. Listen to music, go for a walk in nature, or go out with friends. Increase the laughter in your life by watching a comedy or hanging with friends and family members who make you laugh. Schedule self-care rituals throughout the week that make you feel good.

🔻 Makeover your home by using the Abōde™ line of cleaning products, laundry pods, dishwasher pods, surface cleaner, and dish soap. Take care of your hands with Abōde™ Foaming Hand Wash and Lotion. If tolerated, do a 30-day cleanse each season. See the 30-day cleanse on page 434.

M-O

MORNING SICKNESS

3-5x per day		**Ongoing until symptoms lessen**

Essential Oils: *Ginger, Peppermint, Cardamom, Spearmint, DigestZen®*

Other Solutions: *Ginger Drops, Peppermint Beadlets*

- Apply 1-2 drops of each recommended oil behind your ears and over your navel hourly, diffuse 4-5 drops of each recommended oil into the air and inhale, or place 1 drop of each recommended oil in a veggie capsule and take upon onset of symptoms. Combine 10 drops each of Ginger and Peppermint or 10 drops each of Spearmint and DigestZen® in a 10 ml roller bottle with fractionated coconut oil. Apply to your abdominal area as needed. You can also place 1 drop of Spearmint or Peppermint on your tongue once symptoms start. Take Ginger Drops as needed. Take Peppermint Beadlets as desired.

MOSQUITO BITES

3-5x per day		**As needed**

Essential Oils: *Tea Tree, Purify, Lavender, Roman Chamomile*

Other Solutions: *N/A*

- Choose 1-2 of the recommended oils. Apply 1 drop of each with 10 drops of fractionated coconut oil over the affected area.

- Seek medical attention if you experience a fever, swollen glands, a headache, a rash, vomiting, muscle/joint pain, or diarrhea.

M-O

MOTION SICKNESS

 Hourly as nausea occurs	 *Until symptoms improve*

Essential Oils: *Ginger, Peppermint, Basil, DigestZen®*

Other Solutions: *Ginger Drops, Peppermint Beadlets*

 Place 2 drops of Ginger, Peppermint, Basil, or DigestZen®, or a combination of two of these oils, in the palm of your hand. Massage gently in a circular clockwise motion over your navel region upon the initial onset of motion sickness. Cup your hands over your face and inhale deeply for 1 minute. If symptoms are ongoing, place 5 drops of each recommended oil in a 10 ml roller bottle with fractionated coconut oil and massage over your navel region hourly until symptoms resolve. Diffuse 3-5 drops of each recommended oil in the air and inhale during acute episodes of sickness and to prevent recurring episodes. If you get oils in your eyes or on your face while inhaling from your hands, apply plain coconut oil over your eye or face to soothe the area. Repeat as needed. Take Ginger Drops as needed. Take Peppermint Beadlets as desired.

MOUTH ULCER

 4-5x per day	 *While symptoms persist*

Essential Oils: *Tea Tree, On Guard®, Myrrh*

Other Solutions: *N/A*

 Mix 1 drop of each recommended oil with 5-10 drops of fractionated coconut oil. Apply directly on the sore. Gargle 1-2 drops of any of the recommended oils mixed with water several times daily, apply the recommended oils to your gums, or take internally as needed by swallowing water you gargled with.

M-O

MRSA

4-5x per day	**While symptoms persist**

Essential Oils: *Cinnamon, Oregano, Thyme, On Guard®, Clove*

Other Solutions: *DDR Prime® Softgels, On Guard® Foaming Hand Wash, On Guard® Sanitizing Mist*

Choose 3 of the recommended oils. Mix 5-7 drops of each oil in a 10 ml roller bottle and fill with fractionated coconut oil. Rub down your spine, over the affected area, and on the bottoms of your feet morning and evening. Put 1-2 drops each of Oregano, On Guard®, and Thyme in a capsule and add fractionated coconut oil. Take 3 times per day. Diffuse 4-5 drops of On Guard® throughout the day and at bedtime. Take 1 DDR Prime® Softgel morning and evening. Cover the affected area with a clean bandage. Wash your hands frequently with On Guard® Foaming Hand Wash. Use On Guard® Sanitizing Mist often throughout the day.

M-O

MULTIPLE SCLEROSIS

4-5x per day	*Ongoing*

Essential Oils: *DDR Prime®, Zendocrine®, Frankincense, Sandalwood, Cypress, On Guard®*

Other Solutions: *Lifelong Vitality, DigestZen TerraZyme®, PB Assist®+, Serenity® Softgels, Turmeric Dual Chamber Capsules, Deep Blue® Rub*

- Put 1 drop each of On Guard®, DDR Prime®, Zendocrine®, Frankincense, and Sandalwood in a capsule and take 3 times per day. Take 2 Turmeric Dual Chamber Capsules a day. Mix 5 drops each of On Guard®, DDR Prime®, Zendocrine®, Frankincense, Sandalwood, and Cypress in a 10 ml roller bottle with fractionated coconut oil. Apply to your abdomen, down your spine, and on the bottoms of your feet morning and night.

- Take Lifelong Vitality Supplements twice a day, 2-3 DigestZen TerraZyme® capsules at each meal, and PB Assist® once per day. Eat a variety of fresh fruits, vegetables, lean meat, healthy fats, and rice. Avoid MSG, gluten, corn, fried food, fast food, processed foods, and artificial sweeteners.

- Exercise on days when you feel good. Alternate between light to moderate cardio and strength training as tolerated. Listen to your body and rest when needed. Apply Lemongrass and Deep Blue® Rub to muscles and joints that are sore or inflamed.

- Apply 1-2 drops of Serenity® or Lavender to your pillow at bedtime. Take 1-2 Serenity® Softgels 30 minutes before bed. Use emotional oils as needed. Include meditation, prayer, and spending time in nature as part of your regular routine to rest and manage your stress. Join an online support group or reach out to friends and family for help as needed.

- Makeover your home by using the Abōde™ line of cleaning products, laundry pods, dishwasher pods, surface cleaner, and dish soap. Take care of your hands with Abōde™ Foaming Hand Wash and Lotion. If tolerated, do a 30-day cleanse each season. See the 30-day cleanse on page 434.

M-O

MUMPS

4-5x per day	*While symptoms persist*

Essential Oils: *On Guard®, DDR Prime®, Zendocrine®, Yarrow|Pom, Lavender*

Other Solutions: *On Guard® Protecting Throat Drops, On Guard® Beadlets, On Guard® Tablets, Peppermint Beadlets*

- Mix 5-7 drops each of On Guard®, DDR Prime®, and Zendocrine® in a 10 ml roller bottle and fill with fractionated coconut oil. Apply over swollen glands, down the back of your neck and spine, and on the bottoms of your feet morning and evening and while laying down. Rub 3 drops of Yarrow|Pom over the affected areas. Apply cold packs or warm compresses *(whichever feels best to you)* over the swollen glands. Diffuse 4-5 drops each of On Guard®, Zendocrine®, and Lavender in a diffuser. Take On Guard® Protecting Throat Drops as needed. Take On Guard® Beadlets and Peppermint Beadlets as desired. Take up to 3 On Guard® Tablets per day.

- Drink plenty of liquids. Eat soft foods if it is hard for you to swallow due to swollen glands.

- Get plenty of rest. Place 1 drop of Lavender on your pillow. Diffuse 4-5 drops of Lavender and On Guard® while sleeping or resting.

MUSCLE PAIN

4-5x per day	*As needed*

Essential Oils: *Marjoram, AromaTouch®, Copaiba, Frankincense, Siberian Fir, PastTense®*

Other Solutions: *Lifelong Vitality, DigestZen TerraZyme®, PB Assist®+, Deep Blue® Polyphenol Complex, Deep Blue® Rub, Deep Blue® Stick*

- Choose 2-3 of the recommended oils. Mix 5-7 drops of each oil with fractionated coconut oil in a 10 ml roller bottle and apply over the affected joint(s). Take 2 Deep Blue® Polyphenol Complex capsules per day with food. Uses Deep Blue® Rub or Deep Blue® Stick over the affected area as needed.

- Take Lifelong Vitality Supplements twice a day, 2-3 DigestZen TerraZyme® capsules at each meal, and PB Assist® once per day. Eat a variety of fresh fruits, vegetables, lean meats, healthy fats, and rice. Avoid MSG, gluten, corn, fried food, fast food, processed foods, and artificial sweeteners.

M-O

MUSCLE SPASMS

4-5x per day	**As needed**

Essential Oils: *Marjoram, AromaTouch®, Copaiba, Frankincense, Siberian Fir, PastTense®*

Other Solutions: *Lifelong Vitality, DigestZen TerraZyme®, PB Assist®+, Deep Blue® Rub, Deep Blue® Stick, Deep Blue® Polyphenol Complex*

- Choose 2-3 of the recommended oils. Mix 5-7 drops of each oil with fractionated coconut oil in a 10 ml roller bottle and apply over the affected joint(s). Take 2 Deep Blue® Polyphenol Complex capsules per day with food. Uses Deep Blue® Rub or Deep Blue® Stick over the affected area as needed.

- Take Lifelong Vitality Supplements twice a day, 2-3 DigestZen TerraZyme® capsules at each meal, and PB Assist® once per day. Eat a variety of fresh fruits, vegetables, lean meats, healthy fats, and rice. Avoid MSG, gluten, corn, fried food, fast food, processed foods, and artificial sweeteners.

MUSCLE STIFFNESS

4-5x per day	**As needed**

Essential Oils: *Marjoram, AromaTouch®, Copaiba, Frankincense, Siberian Fir, PastTense®*

Other Solutions: *Lifelong Vitality, DigestZen TerraZyme®, PB Assist®+, Deep Blue® Rub, Deep Blue® Stick, Deep Blue® Polyphenol Complex*

- Choose 2-3 of the recommended oils. Mix 5-7 drops of each oil with fractionated coconut oil in a 10 ml roller bottle and apply over the affected joint(s). Take 2 Deep Blue® Polyphenol Complex capsules per day with food. Use Deep Blue® Rub or Deep Blue® Stick over the affected area as needed.

- Take Lifelong Vitality Supplements twice a day, 2-3 DigestZen TerraZyme® capsules at each meal, and PB Assist® once per day. Eat a variety of fresh fruits, vegetables, lean meats, healthy fats, and rice. Avoid MSG, gluten, corn, fried food, fast food, processed foods, and artificial sweeteners.

M-O

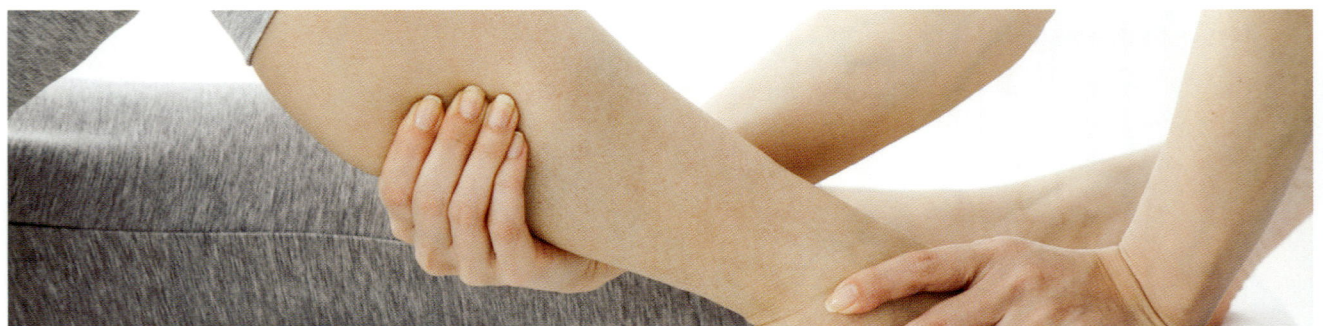

NAUSEA

| 🕐 **3-5x per day** | 📅 *Ongoing until symptoms lessen* |

Essential Oils: *Ginger, Peppermint, Cardamom, Spearmint, DigestZen®*

Other Solutions: *Ginger Drops, Peppermint Beadlets*

 Apply 1-2 drops of each recommended oil behind your ears and over your navel hourly, diffuse 4-5 drops each of the recommended oils into the air and inhale, or place 1 drop of each recommended oil in a veggie capsule and take upon onset of symptoms. Combine 10 drops each of Ginger and Peppermint or 10 drops each of Spearmint and DigestZen® in a 10 ml roller bottle with fractionated coconut oil. Apply to your abdominal area as needed. You can also place 1 drop of Spearmint or Peppermint on your tongue once symptoms start. Take Ginger Drops as needed. Take Peppermint Beadlets as desired.

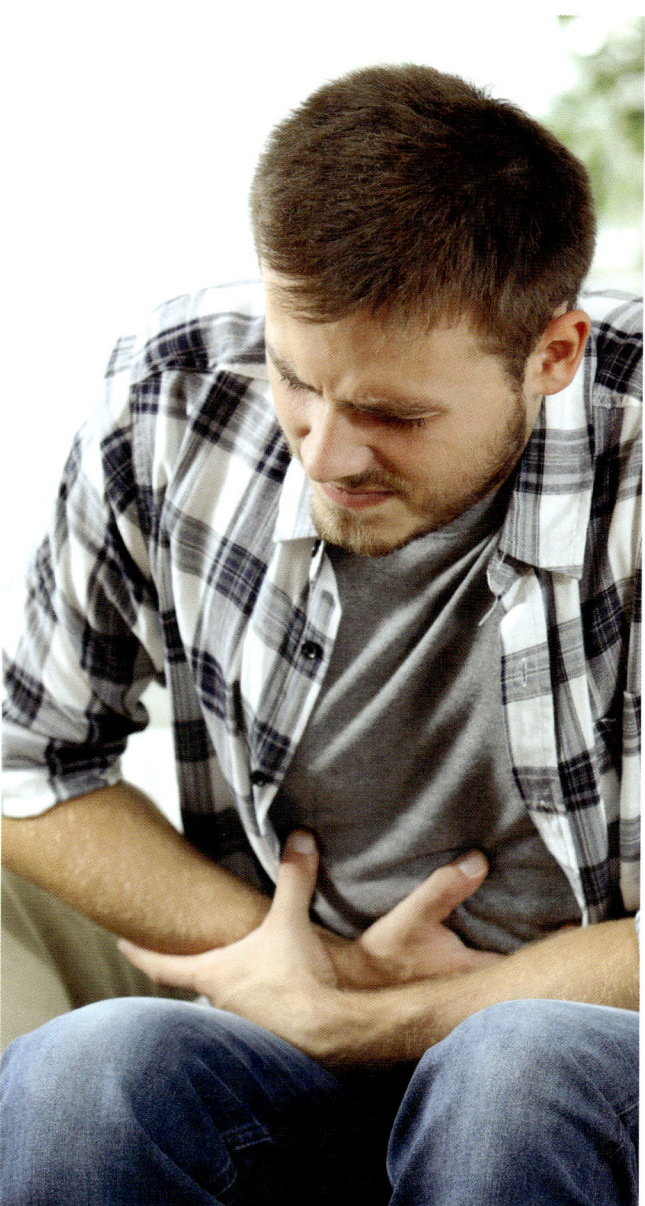

M-O

NECK PAIN

⏰ *4-5x per day*	📅 *As needed*

Essential Oils: *Marjoram, AromaTouch®, Turmeric, Copaiba, Frankincense, Siberian Fir, PastTense®*

Other Solutions: *Lifelong Vitality, DigestZen TerraZyme®, PB Assist®+, Serenity® Softgels, Deep Blue® Rub, Deep Blue® Stick, Deep Blue® Polyphenol Complex*

 Choose 2-3 of the recommended oils. Mix 5-7 drops of each oil with fractionated coconut oil in a 10 ml roller bottle and apply over your neck. Use a PastTense® roller down your neck and the top of your shoulders, under the ridge of your skull, and behind your ears a few times per day. Take 2 Deep Blue® Polyphenol Complex capsules per day with food. Use Deep Blue® Rub or Deep Blue® Stick over the affected area as needed. After applying the oils, lay on your back with a rolled up towel behind your neck. Lay in this position, with your neck in extension, for about 15 minutes and take deep breaths.

 Take Lifelong Vitality Supplements twice a day, 2-3 DigestZen TerraZyme® capsules at each meal, and PB Assist® once per day. Eat a variety of fresh fruits, vegetables, lean meats, healthy fats, and rice. Avoid MSG, gluten, corn, fried food, fast food, processed, foods, and artificial sweeteners.

M-O

NERVOUS FATIGUE

 4-5x per day | *As needed*

Essential Oils: *Peppermint, Rosemary, Basil, Black Pepper, Tangerine*

Other Solutions: *Lifelong Vitality, DigestZen TerraZyme®, PB Assist®+, Serenity® Softgels, Phytoestrogen Essential Complex, Greens, Protein*

Mix 5 drops of each recommended oil with fractionated coconut oil in a 10 ml roller bottle or a 2-ounce spray bottle. Apply topically over your chest, on your wrists, and along your spine with a focus under each side of the rib cage. Use every 4 hours until symptoms resolve. Combine 1 drop of each recommended oil in a veggie capsule with a carrier oil. Take twice daily morning and evening. Diffuse 3 drops of Tangerine and 2 drops each of Basil and Peppermint in the air and inhale. Do not use Peppermint right before bed.

Consume leafy greens, broccoli, legumes, calcium, selenium, omega oils, free-range poultry, grass-fed beef, walnuts, prunes, pumpkin seeds, flaxseed, cashews, B vitamins, bananas, seafood, chia seeds, citrus fruits, ripe fruits, antioxidants, almonds, maca root, whole grain bread, cereals, rice, and vitamins D, A, C, and E. Take 1-2 capsules of Phytoestrogen Essential Complex per day with food. Take Lifelong Vitality Supplements twice a day; 2-3 DigestZen TerraZyme® capsules at each meal; PB Assist® once per day; Lemon oil in water (2 drops per glass); and 1 scoop of Greens in a morning smoothie that includes berries, baby spinach, 1 scoop of vanilla Protein, and 1 cup almond milk.

Do 45 minutes of aerobic activity at your own pace. Start by taking a brisk walk and move up from there (if you feel up to it). Once symptoms lessen, follow the strength training recommendations on page 394 of the Exercise chapter.

Get 7-9 hours of sleep per night for rest and recovery. Apply 1-2 drops of Serenity® and Lavender to your pillow at bedtime. Take 1-2 Serenity® Softgels 30 minutes before bed.

Continue to work with your medical provider for this condition.

M-O

NERVOUSNESS

Daily as needed | *Ongoing while symptoms persist*

Essential Oils: *Hygge™, Bergamot, Serenity®, Balance®, Basil, Adaptiv™ (3-part system), Ylang Ylang, Vetiver, Roman Chamomile, Lavender*

Other Solutions: *Adaptiv™ Capsules, Lifelong Vitality, DigestZen TerraZyme®, PB Assist®+, Serenity® Softgels*

Diffuse 3-4 drops each of Hygge™, Bergamot, Basil, Balance®, and Vetiver throughout the day. Mix 5-7 drops each of Roman Chamomile, Bergamot, Vetiver, and Ylang Ylang with fractionated coconut oil in a 10 ml roller bottle. Rub it down your neck, over your spine, over your wrist pulse points, and on the bottoms of your feet often throughout the day. Buy a diffuser necklace or place a combination of any of the oils on a cotton ball. When you experience the first sign of anxiety, inhale the oils from the cotton ball or necklace and take slow, deep breaths. Do this as often as needed throughout the day. Take Adaptiv™ Capsules as directed. Use an Adaptiv™ roller alone or rotate its use with the homemade roller throughout the day.

Take Lifelong Vitality Supplements twice a day, 2-3 DigestZen TerraZyme® capsules at each meal, and PB Assist® once per day. Eat a variety of fresh fruits, vegetables, lean meats, healthy fats, and rice. Avoid MSG, gluten, corn, fried food, fast food, processed foods, and artificial sweeteners.

Apply 1 drop of Serenity® or Lavender to your pillow at bedtime. Take 1-1-2 Serenity® Softgels 30 minutes before bed. Meditate frequently throughout the week. Get a meditation app or adopt practices recommended in the Rest and Manage Stress chapter (page 410). Take a sauna. Take a long walk. Take deep diaphragmatic breaths often throughout the day.

Makeover your home by using the Abōde™ line of cleaning products, laundry pods, dishwasher pods, surface cleaner, and dish soap. Take care of your hands with Abōde™ Foaming Hand Wash and Lotion. Do a 30-day cleanse each season. See the 30-day cleanse on page 434.

M-O

NEURALGIA

4-5x per day	*Until symptoms resolve*

Essential Oils: *PastTense® roller, Frankincense, Lavender, Wild Orange, Clove, Helichrysum, Copaiba*

Other Solutions: *Turmeric Dual Chamber Capsules*

 Combine 5 drops each of Frankincense, Lavender, Wild Orange, Clove, and Helichrysum with fractionated coconut oil in a 10 ml roller bottle. Apply to the affected area 3 times per day. Rub a PastTense® roller over the affected area 2 times per day or until symptoms diminish. Place 2 drops each of Copaiba and Frankincense under your tongue 2 times per day, morning and evening. Take 2 Turmeric Dual Chamber Capsules daily.

NEUROPATHY

4-5x per day	*Until symptoms improve*

Essential Oils: *Cypress, AromaTouch®, Wintergreen, Deep Blue®, Basil*

Other Solutions: *Lifelong Vitality, DigestZen TerraZyme®, PB Assist®+, Serenity® Softgels, Deep Blue® Rub, Deep Blue® Stick, Deep Blue® Polyphenol Complex*

 Apply a few drops topically to affected areas several times daily.

 Take Lifelong Vitality Supplements twice a day, 2-3 DigestZen TerraZyme® capsules at each meal, and PB Assist® once per day. Take 2 Deep Blue® Polyphenol Complex capsules per day with food. Use Deep Blue® Rub or Deep Blue® Stick over the affected area as needed. Eat a variety of fresh fruits, vegetables, lean meats, healthy fats, and rice. Avoid MSG, gluten, corn, fried food, fast food, processed foods, and artificial sweeteners.

M-O

NIGHT SWEATS

⏰ **3-5x per day**	📅 **As needed**

Essential Oils: *DDR Prime®, Lime, Peppermint , Clary Sage, ClaryCalm®, Whisper®, Spearmint, Jasmine roller*

Other Solutions: *N/A*

 Combine 5-7 drops each of DDR Prime®, Lime, and Peppermint or 5-7 drops each of Spearmint and Clary Sage with fractionated coconut oil in a 10 ml roller bottle. Apply over your lower abdominal region, on your feet, and along your spine in the lower back area 2 times per day. Rotate between using a ClaryCalm® roller and a Jasmine roller throughout the day in-between using the homemade roller. Diffuse 5 drops of Whisper® throughout the day.

M-O

NIGHTTIME URINATION

 2-3x per day

 An hour before bed, at bedtime, and anytime you wake up in the middle of the night

Essential Oils: *Rosemary, Copaiba, Cypress, Juniper Berry, Thyme*

Other Solutions: *Serenity® Softgels*

⊘ Choose 2-3 of the recommended oils. Mix 5-7 drops of each oil in a 10 ml roller bottle and fill with fractionated coconut oil. Apply over your lower abdomen, lower back, and the bottoms of your feet morning and night.

⊘ Drink water throughout the day, but avoid drinking too much liquid within 2 hours of bed. Don't eat or drink caffeine, chocolate milk, or chocolate later in the day.

⊕ Opt for an earlier sleep time and develop a good sleep routine. Take 1 Serenity® Softgel an hour before bed when winding down for the evening. Avoid electronics too close to bedtime.

NOSEBLEED

 As long as needed upon initial onset of symptoms, or 3-5x per day if condition is a common occurrence

⊘ *Until symptoms resolve*

Essential Oils: *Helichrysum, Geranium, Lemon, Myrrh, Lavender*

Other Solutions: *N/A*

 Combine 5 drops each of Helichrysum, Geranium, Cypress, Lemon, and Myrrh in a 10 ml roller bottle with fractionated coconut oil. Shake well and swipe the roller starting at the top of your nose down to the bottom, swipe down the right and left sides of your nose, and swipe under your nose. Continue until symptoms lessen.

⊕ If your nosebleed is the result of an injury or broken nose, seek medical attention without delay.

M-O

OBESITY

🕐 *4-5x per day*	📅 *As needed*

Essential Oils: *MetaPWR™, Cinnamon, Grapefruit, Ginger, Black Pepper, Breathe®*

Other Solutions: *Peppermint Beadlets, Lifelong Vitality, DigestZen TerraZyme®, PB Assist®+, Deep Blue® Rub, Turmeric Dual Chamber Capsules, Deep Blue® Polyphenol Complex, Mito2Max®, Protein, MetaPWR™ Softgels*

 Mix 5-7 drops of each recommended oil except Breathe® in a 10 ml roller bottle with fractionated coconut oil. Rub it over your pulse points, over your abdominal area, and along your spine. Diffuse 5-7 drops of MetaPWR™ and inhale throughout the day. Add 1-2 drops of MetaPWR™ or Grapefruit to your water daily. Take 3-5 MetaPWR™ Softgels daily. Drink Protein *(blend one scoop of shake mix with 1/2 cup of almond, rice, or soy milk or water until smooth and creamy)*. Take Peppermint Beadlets as desired for sugar cravings.

 Take Lifelong Vitality Supplements twice a day, 2-3 DigestZen TerraZyme® capsules at each meal, and PB Assist® once per day. Eat a variety of fresh fruits, vegetables, lean meats, healthy fats, sweet potatoes, and brown rice. Avoid refined sugar, MSG, gluten, corn, fried food, fast food, processed foods, and artificial sweeteners. Pay attention to how you feel when you are eating your food. Stop eating if you feel full. Eat when you feel truly hungry. Eat fiber- and protein-filled foods that make you feel full.

Exercise 3 days a week for 20 minutes to start *(walking, swimming, yoga, biking, and cross-country skiing are good choices)*. Work up to 45 minutes for 4-5 days a week. Use Breathe® on your chest if your breathing is altered due to excess weight. Do strength training 3-4 times per week, starting with light weights and working your way up to heavier weights. Warm up, cool down, and stretch for each exercise session. Apply Deep Blue® Rub after exercise. Take 1 Mito2Max® with breakfast and lunch. If sore, take 2 Deep Blue® Polyphenol Complex capsules or 2 Turmeric Dual Chamber Capsules. Work at your own pace. Rest when needed. Take baby steps in this area.

M-O

OBSESSIVE COMPULSIVE DISORDER *(OCD)*

3-5x per day	*Ongoing as needed*

Essential Oils: *Frankincense, Geranium, Rosemary, Cedarwood, Black Pepper, Ylang Ylang, Hygge™*

Other Solutions: *N/A*

 Choose 3-4 of the recommended oils. Mix 10 drops of each with fractionated coconut oil in a 10 ml roller bottle. Rub it over your upper back, the back of your neck, your wrist pulse points, and your feet. Diffuse 3-4 drops of each chosen oil throughout the day.

Take time to breathe deeply often throughout the day. Do meditation and yoga. Keep a journal to track how you feel. Apply the recommended oils as directed. Take Epsom salt baths. Reduce stress.

OILY HAIR

Daily or 3x per week	*Ongoing until symptoms improve*

Essential Oils: *Petitgrain, Citronella, Lemon, Tea Tree, Arborvitae, Rosemary, Elevation*

Other Solutions: *Salon Essentials Protecting Shampoo, Salon Essentials Smoothing Conditioner, Healthy Hold Glaze, Yarrow|Pom Body Renewal Serum, Yarrow|Pom Botanical Nutritive Duo capsules, Lifelong Vitality, DigestZen TerraZyme®, PB Assist®+*

 Use Protecting Shampoo and Smoothing Conditioner to clean your hair. Apply Healthy Hold Glaze to damp hair. Choose 3-4 of the recommended oils. Put 1-2 drops of each oil into your palm with 1 teaspoon of fractionated coconut oil. Rub your palms together and apply from the middle to the ends of your hair *(dry or wet)* daily or 3 times per week. Leave it in your hair for at least 20 minutes. Shampoo, rinse, and style as usual. You may also use a dry shampoo during the day and use this blend before you go to bed. Massage Yarrow|Pom Body Renewal Serum on your scalp after washing. Take 2 Yarrow|Pom Botanical Nutritive Duo capsules per day.

Take Lifelong Vitality Supplements twice a day, 2-3 DigestZen TerraZyme® capsules at each meal, and PB Assist® once per day. Eat a variety of fresh fruits *(like blueberries, kiwi, and guava)*, carrots, almond butter, lentils, oysters, lean meat, healthy fats, barley, and rice. Avoid MSG, high amounts of sugar, and swordfish *(high amounts of mercury may be linked to hair health)*. Avoid processed foods, artificial sweeteners, and starchy foods.

M-O

ORAL HEALTH

| ⏰ *2x per day and after meals* | 📅 *Ongoing* |

Essential Oils: *Clove, Cinnamon Bark, Myrrh, Tea Tree, Spearmint, On Guard®*

Other Solutions: *On Guard® Natural Whitening Toothpaste, On Guard® Mouthwash, Peppermint Beadlets*

 Combine 1 drop of Cinnamon Bark, Spearmint, or Myrrh in 2 ounces of water. Shake well and gargle twice daily. Use On Guard® toothpaste and On Guard® Mouthwash every morning and evening. Soak your dental floss in warm salt water with either 1 drop of Tea Tree or 1 drop of On Guard® for 5 minutes. Floss after each meal as well as prior to bed and upon waking. Brush your tongue each time you brush your teeth. Place 1 drop of Clove, Cinnamon Bark, or On Guard® on your toothbrush prior to brushing your tongue or teeth. Use Peppermint Beadlets during the day to combat bad breath.

🌱 Eliminate sugar and refined carbohydrates. Avoid sticky candies and sweets like lollipops, caramels, and sugary cough drops. Avoid starchy foods that can get stuck in your mouth, like potato chips. If you eat sugar, eat it with a meal. Eat nuts and seeds as well as salmon and other fatty fish. Eat grass-fed beef, red and green bell peppers, broccoli, sweet potatoes, and probiotic-containing foods (*such as kefir, sauerkraut, fermented yogurt, and kimchi*).

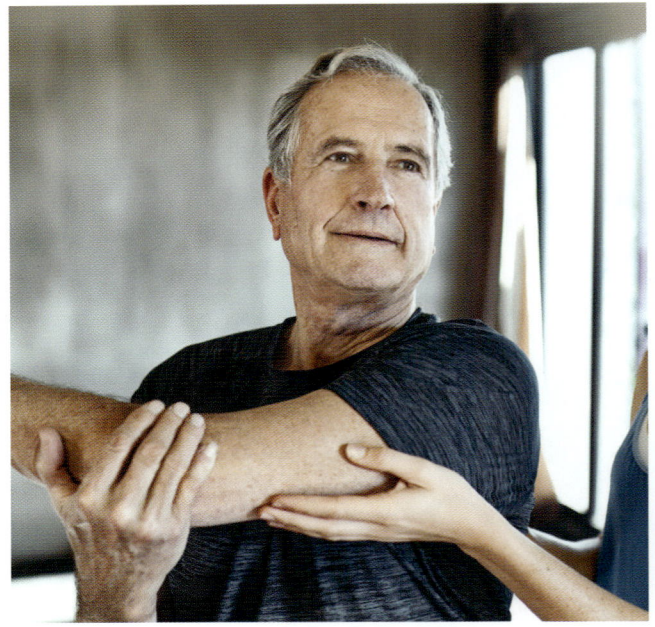

OSTEOARTHRITIS

| ⏰ *4-5x per day* | 📅 *As needed* |

Essential Oils: *Siberian Fir, Wintergreen, Deep Blue®, Marjoram, Cypress, Copaiba, Lemongrass, Frankincense*

Other Solutions: *Deep Blue® Polyphenol Complex, Deep Blue® Rub, Deep Blue® Stick*

 Choose 2-3 of the recommended oils. Mix 5-7 drops of each oil with fractionated coconut oil in a 10 ml roller bottle and apply over the affected area. Take 2 Deep Blue® Polyphenol Complex capsules per day with food. Uses Deep Blue® Rub or Deep Blue® Stick over the affected area as needed.

M-O

OSTEOPOROSIS

 4-5x per day | **Ongoing as needed**

Essential Oils: *Lemongrass, Clove, Geranium, Ginger, Siberian Fir, Black Pepper, Frankincense, Rosemary, Thyme, DDR Prime®, Peppermint, Copaiba*

Other Solutions: *Lifelong Vitality, DigestZen TerraZyme®, PB Assist®+, Serenity® Softgels, Turmeric Dual Chamber Capsules, Bone Nutrient Essential Complex, Phytoestrogen Essential Complex*

⊻ Choose 3-4 of the recommended oils. Mix 10 drops of each oil with fractionated coconut oil in a 10 ml roller bottle. Rub it along your entire spine and on your feet. You can also apply it to your knees, elbows, wrists, or other areas of concern. Take Lifelong Vitality Supplements twice a day. Pre- an peri-menopausal women should take 1-2 Phytoestrogen Essential Complex capsules daily with food. Post-menopausal women should take 2 capsules daily with food. Take 4 Bone Nutrient Essential Complex capsules daily with food. Take 2 Turmeric Dual Chamber Capsules daily (one capsule with two separate meals).

✚ Aim to get 7-9 hours of sleep per night for rest and recovery. Take 1-2 Serenity® Softgels 30 minutes before bed. Take a break from electronics throughout the day. Apply 1 drop of Frankincense over your forehead and meditate 3-4 times per week. Check in with your emotions and use the emotional blends as needed throughout the day.

OVARIAN CYST

 3x per day and nightly before bed | **As needed until symptoms resolve**

Essential Oils: *Frankincense, Clary Sage, Basil, Copaiba*

Other Solutions: *N/A*

⊻ Combine 10 drops each of Frankincense, Clary Sage, Copaiba, and Basil with fractionated coconut oil in a 10 ml roller bottle. Apply below your navel area and on your lower back 3 times per day. Apply once more prior to bed. Place 2 drops each of Copaiba and Frankincense under your tongue 2 times per day, morning and evening.

M-O

OVEREATING

⏰ *3-5x per day*	📅 *As needed*

Essential Oils: *MetaPWR™, Peppermint, Grapefruit, Lemon, Ginger, Cinnamon, Patchouli*

Other Solutions: *Peppermint Beadlets, MetaPWR™ Softgels, MetaPWR™ Metabolic Gum, Lifelong Vitality, DigestZen TerraZyme®, PB Assist®+, Serenity® Softgels*

🌿 Place 2 drops of MetaPWR™ in your water 2-3 times per day and drink. Mix 5-7 drops each of Grapefruit, MetaPWR™, Ginger, and Patchouli in a 10 ml roller bottle and fill with fractionated coconut oil. Apply over your heart, stomach, abdomen, spine, and the bottoms of your feet morning and night. Put 1 drop of Peppermint on your tongue when craving sweets to prevent overeating. Take 1 MetaPWR™ Softgel before meals. Chew MetaPWR™ Metabolic Gum in-between meals. Take Peppermint Beadlets for sugar cravings. Take 1 MetaPWR™ Softgel at meals.

🔄 Take Lifelong Vitality Supplements twice a day, 2-3 DigestZen TerraZyme® capsules at each meal, and PB Assist® once per day. Adopt the 80/20 rule when it comes to eating: eat healthily 80 percent of the time and let yourself have whatever you want 20 percent of the time.

🌙 Apply 1 drop of Serenity® or Lavender to your pillow at bedtime. Take 1-2 Serenity® Softgels 30 minutes before bed. Use emotional oils as needed throughout the day. Include meditation, prayer, and spending time in nature as part of your regular routine to rest and manage your stress. Join an online support group or reach out to friends and family for help as needed.

➕ Don't struggle alone. Reach out for professional help if you feel you are out of control with your eating.

M-O

PAIN

4-5x per day	*As needed*

Essential Oils: *Deep Blue®, Copaiba, Wintergreen, Lavender*

Other Solutions: *Deep Blue® Rub, Deep Blue® Stick, Lifelong Vitality, DigestZen TerraZyme®, PB Assist®+, Turmeric Dual Chamber Capsules, Deep Blue® Polyphenol Complex*

● Choose 2 of the recommended oils. Mix 1-2 drops of each oil with 1 tablespoon of fractionated coconut oil. Apply over the affected area throughout the day. Take 2 Deep Blue® Polyphenol Complex capsules per day, once in the morning and once in the evening. Take 2 Turmeric Dual Chamber Capsules per day as needed. Use Deep Blue® Rub or Deep Blue ®Stick over affected area.

● Take Lifelong Vitality Supplements twice a day, 2-3 DigestZen TerraZyme® capsules at each meal, and PB Assist® once per day. Eat a variety of fresh fruits, vegetables, lean meats, healthy fats, sweet potatoes, and rice. Avoid inflammatory foods such as MSG, gluten, corn, fried food, fast food, processed foods, and artificial sweeteners.

● Do a combination of aerobic exercises, strength training, and balance exercises.

● Place 1 drop of Lavender on your pillow at night. Turn off electronic devices an hour or two before bed. Apply the recommended oils to the affected area before bed or during the night if the pain wakes you.

● If tolerated, do a 30-day cleanse each season. See the 30-day cleanse on page 434.

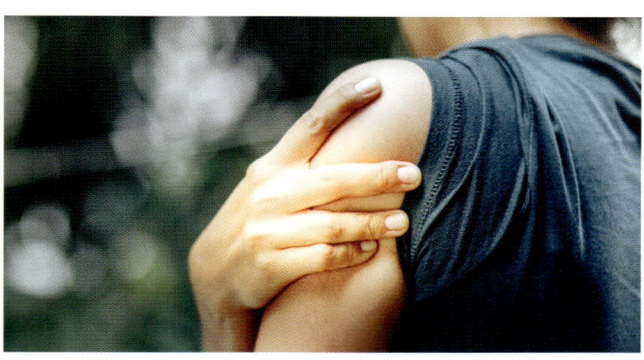

PALPITATIONS

3-5x per day	*Ongoing until symptoms lessen*

Essential Oils: *Lavender, Wild Orange, Ylang Ylang, Adaptiv™, Frankincense, Hygge™*

Other Solutions: *Serenity® Softgels*

● Combine 5 drops of each recommended oil in a 10 ml roller bottle and fill with fractionated coconut oil. Apply over your chest, down the front and back of your neck, and on the bottoms of your feet morning and evening. Diffuse 3-4 drops of each recommended oil and inhale Hygge™ throughout the day.

● Aim to get 7-9 hours of sleep per night for rest and recovery. Take 1-2 Serenity® Softgels 30 minutes before bed. Take a break from electronics throughout the day. Apply 1 drop of Frankincense over your forehead and meditate 3-4 times per week. Check in with your emotions and use the emotional blends as needed throughout the day.

P-R

PANCREATITIS

⏰ *4-5x per day*	📅 *Until condition improves*

Essential Oils: *Zendocrine®, Marjoram, Coriander, Frankincense*

Other Solutions: *Ginger Drops, Peppermint Beadlets*

🌫 Mix 5-7 drops each of Zendocrine®, Marjoram, Coriander, and Frankincense with fractionated coconut oil in a 10 ml roller bottle. Apply over your abdomen, lower back, and feet. Place 1 drop of each recommended oil in a veggie capsule and take 3 times per day. Take Ginger Drops as needed. Take Peppermint Beadlets as desired.

PANIC ATTACKS

⏰ *3-5x per day*	📅 *While symptoms persist*

Essential Oils: *Petitgrain, Serenity®, Neroli Touch, Bergamot, Balance®, Hygge™, Adaptiv™ roller*

Other Solutions: *Adaptiv™ Capsules, Serenity® Softgels*

🌫 Take 1 Adaptiv™ Capsule daily with food. Apply an Adaptiv™ roller over your heart, down the back of your neck, and on your pulse points throughout the day. Choose 2-3 of the recommended oils, include Hygge™. Diffuse 4-5 drops of each oil. Mix 5-7 drops of each chosen oil in a 10 ml roller bottle with fractionated coconut oil. Rub over your heart, down the back of your neck, on your temples, over your pulse points, and on the bottoms of your feet morning and evening. Put 1-2 drops of Bergamot in your water and drink.

🌙 Place 1 drop of Serenity® on your pillow at night or take 2 Serenity® Softgels at bedtime.

P-R

PARASITES

2-3x per day	**Until symptoms resolve**

Essential Oils: *Oregano, Clove, Zendocrine®*

Other Solutions: *N/A*

 Combine 10 drops of each recommended oil with fractionated coconut oil in a 10 ml roller bottle. Apply over your intestinal area 2-3 times daily and then place a warm compress over the area. Place 1 drop of each recommended oil in a veggie capsule and take 3 times per day until the condition resolves. After day 10 of taking the veggie capsule, stop adding Oregano, and wait 10 days until adding it again. Diffuse 3-4 drops of each recommended oil throughout the day.

PARKINSON'S DISEASE

3-5x per day	*Ongoing*

Essential Oils: *Frankincense, Copaiba, Zendocrine®, Marjoram, Melissa, DDR Prime®*

Other Solutions: *Lifelong Vitality, DigestZen TerraZyme®, PB Assist®+, Serenity® Softgels, Turmeric Dual Chamber Capsules, Deep Blue® Polyphenol Complex*

 Put 1 drop each of Frankincense and Copaiba under your tongue morning and evening. Choose 2-3 of the recommended oils. Mix 5-7 drops of each in a 10 ml roller bottle and fill with fractionated coconut oil. Apply topically down your spine, over your heart, over your temples, and under the ridge of your skull. Take 2 Turmeric Dual Chamber Capsules per day.

Eat a healthy diet. Take Lifelong Vitality Supplements twice a day, 2-3 DigestZen TerraZyme® capsules at each meal, and PB Assist® once per day. Eat a variety of fresh fruits, vegetables, lean meats, healthy fats, sweet potatoes, and rice. Avoid inflammatory foods such as MSG, gluten, corn, fried food, fast food, processed foods, and artificial sweeteners.

Get regular exercise combining cardio, strength, balance, and flexibility exercises.

Stick to a regular sleep routine. Aim to get 7-9 hours of sleep each night. Take 2 Serenity® Softgels before bed.

P-R

PEPTIC ULCER

🕐	*Use roller bottle 3-5x daily and use Zendo-crine® internally daily*	📅	*Ongoing while symptoms persist*

Essential Oils: *Zendocrine®, Frankincense, Wintergreen, Lemongrass, Clove*

Other Solutions: *Ginger Drops, Peppermint Beadlets*

 Add 1-2 drops of Zendocrine® to a citrus drink, tea, or water and drink. Put 2 drops of Frankincense under your tongue twice per day, morning and evening. Combine 10 drops each of Lemongrass, Clove, Wintergreen, and Frankincense in a 10 ml roller bottle topped off with fractionated coconut oil. Apply to your abdominal region, along your spine in the center of your back, and on your feet. Take Ginger Drops as needed. Take Peppermint Beadlets as desired.

P-R

PERIMENOPAUSE

3-5x per day	*As needed*

Essential Oils: *ClaryCalm®, Clary Sage, Whisper®, Ylang Ylang, Tulsi, Jasmine, Geranium, Sandalwood, Lavender*

Other Solutions: *Lifelong Vitality, DigestZen TerraZyme®, PB Assist®+, Serenity® Softgels, Phytoestrogen Essential Complex, Bone Nutrient Essential Complex*

⬇ Combine 5-7 drops of Sandalwood, Geranium, Tulsi, Ylang Ylang, and Clary Sage with fractionated coconut oil in a 10 ml roller bottle. Apply over your lower abdominal region, on your feet, and along your spine in the lower back area 2 times per day. Rotate between using a ClaryCalm® roller and a Jasmine roller throughout the day in-between using the homemade roller. Diffuse 5 drops of Whisper® throughout the day.

⊕ Take 1-2 Phytoestrogen Essential Complex capsules daily with food. Post-menopausal women should take 2 Phytoestrogen Essential Complex capsules daily with food. Take 4 Bone Nutrient Essential Complex capsules daily with food. Take Lifelong Vitality Supplements twice a day, 2-3 DigestZen TerraZyme® capsules at each meal, and PB Assist® once per day. Consume avocados, flaxseed, broccoli, pomegranate, salmon, leafy greens, nuts, organic soy, turmeric, quinoa, and brown rice. Avoid excess sugar, simple carbohydrates, trans fats, and processed foods.

⬇ Place 1 drop of Lavender or Serenity® on your pillow at night. Take 2 Serenity® Softgels at bedtime.

⬇ Makeover your home by using the Abōde™ line of cleaning products, laundry pods, dishwasher pods, surface cleaner, and dish soap. Take care of your hands with Abōde™ Foaming Hand Wash and Lotion. Do a 30-day cleanse each season. See the 30-day cleanse on page 434.

PET ALLERGIES

3-5x per day	*During allergy season or when symptoms appear*

Essential Oils: *Lemon, Lavender, Peppermint, DigestZen®*

Other Solutions: *Lifelong Vitality, DigestZen TerraZyme®, PB Assist®+, TriEase® Softgels*

⬇ Diffuse 4 drops each of Lemon, Lavender, and Peppermint when at home or at work. Add 5-7 drops of each recommended oil to a 10 ml roller bottle and fill the rest with fractionated coconut oil. Rub over your temples and forehead, behind your ears, and over your thymus. Take 1-2 TriEase® Softgels as needed. Mix 1 drop of DigestZen® with 10 drops of fractionated coconut oil. Rub over your sinuses and temples morning and evening.

⊕ Take Lifelong Vitality Supplements twice a day, 2-3 DigestZen TerraZyme® capsules at each meal, and PB Assist® once per day. Drink 2 drops of Lemon in water.

P-R

PET ALLERGIES

⏰ **3-5x per day**	📅 *During allergy season or when symptoms appear*

Essential Oils: *Lemon, Lavender, Peppermint, DigestZen®*

Other Solutions: *Lifelong Vitality, DigestZen TerraZyme®, PB Assist®+, TriEase® Softgels*

 Diffuse 4 drops each of Lemon, Lavender, and Peppermint when at home or at work. Add 5-7 drops of each recommended oil to a 10 ml roller bottle and fill the rest with fractionated coconut oil. Rub over your temples and forehead, behind your ears, and over your thymus. Take 1-2 TriEase® Softgels as needed. Mix 1 drop of DigestZen® with 10 drops of fractionated coconut oil. Rub over your sinuses and temples morning and evening.

 Take Lifelong Vitality Supplements twice a day, 2-3 DigestZen TerraZyme® capsules at each meal, and PB Assist® once per day. Drink 2 drops of Lemon in water.

P-R

PLANTAR FASCIITIS

 3-5x per day   *Ongoing as needed*

Essential Oils: *Lemongrass, Copaiba, Wintergreen, AromaTouch®, Siberian Fir*

Other Solutions: *Deep Blue® Rub, Deep Blue® Stick*

- Combine 5 drops of each recommended oil in a 10 ml roller with fractionated coconut oil. Gently apply to the affected area frequently throughout the day. Use Deep Blue® Rub or Deep Blue® Stick in-between using the roller. Ice and elevate the affected area for 20 minutes 2-5 times per day, and immediately after the injury if possible. Massage your foot by using a tennis ball or warm rolled towel. Place the tennis ball or the rolled towel on the ball of your foot and move your foot around to massage the area. You can also rub your thumb along the arch of the affected foot. You can also place 2 drops of each recommended oil onto the rolled towel or use the roller bottle immediately after stretching/warming the affected area.

- Rest your foot by taking 2-3 weeks off from repetitive motions that may have caused the condition or that intensify pain. Stretch your toes by doing the following: cross your affected leg over your unaffected leg.; take a hold of your affected foot and pull your toes back toward your shin; hold for 10 seconds. Repeat 10 times.

PLANTAR WARTS

 3-5x per day   *While symptoms persist*

Essential Oils: *DDR Prime®, Purify, Oregano, Frankincense, On Guard® roller*

Other Solutions: *On Guard™+ Softgels*

- Combine 10 drops of each recommended oil in a 10 ml roller bottle topped off with fractionated coconut oil. Apply directly onto the wart(s) several times per day. Cover the wart(s) with a bandage if you need to wear shoes right away. Take 2 On Guard™+ Softgels daily. Be patient, as warts can take weeks to months to disappear. If warts are a frequent issue, take On Guard™+ Softgels daily along and use the On Guard® roller 3 times per day. Avoid contact with the warts *(yours or others)*; do not touch them with your bare hands, because this can lead to warts on your fingers. Keep your feet clean and dry, and change your socks and footwear every day. Always wear shoes or sandals when walking around public swimming pools or gym showers *(these are common areas of wart-causing virus exposure)*.

P-R

PNEUMONIA

4-5x per day	*Ongoing while symptoms persist*

Essential Oils: *On Guard®, Breathe®, Roman Chamomile, Eucalyptus, Peppermint, Thyme, Lavender, Ginger*

Other Solutions: *On Guard® Beadlets, On Guard™+ Softgels, On Guard® Tablets*

Choose 3-4 of the recommended oils. Mix 10 drops of each oil with fractionated coconut oil in a 10 ml roller bottle. Rub it over the front and back of your chest area, over the top of the lung field. Use every 2-3 hours or until symptoms diminish. Diffuse 3-4 drops of each recommended oil throughout the day. Take 2 On Guard™+ Softgels twice per day. Take On Guard® Beadlets as desired. Take up to 3 On Guard® Tablets per day.

P-R

POISON IVY

⏰ **3-5x per day**	📅 *While symptoms persist*

Essential Oils: *Frankincense, Lavender, Geranium, Roman Chamomile*

Other Solutions: *N/A*

 Create a compress by wetting a soft cloth with cold water and 2 tablespoons of apple cider vinegar. Wring out the cloth leaving just enough water so it is not dripping. Wrap the compress around ice and add 1 drop of each recommended oil to the outside of the compress. Apply to the affected area several times a day for about 15 minutes. You can also combine 5 drops of each recommended oil in a 10 ml glass roller bottle topped off with fractionated coconut oil. Apply to the affected area several times per day.

POISON OAK/SUMAC

⏰ **4-5x per day**	📅 *While symptoms persist*

Essential Oils: *Geranium, Purify, Roman Chamomile, Lavender, Frankincense*

Other Solutions: *N/A*

 Add 5-7 drops of each recommended oil into a glass bowl with cold water and add 2 tablespoons of fractionated coconut oil. Stir the mixture together. Soak a clean washcloth in the mixture and wring the cloth out a little bit, keeping some of the water in the cloth but making sure it's not dripping. Apply over the affected area for 10-15 minutes. Repeat throughout the day.

P·R

 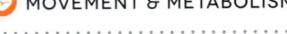
POLYCYSTIC OVARY SYNDROME (*PCOS*)

🕐 **3-5x per day**	📅 *As needed*

Essential Oils: *ClaryCalm®, Clary Sage, Thyme, Basil, Tulsi, Geranium, Zendocrine®, Lavender*

Other Solutions: *DDR Prime® Softgels, Serenity® Softgels, Phytoestrogen Essential Complex, Bone Nutrient Essential Complex, Lifelong Vitality, DigestZen TerraZyme®, PB Assist®+*

💜 Combine 5-7 drops each of Thyme, Basil, Tulsi Zendocrine®, Geranium, Ylang Ylang, and Clary Sage with fractionated coconut oil in a 10 ml roller bottle. Apply over your lower abdominal region, on your feet, and along your spine in the lower back area 2 times per day. Rotate between using this roller and a ClaryCalm® roller throughout the day. Take 1 DDR Prime® Softgel morning and evening.

🍏 Pre- and peri-menopausal women should take one 1-2 Phytoestrogen Essential Complex capsules daily with food. Post-menopausal women should take 2 Phytoestrogen Essential Complex capsules daily with food. Take 4 Bone Nutrient Essential Complex capsules daily with food. Take Lifelong Vitality Supplements twice a day, 2-3 DigestZen TerraZyme® capsules at each meal, and PB Assist® once per day. Consume avocados, flax-seed, broccoli, pomegranate, salmon, leafy greens, nuts, organic soy, turmeric, quinoa, and brown rice. Avoid excess sugar, simple carbohydrates, trans fats, and processed foods.

🌙 Place 1 drop of Lavender or Serenity® on your pillow at night. Take 2 Serenity® Softgels at bedtime.

🔻 Makeover your home by using the Abōde™ line of cleaning products, laundry pods, dishwasher pods, surface cleaner, and dish soap. Take care of your hands with Abōde™ Foaming Hand Wash and Lotion. Do a 30-day cleanse each season. See the 30-day cleanse on page 434.

POLYPS

3-5x per day	Ongoing as needed

Essential Oils: *Rosemary, Ginger, Peppermint, Clove, Lemongrass*

Other Solutions: *DDR Prime® Softgels*

● Take 2 DDR Prime® Softgels per day, 1 in the morning and 1 in the evening. Choose 2-3 of the recommended oils. Mix 5-7 drops of each oil in a 10 ml roller bottle and fill with fractionated coconut oil. Apply over the affected area.

POOR CIRCULATION

3x per day	As needed

Essential Oils: *AromaTouch®, Black Pepper, Cinnamon*

Other Solutions: *N/A*

● Choose 2 of the recommended oils. Apply topically to your hands and feet, the bottoms of your feet, and the affected area throughout the day.

POST-TRAUMATIC STRESS DISORDER *(PTSD)*

3-5x per day	As needed

Essential Oils: *Cedarwood, Peace®, Melissa, Balance®, Madagascar Vanilla, Roman Chamomile, Ylang Ylang, Hygge™*

Other Solutions: *N/A*

● Choose 3-5 of the recommended oils. Mix 5-7 drops of each with fractionated coconut oil in a 10 ml roller bottle. Rub it along your spine, over your wrists, on the back of your neck, and on your feet. Try mixing different combinations together to find an oil combination that works best for you. Diffuse 3 drops each of Melissa, Peace®, Hygge™, Madagascar Vanilla, and Ylang Ylang and inhale throughout the day.

● Continue to seek professional medical attention for the condition as needed, if relevant. Seek immediate medical attention if flashbacks, anxiety, or depressive symptoms worsen in any way or if suicidal thoughts are present.

P-R

POSTPARTUM DEPRESSION

⏰ *3-5x per day*	📅 *Ongoing as needed*

Essential Oils: *Melissa, ClaryCalm®, Clary Sage, Elevation, Cheer®, Frankincense, Adaptiv™ (3-part system), Neroli Touch, Serenity®, Lavender, Peppermint, Hygge™, Madagascar Vanilla*

Other Solutions: *Lifelong Vitality, Serenity® Softgels, DigestZen TerraZyme®, PB Assist®+, Adaptiv™ Capsule*

● Choose 2-3 of the recommended oils. Mix 5-7 drops of each in a 10 ml roller bottle and fill with fractionated coconut oil. Apply to the back of your neck, behind your ears, over your heart, and on the bottoms of your feet morning and evening. You can also use a Neroli Touch roller. Take 1 Adaptiv™ Capsule per day. Diffuse 5 drops of Adaptiv™ daily and inhale. Diffuse 3-5 drops each of Hygge™, Madagascar Vanilla, and Clary Sage throughout the day. Rotate between using an Adaptiv™ roller and the homemade roller throughout the day.

● Take Lifelong Vitality Supplements twice a day, 2-3 DigestZen TerraZyme® capsules at each meal, and PB Assist® once per day. Eat a variety of fresh fruits, vegetables, lean meats, healthy fats, and rice. Avoid MSG, gluten, corn, fried food, fast food, processed foods, and artificial sweeteners.

● Do a combination of aerobic exercises, strength training, and balance exercises.

● Place 1 drop of Lavender or Serenity® on your pillow at night. Take 2 Serenity® Softgels at bedtime. Turn off electronic devices an hour or two before bed. Avoid stressful conversations or television before meals or bed. Develop a good bedtime routine that feels relaxing to you. Find a hobby or meditation program. Listen to music, go for a walk in nature, or go out with friends. Increase the laughter in your life by watching a comedy or hanging with friends and family members who make you laugh. Schedule self-care rituals throughout the week that make you feel good.

● Makeover your home by using the Abōde™ line of cleaning products, laundry pods, dishwasher pods, surface cleaner, and dish soap. Take care of your hands with Abōde™ Foaming Hand Wash and Lotion. If tolerated, do a 30-day cleanse each season. See the 30-day cleanse on page 434.

P-R

PREGNANCY

⏰ **3-5x per day**	📅 *Ongoing during pregnancy*

Essential Oils: *DigestZen®, Cardamom, Ginger, Spearmint, Balance®, Serenity®, Ylang Ylang, Geranium, Lavender, Sandalwood, Breathe®, AromaTouch®*

Other Solutions: *DigestTab, Deep Blue® Rub, Deep Blue® Stick*

 For nausea: Add 25 drops of DigestZen® in a 10 ml roller with fractionated coconut oil. Rub over your abdominal region and on your feet daily. You can also combine 5 drops each of DigestZen®, Cardamom, Spearmint, and Ginger in a 10 ml roller bottle with fractionated coconut oil and apply the same way. Take DigestTab as needed.

For stress: Choose 3 of the following oils: Balance®, Serenity®, Ylang Ylang, Geranium, Lavender, or Sandalwood. Combine 10 drops of each chosen oil in a roller bottle with fractionated coconut oil. Apply to the back of your neck, your chest, your pulse points, and your feet daily. You can also diffuse 3-5 drops of each chosen oil and inhale throughout the day.

For respiratory support: diffuse 5 drops of Breathe® or add 25 drops of Breathe® to a 10 ml roller with fractionated coconut oil and apply over your chest.

For a sore back: Apply Deep Blue® Rub over the affected area or use the Deep Blue® Stick. You can also add 25 drops of AromaTouch® to a 10 ml roller with fractionated coconut oil and apply to the affected area.

P-R

PREMENSTRUAL SYNDROME (PMS)

 3-5x per day   *10 days before menstrual cycle and during cycle*

Essential Oils: *ClaryCalm®, Clary Sage, Magnolia, Rosemary, Marjoram, Lavender, Rose, Tulsi, Ylang Ylang, Geranium, Roman Chamomile*

Other Solutions: *Lifelong Vitality, DigestZen TerraZyme®, PB Assist®+, Phytoestrogen Essential Complex*

Choose 3-4 of the recommended oils. Mix 10 drops of each with fractionated coconut oil in a 10 ml roller bottle. Rub it over your abdominal region, along your spine in the lower back, and on your wrists and feet. Alternate between using this roller and a ClaryCalm® roller. Use a Magnolia roller for stress reduction as needed throughout the day, every 2-3 hours or until symptoms diminish. Apply to the back of your neck and your chest area. Diffuse 3-4 drops of each recommended oil throughout the day and inhale. Drink at least half your body weight in ounces of water per day.

Take Lifelong Vitality Supplements twice a day, 2-3 DigestZen TerraZyme® capsules at each meal, and PB Assist® once per day. Take 1-2 Phytoestrogen Essential Complex capsules daily with food. Consume avocado, flaxseed, broccoli, pomegranate, salmon, leafy greens, nuts, organic soy, turmeric, quinoa, and brown rice. Avoid excess sugar, simple carbohydrates, trans fats, and processed foods.

Do 30-45 minutes of aerobic exercise per day, preferably in nature/fresh air.

Aim to get 7-9 hours of sleep per night for rest and recovery. Take time to Breathe® deeply often throughout the day. Do meditation and yoga. Keep a journal to track how you feel. Take Epsom salt baths. Reduce stress.

Makeover your home by using the Abōde™ line of cleaning products, laundry pods, dishwasher pods, surface cleaner, and dish soap. Take care of your hands with Abōde™ Foaming Hand Wash and Lotion. If tolerated, do a 30-day cleanse each season. See the 30-day cleanse on page 434.

Seek professional medical attention if you have persistent PMS symptoms such as chronic depression, intense anger, and continual negative thoughts.

P-R

PROSTATITIS

 4-5x per day | *As needed*

Essential Oils: *Frankincense, Rosemary, Cypress, Juniper Berry, Lemon, Lemongrass, Basil*

Other Solutions: *DDR Prime® Softgels, Turmeric Dual Chamber Capsules*

💚 Choose 3-4 of the recommended oils. Combine 10 drops of each in a 10 ml roller bottle with fractionated coconut oil. Apply over your lower abdominal region, lower back, and feet several times per day. Take 2 Turmeric Dual Chamber Capsules daily with meals. Take 2 DDR Prime® Softgels daily.

P-R

PSORIASIS

⏰ *Every 4 hours*	📅 *Until symptoms diminish*

Essential Oils: *Turmeric, Rose, Zendocrine®, Lavender, Roman Chamomile, Geranium, Myrrh, Frankincense, Manuka*

Other Solutions: *Yarrow|Pom Body Renewal Serum, Yarrow|Pom Botanical Nutritive Duo , DigestZen TerraZyme®, DDR Prime® Softgels, Zendocrine® Complex, Zendocrine® Softgels, GX Assist®, PB Assist®+, On Guard® Cleaner Concentrate, On Guard® Natural Whitening Toothpaste, On Guard® Mouthwash*

😌 Choose 3-4 of the recommended oils. Mix 10 drops of each with fractionated coconut oil in a 10 ml roller bottle. Rub over the affected area every 4 hours or until symptoms diminish. Use a Rose 10 ml roller over the affected area 3 times per day. Apply Yarrow|Pom Body Renewal Serum on the affected area twice daily. Take 2 Yarrow|Pom Botanical Nutritive Duo capsules per day.

🍎 Eat organic, raw, cultured dairy (*kefir, yogurt*); cultured vegetables; seeds; fruits; herbs; beans; nuts; goji berries; wild blueberries; pecans; cilantro; kidney beans; grass-fed beef; lamb; pumpkin seeds; chickpeas; orange, yellow, and dark leafy green vegetables; cantaloupe; carrots; mango; tomatoes; kale; collard greens; watermelon; salmon; mackerel; herring; sardines; and omega-3 fatty acids. Take raw milk, turmeric, and aloe vera internally. Consider a gluten-free diet.

⬇️ Do this 30-day cleanse: take TerraZyme® at meals; put 2-3 drops of Lemon in your water 3-5 times per day; take 2 DDR Prime® Softgels with meals; take 1 Zendocrine® Complex with morning and evening meals; take 1 Zendocrine® Softgel with meals; take 1 GX Assist® at morning and evening meals for days 10-20; take 1 PB Assist® with meals on days 20-30. Take inventory of your home and remove toxic products. Replace your cleaning products with On Guard® Cleaner Concentrate. Use On Guard® toothpaste and mouthwash. Choose On Guard® cleaning products and organic foods as much as you can. Avoid pesticides, insecticides, heavy metals, toxic food chemicals, MSG, trans fats, fast foods, mold, synthetic vitamins, excess alcohol, and nicotine.

P-R

RADIATION DAMAGE

3-5x per day	*As needed*

Essential Oils: *Zendocrine®, Peppermint, Patchouli, Cilantro, Geranium, Tea Tree*

Other Solutions: *DDR Prime® Softgels*

 Combine 5 drops each of the recommended oils in a 10 ml roller bottle with fractionated coconut oil. Apply around the affected site.

RASH

3-5x per day	*As needed*

Essential Oils: *Frankincense, Tea Tree, Roman Chamomile, Lavender*

Other Solutions: *Yarrow|Pom Body Renewal Serum, Yarrow|Pom Botanical Nutritive Duo*

 Combine 5-7 drops of each recommended oil in a 10 ml roller bottle with fractionated coconut oil. Apply to the affected area several times per day. Place 1 drop of each recommended oil in a veggie capsule and take twice per day, morning and evening. Apply Yarrow|Pom Body Renewal Serum on the affected area twice daily and take 2 Yarrow|Pom Botanical Nutritive Duo capsules per day.

RESPIRATORY ISSUES

3-5x per day	*As needed*

Essential Oils: *Breathe®, Eucalyptus, On Guard®, Tea Tree, Zendocrine®*

Other Solutions: *Breathe® Drops, Breathe® Vapor Stick*

 Choose 3 of the recommended oils. Mix 5-7 drops of each in a 10 ml roller bottle and fill with fractionated coconut oil. Apply over your chest and mid/upper back and the bottoms of your feet morning and evening. Put 1 drop each of Breathe® and Eucalyptus in your palms, rub together, and inhale slowly and deeply 3 times as needed. Take Breathe® Drops as needed. Rub a Breathe® Vapor Stick over your chest and upper back throughout the day. If you get oils in your eyes or on your face while inhaling from your hands, apply plain coconut oil over your eye or face to soothe the area. Repeat as needed.

Avoid dairy products. Add 1-2 drops of Lemon to your water and drink. Drink half your body weight in ounces of water.

P-R

RESTLESS LEG SYNDROME

⏰ *Every 4 hours*	📅 *Ongoing as needed*

Essential Oils: *AromaTouch®, Wintergreen, Cypress, PastTense®, Deep Blue®, Copaiba*

Other Solutions: *Deep Blue® Polyphenol Complex*

💜 Combine 5 drops of each recommended oil in a 10 ml roller bottle with fractionated coconut oil, or combine 25 drops of AromaTouch® or Deep Blue® in a 10 ml roller bottle with fractionated coconut oil. You can also add the oils to a 2-ounce spray bottle with fractionated coconut oil (*but double the amount of oils*). Apply over the affected area every 4 hours, the last time being before bed. Use a PastTense® roller over your legs 3 times per day. Take 2 Deep Blue® Polyphenol Complex capsules a day with meals, in the morning and evening.

RESTLESSNESS

⏰ *4-5x per day*	📅 *Until symptoms diminish*

Essential Oils: *Balance®, Lavender, Serenity®*

Other Solutions: *Serenity® Softgels*

💜 Combine 15 drops each of Balance® and Lavender or 25-30 drops of Serenity®, Balance®, or Lavender in a 10 ml roller bottle with fractionated coconut oil. Apply to the back of your neck, the front of your neck, over your pulse points, and on your feet. Diffuse a combination of recommended oils, 1-3 drops each, or diffuse 5-7 drops of your oil of choice and inhale often throughout the day. Use whatever oil or oil combination proves effective with your body chemistry.

🌙 Aim to get 7-9 hours of sleep per night for rest and recovery. Apply 1-2 drops of Serenity® and Lavender to your pillow at bedtime. Take 1-2 Serenity® Softgels 30 minutes before bed.

RHEUMATIC FEVER

🕐 *3-5x per day*	📅 *Until condition improves*

Essential Oils: *Oregano, Thyme, Arborvitae, Peppermint, DDR Prime®*

Other Solutions: *N/A*

 Combine 5 drops of each recommended oil in a 10 ml roller bottle with fractionated coconut oil. Apply along your spine, on your feet, and on your wrist pulse points.

 Seek medical attention immediately if you experience a chronic sore throat accompanied by small, hard, painless lumps/nodules under the skin in any region of the body; chest pain or heart palpitations; random nosebleeds; or fatigue.

RHEUMATOID ARTHRITIS

🕐 *4-5x per day*	📅 *As needed*

Essential Oils: *Deep Blue®, Marjoram, Cypress, Copaiba, Lemongrass, Frankincense, Siberian Fir*

Other Solutions: *Deep Blue® Rub, Deep Blue® Stick, Deep Blue® Polyphenol Complex*

 Choose 2-3 of the recommended oils. Mix 5-7 drops of each oil with fractionated coconut oil in a 10 ml roller bottle and apply over the affected joint(s). Take 2 Deep Blue® Polyphenol Complex capsules per day with food. Use Deep Blue® Rub or Deep Blue® Stick over the affected area as needed.

RHINITIS

🕐 *3-5x per day*	📅 *Ongoing until symptoms subside*

Essential Oils: *Lemon, Lavender, Peppermint, DigestZen®*

Other Solutions: *Breathe® Drops, Breathe® Vapor Stick, Correct-X, On Guard® Beadlets, On Guard™+ Softgels, TriEase® Softgels, Lifelong Vitality, DigestZen TerraZyme®, PB Assist®+*

 Diffuse 4 drops each of Lemon, Lavender, and Peppermint when at home or at work. Add 10 drops of each recommended oil to a 10 ml roller bottle and fill the rest with fractionated coconut oil. Rub over your temples and forehead, behind your ears, and over your thymus. Take 1-2 TriEase® Softgels as needed. Rub DigestZen® over your sinuses and temples morning and evening. Use a cotton swab to apply a dab of Correct-X into your nose for added immune support. Take On Guard® Beadlets as needed. Take 3 On Guard™+ Softgels throughout the day.

● Take Lifelong Vitality Supplements twice a day, 2-3 DigestZen TerraZyme® capsules at each meal, PB Assist® once per day, and 2 drops of Lemon in water.

P-R

RINGWORM

⏰ **3x per day**	📅 *Until condition improves*

Essential Oils: *Tea Tree, Oregano, Myrrh, Citronella, Lavender, Lemon Eucalyptus*

Other Solutions: *HD Clear® Foaming Face Wash*

 Wash the affected area with HD Clear® Foaming Face Wash. Allow to dry. Mix 3-5 drops of each recommended oil in a 10 ml roller bottle with fractionated coconut oil. Rub it over the affected area every 4 hours.

RSV (*Respiratory Syncytial Virus*)

⏰ *3x per day*	📅 *Ongoing until symptoms resolve*

Essential Oils: *Thyme, Breathe®, Tea Tree*

Other Solutions: *Breathe® Vapor Stick*

 Rub a Breathe® Vapor Stick on your feet several times a day. For children under 1 year old: combine 1 drop of each recommended oil in a 10 ml roller bottle with fractionated coconut oil. Apply to your feet, along your spine over your mid-back region, and over your chest. For children over 1 year old: combine 2 drops of each recommended oil in a 10 ml roller bottle with fractionated coconut oil. Apply to your feet, along your spine over your mid-back region, and over your chest.

⊕ Be sure to monitor your child's symptoms, as RSV can be serious in infants, especially those under 6 months. If you see any of the following symptoms, contact your pediatrician right away: coughing/wheezing that doesn't stop; fever; irritability; poor appetite; lethargy; a sunken chest when breathing; gasping for breath or rapid breathing; blue mouth or fingernails; a cough producing yellow, green, or gray mucus; signs of dehydration, like a lack of tears, a sunken soft spot, or continually dry diapers.

P-R

SCARRING

⏰ **3-5x per day**	📅 ***Until condition improves***

Essential Oils: *Immortelle, Yarrow|Pom, Helichrysum, Frankincense*

Other Solutions: *Yarrow|Pom Body Renewal Serum, Yarrow|Pom Botanical Nutritive Duo*

 Use an Immortelle roller over the affected area daily, morning and evening. Combine 10 drops of Yarrow|Pom and 7 drops of Helichrysum in a 10 ml roller bottle with fractionated coconut oil. Apply to the affected area 2-3 times per day for several weeks. Apply Yarrow|Pom Body Renewal Serum on the affected area twice daily. Take 2 Yarrow|Pom Botanical Nutritive Duo capsules per day.

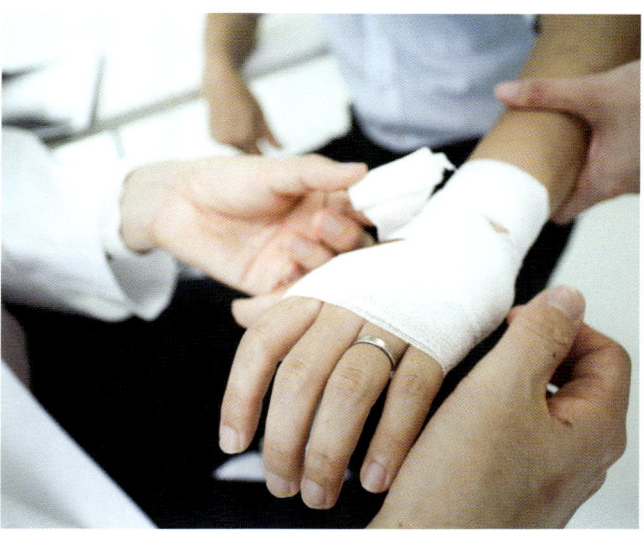

SCHIZOPHRENIA

⏰ **3-5x per day**	📅 ***Ongoing***

Essential Oils: *Melissa, Frankincense, Lavender, Vetiver, Sandalwood, Roman Chamomile, Basil, Bergamot*

Other Solutions: *N/A*

 Choose 4-5 of the recommended oils. Add 5 drops of each in a 10 ml roller bottle with fractionated coconut oil. Apply to your feet, the back of your neck, your chest, and your pulse points often throughout the day. Choose 2-3 of the recommended oils. Diffuse 3 drops of each and inhale throughout the day.

● Continue to seek guidance from your health care provider for this condition.

S-U

SCIATICA

⏰ *4-5x per day*	📅 *Ongoing as needed*

Essential Oils: *Black Pepper, Siberian Fir, Frankincense, Marjoram, Wintergreen*

Other Solutions: *Lifelong Vitality, DigestZen TerraZyme®, PB Assist®+, Turmeric Dual Chamber Capsules, Deep Blue® Polyphenol Complex*

🌀 Combine 5-7 drops each of Black Pepper, Siberian Fir, Frankincense, Marjoram, and Wintergreen in a 10 ml roller bottle with fractionated coconut oil. Apply over the affected area several times per day. Take 2 Turmeric Dual Chamber Capsules per day with meals. Take 2 Deep Blue® Polyphenol Complex capsules a day with meals, in the morning and evening.

🌿 Avoid inflammatory foods. Take Lifelong Vitality Supplements twice a day, 2-3 DigestZen Terra-Zyme® capsules at each meal, and PB Assist® once per day. Eat a variety of fresh fruits, vegetables, lean meats, fatty fish, healthy fats, and brown rice. Avoid MSG, gluten, corn, fried food, fast food, and processed foods. Drink half your weight in ounces of water.

🔄 Stay active by engaging in moderate activity daily, such as walking. Avoid sitting for prolonged periods of time. If you must sit for long stretches, be sure to take a break and stand up/walk around every 20-30 minutes. Get a supportive ergonomic chair. Stretch regularly. Alternate hot and cold therapy throughout the day. Incorporate posture exercises into your daily routine.

➕ Seek professional medical attention from your doctor or chiropractor if the problem persists, if you have pain that radiates down your thigh or leg, if you have bowel or bladder incontinence, if you lose sensation in your groin or legs, or if you do not see an improvement in your condition after a couple of weeks on this protocol. A chiropractor can help determine the type of bulging disc you are suffering from and help you pinpoint some of the underlying causes. Physical therapy and massage can also help.

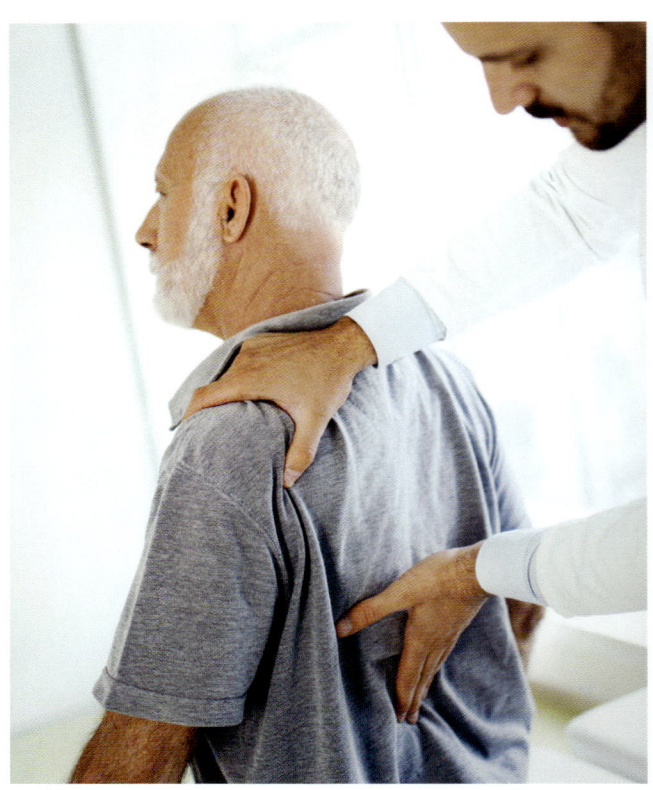

S-U

SEASONAL AFFECTIVE DISORDER

 3-5x per day   **As needed**

Essential Oils: *Adaptiv™ (3-part system), Citrus Bliss®, Wild Orange, Jasmine, Ylang Ylang, Hygge™*

Other Solutions: *Adaptiv™ Capsules, Lifelong Vitality, DigestZen TerraZyme®, PB Assist®+, Serenity® Softgels*

🔽 Use an Adaptiv™ roller frequently throughout the day. Combine 5 drops of each recommended oil *(except Adaptiv™)* in a 10 ml roller bottle topped off with fractionated coconut oil. Apply down the back of your neck, under your skull, behind your ears, over your wrists, and over your heart every 4 hours throughout the day. Apply to the bottoms of your feet morning and evening. Take 1 Adaptiv™ Capsule daily with food and 2 Serenity® Softgels 30 minutes before bed. Diffuse 3-5 drops each of Hygge™, Citrus Bliss® or Wild Orange, Adaptiv™, and Ylang Ylang throughout the day.

🍏 Eat omega-3 fatty acids, almonds, asparagus, beets, cabbage, peaches, carrots, bananas, onions, fennel, nuts, ocean fish, ginger, white beans, cauliflower, white sesame seeds, grass-fed beef, farm-raised poultry, brown rice, pears, celery, eggs, flaxseed, ginger, scallions, potatoes, sweet potatoes, avocado, pork chops, canned sardines, ham, cheddar cheese, fortified milk, fortified yogurt, fortified cereals, and almond milk. Take Lifelong Vitality Supplements twice a day, 2-3 DigestZen TerraZyme® Capsules at each meal, PB Assist® once per day, and Lemon in water *(2 drops per glass)*. Eat foods high in vitamin D and omega-3 fatty acids, like salmon, tuna, cod, trout, other types of fatty fish, and cod liver oil, to support your mood.

🔸 Get outdoors as much as possible, especially on sunny days. Follow the recommendations in the Exercise chapter (page 385).

🌙 Aim to get 7-9 hours of sleep per night for rest and recovery. Apply 1-2 drops of Serenity® and Lavender to your pillow at bedtime. Take 1-2 Serenity® Softgels 30 minutes before bed.

➕ If symptoms worsen or do not improve, seek medical attention.

S-U

SEBACEOUS CYST

⏰ *3-5x per day*	📅 *Ongoing as needed*

Essential Oils: *Fennel, Cedarwood, Basil, Black Pepper, Coriander*

Other Solutions: *Yarrow|Pom Body Renewal Serum, Yarrow|Pom Botanical Nutritive Duo capsules*

🌿 Choose 2-3 of the recommended oils. Mix 5-7 drops of each oil in a 10 ml roller bottle and fill with fractionated coconut oil. Apply over the affected area. Apply Yarrow|Pom Body Renewal Serum on the affected area. Take 2 Yarrow|Pom Botanical Nutritive Duo capsules per day.

SHIN SPLINTS

⏰ *3-5x per day*	📅 *While symptoms persist*

Essential Oils: *AromaTouch®, Lemongrass, Wintergreen, Basil*

Other Solutions: *Deep Blue® Rub, Deep Blue® Stick, Deep Blue® Polyphenol Complex*

🌿 Ice your shins several times per day. Mix 7-10 drops of each recommended oil in a 10 ml roller bottle and fill with fractionated coconut oil. After icing, apply the roller bottle blend and Deep Blue® Rub or Deep Blue® Stick over your shins. Take 2 Deep Blue® Polyphenol Complex capsules a day with meals, in the morning and evening.

🔶 Do light walking and yoga. Make sure to warm up, cool down, and stretch for each exercise session. Ice your shins after exercise. Do balance exercises daily. Consider changing your shoes. Avoid running and exercises that put stress on your shins.

S-U

SHINGLES

4-5x per day	*Until condition resolves*

Essential Oils: *Black Pepper, Tea Tree, Melissa, Geranium, Lavender*

Other Solutions: *N/A*

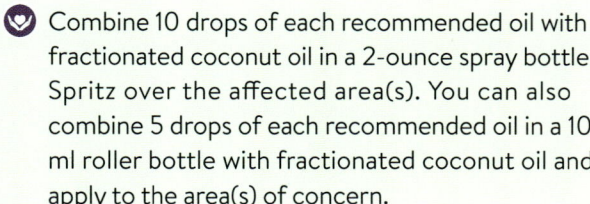 Combine 10 drops of each recommended oil with fractionated coconut oil in a 2-ounce spray bottle. Spritz over the affected area(s). You can also combine 5 drops of each recommended oil in a 10 ml roller bottle with fractionated coconut oil and apply to the area(s) of concern.

SHOCK

4-5x per day	*Until symptoms improve*

Essential Oils: *Peppermint, Magnolia, Peace®*

Other Solutions: *N/A*

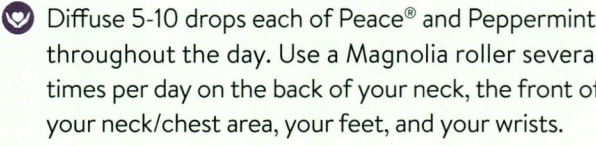 Diffuse 5-10 drops each of Peace® and Peppermint throughout the day. Use a Magnolia roller several times per day on the back of your neck, the front of your neck/chest area, your feet, and your wrists.

SINUS CONGESTION

3-5x per day	*Ongoing as needed*

Essential Oils: *Cardamom, Breathe®, Rosemary, Eucalyptus, Peppermint, Thyme, Cilantro, Lemon*

Other Solutions: *Breathe® Drops, Breathe® Vapor Stick, Peppermint Beadlets*

Use a non-drying nasal spray (*like a 1.5-ounce bottle of Xlear® from your local drugstore*) with 1 drop of Cilantro and 1 drop of Lemon in it. Shake well and spray 3 times per day to clear sinuses, break up mucus, and reduce inflammation. Diffuse 3 drops each of 3-4 oils of your choice and inhale several times daily. Combine 5 drops each of Cardamom, Breathe®, Rosemary, and Eucalyptus or 5 drops each of Peppermint and Thyme in a 10 ml roller with fractionated coconut oil. Apply topically to back of your neck, under your nose, on the bridge of your nose, and on your chest as needed. You can also mix 1 drop of DigestZen® with 1/4 teaspoon of fractionated coconut oil and apply over the affected area. Take Breathe® Drops as needed. Rub a Breathe® Vapor Stick over your sinus area 3-4 times per day. Take Peppermint Beadlets as desired.

S-U

SINUSITIS

3-5x per day	Ongoing as needed

Essential Oils: *Cardamom, Breathe®, Rosemary, Eucalyptus, Peppermint, Thyme, Lemongrass, Cilantro, Lemon*

Other Solutions: *Breathe® Drops, Breathe® Vapor Stick, Peppermint Beadlets*

● Use a non-drying nasal spray with 1 drop of Cilantro and 1 drop of Lemon in it. Shake well and spray 3 times per day to clear sinuses, break up mucus, and reduce inflammation. Choose 2-3 of the recommended oils. Mix 5-7 drops of each in a 10 ml roller bottle and fill with fractionated coconut oil. Apply topically to the back of your neck, under your nose, on the bridge of your nose, and on your chest as needed. Choose 3-4 of the recommended oils. Diffuse 3 drops of each and inhale through-out the day. Take Breathe® Drops as needed. Rub a Breathe® Vapor Stick over your sinus area 3-4 times per day. Take Peppermint Beadlets as desired.

S-U

SKIN BLEMISH

⏰ **4-5x per day**	📅 **Until blemish disappears**

Essential Oils: *Rose Touch, Yarrow|Pom, Laurel Leaf*

Other Solutions: *HD Clear® Foaming Face Wash, HD Clear® Facial Lotion*

 Wash the affected area with HD Clear® Foaming Face Wash. Allow to dry. Combine 15 drops each of Yarrow|Pom and Laurel Leaf in a 10 ml roller bottle with fractionated coconut oil. Apply to the affected region frequently. Use a Rose Touch roller twice per day over the affected area. Apply HD Clear® Facial Lotion to the affected area.

SLEEP APNEA

⏰ **3-5x per day**	📅 **As needed**

Essential Oils: *Breathe®, Eucalyptus, Cardamom, Serenity®, Madasgascar Vanilla*

Other Solutions: *Breathe® Drops, Breathe® Vapor Stick, Serenity® Softgels*

 Choose 2 of the recommended oils. Mix 5-7 drops of each in a 10 ml roller bottle and fill with fractionated coconut oil. Apply over your chest, your mid/upper back, and the bottoms of your feet morning and evening. Put 1 drop each of Breathe® and Eucalyptus in your palms, rub them together, and inhale from your palms slowly and deeply 3 times or as needed. Use Breathe® Drops and a Breathe® Vapor Stick as needed. If you get oils in your eyes or on your face while inhaling from your hands, apply plain coconut oil over your eye or face to soothe the area. Repeat as needed. Diffuse 5 drops each of Breathe®, Serenity® and Madagascar Vanilla overnight.

🍎 Avoid dairy products. Add 1-2 drops of Lemon to your water, and drink half your body weight in ounces of water.

🌙 Diffuse 4-5 drops each of Serenity® and Breathe® at bedtime, or put 1 drop of each on your pillow. Take 2 Serenity® Softgels before bed.

⊕ Watch for the following symptoms: severe shortness of breath, chest tightness, or coughing and wheezing. If you are unable to speak more than a few short sentences or have to strain your chest muscles to breathe, seek medical attention right away.

S-U

SNORING

🕐 *3-5x per day*	📅 *As needed*

Essential Oils: *Breathe®, Eucalyptus, Cardamom, Serenity®*

Other Solutions: *Breathe® Drops, Breathe® Vapor Stick, Serenity® Softgels*

- 🌼 Choose 2 of the recommended oils. Mix 5-7 drops of each in a 10 ml roller bottle and fill with fractionated coconut oil. Apply over your chest, your mid/upper back, and the bottoms of your feet morning and evening. Put 1 drop each of Breathe® and Eucalyptus in your palms, rub them together, and inhale from your palms slowly and deeply 3 times or as needed. Use Breathe® Drops and the Breathe® Vapor Stick as needed. If you get oils in your eyes or on your face while inhaling from your hands, apply plain coconut oil over your eye or face to soothe the area. Repeat as needed.

- 🌿 Avoid dairy products. Add 1-2 drops of Lemon to your water, and drink half your body weight in ounces of water.

- 🌙 Diffuse 4-5 drops each of Serenity® and Breathe® at bedtime, or put 1 drop of each on your pillow. Take 2 Serenity® Softgels before bed.

- ➕ Watch for the following symptoms: severe shortness of breath, chest tightness, or coughing and wheezing. If you are unable to speak more than a few short sentences or have to strain your chest muscles to breathe, seek medical attention right away.

SORE FEET

🕐 *4-5x per day*	📅 *As needed*

Essential Oils: *Deep Blue®, Marjoram, Cypress, Copaiba, Lemongrass, Frankincense, Siberian Fir*

Other Solutions: *Deep Blue® Polyphenol Complex, Deep Blue® Rub, Deep Blue® Stick*

- 🌼 Choose 2-3 of the recommended oils. Mix 5-7 drops of each oil with fractionated coconut oil in a 10 ml roller bottle. Apply over the affected joint(s). Take 2 Deep Blue® Polyphenol capsules per day with food. Use Deep Blue® Rub or Deep Blue® Stick over the affected area as needed.

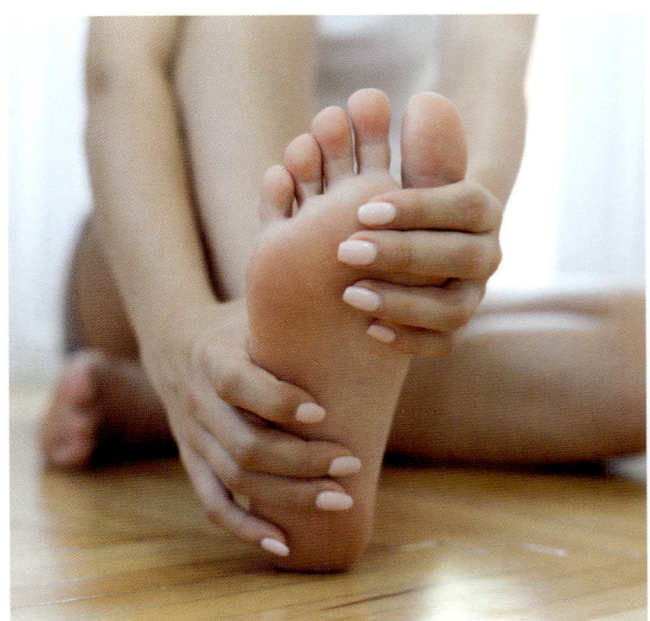

S-U

SORE MUSCLES

⏰ 4-5x per day	📆 As needed

Essential Oils: *Marjoram, AromaTouch®, Copaiba, Frankincense, Siberian Fir, PastTense®*

Other Solutions: *Deep Blue® Polyphenol Complex, Deep Blue® Rub, Deep Blue® Stick, Lifelong Vitality, DigestZen TerraZyme®, PB Assist®+*

💟 Choose 2-3 of the recommended oils. Mix 5-7 drops of each oil with fractionated coconut oil in a 10 ml roller bottle. Apply over the affected joint(s). Take 2 Deep Blue® Polyphenol capsules per day with food. Use Deep Blue® Rub or Deep Blue® Stick over the affected area as needed.

🌿 Take Lifelong Vitality Supplements twice a day, 2-3 DigestZen TerraZyme® capsules at each meal, and PB Assist® once per day. Eat a variety of fresh fruits, vegetables, lean meats, healthy fats, and rice. Avoid MSG, gluten, corn, fried food, fast food, processed foods, and artificial sweeteners.

SORE THROAT

⏰ 3-5x per day	📆 Until symptoms resolve

Essential Oils: *Oregano, On Guard®, Tea Tree, Cilantro, Wild Orange, Clove, Copaiba*

Other Solutions: *Breathe® Drops, On Guard® Protecting Throat Drops, On Guard® Tablets, On Guard™+ Softgels*

💟 Combine 1 drop of each recommended oil in a veggie capsule with a carrier oil and take 3 times per day. Mix 2 drops each of Wild Orange, On Guard®, and Lemon with water and gargle; or add those oils to a teaspoon of honey and swallow; or diffuse 3 drops each of the same oils and inhale; or combine 5 drops of each of the same oils in a 10 ml roller bottle topped off with fractionated coconut oil and apply topically to your throat, chest, and the back of your neck several times daily as needed. Place 2 drops of Copaiba under your tongue 3 times per day. Take Breathe® Drops as needed. Take On Guard® Protecting Throat Drops as needed along with On Guard™+ Softgels as directed and up to 3 On Guard® Tablets per day.

S-U

SPRAINS

⏰ *3x per day*	📅 *Ongoing until symptoms improve*

Essential Oils: *Lemongrass, Cardamom, Marjoram, Peppermint, Frankincense, Cypress, AromaTouch®*

Other Solutions: *Deep Blue® Rub, Deep Blue® Stick*

❤ Combine 25-30 drops of AromaTouch® in a 10 ml roller bottle with fractionated coconut oil, or combine 5 drops each of the rest of the recommended oils besides AromaTouch® in a 10 ml roller bottle with fractionated coconut oil. Rub over the affected area every 4 hours or before activities that may exacerbate symptoms. Use Deep Blue® Rub or Deep Blue® Stick as needed.

STAPH INFECTION

⏰ *4-5x per day*	📅 *While symptoms persist*

Essential Oils: *Cinnamon, Oregano, Thyme, On Guard®, Clove*

Other Solutions: *DDR Prime® Softgels, On Guard® Foaming Hand Wash, On Guard® Sanitizing Mist*

❤ Choose 3 of the recommended oils. Mix 5-7 drops of each oil in a 10 ml roller bottle and fill with fractionated coconut oil. Rub down your spine, over the affected area, and on the bottoms of your feet morning and evening. Put 1-2 drops each of Oregano, On Guard®, and Thyme in a capsule and add fractionated coconut oil. Take 3 times per day. Diffuse 4-5 drops of On Guard® throughout the day and at bedtime. Take 1 DDR Prime® Softgel morning and evening. Cover the affected area with a clean bandage. Wash your hands frequently with On Guard® Foaming Hand Wash. Use On Guard® Sanitizing Mist often throughout the day.

➕ If you develop a fever or experience shortness of breath, cough, chills, or a rash, seek medical attention right away.

S-U

STOMACHACHE

⏰ **3-5x per day**	📅 **As needed**

Essential Oils: *Ginger, DigestZen®, Peppermint, Fennel*

Other Solutions: *Ginger Drops, Peppermint Beadlets, Peppermint Softgels*

 Combine 5-7 drops each of Ginger, DigestZen®, Peppermint, and Fennel in a 10 ml roller bottle with fractionated coconut oil. Apply to your abdominal/navel area. Use a warm compress on your stomach prior to use to increase absorption and efficacy. For adults, take up to 2 Peppermint Softgels. For children 8 years and older, take 1 Peppermint Softgel. For best results, take Peppermint Softgels 30-60 minutes before meals if the meal may result in an upset stomach. Take Ginger Drops as needed. Take Peppermint Beadlets as desired.

STREP THROAT

⏰ **4-5x per day**	📅 **Until symptoms resolve**

Essential Oils: *Oregano, On Guard®, Tea Tree, Cilantro, Wild Orange, Clove, Copaiba*

Other Solutions: *On Guard® Protecting Throat Drops, On Guard™+ Softgels, On Guard® Tablets*

 Combine 1 drop of each recommended oil in a veggie capsule with a carrier oil and take internally 3 times per day. Mix 2 drops each of Wild Orange, On Guard®, and Lemon with water and gargle; or add those oils to a teaspoon of honey and swallow; or diffuse 3 drops of the same oils in the air and inhale; or combine 5 drops each of the same oils in a 10 ml roller bottle topped off with fractionated coconut oil and apply topically to your throat, chest, and the back of your neck several times daily as needed. Place 2 drops of Copaiba under your tongue 3 times per day. Take On Guard® Protecting Throat Drops as needed along with On Guard™+ Softgels and up to 3 On Guard® Tablets per day.

S-U

STRESS FRACTURES

⏰ *3-5x per day*	📅 *Ongoing until condition improves*

Essential Oils: *Siberian Fir, Cypress, Helichrysum, Wintergreen, Frankincense, Black Pepper*

Other Solutions: *Turmeric Dual Chamber Capsules, Lifelong Vitality Supplements*

Combine 5-7 drops of each recommended oil in a 10 ml roller bottle with fractionated coconut oil. Apply to the affected area and the bottoms of your feet several times per day. Take 2 Turmeric Dual Chamber capsules per day. Take Lifelong Vitality Supplements twice per day.

Consume kale, spinach, raw milk, sardines, yogurt, kefir, flaxseed, grass-fed beef, almonds, black beans, avocados, Swiss chard, pumpkin seeds, chia seeds, vegetable juices, bell peppers, oranges, asparagus, and fatty fish (*salmon, tuna, and mackerel*).

Get about 20 minutes of safe sun exposure daily to encourage healing.

S-U

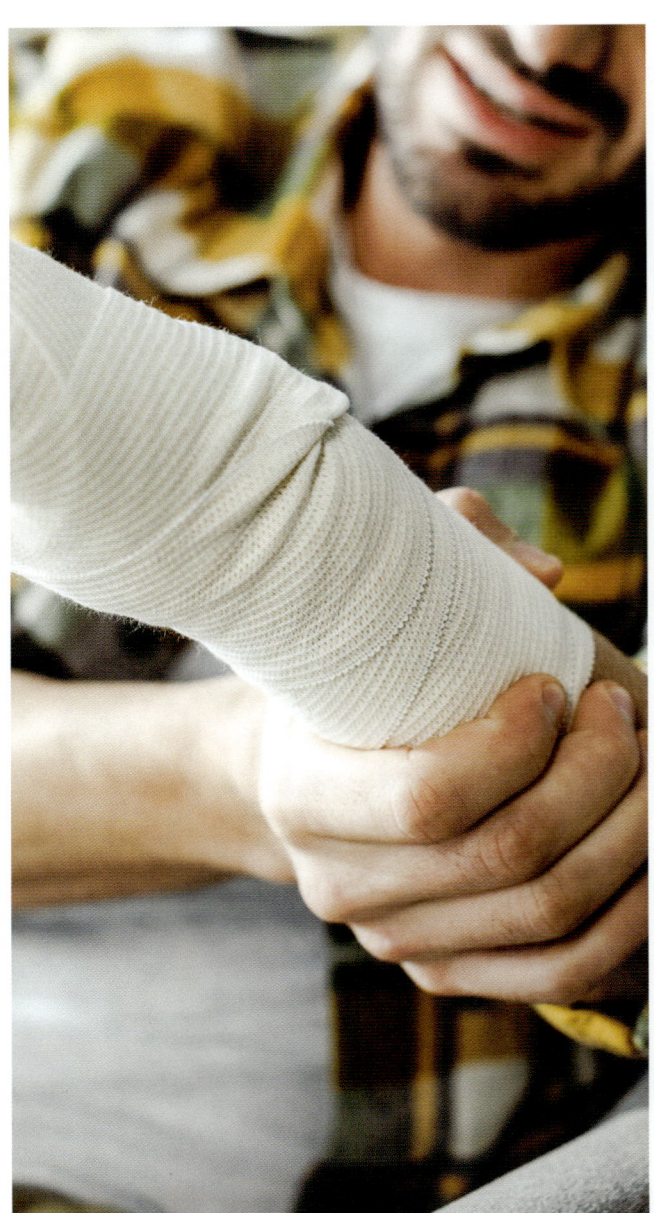

STRESS RELIEF

3-5x per day	*Ongoing until stress resolves*

Essential Oils: *Adaptiv™ (3-part system), Basil, Bergamot, Vetiver, Black Spruce, Lavender, Ylang Ylang, Roman Chamomile, Hygge™, PastTense® roller, Magnolia roller*

Other Solutions: *Adaptiv™ Capsule, Deep Blue® Rub, Deep Blue® Stick*

⊙ Take 1 Adaptiv™ Capsule daily with food. Use an Adaptiv™ roller frequently throughout the day. Choose 3-4 of the recommended oils and diffuse 3-4 drops of each with 3-4 drops of Adaptiv™ throughout the day. Choose 3 of the recommended oils in addition to Basil and mix 10 drops of each with fractionated coconut oil in a 10 ml roller bottle. Rub it over your chest, on the back of your neck, along your spine, and on your feet several times per day. Use PastTense® immediately before a predicted stressful event. Use a Magnolia roller prior to bed. Use Deep Blue® Rub or Deep Blue® Stick over back of neck and upper back/shoulder area if this is a typical area you carry stress.

⊙ Do 45 minutes of aerobic activity, 5-6 times per week (*jogging, walking, biking, hiking, dance, yoga, cross-country skiing, basketball, swimming*). Do moderate strength training 3-4 times per week (weights, yoga, TRX, exercise class). Warm up, cool down, and stretch for each exercise session. See Chapter Five for more information (page 394).

⊙ Breathe deeply often throughout the day. Meditate and do yoga. Apply a cool compress/ice pack to your head as needed several times per day to relieve pain. Apply heat and Deep Blue® Rub to sore neck muscles if relevant. Apply recommended oils as directed. Take Epsom salt baths.

S-U

STRETCH MARKS

⏰ **3-5x per day**	📅 *Ongoing until condition improves*

Essential Oils: *Neroli Touch, Frankincense, Helichrysum, Geranium, Lemon*

Other Solutions: *Yarrow|Pom Body Renewal Serum, Yarrow|Pom Botanical Nutritive Duo*

 Combine 10 drops each of Frankincense and Helichrysum with 5 drops each of Geranium and Lemon in a 10 ml roller bottle with fractionated coconut oil. Apply to the affected area several times a day. Use a Neroli Touch roller a few times a day as well. Apply Yarrow|Pom Body Renewal Serum on the affected area twice daily. Take 2 Yarrow|Pom Botanical Nutritive Duo capsules per day.

STROKE

⏰ **4-5x per day**	📅 *Ongoing*

Essential Oils: *Frankincense, Helichrysum, Cypress*

Other Solutions: *N/A*

 Combine 15 drops of Frankincense and 10 drops each of Helichrysum and Cypress in a 10 ml roller bottle and fill with fractionated coconut oil. Use on the back and front of your neck, along your skull line, on your feet, and on your pulse points. Diffuse 5-10 drops of Frankincense and inhale daily. Place 2 drops of Frankincense under your tongue twice daily.

 To know whether you need to seek medical attention, you must understand the warning signs of a stroke, even if the symptoms fluctuate or disappear. The sooner treatment can begin, the better the prognosis for recovery. Use the "FAST" test to determine whether you or someone you love is having a stroke.

S-U

STYE

⏰ 4-5x per day	📅 While symptoms persist

Essential Oils: *Tea Tree, DDR Prime®, Patchouli, Frankincense, Myrrh*

Other Solutions: *Yarrow|Pom Body Renewal Serum*

 Choose 2-3 of the recommended oils. Mix 5-7 drops of each oil in a 10 ml roller bottle and fill with fractionated coconut oil. Apply around the eye area *(do not get too close to the eye; never put oils in your eye)*. Apply Yarrow|Pom Body Renewal Serum around the eye area.

SUNBURN

⏰ 3-5x per day	📅 While symptoms persist

Essential Oils: *Peppermint, Lavender, Helichrysum*

Other Solutions: *N/A*

 Combine 10 drops each of Peppermint, Helichrysum, and Lavender in a 10 ml roller bottle with fractionated coconut oil. Apply to the affected area 3-5 times per day. If applying the roller is uncomfortable, combine 20 drops of Peppermint and 10 drops each of Helichrysum and Lavender in a 4-ounce amber glass spray bottle. Spritz over the affected area. Keep both the roller and 4-ounce spray bottle in the refrigerator for an enhanced cooling effect upon application.

S-U

SWIMMER'S EAR

⏰ *3-5x per day*	📅 *While symptoms persist*

Essential Oils: *Tea Tree, Basil, Helichrysum, Rosemary*

Other Solutions: *On Guard™+ Softgels, On Guard® Beadlets*

 Choose 2-3 of the recommended oils. Mix 5-7 drops of each oil in a 10 ml roller bottle and fill with fractionated coconut oil. Rub on the bottoms of your feet morning and evening. Roll down the back of your neck, under your skull, and behind your ears throughout the day. Take 3 On Guard™+ Softgels throughout the day. Take On Guard® Beadlets as needed.

SWOLLEN EYES

⏰ *3-5x per day*	📅 *While symptoms persist*

Essential Oils: *Immortelle, Green Mandarin, Patchouli, Geranium*

Other Solutions: *N/A*

 Choose 2-3 of the recommended oils. Mix with 1 tbsp fractionated coconut oil and apply 1 drop of each oil topically around the opening of your eye. Put 1-2 drops of Green Mandarin in your water and drink throughout the day.

S-U

TEETH GRINDING

🕐 *3x per day and nightly before bed*	📅 *As needed*

Essential Oils: *Bergamot, Serenity®, Balance®, Basil, Adaptiv™ (3-part system), Ylang Ylang, Vetiver, Roman Chamomile*

Other Solutions: *Adaptiv™ Capsules*

 Diffuse 3-4 drops each of the recommended oils; diffuse 6-7 drops of Adaptiv™; or diffuse 3 drops of Adaptiv™ with 3 drops each of 1-2 recommended oils of your choice. Diffuse intermittently throughout the day. Choose 3-4 of the recommended oils. Mix 5-7 drops of each oil with fractionated coconut oil in a 10 ml roller bottle. Rub it over your neck, spine, pulse points, and feet often throughout the day. Buy a diffuser necklace or place a combination of any of the oils on a cotton ball. Take Adaptiv™ Capsules as directed. Use an Adaptiv™ roller alone or rotate its use with the homemade roller throughout the day.

TEETHING PAIN

🕐 *4-5x per day*	📅 *As needed*

Essential Oils: *Roman Chamomile, Lavender, Copaiba, Clove*

Other Solutions: *N/A*

Combine 2 drops each of Roman Chamomile, Lavender, and Copaiba in a 10 ml roller bottle with fractionated coconut oil. Rub along the jawline on the side where teething is occurring. Place 1 drop of Clove in a few drops of fractionated coconut oil. Rub around the gum area where teething is occurring to relieve pain.

S-U

TENDONITIS

⏰ **3-5x per day**	📅 *Until symptoms lessen*

Essential Oils: *Lemongrass, Cardamom, Marjoram, Peppermint, Frankincense, Cypress, AromaTouch®, Deep Blue®*

Other Solutions: *Deep Blue® Polyphenol Complex, Turmeric Dual Chamber Capsules, Deep Blue® Rub, Deep Blue® Stick*

- Mix 25-30 drops of either AromaTouch® or Deep Blue® in a 10 ml roller bottle with fractionated coconut oil, or mix 5-7 drops each of Lemongrass, Cardamom, and Marjoram with 5-7 drops each of 2 additional recommended oils of your choice in a 10 ml roller bottle with fractionated coconut oil. Rub over the affected area every 4 hours or before activities that may exacerbate symptoms. Take 2 Turmeric Dual Chamber Capsules per day, each with a meal. Take 2 Deep Blue® Polyphenol Complex capsules a day with meals, in the morning and evening. Use Deep Blue® Rub or Deep Blue® Stick as needed over affected area.

- Consume all types of vegetables, especially green leafy kinds, like kale, broccoli, spinach, and other greens. Eat high-quality proteins, like wild-caught fish, raw dairy, cage-free eggs, or grass-fed beef. Eat foods rich in vitamin C, like berries, citrus fruits, squash, green veggies, and bell peppers. Eat pineapple, which is good for swelling.

- Try to pinpoint the activity that caused tendonitis, and temporarily stop doing that activity. Don't rest for too long, because this can leave your tendons stiff. Work slowly back into the activity after the swelling is under control. Using a barrier (*such as a piece of clothing*), ice the area of concern right away for 20 minutes if you notice swelling. Consider wearing a brace or splint for extra support around your tendons. Isolating an inflamed tendon helps support healing and reduce swelling.

- Seek care from a chiropractic doctor who can assess your posture and give you tips for performing activities in a safer way.

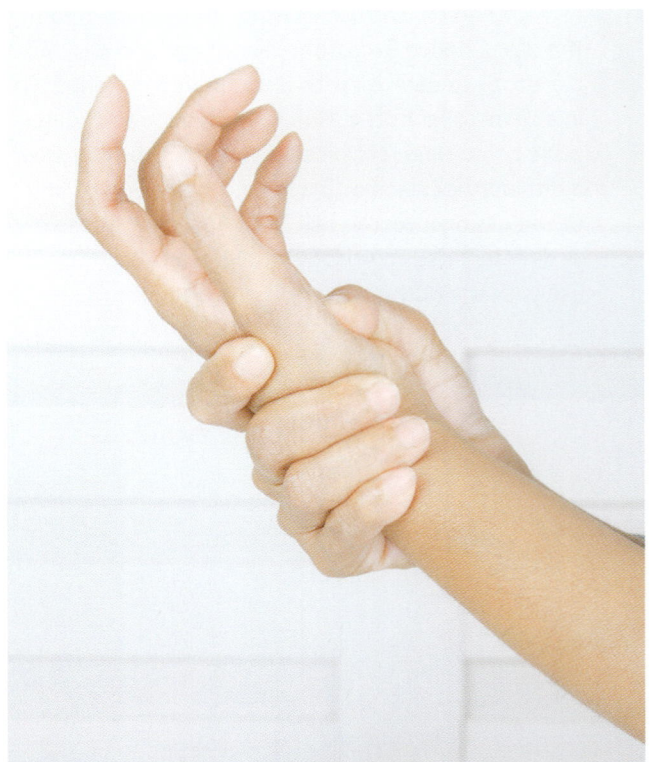

S-U

TENNIS ELBOW

⏰ *3-5x per day*	📅 *Until symptoms lessen*

Essential Oils: *Lemongrass, Cardamom, Marjoram, Peppermint, Frankincense, Cypress, AromaTouch®, Deep Blue®*

Other Solutions: *Deep Blue® Polyphenol Complex, Turmeric Dual Chamber Capsules, Deep Blue® Rub, Deep Blue® Stick*

⬇ Mix 25-30 drops of either AromaTouch® or Deep Blue® in a 10 ml roller bottle with fractionated coconut oil, or mix 5-7 drops each of Lemongrass, Cardamom, and Marjoram with 5-7 drops each of 2 additional recommended oils of your choice in a 10 ml roller bottle with fractionated coconut oil. Rub over the affected area every 4 hours or before activities that may exacerbate symptoms. Take 2 Turmeric Dual Chamber Capsules per day, each with a meal. Take 2 Deep Blue Polyphenol Complex® capsules a day with meals, in the morning and evening. Use Deep Blue® Rub or Deep Blue® Stick as needed.

🍏 Consume all types of vegetables, especially green leafy kinds, like kale, broccoli, spinach, and other greens. Eat high-quality proteins, like wild-caught fish, raw dairy, cage-free eggs, or grass-fed beef. Eat foods rich in vitamin C, like berries, citrus fruits, squash, green veggies, and bell peppers. Eat pineapple, which is good for swelling.

🔸 Try to pinpoint the activity that caused tendonitis, and temporarily stop doing that activity. Don't rest for too long, because this can leave your tendons stiff. Work slowly back into the activity after the swelling is under control. Using a barrier *(such as a piece of clothing)*, ice the area of concern right away for 20 minutes if you notice swelling. Consider wearing a brace or splint for extra support around your tendons. Isolating an inflamed tendon helps support healing and reduce swelling.

✚ Seek care from a chiropractic doctor who can assess your posture and give you tips for performing activities in a safer way.

S-U

TENSION *(Muscles)*

⏰ **4-5x per day**	📅 *As needed*

Essential Oils: *Marjoram, AromaTouch®, Copaiba, Frankincense, Siberian Fir, PastTense® roller*

Other Solutions: *Deep Blue® Polyphenol Complex, Deep Blue® Rub, Deep Blue® Stick, Lifelong Vitality, DigestZen TerraZyme®, PB Assist®+*

 Choose 2-3 of the recommended oils. Mix 5-7 drops of each oil with fractionated coconut oil in a 10 ml roller bottle. Apply over the affected joint(s). Take 2 Deep Blue® Polyphenol capsules per day with food. Use Deep Blue® Rub or Deep Blue® Stick over the affected area as needed.

 Take Lifelong Vitality Supplements twice a day, 2-3 DigestZen TerraZyme® capsules at each meal, and PB Assist® once per day. Eat a variety of fresh fruits, vegetables, lean meats, healthy fats, and rice. Avoid MSG, gluten, corn, fried food, fast food, processed foods, and artificial sweeteners.

THRUSH

⏰ **3-5x per day**	📅 *Until condition resolves*

Essential Oils: *Lemon, Spikenard, Arborvitae, Clary Sage, Tea Tree, Myrrh*

Other Solutions: *N/A*

 Gargle 1 drop of Lemon in water several times per day. Combine 5 drops each of Spikenard, Arborvitae, Clary Sage, Tea Tree, and Myrrh in a 10 ml roller bottle with fractionated coconut oil *(cut recipe in half for children)*. Apply over the back of your neck, the front of your neck, and your throat area.

S-U

TICK BITES

⏰ *Frequently for the first hour following the bite*   📅 *1 hour after the bite*

Essential Oils: *Tea Tree, Purify, TerraShield®*

Other Solutions: *On Guard™+ Softgels, DDR Prime® Softgels*

 As soon as you see the tick, remove it carefully and promptly. Use tweezers to remove the tick as close to the skin as possible. Pull the tick out using a slow, steady upward motion *(avoid twisting)*. Seal the tick in a container and place it in freezer if you wish to confirm the type of tick with a medical professional. *To transmit Lyme disease, a deer tick must be attached for 36-48 hours. If you find an attached tick that looks swollen, it may have fed long enough to transmit bacteria.* Wash your hands and the bite site, using warm water and soap or rubbing alcohol. Apply 1 drop each of Tea Tree and Purify topically to the tick bite frequently for the first hour after removing the tick. Take 2 On Guard™+ Softgels and 2 DDR Prime® Softgels immediately. Continue taking 2 On Guard® Softgels twice daily and 2 DDR Prime® Softgels twice daily for 2 weeks. To repel ticks and prevent further bites, mix 30 drops of TerraShield® in a 10 ml roller bottle with fractionated coconut oil. Apply before heading outdoors and several times while you are outdoors. You can also double the recipe and add 60 drops of TerraShield® to a 2-ounce glass spray bottle and fill with water.

⊕ It is important to identify what kind of tick bit you, particularly if you get a tick bite where deer ticks *(potentially carrying Lyme disease)* are prevalent *(such as the Northeast/Midwest United States)*. If you experience any of the following symptoms, follow this protocol and seek medical attention right away: bull's-eye-shaped rash that appears like a red ring around a clear area with a red center *(roughly 70% of Lyme disease patients develop this rash)*.

S-U

TINNITUS

⏰ *Every 2 hours*	📅 *While symptoms persist*

Essential Oils: *Helichrysum, Lavender, Ylang Ylang, Peppermint, Ginger, Frankincense, Rosemary, On Guard®*

Other Solutions: *N/A*

 Choose 3-4 of the recommended oils. Mix 5 drops of each in a 10 ml roller bottle with fractionated coconut oil and rub behind your ears, the back of your neck along the spine, and at base of your skull. Use every 2 hours while symptoms persist. Place 1 drop of Helichrysum on your finger and rub behind your ear several times per day.

 Avoid rapid movements or exercises with positional changes, as these can worsen symptoms.

TOBACCO ADDICTION

⏰ *3-5x per day*	📅 *Ongoing*

Essential Oils: *Black Pepper, Clove, On Guard®, Cilantro*

Other Solutions: *Peppermint Beadlets*

 Mix 10 drops of each recommended oil with fractionated coconut oil in a 10 ml roller bottle. Rub over your wrists, spine, the bottoms of your feet in the morning and evening, and the back and front of your neck. Diffuse 3-4 drops of each recommended oil throughout the day. Take Peppermint Beadlets as desired.

TONSILLITIS

⏰ *3-5x per day*	📅 *Until symptoms resolve*

Essential Oils: *On Guard®, Lemon, Tea Tree*

Other Solutions: *On Guard™+ Softgels, On Guard® Tablets, On Guard® Protecting Throat Drops*

 Add 1 drop each of On Guard®, Tea Tree, and Lemon to water, gargle for 30-60 seconds, and swallow, or place 1 drop of each oil in a veggie capsule and take 2 times per day. Combine 10 drops of each recommended oil in a 10 ml roller bottle with fractionated coconut oil. Apply topically to your throat, chest, and the back of your neck several times daily. Take up to 3 On Guard® Tablets per day. Take 2 On Guard™+ Softgels daily. Use On Guard® Protecting Throat Drops several times per day.

 S-U

TOOTH DECAY

⏰ *3-5x per day*	📅 *While symptoms persist*

Essential Oils: *Clove, On Guard®, Tea Tree*

Other Solutions: *On Guard® Natural Whitening Toothpaste, On Guard® Mouthwash*

 Brush your teeth with On Guard® toothpaste 3 times per day. Use On Guard® Mouthwash after brushing your teeth, 3 times per day. Place 1 drop each of Clove, On Guard®, and Tea Tree over the affected teeth throughout the day.

 Eliminate sugar and refined carbohydrates. Avoid sticky candies and sweets like lollipops, caramels, and sugary cough drops. Avoid starchy foods that can get stuck in your mouth, like potato chips. If you eat sugar, eat it with a meal.

TOOTHACHE

⏰ *4-5x per day*	📅 *Until symptoms improve*

Essential Oils: *Clove, Tea Tree, On Guard*

Other Solutions: *N/A*

 Combine 1 drop each of Clove, Tea Tree, and On Guard® with 25-30 drops of fractionated coconut oil. Apply directly to the gums surrounding the tooth that aches. Combine 10 drops of each of the recommended oils in a 10 ml roller bottle with fractionated coconut oil. Shake well with the cap on and apply to your jaw near the affected tooth.

TUBERCULOSIS

⏰ *3-5x per day*	📅 *Ongoing until symptoms resolve*

Essential Oils: *Thyme, Black Pepper, Rosemary, Eucalyptus, Breathe®*

Other Solutions: *Breathe® Drops, Breathe® Vapor Stick*

 Use a Breathe® Vapor Stick and Breathe® Drops as necessary. Combine 5 drops of each recommended oil in a 10 ml roller bottle with fractionated coconut oil. Apply topically over your chest, upper back, feet, and the back of your neck. Diffuse 3 drops each of Breathe®, Eucalyptus, and Rosemary and inhale throughout the day.

S-U

ULCERS

4-5x per day	**Until symptoms resolve**

Essential Oils: *Zendocrine®, Frankincense, Wintergreen*

Other Solutions: *Peppermint Beadlets, Ginger Drops*

 Combine 10 drops of each recommended oil in a 10 ml roller bottle with fractionated coconut oil. Apply topically to your abdomen, lower back, and feet. Use Peppermint Beadlets several times per day, as needed. Use Ginger Drops as needed throughout the day for soothing relief.

ULCERS *(Gastric)*

4-5x per day	**Until symptoms resolve**

Essential Oils: *Zendocrine®, Frankincense, Wintergreen*

Other Solutions: *Peppermint Beadlets, Ginger Drops*

 Combine 10 drops of each recommended oil in a 10 ml roller bottle with fractionated coconut oil. Apply to your abdomen, lower back, and feet. Use Peppermint Beadlets several times per day, as needed. Use Ginger Drops as needed throughout the day for soothing relief.

URINARY TRACT INFECTION

4-5x per day	**While symptoms persist**

Essential Oils: *Juniper Berry, On Guard®, Basil, Rosemary, Frankincense, Lemon, Lemon Eucalyptus, Citronella*

Other Solutions: *On Guard™+ Softgels, On Guard® Tablets*

 Choose 3-4 of the recommended oils. Mix 10 drops of each with fractionated coconut oil in a 10 ml roller bottle. Rub over your abdominal area and on your lower back over your spine every 2-3 hours or until symptoms diminish. Take 2 On Guard™+ Softgels 3 times per day. Take up to 3 On Guard® Tablets per day. Add 1 drop of Lemon to warm water or tea and sip throughout the day. Drink at least half your body weight in ounces of water per day.

 Avoid sugary foods.

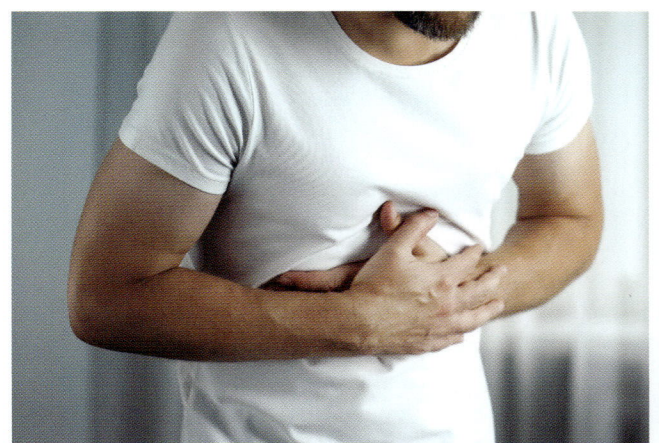

S-U

VAGINAL YEAST INFECTION

 4-5x per day   *While symptoms persist*

Essential Oils: *Tea Tree, Oregano, On Guard®, Basil, Rosemary, Frankincense, Lemon, Lemon Eucalyptus*

Other Solutions: *On Guard™+ Softgels, On Guard® Tablets, DDR Prime® Softgels*

🌢 Choose 3-4 of the recommended oils. Mix 10 drops of each with fractionated coconut oil in a 10 ml roller bottle. Rub over your abdominal area and on your lower back over your spine every 2-3 hours or until symptoms diminish. Take 2 On Guard™+ Softgels 3 times per day. Take up to 3 On Guard® Tablets per day. Add 1 drop of Lemon to warm water or tea and sip throughout day. Drink at least half your body weight in ounces of water per day. Take 2 DDR Prime® Softgels per day.

🔻 Avoid sugary foods.

VARICOSE VEINS

 4-5x per day   *As needed*

Essential Oils: *Cypress, Helichrysum, Siberian Fir*

Other Solutions: *N/A*

🌢 Mix 15 drops of Cypress and 10 drops each of Helichrysum and Siberian Fir in a 10 ml roller bottle with fractionated coconut oil. Apply to the affected area several times per day.

VERTIGO

 3-5x per day   **As needed**

Essential Oils: *Basil, Balance®, Ginger, Cedarwood*

Other Solutions: *Ginger Drops*

🌢 Choose 2-3 of the recommended oils. Mix 5-7 drops of each oil in a 10 ml roller bottle and fill with fractionated coconut oil. Apply behind your ears, down the back of your neck, under your skull, under your nose, and on your wrists throughout the day. Take Ginger Drops as needed.

VIRUS

⏰ *4-5x per day*	📅 *As needed until condition improves*

Essential Oils: *On Guard®, Oregano, Clove, Tea Tree, Frankincense, Lime, Eucalyptus, Breathe®, Lavender*

Other Solutions: *On Guard™+ Softgels, On Guard® Tablets, DDR Prime® Softgels, On Guard® Protecting Throat Drops, On Guard® Beadlets, On Guard® Sanitizing Mist, Lifelong Vitality, DigestZen TerraZyme®, PB Assist®+*

🌙 Combine 5 drops each of On Guard®, Oregano, Clove, Tea Tree, and Frankincense in a 10 ml roller bottle with fractionated coconut oil. Apply to your wrists, chest, the back of your neck, and your feet frequently throughout the day. If the virus affects respiration: combine 5 drops each of On Guard®, Lime, Eucalyptus, and Breathe® in a 10 ml roller bottle with fractionated coconut oil. Apply over your chest, the back of your neck, and on your feet. Diffuse 5-7 drops of Breathe® and inhale throughout the day. Take 2 On Guard™+ Softgels, twice a day. Take up to 3 On Guard® Tablets per day. Take 2 DDR Prime® Softgels daily. Use On Guard® Protecting Throat Drops and On Guard® Beadlets as needed and when out in public. Wash your hands for at least 30 seconds frequently throughout the day. Refrain from touching your eyes, nose, or mouth. Keep a safe distance from others. Carry On Guard® Sanitizing Mist with you and use as needed on the go.

🌿 Take Lifelong Vitality Supplements twice a day, 2-3 DigestZen TerraZyme® capsules at each meal, and PB Assist® once per day. Eat oysters, beef, chicken, tofu, pork, nuts, seeds (*pumpkin seeds, chia seeds*), lentils, yogurt, oatmeal, mushrooms, red bell peppers, oranges, kiwi, spinach, strawberries, raspberries, blackberries, tomatoes, broccoli, snow peas, asparagus, and fatty fish (*salmon, tuna, mackerel*). Consume herbs and spices like oregano, garlic, thyme, rosemary, ginger, and turmeric. Balance the intake of omega-3 fats from seeds and nuts like walnuts, hemp seeds, flaxseed, and chia seeds. Eat sauerkraut, kefir, kimchi, and yogurt. Drink at least half your body weight in ounces of water per day with 1 drop of Lemon or 1 drop of Grapefruit in it. Avoid sugary and processed foods.

🔶 Do a moderate exercise 4-5 times per week.

🌙 Try to have about 20 minutes of safe sun exposure daily to encourage healing. Aim to get 7-9 hours of sleep per night for rest and recovery.

V-Y

VOMITING

 4-5x per day | *Ongoing until symptoms resolve*

Essential Oils: *DigestZen®, Peppermint, Ginger*

Other Solutions: *Ginger Drops*

⊘ Place 1 drop of either DigestZen®, Peppermint, or Ginger in warm water and swallow. Combine 5-7 drops of each recommended oil in a 10 ml roller bottle with fractionated coconut oil. Apply topically to your abdominal area. Diffuse 3-5 drops of each recommended oil and inhale while symptoms are occurring.

WARTS

 4-5x per day | *Ongoing until wart disappears*

Essential Oils: *Oregano, Frankincense, Arborvitae, Lemon*

Other Solutions: *N/A*

⊘ Add 5-7 drops of each recommended oil in a 10 ml roller bottle with fractionated coconut oil. Apply directly to the warts 4-5 times per day until the warts disappear.

WASP STING

 3x per day | *Ongoing as needed*

Essential Oils: *Lavender, Purify, Basil, Roman Chamomile*

Other Solutions: *N/A*

⊘ Choose 2 of the recommended oils. Mix 1-2 drops of each oil with a tablespoon of fractionated coconut oil in your palm. Apply over the bee sting as soon as possible.

⊕ Seek immediate medical attention if you experience shortness of breath; itching; hives; dizziness; flushed face; pale skin; wheezing; or swelling in your face, throat, or tongue.

V-Y

WATER RETENTION

⏰ **3-5x per day**	📅 *While symptoms persist*

Essential Oils: *Lemon, Cypress, MetaPWR™, Juniper Berry, Grapefruit, Celery Seed, Green Mandarin*

Other Solutions: *Serenity® Softgels*

🌀 Choose Grapefruit, Lemon, Green Mandarin, Celery Seed, or MetaPWR™. Put 1-2 drops of the chosen oil in water and drink. Mix 5-7 drops each of Grapefruit, Cypress, and Juniper Berry in a 10 ml roller bottle and fill with fractionated coconut oil. Roll over the affected area throughout the day.

🍃 Consume dark green leafy vegetables, bananas, avocados, tomatoes, yogurt, dark chocolate, nuts, dairy products, and whole grains. Drink half your body weight in ounces of water. Add grapefruit, cucumber, or lemon wedges to your water along with your essential oils.

🔥 Make sure to adopt an exercise program consisting of cardio, strength, and balance exercises. If you have swelling in your legs or feet, elevate them while sitting or use compression stockings.

🌙 Make sure to get adequate sleep and rest. Take 2 Serenity® Softgels at bedtime.

🔻 If tolerated, do a 30-day cleanse each season. See the 30-day cleanse on page 434.

V-Y

WEIGHT ISSUES

⏰ *4-5x per day*	📅 *As needed*

Essential Oils: *MetaPWR™, Cinnamon, Grapefruit, Ginger, Black Pepper, Breathe®*

Other Solutions: *MetaPWR™ Softgels, Protein, MetaP-WR™ Metabolic Gum, Deep Blue® Rub, Mito2Max®, Lifelong Vitality, DigestZen TerraZyme®, PB Assist®+, Turmeric Dual Chamber Capsules, Deep Blue® Polyphenol Complex*

🔽 Mix 5-7 drops of each recommended oil, with the exception of Breathe®, in a 10 ml roller bottle with fractionated coconut oil. Rub it over your pulse points, over your abdominal area, and along your spine. Diffuse 5-7 drops of MetaPWR™ and inhale throughout the day. Add 1 drop of MetaPWR™ or Grapefruit to your water daily. Take 3-5 MetaPWR™ Softgels daily. Drink Protein *(blend one scoop of shake mix with 1/2 cup of almond, rice, soy milk, or water until smooth and creamy)*. Chew MetaPWR™ Metabolic Gum between meals. Take Mito2Max® twice daily.

🍏 Take Lifelong Vitality Supplements twice a day, 2-3 DigestZen TerraZyme® capsules at each meal, and PB Assist® once per day. Eat a variety of fresh fruits, vegetables, lean meats, healthy fats, sweet potatoes, and brown rice. Avoid refined sugar, MSG, gluten, corn, fried food, fast food, processed foods, and artificial sweeteners. Pay attention to how you feel when you are eating your food. Stop eating if you feel full. Eat when you feel truly hungry. Eat fiber- and protein-filled foods that make you feel full.

🐾 Exercise 3 days a week for 20 minutes to start *(walking, swimming, yoga, biking, and cross-country skiing are good choices)*. Work up to 45 minutes for 4-5 days a week. Use Breathe® on your chest if your breathing is altered due to excess weight. Do strength training 3-4 times per week, starting with light weights and working your way up to heavier weights. Warm up, cool down, and stretch for each exercise session. Apply Deep Blue® Rub after exercise. If sore, take 2 Deep Blue® Polyphenol Complex capsules or 2 Turmeric Dual Chamber Capsules. Work at your own pace. Rest when needed. Take baby steps in this area.

V-Y

WHIPLASH

4-5x per day	*Until symptoms improve*

Essential Oils: *PastTense®, Lemongrass, AromaTouch®, Wintergreen, Cypress, Marjoram, Copaiba*

Other Solutions: *Deep Blue® Rub, Deep Blue® Stick, Deep Blue® Polyphenol Complex, Turmeric Dual Chamber Capsules*

💠 Fill a 4-ounce glass jar with hard coconut oil until 3/4-Full. Add 2 quarter-sized drops of Deep Blue® Rub and 10 drops each of Lemongrass, Marjoram, Wintergreen, Cypress, AromaTouch®, and Copaiba. Stir well. Apply liberally over the affected area, massaging it into the soft tissues. Use PastTense® over your forehead and temples and down your neck for headaches. Take 2 Deep Blue® Polyphenol Complex capsules a day with meals, in the morning and evening. Take 2 Turmeric Dual Chamber Capsules per day. Use Deep Blue® Rub or Deep Blue® Stick over affected area.

V-Y

WHOOPING COUGH

4-5x times per day	While symptoms persist

Essential Oils: *Clary Sage, Roman Chamomile, Breathe®, Blue Tansy, Cardamom, Lemon*

Other Solutions: *Breathe® Drops, Breathe® Vapor Stick, On Guard® Protecting Throat Drops, On Guard® Beadlets*

🔽 Mix 1 drop of Breathe® with 1 tablespoon of fractionated coconut oil in your palms. Rub over your chest and mid/upper back, under your nose, and behind your ears. Cup your hands and inhale 3 deep breaths. Choose 3-4 of the recommended oils. Mix 5-7 drops of each oil in a 10 ml roller bottle and fill with fractionated coconut oil. Rub on the bottoms of your feet morning and evening. Put 2 drops of Lemon in your water and drink. Take Breathe® Drops as needed. Rub a Breathe® Vapor Stick over your chest and upper back throughout the day. Take On Guard® Protecting Throat Drops as needed. Take On Guard® Beadlets as desired. If you get oils in your eyes or on your face while inhaling from your hands, apply plain coconut oil over your eye or face to soothe the area. Repeat as needed.

🍏 Avoid dairy while symptoms persist.

V-Y

WITHDRAWAL SYMPTOMS

3x per day	*Until symptoms resolve*

Essential Oils: *Zendocrine®, Frankincense, Spikenard*

Other Solutions: *Ginger Drops, Peppermint Beadlets*

- Combine 10 drops of each recommended oil in a 10 ml roller bottle with fractionated coconut oil. Apply over your abdominal region, lower back, feet, and chest. Use Ginger Drops as needed throughout the day. Consume Peppermint Beadlets as needed.

WORKOUT RECOVERY

Post workout	*Ongoing as needed*

Essential Oils: *AromaTouch®, Marjoram, Lemongrass, Siberian Fir, Copaiba*

Other Solutions: *Deep Blue® Rub, Deep Blue® Stick, Deep Blue® Polyphenol Complex, Serenity® Softgels*

- Choose 2-3 of the recommended oils. Mix 5-7 drops of each in a 10 ml roller bottle and fill with fractionated coconut oil. Apply it over the affected muscles, joints, and soft tissues. Follow it up by applying Deep Blue® Rub or Deep Blue® Stick over the affected areas. Take 2 Deep Blue® Polyphenol Complex capsules a day with meals, in the morning and evening.

- Take 2 Serenity® Softgels at bedtime.

A - Y

WORMS

3-5x per day	As needed

Essential Oils: *Oregano, Tea Tree, Thyme*

Other Solutions: *N/A*

🟣 Combine 1 drop of each recommended oil in a veggie capsule and take 3 times per day. Add 10 drops of each recommended oil to a 10 ml roller bottle topped off with fractionated coconut oil. Apply to your abdomen frequently throughout the day.

WOUNDS

3-5x per day	Until symptoms improve

Essential Oils: *Tea Tree, Myrrh, Helichrysum*

Other Solutions: *Correct-X*

🟣 Combine 10 drops each of Tea Tree, Myrrh, Helichrysum in a 10 ml roller bottle with fractionated coconut oil. Apply to the affected area as recommended. Put a small amount of Correct-X on the affected area a few times per day.

YEAST

3x per day	Until symptoms resolve

Essential Oils: *Tea Tree, Lemon Eucalyptus, Siberian Fir, DDR Prime®, Thyme, Oregano, Pink Pepper, Geranium, Clove*

Other Solutions: *Lifelong Vitality, DigestZen TerraZyme®, PB Assist®+*

🟣 Mix 7 drops each of Lemon Eucalyptus, Tea Tree, Thyme, Oregano, and Geranium with fractionated coconut oil in a 10 ml roller bottle. Rub along your spine, over your abdominal region, on your wrists, and on your feet every 2-3 hours or until symptoms diminish. Place 1 drop each of Siberian Fir, Clove, DDR Prime®, and Pink Pepper in a capsule with a carrier oil and take twice daily with meals.

🟢 Take Lifelong Vitality Supplements twice a day and 2-3 DigestZen TerraZyme® capsules at each meal. Take 1-2 GX Assist softgels every day for 10 days and follow it up with 1 PB Assist® per day for 20 days. Eat a variety of fresh fruits, vegetables, lean meats, healthy fats, and rice. Avoid MSG, gluten, corn, fried food, fast food, processed foods, and artificial sweeteners.

🔴 Makeover your home by using the Abōde™ line of cleaning products, laundry pods, dishwasher pods, surface cleaner, and dish soap. Take care of your hands with Abōde™ Foaming Hand Wash and Lotion. If tolerated, do a 30-day cleanse each season. See the 30-day cleanse on page 434.

Chapter **3**

NATURAL SOLUTIONS

"I believe that for every illness or ailment known to man,
that God has a plant out here that will heal it. We just need
to keep discovering the properties for natural healing."
—Vannoy Gentles Fite

SINGLES AND BLENDS

Abōde™
Refreshing Blend

Adaptiv™
Calming Blend

 TOP USES

Refreshing Environment—Diffuse to energize, uplift, and refresh home, office, and/or personal spaces.

Body, Air & Odor Cleansing, Airborne Pathogens—Diffuse. Dilute and apply to underarm area or add to body wash.

Dishwasher Boost—Add a few drops onto dishwasher soap before starting cycle.

Urinary Issues & Parasites—Dilute and apply to bottoms of feet, and/or over kidney area or lower abdomen.

Viruses & Bacteria, Respiratory Congestion & Lymphatic Toxicity—Diffuse. Dilute and apply to bottoms of feet, chest and back, and/or underarms.

 TOP USES

Chaotic Environments & Situations, Lack of Tranquility—Diffuse, and apply to bottoms of feet.

Loss of Composure, Poor Coping Capacity & Anxiety—Diffuse, and apply up spine, on back of neck, and bottoms of feet.

Menstruation & Menopause-related Moodiness & Depression—Apply to abdomen, reflex points for ovaries, and to bottoms of feet.

Addictive, Obsessive/ Compulsive Behaviors/ Overthinking—Diffuse, and apply over liver area and to bottoms of feet.

 MAIN INGREDIENTS ·······························

Distilled Lime, Litsea, Cassia, Lemon Eucalyptus, Tea Tree, Arborvitae, Eucalyptus, Cilantro, Lavandin, Lemon Myrtle

 MAIN INGREDIENTS ·······························

Wild Orange, Lavender, Copaiba, Spearmint, Magnolia, Rosemary, Neroli, Sweetgum

⚠ **SAFETY** ···

Not safe for internal use. Dilution recommended. Possible skin irritation. Avoid exposure to sunlight or UV rays for up to 12 hours after application.

⚠ **SAFETY** ···

Not safe for internal use.

Air-X™
Air Blend

 TOP USES

Asthma, Cough, Bronchitis, Pneumonia, Sinusitus—Diffuse, and apply diluted to forehead, chest, and back.

Injured Respiratory Tissue Due to Oxidative Stress—Diffuse or inhale, and apply to bottoms of feet, chest, and back. Dilute if needed.

Congestion & Digestion Discomfort—Take in a capsule or under tongue. Apply diluted to chest or abdomen.

Odors & Airborne Pathogens—Diffuse or inhale, and apply to bottoms of feet, chest, and back. Dilute if needed.

 ⭐ **MAIN INGREDIENTS**

Litsea, Tangerine, Grapefruit, Frankincense, Cardamom

⚠️ **SAFETY**

Avoid exposure to sunlight or UV rays for up to 12 hours after application.

Align
Yoga Centering Blend

 TOP USES

Scattered & Overwhelmed—Apply under nose and across forehead. Inhale deeply from cupped hands.

Aligned, Singleminded, Tranquil & Focused—Diffuse. Apply to crown, neck area, and/or forehead.

Perfume—Apply to pulse points, chest, behind ears, and/or on ankles.

Accepted & Worthy—Diffuse. Apply under nose, over heart, spleen, and/or solar plexus.

Meditation & Prayer—Diffuse, or inhale deeply. Apply over heart and forehead.

Apathetic & Low Energy—Diffuse. Apply to pulse points, over heart, and on bottoms of feet.

⭐ **MAIN INGREDIENTS**

Bergamot, Coriander, Marjoram, Peppermint, Jasmine, Rose

⚠️ **SAFETY**

Not safe for internal use. Avoid exposure to sunlight or UV rays for up to 12 hours after application.

Amavi®

Men's Fortifying Blend

 TOP USES

Cologne or Aftershave—Apply to pulse points, neck and behind ears, or apply to face.

Discouraged, Enraged, Agitated & Irritated—Diffuse. Apply over heart, to back of neck, spine, and/or bottoms of feet.

Scattered, Rushed, Stressed—Diffuse. Apply to pulse points and/or bottoms of feet.

Focused Heart, Mind & Body—Diffuse. Apply over heart, to forehead, and/or bottoms of feet.

Mental Clarity, Meditation & Tranquility—Diffuse. Apply to forehead, over heart, and bottoms of feet.

Women's Perfume—Blend with jasmine or Beautiful.

⭐ **MAIN INGREDIENTS**

Buddha Wood, Balsam Fir, Black Pepper, Hinoki, Patchouli, Cocoa Extract

⚠ **SAFETY**

Not safe for internal use.

Anchor

Yoga Steadying Blend

 TOP USES

Meditation, Prayer & Focus—Diffuse. Apply to forehead, behind ears, along spine, and/or bottoms of feet.

Anchored, Courageous & Authentic, Stable—Diffuse. Apply to ankles, along spine and/or bottoms of feet.

Perfume—Apply to pulse points, chest, and behind ears.

Composed, Calm & Rested—Diffuse. Apply to back of neck, along spine, and/or bottoms of feet.

Rooted to the Earth, Grounded, Speaking Truth—Diffuse. Apply to throat area, along spine, and/or bottoms of feet.

⭐ **MAIN INGREDIENTS**

Lavender, Cedarwood, Frankincense, Cinnamon Bark, Sandalwood, Black Pepper, Patchouli

⚠ **SAFETY**

Not safe for internal use.

Arborvitae

Thuja plicata

 TOP USES

Candida & Fungal Issues—Apply to bottoms of feet or area of concern.

Viruses & Fever—Apply to bottoms of feet. Diffuse.

Cold Sores & Warts—Apply to area of concern frequently.

Insect Repellent—Diffuse. Spray on surfaces, and/or apply to exposed areas or clothing.

Respiratory Issues & Cough—Apply to chest and back.

Skin Cancer, Sunscreen—Apply to affected area.

Lymphatic Congestion—Apply under nose, on back of neck, and/or bottoms of feet.

Psoriasis & Hair Loss—Apply to troubled skin or scalp, or add with shampoo.

 **PROPERTIES**

Antiviral, Antifungal, Antibacterial, Stimulant

 MAIN CONSTITUENTS

Methyl thujate, Methyl-myrtenate, Terpinen-4-ol

⚠ **SAFETY**

Not safe for internal use. Dilution recommended. Possible skin sensitivity.

Arise

Yoga Enlightening Blend

 TOP USES

Connectedness with Self and Higher Power—Diffuse. Apply to crown, over heart, and along spine.

Intentional, Action-Oriented & Manifesting—Diffuse. Apply to ankles, along spine, and bottoms of feet.

Perfume—Apply to pulse points, chest, behind ears, and/or on ankles.

Uplifted, Courageous & Empowered—Diffuse. Apply to forehead, over heart, and bottoms of feet.

Overwhelmed, Mental Chatter, Lack of Clarity & Focus—Diffuse. Apply to forehead, toes, and behind ears.

 MAIN INGREDIENTS

Grapefruit, Lemon, Osmanthus, Melissa, Siberian Fir

⚠ **SAFETY**

Not safe for internal use. Avoid exposure to sunlight or UV rays for up to 12 hours after application.

Sourced— Canada

AromaTouch®
....
Massage Blend

 TOP USES

Muscle Tension, Aches & Cramps—Apply to areas of concern.

Headache, Neck & Back Pain, Arthritis—Apply to neck, shoulders, and along spine.

Neuropathy & Restless Leg—Apply to areas of concern to stimulate nerves and circulation.

Connective Tissue, Ligament & Tendon Issues—Apply to areas of concern.

Lymphatic Congestion—Apply to bottoms of feet and/or under arms, back of knees, and neck.

High Blood Pressure—Apply to bottoms of feet.

⭐ **MAIN INGREDIENTS** ....

Cypress, Peppermint, Marjoram, Basil, Grapefruit, Lavender

⚠ **SAFETY** ....

Not safe for internal use. Avoid exposure to sunlight or UV rays for up to 12 hours after application.

Balance®
....
Grounding Blend

 TOP USES

Stress & Anxiety—Apply to bottoms of feet. Diffuse, or inhale from cupped hands.

Jet Lag & Travel Anxiety—Inhale from cupped hands and/or apply under nose.

Mood Swings—Diffuse. Apply under nose and/or back of neck.

Neurological Conditions, Convulsions, Epilepsy, Parkinson's, Brain Injury—Apply to back of neck, along spine, and/or bottoms of feet, especially on toes.

Feeling Unstable or Inflexible—Apply to bottoms of feet, and/or diffuse.

⭐ **MAIN INGREDIENTS** ....

Spruce, Ho Wood, Frankincense, Blue Tansy, Blue Chamomile, Osmanthus

⚠ **SAFETY** ....

Not safe for internal use.

Basil
Ocimum basilicum

 **TOP USES**

Adrenal & Chronic Fatigue— Apply under nose, to bottoms of feet, back of neck, forehead, and/or over the adrenal area.

Loss of Sense of Smell— Apply under nose and to toes to regain or increase sense of smell.

Earache & Congestion, Allergies, Chronic Colds, Chills, Malaria— Apply behind and around ear area, swab ear canal. Apply to spine, bottoms of feet, and chest. Take in a capsule.

Low Blood Pressure, Dizziness, Fainting, Migraines— Apply to temples and back of neck, and/or bottoms of feet.

 **PROPERTIES** ···

Stimulant, Neurotonic, Steroidal, Regenerative, Antispasmodic, Anti-inflammatory, Antibacterial, Digestive Stimulant

MAIN CONSTITUENTS

Linalool, 1,8-cineole (eucalyptol), Bergamotene

⚠ **SAFETY**

Dilution recommended. Possible skin sensitivity. Caution with pregnancy and epilepsy.

Beautiful
Captivating Blend

 TOP USES

Energize & Uplift Mood & Environment— Apply to pulse points, back of neck, and/or bottoms of feet. Diffuse.

Stressed & Anxious— Apply to forehead, back of neck, and over heart. Diffuse.

Encourage Being True to Self— Apply to pulse points, back of neck, along spine, and/or bottoms of feet. Diffuse.

Focused Heart, Mind & Body— Apply to forehead, back of neck, and/or bottoms of feet. Diffuse.*

Meditation & Tranquility, Empowerment & Self Worth— Apply to pulse points, back of neck, along spine, and/or bottoms of feet. Diffuse.

*Apply roller blend to diffuser jewelry.

⭐ **MAIN INGREDIENTS** ·····························

Lime, Osmanthus, Bergamot, Frankincense

⚠ **SAFETY** ···

Not safe for internal use. Avoid exposure to sunlight or UV rays for up to 12 hours after application.

Sourced— Egypt

Bergamot
Citrus bergamia

 **TOP USES**

Addictions & Dopamine—Apply to back of neck and bottoms of feet, or diffuse.

Self-Worth Issues & Depression—Apply over heart or gut and diffuse.

Coughs & Bronchitis, Tonsilitis, Sore Throat—Apply to chest and/or throat area. Gargle and take in a capsule.

Appetite Excess or Loss & Anorexia—Breathe in and take in a capsule.

Acne, Oily Skin, Psoriasis & Eczema, Wounds, Boils—Apply to affected area.

Insomnia—Inhale or diffuse before sleep.

Bladder & Urinary Tract Infections—Take in a capsule.

 **PROPERTIES** ·······························

Neurotonic, Anti-inflammatory, Antidepressant, Antibacterial, Antifungal, Digestive Stimulant

 MAIN CONSTITUENTS

Limonene, Linalyl acetate, Linalool, Terpinene, β-pinene

⚠ **SAFETY**

Possible skin sensitivity. Avoid sunlight or UV rays to applied area for up to 12 hours.

Bergamot Mint
Mentha citrata

 TOP USES

Clear & Revitalize Mind, Meditation & Mindfulness—Diffuse, or apply under nose, on forehead, back of neck, and/or toes.

Calm, Center, & Relax—Diffuse, or apply to pulse points, back of neck, along spine, and/or bottoms of feet.

Low Energy, Lack of Motivation, Pessimism—Diffuse, or apply under nose, over heart, and across forehead.

Muscle Aches & Pains, Tension—Apply to areas of concern.

Unsettled or Restless, Sleep Issues—Diffuse. Apply under nose and on bottoms of feet.

 PROPERTIES ·······························

Antioxidant, Calming, Invigorating, Analgesic, Antidepressant

 MAIN CONSTITUENTS

Linalool, Linalyl acetate

⚠ **SAFETY**

Not safe for internal use.

Sourced— Italy

Sourced— India

Birch

Betula lenta

 TOP USES

Connective Tissue, Muscle, or Tendon Injuries, Whiplash—Apply to affected area.

Broken Bones & Tooth Pain—Apply to area of concern.

Arthritis & Rheumatism, & Gout—Apply to affected area.

Edema, Blood, Toxicity, Congested Lymph—Apply to bottoms of feet or ankles.

Muscle Pain, Spasms, Lack of Tone—Apply to area(s) of concern for steroidal support.

Fever—Apply on spine.

Weak-willed, Unsupported—Diffuse, or inhale from cupped hands. Apply to bottoms of feet.

 **PROPERTIES**

Analgesic, Neurotonic, Anti-rheumatic, Stimulant, Steroidal, Warming

 MAIN CONSTITUENTS

Methyl salicylate

SAFETY

Not safe for internal use. Avoid during pregnancy. Not for use by epileptics.

Sourced— Canada

Black Pepper

Piper nigrum

 TOP USES

Constipation, Diarrhea, Gas—Take in capsule or apply to abdomen.

Respiratory & Lymphatic Drainage, Lack of Perspiration—Use a drop under tongue. Inhale or diffuse.

Cataracts—Take in a capsule. Apply under second and third toes.

Poor Circulation & Cold Extremities, Dizziness, Aphrodisiac—Apply to increase circulation and blood flow to areas of concern or interest.

Smoking & Addictions—Take under tongue. Inhale or diffuse.

Food Flavor—Enchance foods by adding a drop for flavor.

 PROPERTIES

Antioxidant, Antispasmodic, Digestive Stimulant, Expectorant, Neurotonic, Rubefacient, Stimulant

 MAIN CONSTITUENTS

β-Caryophyllene, Limonene, Sabinene, α-pinene, ß-Pinene, δ-3-carene

SAFETY

Dilution recommended. Possible skin sensitivity if old or oxidized.

Sourced— Madagascar

Black Spruce
Picea mariana

 TOP USES

Overstriving, Adrenal/Nervous Exhaustion & Fatigue, Melancholic—Diffuse, and apply to forehead, over heart, and/or above kidney area.

Chronic Joint/Back Pain—Apply to areas of concern.

Insecurity & Indecisiveness—Diffuse, and apply over heart and on pulse points.

Feeling Disconnected from Potential, Thwarted, Stuck, Unforgiving—Diffuse, and apply to pulse points and over heart.

Asthma, Bronchitis, Sinusitis, Spastic & Moist Coughs—Apply to warm/wet washcloth and place on chest, or add to hot water, cover head with towel, and inhale vapors.

 **PROPERTIES**

Anti-inflammatory, Steroidal, Expectorant, Calming, Grounding, Restorative

MAIN CONSTITUENTS

Bornyl acetate, a-pinene, Camphene, δ-3-carene

⚠ **SAFETY**

Not safe for internal use.

Blue Tansy
Tanacetum annuum

 TOP USES

Allergies, Itching, Rashes, Watery Eyes, Sneezing—Apply to bottoms of feet and/or affected areas. Diffuse.

Acne, Eczema, Psoriasis, Sunburn—Apply to affected areas.

Asthma & Respiratory Issues, Hiccups—Diffuse, and apply to chest.

Fibromyalgia, Sciatica, Arthritis, & Rheumatism—Apply to affected areas.

Fungal & Skin Infections—Apply to affected areas.

Tension & Sinus Headaches, Migraines, Toothache—Massage into temples, forehead, sides of nose or jaw.

 PROPERTIES

Sedative, Relaxant, Antidepressant, Aphrodisiac, Decongestant, Stomachic

MAIN CONSTITUENTS

Sabinene, Chamazulene, p-Cymene, a-Phellandrene, ß-Pinene, Camphor

⚠ **SAFETY**

Not safe for internal use. Can be harmful to small animals. Possible skin sensitivity. May stain surfaces, fabrics, and skin.

Sourced— Canada

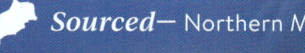

Sourced— Northern Morocco

Brave™
....
Children's Courage Blend

 TOP USES

Discouraged & Low Energy— Apply under nose, to back of neck, over heart, and/or bottoms of feet.

Tired & Weary—Apply under nose, to back of neck, forehead, and/or bottoms of feet.

Lack of Determination & Conviction—Apply under nose, along spine, over heart, and/or bottoms of feet.

Afraid & Scared—Apply under nose, to back of neck, along spine, and/or bottoms of feet.

Lack of Confidence & Motivation—Apply under nose, to chest, back, and/or bottoms of feet.

Confused & Overwhelmed— Apply under nose, to back of neck, and forehead.

⭐ **MAIN INGREDIENTS** ······························

Wild Orange, Amyris, Osmanthus, Cinnamon

 ⚠ **SAFETY** ······························

Not safe for internal use. Avoid exposure to sunlight or UV rays for up to 12 hours after application.

Breathe®
....
Respiration Blend

 TOP USES

Pneumonia & Asthma— Diffuse, and/or apply under nose, and on chest and back.

Allergies & Pollen Sensitivity— Inhale from cupped hands and/or apply under nose and on forehead. Diffuse.

Sleep Issues—Diffuse, and/or apply to bottoms of feet before bed.

Bronchitis & Influenza— Diffuse, and/or apply to chest, back, and on bottoms of feet.

Sinusitis & Nasal Polyps— Apply across forehead and under nose.

Cough & Congestion, Runny Nose—Diffuse, and/or apply under or over bridge of nose, to chest, and bottoms of feet.

⭐ **MAIN INGREDIENTS** ······························

Laurel Leaf, Peppermint, Eucalyptus, Tea Tree, Lemon, Cardamom, Ravintsara

 ⚠ **SAFETY** ······························

Not safe for internal use. Dilution recommended. Possible skin sensitivity. Avoid exposure to sunlight or UV rays for up to 12 hours after application.

Calmer™

Children's Restful Blend

 TOP USES

Unsettled & Restless, Sleep Issues—Apply under nose and to bottoms of feet.

Stressed & Anxious—Apply under nose, to back of neck and forehead.

Fussy, Easily Upset & Startled— Apply to chest, and/or bottoms of feet.

Uptight & Wound Up, Moody—Apply under nose and across forehead, or inhale deeply from cupped hands.

Muscles Aches & Growing Pains—Apply to areas of concern.

Angry, Agitated & Irritable—Apply to bottoms of feet, spine, and under nose.

⭐ **MAIN INGREDIENTS** ·····················

Lavender, Cananga, Buddha Wood, Roman Chamomile

 SAFETY ······································

Not safe for internal use.

Cardamom

Elettaria cardamomum

 **TOP USES**

Respiratory Congestion & Breathing Difficulties—Apply to chest, bridge of nose, forehead, and diffuse.

Stomach Ache & Constipation—Take in a capsule, and/or apply to abdomen.

Colitis & Diarrhea, Loss of Appetite—Apply to abdomen, and/or take in a capsule.

Gastritis & Stomach Ulcers—Take in a capsule. Apply to abdomen.

Menstrual & Muscular Pain—Apply to area of concern.

Sore Throat & Fevers—Gargle and apply to throat area, back of neck, forehead, and/or bottoms of feet.

⭐ **PROPERTIES** ··································

Digestive Stimulant, Antispasmodic, Anti-inflammatory, Decongestant, Expectorant, Tonic, Stomachic, Carminative

MAIN CONSTITUENTS

α-Terpinyl acetate, Linalyl acetate, 1,8-cineole (eucalyptol)

 SAFETY

N/A

Sourced— Guatemala

Cassia
Cinnamomum cassia

 TOP USES

Cold Extremities & Poor Circulation—Apply diluted to bottoms of feet.

Upset Stomach & Vomiting—Take in a capsule.

Detox for Ear, Nose, Throat, Lungs & Lymph—Take in a capsule.

Slow Metabolism—Take in a capsule before meals.

Water Retention & Kidney Infection—Take in a capsule, or apply on bottoms of feet to kidney reflex points.

Viruses & Bacteria, Fungus & Candida—Take in a capsule, and diffuse.

Imbalanced Blood Sugar & Insulin Resistance—Take in a capsule before meals.

 **PROPERTIES**

Decongestant, Carminative, Detoxifier, Cardiotonic, Antimicrobial, Antiviral, Antifungal, Antispasmodic

 MAIN CONSTITUENTS

Transcinnameldehyde, Cinnamyl acetate

⚠ **SAFETY**

Dilution recommended. Possible skin sensitivity. Can reduce milk supply in lactating women.

Cedarwood
Juniperus virginiana

 TOP USES

ADD, ADHD, Low Gaba or Dopamine Levels—Apply to back of neck, across forehead, and Diffuse, or inhale.

Psoriasis & Eczema, Skin Infections—Apply to affected area.

Ulcers—Inhale or apply to back of neck, bottoms of feet, and/or abdomen.

Cough, Sinus & Lung Issues—Apply to chest and forehead. Diffuse, and/or inhale from cupped hands.

Stroke & Seizures, Anxiety—Apply on back of neck and bottoms of feet.

Joint Inflammation, Stiff Neck, Muscle Tension—Apply to area of concern.

 **PROPERTIES**

Anti-inflammatory, Diuretic, Astringent, Antiseptic, Insecticidal, Sedative

MAIN CONSTITUENTS

a-cedrene, Cedrol, Thujopsene

⚠ **SAFETY**

Not safe for internal use. Dilution recommended. Possible skin sensitivity.

Celery Seed

Apium graveolens

 TOP USES

Celery Seed Tonic—Take 4 drops per 8 ounces of purified water.

Ulcers, GERD, Stomach or Intestinal Lining Issues—Take in capsule and apply to abdomen.

Blood & Liver Toxicity—Take in capsule and apply to bottoms of feet and over liver.

Water Retention & Edema, Urinary Issues—Take in water or juice. Apply on lower abdomen and bottoms of feet.

Weak & Stiff Joints, Gout, Arthritis & Rheumatism, Osteoporosis—Apply to bottoms of feet and areas of concern.

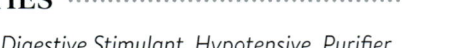 **PROPERTIES**

Diuretic, Detoxifier, Digestive Stimulant, Hypotensive, Purifier

 **MAIN CONSTITUENTS**

Limonene, ß-Selinene

 **SAFETY**

N/A

Cheer®

Uplifting Blend

 TOP USES

Depression & Discouragement—Diffuse, or inhale from cupped hands. Apply to pulse points, under nose and/or across forehead.

Hysteria & Anxiety—Diffuse, or inhale from cupped hand. Apply to pulse points, under nose, and/or across forehead.

Disconnection—Diffuse, or inhale from cupped hands. Apply to pulse points, under nose, and/or across forehead.

PMS—Diffuse, or inhale from cupped hands. Apply on lower abdomen.

Cellular Health—Apply to bottoms of feet.

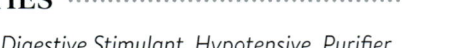 **MAIN INGREDIENTS**

Wild Orange, Clove, Star Anise, Ginger, Bergamot, Ylang Ylang, Frankincense, Lemongrass, Tonka Bean, Vanilla

 SAFETY

Not safe for Internal use. Avoid exposure to sunlight or UV rays for up to 12 hours after application.

Sourced— India

Cilantro

Coriandrum sativum

TOP USES

Heavy Metal Toxicity & Free Radical Damage—Take in a capsule.

Autism, Parkinson's, Alzheimer's, Multiple Sclerosis—Take in a capsule and apply to toes.

Gas, Bloating & Constipation—Apply over abdomen.

Allergies—Apply over liver and to bottoms of feet to ease allergies by reducing liver toxicity.

Liver & Kidney Support—Take in a capsule or apply over liver or kidney area.

Fungal & Bacterial Infections, Candida—Take in a capsule, and apply to infected area.

PROPERTIES

Antioxidant, Antifungal, Detoxifying, Antibacterial

MAIN CONSTITUENTS

Linalool, Trans-2-Decenal

SAFETY

N/A

Sourced— USA

Cinnamon Bark

Cinnamomum zeylanicum

TOP USES

Diabetes & High Blood Sugar—Take in a capsule.

Cold & Flu, Viruses, Respiratory Infection—Take in a capsule or apply to bottoms of feet. Diffuse.

Poor Circulation, Cold Extremities, Heart Issues—Apply diluted to bottoms of feet. Take in a capsule.

Oral Infections—Gargle a drop in water.

Fungal & Bacterial Infection Parasites, Scabies—Take in a capsule. Apply highly diluted to area of concern.

Kidney Infection or Bladder—Take in a capsule.

Candida & Vaginitis—Take in a capsule.

PROPERTIES

Antiseptic, Antimicrobial, Antioxidant, Antifungal, Antiviral, Aphrodisiac

MAIN CONSTITUENTS

Transcinnamaldehyde, Cinnamyl acetate, Eugenol

SAFETY

Dilution recommended. Possible skin sensitivity.

Sourced— Madagascar

Citronella

Cymbopogon winterianus

Citrus Bliss®

Invigorating Blend

 **TOP USES**

Side Effects from Drugs, Alcohol, Narcotics & Toxins—Diffuse, and apply to bottoms of feet and affected areas.

Greasy Hair & Lice, Detangler—Add to shampoo or conditioner.

Acne, Athlete's Foot & Nail Fungus—Apply to areas of concern.

Digestive & Intestinal Inflammation, Reaction to Spicy Foods & Carrageenan—Apply to bottoms of feet and over upper abdomen and liver area.

Flea & Tick Repellent—Diffuse, and apply to exposed areas. Add to glass spray bottle to treat surfaces or apply to clothing.

 TOP USES

Eating Disorders—Diffuse, or inhale from cupped hands. Apply to the abdomen.

Stress, Anxiety & Depression—Diffuse. Apply under nose, and/or back of neck.

Air Freshener—Diffuse to clear air of odors and uplift.

Perfume—Apply to pulse points.

Lymphatic & Immune Boost—Diffuse. Apply under nose, on back of neck, and/or bottoms of feet.

Low Energy & Exhaustion—Diffuse. Apply under nose and/or back of neck to energize and uplift.

Antiseptic Cleanser—Mix with water in a glass bottle and apply to surfaces.

⭐ **PROPERTIES**

Insect Repellent, Insecticidal, Detoxifier, Cleanser, Bactericidal, Antifungal, Astringent, Fungicidal, Deodorant

⭐ **MAIN INGREDIENTS**

Wild Orange, Lemon, Grapefruit, Bergamot, Red Mandarin, Green Mandarin, Litsea, Tonka Bean, Vanilla

 MAIN CONSTITUENTS

Citronellal, Geraniol

⚠ **SAFETY**

Not safe for internal use. Dilution recommended for possible skin sensitivity.

⚠ **SAFETY**

Not safe for internal use. Avoid exposure to sunlight or UV rays for up to 12 hours after application.

Sourced— Indonesia

Citrus Bloom™
Springtime Blend

 TOP USES

Closed Mindedness, Hopelessness or Resignation—Diffuse, or inhale deeply from cupped hands. Apply to belly button, over heart, and on forehead to open up to new possibilities.

Chaotic Environments & Situations—Diffuse, and/or apply to forehead, bottoms of feet, and over heart.

Self-Worth Issues—Diffuse, and/or inhale. Apply over solar plexus and heart areas, and back of neck to create connections with heart, mind, and body.

Afternoon Slump & Pessimistic Outlook—Diffuse, and inhale. Apply under nose, on forehead, and over heart.

⭐ **MAIN INGREDIENTS** ·······················

Wild Orange, Grapefruit, Lavender, Roman Chamomile, Magnolia

⚠ **SAFETY** ·······················

Not safe for internal use. Avoid exposure to sunlight or UV rays for up to 12 hours after application.

ClaryCalm®
Women's Monthly Blend

TOP USES

Imbalanced Hormones—Apply to back of neck, reflex points, lower abdomen, and/or bottoms of feet.

Heavy Periods, PMS & Cramps, Breast Tenderness—Apply to lower abdomen, back of neck, and/or bottoms of feet. For added soothing, combine with marjoram and cover with a moist, warm washcloth.

Pre & Perimenopause—Apply to abdomen, back of neck, and/or bottoms of feet.

Hot Flashes—Apply to lower abdomen, back and sides of neck, and/or bottoms of feet.

Mood Swings—Apply over heart, across forehead, on back of neck, and/or bottoms of feet.

⭐ **MAIN INGREDIENTS** ·······················

Clary Sage, Lavender, Bergamot, Roman Chamomile, Ylang Ylang, Cedarwood, Geranium, Fennel, Carrot Seed, Palmarosa, Vitex

⚠ **SAFETY** ·······················

Not safe for internal use. Avoid exposure to sunlight or UV rays for up to 12 hours after application.

Clary Sage
....
Salvia sclarea

 TOP USES

Endometriosis & Breast Cancer—Apply diluted to breasts, or take in capsule to regulate estrogen.

Breast Issues or Enlargement—Apply to breast areas.

PMS & Cramps, Perimenopause, Menopause—Take in a capsule, or apply to abdomen or bottoms of feet.

Parkinson's, Seizures & Convulsions, Thick Blood—Apply to back of neck to support healthy brain function.

Child Birth & Low Milk Supply—Apply diluted down spine or over abdomen to help bring on labor. Apply to each breast for increased lactation.

 PROPERTIES ....

Emmenagogue, Galactagogue, Neurotonic, Mucolytic, Anticoagulant, Sedative, Antispasmodic

 MAIN CONSTITUENTS

Linalyl acetate, Linalool

⚠ **SAFETY**

Exercise caution during earlier stages of pregnancy.

Clove
....
Eugenia caryophyllata

 TOP USES

Alzheimer's & Memory Loss—Dilute and apply to bottoms of feet. Take in a capsule.

Cold & Flu, Viral or Respiratory Infection, Lupus—Apply diluted to bottoms of feet, or take in a capsule. Diffuse.

Thyroid Issues & Metabolism—Apply to diluted to base of big toe and/or take in a capsule.

Tooth Pain & Cavities—Dilute and apply to affected area to numb and ease pain.

Candida & Parasites, Intestinal Infection, Hepatitis—Take in a capsule.

Smoking Addiction—Take with black pepper under tongue.

Lymphoma & Leukemia—Take in a capsule.

 PROPERTIES ....

Antioxidant, Antiviral, Antifungal, Expectorant, Nervine, Anti-parasitic, Vermicide

 MAIN CONSTITUENTS

Eugenol, Eugenyl acetate, β-caryophyllene

⚠ **SAFETY**

Dilution recommended. Possible skin sensitivity. To reduce liver stress, use Zendocrine®.

Sourced— France

Sourced— Madagascar

Console®
Comforting Blend

 TOP USES

Grief & Sadness, Heartache—Diffuse, or apply under nose and over heart.

Emotional Release & Reassurance—Diffuse, and apply under nose, over heart, and across forehead.

Fear & Emotional Pain Relief—Diffuse, or apply under nose and to chest.

Brain Impairment—Apply to forehead, back of neck, and toes.

Spiritual Connectivity & Meditation—Apply to forehead and chest. Diffuse, and/or inhale from cupped hands.

Low Libido—Diffuse, or apply to abdomen.

 MAIN INGREDIENTS ....

Frankincense, Patchouli, Ylang Ylang, Labdanum, Amyris, Sandalwood, Rose, Osmanthus

⚠ **SAFETY** ....

Not safe for internal use. Avoid exposure to sunlight or UV rays for up to 12 hours after application.

Copaiba
Copaifera reticulata, offincinalis, coriacea, landsdorffii

 TOP USES

Pain & Inflammation, Arthritis, Gout & Muscle Cramps—Diffuse, inhale from cupped hands, and/or apply to area of concern.

Liver Toxicity & Issues, Cancer—Take in a capsule or in water.

Tendonitis, Plantar Fasciitis & Heel Spurs—Apply to area of concern.

Respiratory & Tonsil Issues, Sore Throat—Diffuse, or inhale from cupped hands. Apply to throat area, under nose, and/or chest.

Dopamine Deficiency & Additions—Take in a capsule.

Bedwetting & Incontinence—Apply to abdomen and/or take in a capsule.

 PROPERTIES ....

Anti-inflammatory, Antiarthritic, Analgesic, Antifungal, Antibacterial, Antioxidant, Anti-carcinoma, Carminative, Anti-microbial

 MAIN CONSTITUENTS

β-caryophyllene

⚠ **SAFETY**

Dilution recommended. Possible skin sensitivity. To reduce liver stress, use Zendocrine®.

 Sourced— Brazil

Coriander

Coriandrum sativum

 TOP USES

Gas & Nausea, Colic, Diarrhea, Food Poisoning—Apply to abdomen. Take in a capsule.

High Blood Sugar & Diabetes—Take in a capsule before meals.

Itchy Skin & Rashes, Acne, Candida, Fungal Issues—Apply to area of concern.

Cartilage & Joint Pain or Injury—Apply directly to area of concern.

Neuropathy—Apply to bottoms of feet. Take in a capsule.

Loss of Appetite, Anorexia—Take in a capsule, and/or inhale from cupped hands.

 **PROPERTIES**

Analgesic, Antioxidant, Anti-inflammatory, Digestive Stimulant, Antibacterial, Antispasmodic

 MAIN CONSTITUENTS

Linalool, α-pinene, γ-terpinene, Camphor

⚠ **SAFETY**

N/A

Sourced— Russia

Cypress

Cupressus sempervirens, lusitanica

 TOP USES

Restless Leg, Poor Circulation & Cold Extremities—Apply to areas of concern.

Poor Urine Flow, Edema & Toxemia—Apply to lower abdomen, legs, and/or bottoms of feet.

Cellulte, Lack of Perspiration—Apply over areas of concern.

Bed Wetting & Incontinence—Apply over bladder area and/or bladder reflex point on foot.

Varicose Veins & Hemorrhoids, Broken Capillaries, Nose Bleed—Apply over areas of concern.

Stroke & Concussion—Apply to back of neck, forehead, and on bottoms of feet.

 **PROPERTIES**

Antibacterial, Antiseptic, Anti-rheumatic, Stimulant, Vasoconstrictor, Tonic

 MAIN CONSTITUENTS

α-pinene, δ-3-carene

⚠ **SAFETY**

Not safe for internal use.

Sourced— Kenya

DDR Prime®
....
Cellular Complex Blend

 TOP USES

Cancer & Tumors—Take in a capsule. Apply diluted to back of neck, along spine, and/or on bottoms of feet.

Low Progesterone, Estrogen & Thyroid Issues—Take in a capsule, and/or apply to bottoms of feet.

Candida & Fungal Issues—Apply to bottoms of feet, and/or take in a capsule.

Pain & Inflammation—Apply to diluted to area of concern.

Nerve Damage, Brain Injury—Apply diluted to affected area. Take in a capsule.

Autoimmune Disorders—Take in a capsule. Apply diluted to back of neck, along spine, and/or on bottoms of feet.

⭐ **MAIN INGREDIENTS** ·······················

Frankincense, Wild Orange, Litsea, Thyme, Clove, Summer Savory, Niaouli, Lemongrass

 ⚠ **SAFETY** ·······························

Dilution recommended. Possible skin sensitivity. Avoid exposure to sunlight or UV rays for up to 12 hours after application.

Deep Blue®
....
Soothing Blend

 TOP USES

Muscle, Back & Joint Pain—Apply to areas of discomfort.

Arthritis & Rheumatism, Gout—Apply to areas of discomfort.

Neuropathy & Carpal Tunnel—Apply to areas of discomfort.

Bruising & Broken Bones—Apply to affected area to reduce inflammation and scar tissue.

Fibromyalgia & Lupus—Apply to areas of discomfort.

Whiplash & Tense, Strained, or Sprained Muscles—Apply to areas of discomfort.

⭐ **MAIN INGREDIENTS** ·······················

Wintergreen, Camphor, Peppermint, Ylang Ylang, Helichrysum, Blue Tansy, Blue Chamomile, Osmanthus

 ⚠ **SAFETY** ·······························

Not safe for internal use. Possible skin sensitivity.

DigestZen®
Digestion Blend

 TOP USES

Bloating, Gas, Heartburn, Nausea & Indigestion—Apply over abdomen, and take in a capsule.

Reflux & Colic—Take in water or in a capsule. Apply diluted to an infant's abdomen or bottoms of feet.

Dry Or Sore Throat—Drop directly onto back of throat.

Morning Sickness & Heartburn—Apply to chest, pulse points, abdomen, and/or take in a glass of water.

Motion & Travel Sickness—Inhale or apply under nose and/or drink in water or drop under tongue.

Colitis & Irritable Bowel—Take in a capsule, water, and/or massage into abdomen.

 ⭐ **MAIN INGREDIENTS** ·····················

Peppermint, Coriander, Ginger, Caraway, Cardamom, Fennel, Anise

⚠ **SAFETY** ·····················

Possible skin sensitivity. Dilute for sensitive skin.

Dill
Anethum graveolens

 TOP USES

Muscle Spasms—Apply to calm muscles.

Nervousness—Inhale from cupped hands or apply under nose or back of neck with Roman chamomile to calm.

Sugar Addiction & Pancreas Issues—Take in a capsule.

Cholesterol & High Blood Pressure—Take in a capsule.

Low Breast Milk Supply—Apply to chest, and/or take in a capsule.

Detox & Electrolyte Balance—Take in a capsule as part of a detox program.

Respiratory Issues—Apply diluted to chest, and/or take in a capsule. Diffuse.

⭐ **PROPERTIES** ·····················

Antispasmodic, Expectorant, Stimulant, Galactagogue, Carminative, Emmenagogue, Hypertensive, Antibacterial

 **MAIN CONSTITUENTS**

Limonene, Carvone, a-phellandrene

⚠ **SAFETY**

N/A

Sourced— India

Douglas Fir

Pseudotsuga menziesii

 TOP USES

Mental Fog & Low Energy—Apply to temples and forehead or diffuse to clear mind and revive enthusiasm.

Depression & Tension—Apply to temples, forehead, and back of neck, or diffuse to relax and ground.

Constipation—Apply diluted to abdomen.

Respiratory Infection & Cough—Apply to throat, chest, and/or diffuse.

Muscle & Joint Soreness—Massage with wintergreen to affected area.

Rheumatic & Arthritic Conditions—Apply to affected areas.

 PROPERTIES

Antioxidant, Analgesic, Antimicrobial, Antiseptic, Anticatarrhal, Astringent, Diuretic, Expectorant, Laxative, Sedative, Stimulant, Tonic

MAIN CONSTITUENTS

β-pinene, α-pinene, δ-3-carene, Sabinene

 **SAFETY**

Not for internal use.

Elevation

Joyful Blend

 TOP USES

Elevate Mood & Mind—Diffuse, or inhale. Apply under nose, on pulse points, back of neck, and/or forehead.

Energize & Refresh—Diffuse, and inhale from cupped hands. Apply under nose, across forehead, and/or on neck and chest.

Depression & Mood Disorders—Diffuse, or inhale. Apply to back of neck, on forehead, and over heart.

Grief & Sorrow—Diffuse, and inhale. Apply over heart and on back of neck.

Stimulate & Uplift—Apply under nose, on back of neck, forehead, and/or inhale from cupped hands or diffuse.

★ MAIN INGREDIENTS

Lavandin, Tangerine, Lavender, Amyris, Clary Sage, Hawaiian Sandalwood, Ylang Ylang, Ho Wood, Osmanthus, Lemon Myrtle, Melissa

 SAFETY

Not safe for internal use. Avoid exposure to sunlight or UV rays for up to 12 hours after application.

Sourced— New Zealand

Eucalyptus
....
Eucalyptus radiata, polybractea, kochii, loxophleba, globulus

 TOP USES

Congestion, Cough, Bronchitis, Pneumonia, Asthma, Sinusitis—Apply to chest, bridge of nose, forehead, and bottoms of feet. Diffuse, or inhale from cupped hands.

Shingles, Malaria, Cold & Flu, Herpes—Apply to bottoms of feet or spine. Diffuse.

Lice & Parasites, Mosquito Repellent—Apply to affected areas, scalp, or bottoms of feet.

Fevers & Heat Sensitivity—Apply down the spine for cooling effect.

Bites, Wounds & Cuts, Blisters—Apply to area of concern.

 **PROPERTIES** ....

Antiviral, Antibacterial, Expectorant, Analgesic, Insecticidal, Hypotensive, Disinfectant, Catalyst

MAIN CONSTITUENTS

1,8-cineole (Eucalyptol) a-terpineol, a-pinene

⚠ **SAFETY**

Not safe for internal use. Dilution recommended. Possible skin sensitivity.

Fennel
....
Foeniculum vulgare

 TOP USES

Nausea, Colic & Flatulence, Vomiting—Take in a capsule or water. Apply to abdomen. Dilute for infant.

Menstrual Issues & PMS—Take in a capsule, and/or apply to lower abdomen.

Menopause & Premenopause—Take in a capsule. Apply to lower abdomen.

Cramps & Spasms, Lack of Uterus Tone—Dilute and rub onto area of need.

Low Breast Milk Supply—Take in a capsule or water.

Overly Acidic, Toxicity, Kidney Stones, Gout—Take in a capsule or glass of water.

 PROPERTIES ....

Antispasmodic, Emmenagogue, Galactagogue, Diuretic, Mucolytic, Digestive, Anti-inflammatory

MAIN CONSTITUENTS

Trans-Anethole, a-pinene, Limonene

⚠ **SAFETY**

Dilution recommended. Possible skin sensitivity. Caution during pregnancy and with children under 5 years old. Not for use with epileptics.

Forgive®
Renewing Blend

Frankincense
Boswellia carterii, sacra, paprifera, frereana

 TOP USES

Lack of Forgiveness, Repressed Emotions, Holding a Grudge—Apply to temples, back of neck, over heart, and/or diffuse.

Anger, Frustration, Irritability, Excessive Judgment, Punishing—Diffuse, or inhale. Apply under nose, across forehead, on back of neck, and/or over heart.

Spiritual & Emotional Toxicity Held in Body Tissues—Diffuse, and apply under nose and/or to chest. Apply to affected area.

Addictions & Unhealthy Attachments—Diffuse, and apply to pulse points and/or over heart.

Ulcer & Liver Issues—Apply over upper abdomen and/or liver area.

⭐ **MAIN INGREDIENTS**

Spruce, Bergamot, Juniper Berry, Myrrh, Arborvitae, Nootka, Thyme, Citronella

 ⚠ **SAFETY**

Not safe for internal use. Dilution recommended. Possible skin sensitivity. Avoid exposure to sunlight or UV rays for up to 12 hours after application.

 TOP USES

Cancer & Tumors, Cellular & Immune Health—Take in a capsule or under tongue with oil(s) that target area of need. Massage over affected area.

Seizures & Trauma, Concussion—Drop under the tongue and apply along hairline.

Alzheimer's, Dementia, Parkinson's & Brain Injury, Lack of Motor Control—Use or apply under nose and on back of neck. Diffuse, or inhale from cupped hands.

Wounds, Wrinkles, Skin Ulcers, Boils, Moles—Apply to affected areas.

⭐ **PROPERTIES**

Immunostimulant, Anticarcinogenic, Anti-carcinoma, Anti-inflammatory, Antidepressant, Restorative

 **MAIN CONSTITUENTS**

α-pinene, Limonene, α-thujene, octylacetate

 ⚠ **SAFETY**

N/A

Sourced— Omar/Somalia

Geranium

Pelarogonium graveolens

 TOP USES

Blood Toxicity, Bleeding, Varicose Veins & Broken Capillaries—Take in a capsule. Apply to troubled areas.

Liver & Gallbladder Issues, Gallstones, Bile Duct Obstruction—Take in a capsule.

Cuts & Wounds, Burns, Scars—Apply to area of concern.

Hormone Imbalance, Adrenal Fatigue, Excessive Emotionality—Diffuse, or inhale, and take in a capsule.

Endometriosis, Irregular or Prolonged Menstruation, PMS, Pelvic Pain, Sterility—Take in a capsule. Apply to lower abdomen and reflex points.

 PROPERTIES

Hemostatic, Detoxifier, Regenerative, Anti-allergenic, Antihemorrhagic, Antitoxic

 MAIN CONSTITUENTS

Citronellol, Cironellyl formate, Geraniol, Guaiadene, Menthone

⚠ **SAFETY**

Dilution recommended. Possible skin sensitivity.

Ginger

Zingiber officinale

 TOP USES

Nausea, Indigestion, Vomiting, Morning Sickness, Loss of Appetite, Anorexia—Diffuse. Take in a glass of water or capsule. Apply diluted to abdomen and/or bottoms of feet.

Motion Sickness & Vertigo—Inhale from cupped hands, and/or take in a capsule.

Spasms, Cramps & Sore Muscles, Sprain—Dilute and apply to area of discomfort.

Constipation, Diarrhea & Intestinal Cramps—Apply diluted over abdomen or take in a glass of warm water or capsule.

Heartburn & Reflux—Take in a capsule or under tongue as often as needed.

 PROPERTIES

Anti-inflammatory, Antispasmodic, Digestive Stimulant, Laxative, Analgesic, Stimulant, Decongestant, Neurotonic

 MAIN CONSTITUENTS

α-zingiberene, β-sesquiphellandrene

⚠ **SAFETY**

Dilution recommended. Possible skin sensitivity.

Sourced— Madagascar

Sourced— Kenya

Grapefruit
Citrus x paradisi

 TOP USES

Weight Loss & Obesity— Take in water or a capsule.

Food Addictions & Sugar Cravings, Anorexia & Bulimia—Diffuse. Take in a capsule or sip in water.

Breast Issues—Apply to breast area and take in a capsule. Use with pink pepper.

Cancer & Cellular Health— Take in a capsule.

Detoxification & Cellulite, Sagging Skin—Drink in water, or take in a capsule. Apply diluted to problem areas and/or bottoms of feet.

Gallstones & Gallbladder Support—Take with geranium in a capsule.

 **PROPERTIES**

Diuretic, Antioxidant, Antiseptic, Astringent, Antitoxic, Purifier, Expectorant

MAIN CONSTITUENTS

d-limonene

⚠ **SAFETY**

Avoid exposure to sunlight or UV rays for up to 12 hours after application.

🇺🇸 *Sourced*— USA

Green Mandarin
Citrus nobilis

 TOP USES

Depressed, Agitated, Afraid, Nervous, Inner Child Work— Take under tongue. Apply to pulse points. Inhale from cupped hands, or diffuse.

Situational Anxiety—Apply under nose, diffuse, or inhale from cupped hands.

Perfume—Apply with neroli to pulse points.

Gas, Poor Digestion, Constipation, Heartburn & Ulcers—Apply over area of concern, and/or take in water or under tongue.

Poor Circulation, Congested Lymphs, Water Retention & Edema—Take with black pepper under tongue or in a capsule.

 PROPERTIES

Uplifting, Refreshing, Digestive Stimulant, Cleanser, Expectorant, Calming

MAIN CONSTITUENTS

Limonene, γ-Terpinene

⚠ **SAFETY**

N/A

🇧🇷 *Sourced*— Brazil

Guaiacwood
Bulnesia Sarmientoi

 TOP USES

Nervous Tension & Exhaustion, Headaches—Apply diluted across forehead and on temples. Diffuse, and/or inhale from cupped hands

Allergies, Lung Cancer, Cough & Lymphatic Congestion—Diffuse. Apply to chest, back, and/or to bottoms of feet. Combine with cardamom or eucalyptus.

Fibromyagia, Rheumatic, Joint & Tendon Pain, Inflammation, Gout—Apply to areas of concern and/or bottoms of feet.

Poor Circulation, Wound Healing, Edema—Apply diluted to areas of concern, bottoms of feet, and lower extremities.

Dry, Irritated & Aging Skin, Eczema Psoriasis—Apply to areas of concern.

 **PROPERTIES**

Anti-allergenic, Anti-carcinoma, Anti-inflammatory, Antioxidant, Anti-tumor, Neuroprotective, Regenerative

⚠ **SAFETY**

Not safe for internal use.

Harvest Spice
Renewing Blend

 TOP USES

Warm & Invite, Safeguard—Diffuse, and/or apply to pulse points, back of neck, along spine, and/or bottoms of feet.

Delight & Snuggle—Diffuse, and/or drop onto seasonal decor or potpourri as a passive diffuser. Apply diluted on bottoms of feet prior to covering with warm socks or wrapping up in a blanket.

Uplift & Stimulate Mind, Mood & Body—Apply under nose, back of neck, and/or inhale from cupped hands.

Immune Boost, Cold & Flu Prevention—Diffuse, and/or apply to bottoms of feet, back of neck, and/or along the spine.

 MAIN INGREDIENTS

Cinnamon Bark, Clove, Eucalyptus, Cedarwood, Cassia, Nutmeg

⚠ **SAFETY**

Not safe for internal use. Dilution recommended. Possible skin sensitivity.

Sourced— Paraguay

HD Clear®

Skin Clearing Blend

 TOP USES

Acne & Pimples—Apply to areas of concern.

Oily Skin & Overactive Sebaceous Glands—Apply to areas of concern.

Skin Blemishes & Irritations—Apply to areas of concern.

Dermatitis & Eczema—Apply to areas of concern.

Fungal & Bacterial Issues—Apply to areas of concern.

⭐ **MAIN INGREDIENTS**

Black Cumin, Ho Wood, Tea Tree, Litsea, Eucalyptus, Geranium

⚠ **SAFETY**

Not safe for internal use. Possible skin sensitivity.

Helichrysum

Helichrysum italicum

 TOP USES

Nosebleeds, Bleeding & Hemorrhaging, Broken Capillaries, Phlebitis, Hematoma, Stroke—Apply to area of concern. Take in a capsule.

Scars, Wounds & Bruising, Burns—Apply to area of concern.

Alcohol Addiction & Cirrhosis—Apply to abdomen and over liver area.

Varicose Veins & Hemorrhoids—Massage with cypress into affected areas.

Wrinkles & Stretch Marks, Age Spots—Apply to area of concern.

⭐ **PROPERTIES**

Antispasmodic, Anticatarrhal, Neuroprotective, Neurotonic, Vasoconstrictor, Hemostatic, Nervine, Analgesic

 MAIN CONSTITUENTS

Neryl acetate, α-pinene, γ-curcumene

⚠ **SAFETY**

N/A

 Sourced— Corsica, Albania

Hinoki
Chamaecyparis obtusa

 TOP USES

Overactive Mind, Overstimulated or Frazzled Nerves—Diffuse, or inhale deeply from palms. Apply to bottoms of feet and base of skull.

Bronchitis, Sinusitis, Cough & Colds—Diffuse. Apply to chest, back, and bottoms of feet.

Overly Tired, Moody, Unsettled at Bedtime—Diffuse. Apply to bottoms of feet, and/or combine with Epsom salts in a warm bath.

High Blood Pressure & Poor Circulation, Edema & Water Retention—Apply over heart, on lower legs, and bottoms of feet.

 PROPERTIES ··

Anti-inflammatory, Antifungal, Grounding, Deodorant, Antibacterial, Uplifting, Stimulant

MAIN CONSTITUENTS

α-pinene, Δ-cadinene, Δ-amorphene, α-muurolene

 SAFETY

Not safe for internal use.

Holiday Joy
Holiday Blend

 TOP USES

Invite Joyful Gatherings—Diffuse, or inhale from cupped hands.

Protecting—Apply to back of neck, pulse points, and/or bottoms of feet.

Immune Boost—Diffuse, or inhale from cupped hands.

Tension & Stress—Apply to pulse points, and diffuse.

Headache & Migraine—Apply diluted to temples and back of neck.

Cold & Flu Prevention—Diffuse, or inhale from cupped hands.

Neck & Shoulder Discomfort, Arthritis—Apply diluted to areas of discomfort.

 MAIN INGREDIENTS ··

Wild Orange, Clove, Siberian Fir, Frankincense, Styrax, Ginger Co2, Balsam Peru, Cistus

⚠ **SAFETY** ··

Not safe for internal use. Dilution recommended. Possible skin sensitivity. Avoid exposure to sunlight or UV rays for up to 12 hours after application.

Sourced— Japan

Holiday Peace
Holiday Blend

 TOP USES

Tranquil, Harmonious, Grounded & Calm—Diffuse, and/or apply to pulse points, back of neck, along spine, and/or bottoms of feet.

Peaceful & Festive—Diffuse, and/or apply to diffusing ornaments, garlands, and/or holiday decor. Apply to wrist pulse points to exude a holiday aroma.

Uplift & Stimulate Mind, Mood & Body—Apply under nose, on back of neck, and/or inhale from cupped hands.

Congested Airways & Respiratory Issues—Diffuse, and inhale from cupped hands. Apply to bridge of nose or forehead, and chest.

 MAIN INGREDIENTS

Siberian Fir, Grapefruit, Douglas Fir, Himalayan Fir, Frankincense, Vetiver

⚠ **SAFETY**

Not safe for internal use. Dilution recommended. Possible skin irritation. Avoid exposure to sunlight or UV rays for up to 12 hours after application.

Hope™
Uplifting Blend

 TOP USES

Grief & Loneliness, Hopelessness & Depression—Diffuse, and apply under nose, back of neck, and on bottoms of feet.

Self-worth Issues, Meditation, Prayer—Apply to solar plexus, over heart, on back of neck and bottoms of feet.

Wrinkles, Wounds, Scars, Stretch Marks—Apply to affected areas. To increase potency, combine with myrrh or sandalwood.

Low Libido & Hormone Imbalance—Apply to lower abdomen and pulse points.

 MAIN INGREDIENTS

Bergamot, Frankincense, Vanilla Bean Absolute

⚠ **SAFETY**

Avoid exposure to sunlight or UV rays for up to 12 hours after application.

Hygge™
....
Cozy Blend

 TOP USES

Relaxation & Togetherness, Closeness—Diffuse while applying to base of neck, shoulders, and bottoms of feet on self and/or others while gathered. Follow up with fuzzy socks, blankets, and cuddle time.

Pondering, Creative, Warm & Collected—Diffuse, and apply to base of neck, and/or pulse points.

Seasonal Depression & Winter Blahs—Diffuse, and/or inhale from cupped hands. Apply over heart and forehead, on base of neck, and/or bottoms of feet.

Mindful & Minimalistic, Meditation—Diffuse, and/or inhale from cupped hands. Apply to base of neck, bottoms of feet, and/or pulse points.

 MAIN INGREDIENTS ·····································

Wild Orange, Cedarwood, Amyris, Frankincense, Myrrh, Cistus, Vetiver, Tonka Bean

⚠ **SAFETY** ···

Not safe for internal use.

Immortelle
....
Anti-aging Blend

 TOP USES

Wrinkles & Fine Lines, Age Spots—Apply to face, neck, and hands as part of skin care routine.

Sunburn & Damage & Skin Cancer—Apply to affected areas.

Wounds & Cuts, Scars & Stretch Marks—Apply to affected areas.

Facial Redness & Capillaries, Blemishes & Acne, Blotchy Skin—Apply to affected areas.

Postpartum Perineum Recovery—Apply to affected areas.

Cataracts—Apply under eyes and under second & third toes.

Meditation—Apply under nose or to pulse points.

 MAIN INGREDIENTS ·····································

Frankincense, Hawaiian Sandalwood, Lavender, Myrrh, Helichrysum, Rose, Sandalwood, Yarrow|Pom

⚠ **SAFETY** ···

Not safe for internal use.

InTune®
Focus Blend

 TOP USES

Lack of Mental Clarity, Focus or Concentration, Over-whelmed—Apply under nose and back of neck.

ADD/ADHD, Hyperactivity—Apply to back of neck, spine, and/or bottoms of feet. Inhale from cupped hands.

Over & Under Active Brain Activity—Apply to back of neck and spine.

Over & Under Active Brain Activity—Apply under nose, back of neck, and/or on bottoms of feet.

Depression—Apply under nose, on bottoms of feet, and back of neck. Inhale from cupped hands.

Stressful Classroom Environment—Apply to back of neck and under nose.

 MAIN INGREDIENTS

Amyris, Patchouli, Frankincense, Lime, Ylang Ylang, Hawaiian Sandalwood, Roman Chamomile

⚠ **SAFETY**

Not safe for internal use. Avoid exposure to sunlight or UV rays for 12 hours after application.

Island Mint®
Summertime Blend

 TOP USES

Calm, Relaxing & Renewing Atmosphere—Diffuse during a party, gathering, or staycation to solicit feelings of a relaxed and refreshing getaway.

Energize & Uplift Mood and Environment—Diffuse, or apply to pulse points, along spine, on back of neck, and/or bottoms of feet.

Renewed Focus—Diffuse. Apply to back of neck, across forehead, and to bottoms of feet as needed.

Tired & Low Energy, Midday Slump—Diffuse, or inhale from cupped hands. Apply under the nose or on back of neck.

 MAIN INGREDIENTS

Lime, Distilled Lemon, Peppermint, Spruce

⚠ **SAFETY**

Not safe for internal use. Avoid exposure to sunlight or UV rays for up to 12 hours after application.

Jasmine
Jasminum grandiforum

 TOP USES

Uterine Health, Labor & Delivery, Breast Milk—Apply diluted over abdomen and to reflex points, or diffuse.

Lack of Self Assurance, Poor Self Expression, Laryngitis—Wear as a personal perfume, and apply to neck/throat area. Blend as desired.

Hormone Imbalance, PMS, Menstrual Cramps—Apply to lower abdomen. Inhale.

Lack of Sexual Interest or Drive, Frigidity—Apply diluted during a romantic massage.

Fine Lines & Wrinkles, Oily Skin—Add to moisturizer and apply.

 PROPERTIES

Antidepressant, Aphrodisiac, Antispasmodic, Calming, Regenerative, Carminative

 MAIN CONSTITUENTS

Benzyl acetate, Benzyl benzoate

 SAFETY

Not safe for internal use. Best diluted due to aromatic potency.

Juniper Berry
Juniperus communis

 TOP USES

Jaundice, Liver Issues & Kidney Toxicity—Take in a capsule or under tongue.

Enlarged Prostate, Poor Urine Flow, Hair Loss—Take in a capsule or under tongue.

Sore Joints & Muscles, Gout—Apply to area of concern. Take in a capsule.

Urinary, Bladder, Kidney Infections & Stones—Take in a capsule, and/or apply over area of concern.

Excess Uric Acid, Water Retention, Lack of Perspiration—Combine with lemon. Apply and take in a capsule.

 PROPERTIES

Detoxifier, Diuretic, Antiseptic, Antispasmodic, Astringent, Anti-rheumatic, Carminative, Anti-parasitic

 MAIN CONSTITUENTS

a-pinene, Sabinene

 SAFETY

N/A

Sourced— Egypt

Sourced— Albania

Kumquat
Fortunella japonica

 TOP USES

Winter Blahs, Inauthenticity & Pretense, Lack of Perspective—Diffuse, or inhale from cupped hands. Apply over heart and on forehead.

Brain Fog & Poor Focus—Combine with green mandarin and vetiver. Diffuse, or inhale. Apply under nose.

Diabetes, Imbalanced Insulin & Glucose Levels, High Cholesterol—Take in a capsule with fennel.

Ulcers—Take in a capsule.

Bacterial, Fungal & Viral Infections, Parasites—Apply to areas of concern. Take in a capsule.

 **PROPERTIES**

Antiseptic, Antimicrobial, Immunostimulant, Digestive Stimulant, Refreshing

MAIN CONSTITUENTS

Limonene

 SAFETY

Avoid exposure to sunlight or UV rays for up to 12 hours after application.

Sourced— India

Laurel Leaf
Laurus nobilis

 TOP USES

Congestion, Cough, Bronchitis & Pneumonia—Apply to chest and down bridge of nose. Diffuse, or inhale from cupped hands.

Viruses, Cold & Flu, Earaches—Combine with Siberian fir and diffuse, or inhale from cupped hands. Apply under nose, to chest, or around ear.

Acne, Rash, Poison Oak or Ivy, Bruising—Apply to affected areas as often as needed. Consider combining with a soothing oil.

Confident & Courageous, Uplifting Environment—Diffuse, and apply under nose and over heart.

 PROPERTIES

Anticatarrhal, Antiviral, Expectorant, Antibacterial, Analgesic, Antioxidant, Detoxifier, Antimicrobial

MAIN CONSTITUENTS

1,8-cineole (eucalyptol), α-Terpinyl acetate

 SAFETY

Not safe for internal use.

Sourced— Albania

Lavender
Lavandula angustifolia

 TOP USES

Sleep Issues, Insomnia, Restlessness, Jet Lag—Apply under nose, on bottoms of feet, and/or diffuse to promote better sleep.

Upset, Uptight, Stressed & Anxious, Teeth Grinding—Apply over heart and on back of neck. Inhale from cupped hands and diffuse.

Sunburns & Sunstroke, Burns & Scars, Stretch Marks—Apply to area of concern.

Allergies & Hay Fever, Earache—Take in a capsule or under tongue. Inhale from cupped hands.

Cuts, Wounds & Blisters, Diabetic Sores, Bruises—Apply to area of concern.

 PROPERTIES

Sedative, Antihistamine, Cytophylactic, Hypotensive, Nervine, Relaxant, Soothing, Antibacterial, Regenerative

 MAIN CONSTITUENTS

Linalool, Linalyl acetate, Ocimene

 SAFETY

N/A

Lemon
Citrus limon

 TOP USES

Liver & Kidney Toxicity, Cellulite—Take in a capsule. Apply to bottoms of feet or areas of concern.

Toxicity & Low Glutathione Levels—Take in a capsule or under tongue.

Flavoring—Add to favorite recipe or beverage.

Kidney & Gallstones—Apply diluted over kidney area with eucalyptus, or take in a capsule with geranium for gallstones.

Edema & Water Retention, High Blood Pressure—Take in a capsule or glass of water. Apply to lower legs and bottoms of feet.

 PROPERTIES

Antiseptic, Diuretic, Antioxidant, Antibacterial, Detoxifier, Disinfectant, Mucolytic, Astringent, Degreaser

 MAIN CONSTITUENTS

Limonene, β-pinene, γ-terpinene

SAFETY

Avoid exposure to sunlight or UV rays for up to 12 hours after application.

 Sourced— Bulgaria

Sourced— Italy

Lemon Eucalyptus

Eucalyptus citriodora

 TOP USES

Insect, Ticks & Mosquitoes Repellent—Diffuse. Apply to exposed areas of skin and on clothing. Spray on outdoor surfaces.

Airborne Pathogens & Viruses, Malaria—Diffuse. Apply on bottoms of feet, especially when vulnerable to exposure.

Bronchitis, Asthma, Coughs, Sinusitis, Flu—Diffuse, and/or apply on chest and back.

Fear & Feeling Unsafe or Overly Vulnerable to Outside Influences, Unprotected Spaces—Diffuse, or inhale from cupped hands, and/or apply.

 **PROPERTIES**

Expectorant, Analgesic, Insect Repellent, Rubefacient, Cleanser

 MAIN CONSTITUENTS

Citronellal, Citronellol

⚠ **SAFETY**

Not safe for internal use.

Lemongrass

Cymbopogon flexuosus

 TOP USES

Connective Tissue Injury & Whiplash—Apply diluted to affected area.

Joint, Tendon & Ligament Pain, Carpal Tunnel, Frozen Shoulder—Apply diluted to affected area.

Cancer & Tumors, Free Radicals—Take in a capsule.

Lymphatic & Respiratory Congestion, Toxic Accumulations—Take in a capsule, and/or apply to bottoms of feet.

Hypo or Hyperthyroid, Hashimoto's, Grave's Disease—Take in a capsule. Apply under big toe.

Colitis & Lactose Intolerance—Take in a capsule.

 **PROPERTIES**

Anti-inflammatory, Antimicrobial, Analgesic, Anti-carcinoma, Antimutagenic, Decongestant, Regenerative, Anti-rheumatic

 MAIN CONSTITUENTS

Geranial, Neral, Geraniol

⚠ **SAFETY**

Dilution recommended. Possible skin sensitivity.

Sourced— Kenya

Sourced— India

Lime
Citrus aurantifolia

TOP USES

Sore Throat, Cold & Flu, Fever—Gargle, take in a capsule, or lick off back of hand.

Respiratory/Lymph Congestion, Croup—Take in a capsule, or apply over areas of concern with Breathe®.

Insect Bites & Stings, Cellultis—Apply to area of concern.

Liver & Blood Toxicity, Cellulite, Low Glutathione Levels—Take in a capsule or under tongue. Apply to affected areas.

Urinary & Digestive Issues—Take in a glass of water or capsules.

Head Lice—Add 20 drops tea tree to bottle of shampoo.

 ### PROPERTIES

Anti-inflammatory, Antiseptic, Antioxidant, Antibacterial, Tonic, Uplifting, Detoxifier, Disinfectant, Diuretic

 ### MAIN CONSTITUENTS

Limonene, β-pinene, γ-terpinene

 ### SAFETY

Avoid exposure to sunlight or UV rays for up to 12 hours after application.

Litsea
Litsea cubeba

TOP USES

Asthma Attack, Spastic Coughs, Bronchitis, Allergies—Apply diluted to chest with Breathe®, or inhale from cupped hands.

Acute & Chronic Back or Muscle Pain—Apply diluted to affected area.

Lung Cancer—Apply diluted to chest and back.

High Blood Pressure, Irregular Heartbeat, Anxiety—Apply to chest, back of neck under nose, and/or bottoms of feet.

Cold, Chills & Infections—Apply to chest, back of neck, or along spine.

Eczema, Acne & Oily Skin—Apply diluted to affected areas.

 ### PROPERTIES

Refreshing, Detoxifier, Uplifting, Antibacterial, Antifungal, Antispasmodic, Disinfectant, Digestive Stimulant

 ### MAIN CONSTITUENTS

Geranial, Neral, Limonene

 ### SAFETY

Dilution recommended. May stain surfaces, fabrics, and skin.

Magnolia

Michelia x alba

 TOP USES

Anxiety, Depression & Lack of Energy—Apply to back of neck, forehead, under nose, and/or over heart. Inhale from cupped hands.

PMS & Menstrual Cramps, Hormone Imbalances— Apply in clockwise motion over lower abdomen, wrists, and/or ankles.

Irritability, Anger & Rage, Hysteria, Panic, Grief & Shock—Apply to back of neck, forehead, under nose, over heart, and/or bottoms of feet. Inhale from cupped hands.

Acne and Dry Skin, Wrinkles— Add to skincare routine and apply.

 PROPERTIES

Sedative, Relaxant, Antidepressant, Aphrodisiac, Decongestant, Stomachic

MAIN CONSTITUENTS

Linalool

⚠ **SAFETY**

Not safe for internal use. Avoid keeping in hot places to prevent oxidation.

Sourced— China

Manuka

Leptospermum scoparium

 TOP USES

Achy Joints & Muscle Pain—Massage diluted into affected areas.

Dandruff, Scalp Issues— Apply to scalp, or add to shampoo or conditioner.

Athlete's Foot, Toe Fungus— Apply to bottoms of feet, and/or drop into foot soak.

Irritated & Chaffed Skin, Acne, Rashes—Apply to affected area(s). Dilute as needed.

Intestinal, Respiratory, Urinary Tract, Bacterial Infection— Apply to bottoms of feet, abdomen, and/or chest.

Bites, Stings & Burns—Apply to affected area.

 PROPERTIES

Anti-allergenic, Antihistamine, Antibacterial, Anti-inflammatory, Antifungal, Antiviral, Relaxant

MAIN CONSTITUENTS

Leptospermone, E-calamenene, a-pinene, Cadina-3, 5-diene

⚠ **SAFETY**

Not safe for internal use.

Sourced— New Zealand

Marjoram
Origanum majorana

 TOP USES

Carpal Tunnel, Bone Spurs, Tendinitis & Arthritis—Apply to areas of discomfort.

Muscle Cramps & Sprains—Apply to areas of concern.

High Blood Pressure & Edema, Heart Issues, Prolapsed, Mitral Value—Apply over heart, to pulse points, and/or bottoms of feet. Take in a capsule.

Croup & Bronchitis, Asthma—Apply to neck, chest, and upper back.

Pancreatitis & Liver/Spleen Obstructions—Apply over affected area.

Overactive Sex Drive—Apply to lower abdomen and/or bottoms of feet. Inhale.

 PROPERTIES

Vasodilator, Antispasmodic, Digestive Stimulant, Antibacterial, Antifungal, Hypotensive, Sedative

MAIN CONSTITUENTS

Terpinen-4-ol, Trans-sabinene hydrate, γ-terpinene

 SAFETY

Caution during earlier stages of pregnancy.

Melissa
Melissa officinalis

 TOP USES

Fevers, Colds & Viral Infections—Apply diluted along spine, bottoms of feet, or take in a capsule.

Cold Sores & Fever Blisters, Herpes, Chickenpox—Apply directly to sores or take in a capsule.

Bites, Stings & Warts—Apply directly to area of concern.

Depression, Anxiety Shock & PTSD, Overcome by Darkness, Despair—Apply to back of neck and ears. Diffuse. Apply to thumb pad and press to roof of mouth. Then hold for 5-10 seconds.

Allergies & Asthma—Inhale from cupped hands, and/ or apply to chest. Take in a capsule or under tongue.

 PROPERTIES

Antioxidant, Antibacterial, Antidepressant, Antispasmodic, Antihistamine, Antiviral, Hypotensive, Nervine, Sedative

MAIN CONSTITUENTS

Geranial, Germacrene, Neral, β-Caryophyllene

 SAFETY

N/A

Sourced— Egypt

Sourced— Bulgaria

MetaPWR™

Metabolic Blend

 TOP USES

Weight Loss, Obesity, & Slow Metabolism—Take 5 drops up to 5 times daily in capsule or water.

Cellulite, Adipose Fat Deposits—Apply diluted to areas of concern.

Eating Disorders—Take in a capsule or with water. Apply to bottoms of feet or diffuse.

Excess or Diminished Appetite & Cravings—Drop under tongue, or add to drinking water. Inhale from bottle, or apply under nose.

Congestion & Colds—Take in a capsule or in water.

Urinary Tract Infection—Take in a capsule or in water.

⭐ **MAIN INGREDIENTS** ························

Grapefruit, Lemon, Peppermint, Ginger, Cinnamon Bark

⚠ **SAFETY** ·····························

Dilution recommended for topical use. Avoid exposure to sunlight or UV rays for up to 12 hours after application.

Midnight Forest

Nature Blend

 TOP USES

Forest Therapy—Diffuse. Apply under nose, over heart, on back of neck, and/or bottoms of feet.

Lack of Energy, Creativity, Productivity, or Concentration—Apply under nose, on back of neck and forehead. Diffuse or inhale deeply from cupped hands.

Anxiety, Brain Fog & Exhaustion—Diffuse and/or inhale from cupped hands. Apply under nose, across forehead, back of neck, and/or bottoms of feet.

Sore Joints, Sprains & Injuries—Dilute and aplly on affected areas.

Airborne Pathogens—Diffuse in affected space.

 ⭐ **MAIN INGREDIENTS** ························

Siberian Fir, Cypress, Juniper Berry, Black Spruce, Wild Orange, Frankincense, Pimeno Leaf, Pimento Fruit, Cistus, Caraway, Labdanum

⚠ **SAFETY** ·····························

Not safe for internal use. Dilution recommended. Possible skin sensitivity. Avoid exposure to sunlight or UV rays for up to 12 hours after application.

Motivate®
Encouraging Blend

 TOP USES

Lack of Confidence, Courage or Motivation—Diffuse. Apply under nose, on forehead, back of neck, and/or over heart.

Confusion & Overwhelm—Inhale. Apply under nose, on forehead, back of neck, and/or chest.

Digestive Issues—Apply to upper abdomen and/or on bottoms of feet.

Depletion & Stagnation—Inhale from cupped hands and apply to bottoms of feet.

Depression & Stagnation—Diffuse, and/or apply over heart area, on forehead, and back of neck.

Adrenal Exhaustion—Inhale from cupped hands. Apply under nose, over adrenal area, and/or to bottoms of feet.

⭐ **MAIN INGREDIENTS**

Peppermint, Wild Orange, Clementine, Lemon, Rosemary, Coriander, Basil, Spearmint, Lemongrass, TonkaBean, Cardamom, Melissa, Vanilla

 SAFETY

Not safe for internal use. Avoid sunlight or UV rays to applied area for up to 12 hours.

Myrrh
Commiphora myrrha

 TOP USES

Gum Disease & Bleeding, Gingivitis, Mouth Ulcers—Apply directly to gums.

Fine Lines & Dry Skin, Stretch Marks, Cracked Heels—Apply to areas of concern.

Thyroid Issues, Hashimoto's—Apply to base of neck and bottoms of feet.

Digestive Upset & Cramping, Ulcers, Diarrhea—Apply to abdomen, and/or take in capsule.

Eczema, Skin Ulcers, Syphillis, Leprosy—Apply to affected area, especially weeping areas.

Meditation—Diffuse, and inhale from cupped hands.

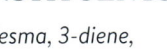 **PROPERTIES**

Anti-inflammatory, Antiviral, Antimicrobial, Expectorant, Anti-infectious, Carminative, Antifungal

 MAIN CONSTITUENTS

Furanoedudesma, 3-diene, Curzerene, Lindestrene

 **SAFETY**

N/A

 *Sourced*— Somaliland

Neroli
Citrus aurantium

 TOP USES

Loss of Sexual Interest or Arousal, Erectile Dysfunction—Apply under nose, to reproductive areas, and/or wear as a personal scent on pulse points. Inhale from cupped hands.

Deodorant, Perfume—Apply diluted to underarms and/or wrist and neck pulse points.

Unsettled, Stressed Out, Depressed, Elevated Cortisol Levels—Diffuse, and/or inhale from cupped hands. Apply diluted to chest, solar plexus, back of neck, temples, and/or under neck.

Damaged, Dry, Wrinkled, Sagging & Scarred Skin—Apply diluted to area of concern.

⭐ **PROPERTIES**

Antidepressant, Anti-inflammatory, Antimutagenic, Aphrodisiac, Cytophylactic, Neurotonic, Regenerative, Sedative, Warming

 MAIN CONSTITUENTS

Linalool, Linalyl acetate, Limonene, Nerolidol, Terpineol, Terpinyl acetate

⚠ **SAFETY**

Not safe for internal use. Dilution recommended. Possible skin sensitivity.

Sourced— Egypt

Northern Escape
Woodland Blend

 TOP USES

Forest Therapy—Diffuse. Apply under nose, over heart, on back of neck, and/or bottoms of feet.

Mental Stress & Cluttered Thinking—Diffuse, or inhale from cupped hands. Apply under nose, across forehead, and/or on back of neck.

Joints, Muscle Aches & Pains—Apply to area of concern.

Overstimulation From Screentime—Apply under nose, across forehead, and on back of neck.

Uninspired or Unmotivated—Diffuse. Apply under nose, on forehead and back of neck, and/or over heart.

Polluted Air & Odors—Diffuse in areas or spaces in need of air purification.

⭐ **MAIN INGREDIENTS**

Black Spruce, Siberian Fir, Balsam Fir, Lavandin, Cedarwood, Cypress, Hinoki, Frankincense, Nootka, Cananga, Clove

 SAFETY

Not safe for internal use.

On Guard®
Protective Blend

 TOP USES

Airborne Pathogens— Diffuse, and apply to chest and under nose.

Seasonal Immune Boost— Diffuse, and take in water or in a capsule.

Colds & Flu—Take in a capsule, and/or apply to bottoms of feet.

Staph, Strep Throat & Cough— Gargle in water. Apply to chest, throat, and/or take in a capsule or with water.

Cold Sores, Warts & Infected Wounds—Apply diluted to affected areas.

Oral Health & Toothbrush Cleaning—Gargle, and/or use as a mouthwash. Apply to bristles.

 **MAIN INGREDIENTS**

Wild Orange, Clove, Cinnamon Leaf, Cinnamon Bark, Eucalyptus, Rosemary

⚠ **SAFETY**

Dilution recommended. Possible skin sensitivity. Avoid exposure to sunlight or UV rays for up to 12 hours after application.

Oregano
Origanum vulgare

 TOP USES

Viral & Bacterial Infection, Cold/Flu—Take in a capsule and/or sip in warm water from a mug that contains one drop each oregano, peppermint, On Guard®, and/or lemon.

Strep Throat & Tonsillitis— Gargle and/or take in a capsule.

Intestinal Worms & Parasites—Take in a capsule.

Staph Infection & MRSA— Apply diluted to affected area and/or take in a capsule.

Warts, Calluses & Canker Sores—Apply diluted to affected areas. Inhale steam from a bowl that contains hot water and one drop each of oregano, Breathe®, and/or On Guard®.

 **PROPERTIES**

Antibacterial, Antifungal, Anti-parasitic, Antiviral, Immunostimulant

MAIN CONSTITUENTS

Carvacrol, Thymol

 SAFETY

Dilution recommended. Possible skin sensitivity. To reduce liver stress, use with Zendocrine®.

🗺 *Sourced*— Turkey

Passion®

Inspiring Blend

PastTense®

Tension Blend

 TOP USES

Apathy, Depression & Energy Issues—Diffuse, or inhale from cupped hands to energize and uplift.

Low Libido & Sexual Performance, Frigidity—Diffuse, and/or inhale from cupped hands. Apply to bottoms of feet, and/or lower abdomen.

Mental Fog & Memory Issues—Apply to big toe and under nose. Diffuse, and/or inhale from cupped hands.

Sluggish Digestion & Elimination—Apply diluted to lower abdomen.

Lung & Sinus Congestion—Diffuse, or inhale from hands.

 ★ **MAIN INGREDIENTS**

Ginger, Jasmine, Sandalwood, Ylang Ylang, Wild Orange, Magnolia, Lemon, Cardamom, Bergamot, Damiana, Tonka Bean, Vanilla, Cinnamon Bark

⚠ **SAFETY**

Not safe for internal use. Dilution recommended. Possible skin sensitivity.

 TOP USES

Headaches & Migraines—Apply to temples, forehead, back of neck, and/or reflex points.

Muscles Aches, Swelling & Cramping—Apply to areas of concern.

Hangover—Apply under nose and to back of neck.

Hot Flashes & Cooling—Apply to abdomen and/or back of neck to cool and calm.

Bruises & Burns—Apply to area of concern.

Tension & Stress—Apply to pulse points, and/or inhale from cupped hands.

Restful Sleep—Apply to back of neck.

 ★ **MAIN INGREDIENTS**

Wintergreen, Lavender, Peppermint, Frankincense, Cilantro, Marjoram, Roman Chamomile, Basil, Rosemary

⚠ **SAFETY**

Not safe for internal use. Possible skin sensitivity.

Patchouli
Pogostemon cablin

 ### TOP USES

Anxiety & Dopamine Deficiency, Nervous Exhaustion, Depression—Diffuse. Apply under nose, on back of neck, and/or bottoms of feet.

Dry Skin & Impetigo, Acne, Eczema—Apply to areas of concern, or add to body or face wash.

Shingles & Herpes—Apply to area of concern bottoms of feet, and/or take in a capsule.

Oily Hair & Dandruff—Add to shampoo or conditioner.

Nerve & CNS Issues—Apply to bottoms of feet. Take in a capsule.

Appetite & Weight Issues—Take in a capsule or under tongue.

PROPERTIES

Aphrodisiac, Sedative, Diuretic, Antifungal, Antispasmodic, Insecticidal, Antidepressant

 ### MAIN CONSTITUENTS

Patchouli alcohol, α-Bulnesene, α-Guaiene

SAFETY

N/A

Peace®
Reassuring Blend

 ### TOP USES

Insecurity & Worry—Apply under nose, on back of neck, and/or forehead. Diffuse, or inhale from cupped hands.

Nervousness & Irritability—Apply under nose, on back of neck, and/or forehead. Diffuse, or inhale from cupped hands.

ADD, ADHD & Focus Issues—Diffuse, or inhale and apply to forehead and/or back of neck.

Stress, Mental Strain & Hyperactivity—Apply under nose, on back of neck, and/or forehead. Diffuse, or inhale from cupped hands.

Addictions & Anorexia—Apply under nose, and/or inhale from cupped hands.

Childbirth & Recovery—Apply to lower abdomen, massage into feet, and/or diffuse.

MAIN INGREDIENTS

Vetiver, Lavender, Ylang Ylang, Frankincense, Clary Sage, Marjoram, Labdanum, Spearmint

 ### SAFETY

Nat safe for internal use. Caution during earlier stages of pregnancy.

Sourced— Indonesia

Peppermint
Menta piperita

 TOP USES

Nausea, Indigestion, Vomiting, Heartburn, Gastritis, IBS—Take in a capsule or water, and/or apply over upper abdomen. Dilute as needed.

Mental or Chronic Fatigue, Jetlag, Fainting, Shock—Inhale, or apply diluted under nose or on back of neck.

Fevers & Hot Flashes—Apply on back of neck, spine, and/or bottoms of feet. Dilute if needed.

Headaches & Migraines—Apply to temples, above ears, and/or on back of neck.

Burns & Sunburn, Heatstroke—Apply neat or diluted to affected area and/or back of neck to cool.

 **PROPERTIES**

Anti-inflammatory, Analgesic, Antispasmodic, Warming, Invigorating, Cooling, Expectorant, Vasoconstrictor, Stimulant

MAIN CONSTITUENTS

Menthol, Menthone, 1,8-cineole (eucalyptol)

⚠ **SAFETY**

Because of its stimulating properties, avoid use at bedtime. Dilution recommended. Possible skin sensitivity.

 Sourced— USA

Petitgrain
Citrus aurantium

 TOP USES

Bacterial Infections & Wounds—Apply to affected area, or take in a capsule.

Spastic Cough & Congestion—Apply to chest, diffuse, or take in a capsule.

Abdominal & Muscular Cramps or Spasms—Apply diluted to affected area.

Convulsions & Seizures—Apply to back of neck and/or bottoms of feet.

Fearful & Anxious Thinking—Diffuse, or inhale from cupped hands.

Sudden Anger, Shock, Hysteria—Diffuse, or inhale from cupped hands.

 PROPERTIES

Antidepressant, Antiseptic, Antispasmodic, Cardiotonic, Detoxifier, Immunostimulant, Nervine, Sedative, Tonic, Uplifting

MAIN CONSTITUENTS

Linalyl acetate, Linalool, a-terpineol

⚠ **SAFETY**

Dilution recommended. Possible skin sensitivity.

 Sourced— Paraguay

Pink Pepper
Schinus molle

Purify
Cleansing Blend

 TOP USES

Lymphatic Congestion, Cancer, Candida—Combine with frankincense, and take in water or a capsule.

Pain Med Addiction—Combine with copaiba and black pepper and take in a capsule.

Flavoring—Add to favorite recipe as a subtle pepper flavor.

Crohn's Disease, Nausea & Vomiting, Gas & Bloating, Poor Appetite—Apply to areas of concern. Take under tongue or in a capsule.

Gout, Rheumatism & Arthritis—Apply to areas of concern, and/or take in a capsule.

 TOP USES

Germs & Microbes—Diffuse. Spray on surfaces from glass spray bottle filled with water.

Air Pollution & Odors—Diffuse to clear the air.

Acne—Add to skin care routine, and apply to areas of content.

Bug Bites & Stings—Apply with lavender to affected areas.

Surface Cleaning—Add 6-8 drops and 1 T vinegar to glass spray bottle filled with water.

Insect Repellent—Diffuse. Apply to clothing and/or exposed areas of skin.

Laundry—Add 2-4 drops to each load of laundry to dispel odors and kill germs.

⭐ **PROPERTIES** ······································

Invigorating, Purifier, Anti-inflammatory, Antioxidant, Refreshing, Antimicrobial, Digestive Stimulant

⭐ **MAIN INGREDIENTS** ·······················

Lemon, Siberian Fir, Citronella, Lime, Tea Tree, Cilantro

 MAIN CONSTITUENTS

Limonene, α-Phellandrene, Myrcene

 SAFETY

Because of stimulating properties, avoid use at bedtime. Dilution recommended.

 SAFETY ··································

Not safe for internal use. Avoid exposure to sunlight or UV rays for up to 12 hours after application.

Sourced— Kenya

Ravintsara
Cinamomum camphora

 TOP USES

Cold & Flu, Respiratory or Ear Issues—Diffuse, or inhale from cupped hands. Apply under nose, to chest and back, and/or around ears.

Situational Anxiety & Worry—Diffuse, or inhale from cupped hands. Apply under nose and on back of neck.

Restful Sleep, Sleep Apnea—Diffuse with Serenity®, and/or apply on bottoms of feet.

Sore Joints & Muscles, Lymphatic Congestion—Apply to areas of concern. Dilute as needed.

Fungus & Parasites, Staph, Eczema—Apply to areas of concern. Dilute as needed.

 **PROPERTIES**

Antibacterial, Energizing, Mucolytic, Relaxant, Cleanser, Analgesic, Antifungal, Anti-parasitic, Antimicrobial

 **MAIN CONSTITUENTS**

1,8-cineole (eucalyptol), Sabinene, a-terpineol

SAFETY

Not safe for internal use. Dilution recommended. Possible skin sensitivity.

Sourced— Madagascar

Red Mandarin
Citrus reticulata

 TOP USES

Acne & Oily Skin, Wounds—Apply to areas of concern.

Bloating, Gas, Hiccups & Indigestion, IBS, Colic, Leaky Gut—Apply to chest, back, and/or forehead. Take under tongue or in a capsule.

Bacterial, Fungal & Viral Infections—Apply to areas of concern. Take in a capsule.

Congestion, Severe & Spastic Coughs—Apply to chest, back, and/or forehead. Take under tongue.

Wrinkles, Age Spots, Scars, Stretch Marks—Add to daily skin care products, and apply to areas of concern.

 **PROPERTIES**

Antimicrobial, Antiseptic, Detoxifying, Digestive Stimulant, Cyptophylactic, Immunostimulant, Antispasmodic, Uplifting

 MAIN CONSTITUENTS

Limonene

SAFETY

Avoid exposure to sunlight or UV rays or up to 12 hours after application.

Sourced— Brazil

Rescuer™

Children's Soothing Blend

 **TOP USES**

Muscle Aches & Tension—Apply to areas of concern.

Growing Pains—Apply to areas of concern.

Headache & Neck Pain—Apply to back of neck, forehead, temples, and shoulders.

Bruises & Injuries—Apply to areas of concern.

Shock, Distress & Fear—Apply under nose, back of neck, forehead, and/or bottoms of feet.

Bath & Bedtime Routine—Apply to bottoms of feet before or after a warm bath or at bedtime.

⭐ **MAIN INGREDIENTS** ·····································

Copaiba, Lavender, Spearmint, Zanthoxylum

⚠ **SAFETY** ··

Not safe for internal use.

Roman Chamomile

Anthemis nobilis

TOP USES

Stress & Stock, Hysteria—Diffuse, or inhale from cupped hands. Apply to back of neck.

Allergies & Itchy Eyes, Hives or Rashes—Take in a capsule. Apply diluted around eyes to bottoms of feet or areas of concern.

Sciatica & Lower Back Pain—Apply to areas of concern.

Dry, Irritated & Aging Skin, Eczema, Psoriasis, Sore Nipples—Apply to areas of concern.

High Blood Pressure—Apply over heart, on back of neck, and/or bottoms of feet. Take in a capsule.

PMS & Cramps, Sprains—Apply to lower abdomen or areas of discomfort.

⭐ **PROPERTIES** ·····································

Antihistamine, Antibacterial, Antifungal, Sedative, Immunostimulant

MAIN CONSTITUENTS

4-methyl amyl angelate, Isobutyl angelate, Isoamyl tiglate

⚠ **SAFETY**

N/A

Sourced— USA

Rose

Rosa damascena

TOP USES

Low Libido, Sexual Debilities, Frigidity, Lack of Sexual Confidence—Diffuse, or inhale from cupped hands. Apply to lower abdomen, bottoms of feet, or areas of interest.

Bacterial Infections, MRSA/Staph, Poison Oak—Apply a drop to areas of concern.

Grief & Depression, Broken-Hearted, Lonely, Heart Issues & Palpitations—Diffuse, and apply to back of neck, forehead, and/or over heart.

Childbirth & Baby Blues—Diffuse, and apply to back of neck and over heart.

Perfume—Combine with jasmine or neroli and apply as desired.

 ## PROPERTIES

Antidepressant, Aphrodisiac, Antispasmodic, Emmenagogue, Sedative, Tonic

MAIN CONSTITUENTS

Citronellol, Geraniol, Nonadecane, Nerol

SAFETY

Not safe for internal use. Dilution recommended due to highly concentrated and powerful aroma.

 Sourced— Bulgaria

Rosemary

Rosmarinus officinalis

TOP USES

Mental, Adrenal & Chronic Fatigue, Headache—Diffuse. Apply under nose and/or on neck and shoulders. Take in a capsule.

Respiratory Infections & Conditions, Loss of Smell—Apply to chest, bottoms of feet, and/or diffuse.

Poor Memory & Lack of Focus—Apply under nose and across forehead, and/or diffuse.

Prostate Issues & Nighttime Urination—Apply to bottoms of feet. Take in a capsule.

Hair Thinning & Loss, Dandruff, Oily Hair—Apply to scalp and/or add to shampoo.

 ## PROPERTIES

Analgesic, Anticatarrhal, Stimulant, Neurotonic

MAIN CONSTITUENTS

1,8-cineole (eucalyptol), a-pinene, Camphor

SAFETY

Caution with use with epileptics, during pregnancy and high blood pressure.

 **Sourced**— Bulgaria

Sandalwood

Santalum album, santalum, paniculatum

TOP USES

Dry Skin & Scalp, Rashes—Use topically or add to shampoo.

Scars & Blemishes, Vitiligo, Moles, UV Skin Damage—Apply directly to affected area.

Wound Care & Skin Infections—Apply to affected area.

Spasms & Cramps—Apply over area of concern.

Cancer & Tumors—Take in a capsule, and/or apply to bottoms of feet and back of neck.

Alzheimer's, Confusion, Pituitary & Pineal Gland Issues—Take in a capsule. Apply to bottoms of feet, back of neck, and forehead.

PROPERTIES

Anti-inflammatory, Anti-carcinoma, Astringent, Antidepressant, Calming, Sedative

MAIN CONSTITUENTS

α- & ß-santalols, α- & ß-santalenes

SAFETY

N/A

Serenity®

Restful Blend

TOP USES

Insomnia & Sleep Issues—Diffuse. Apply under nose, down spine, and/or bottoms of feet.

Stress & Anxiety, Restlessness—Apply under nose, on back of neck, and/or diffuse.

Fussy Baby & Restless Child—Diffuse. Apply to bottoms of feet or down spine to calm. Dilute as desired.

Tension & Mood Swings—Diffuse, or inhale from cupped hands. Apply to back of neck and/or over heart.

Fears & Nervousness—Apply to back of neck, diffuse, and/or inhale from cupped hands.

Bath & Bedtime Routine—Use in bath or apply to back of neck, along spine, and bottoms of feet to relax and unwind at night.

MAIN INGREDIENTS

Lavender, Cedarwood, Ho Wood, Ylang Ylang, Marjoram, Roman Chamomile, Vetiver, Sandalwood, Tonka Bean, Vanilla

SAFETY

Not safe for internal use. Possible skin sensitivity.

Sourced— India, Hawaii

Siberian Fir

Abies sibirica

 TOP USES

Pain & Inflammation, Rheumatism, Arthritis & Gout, Tired & Achy Muscles—Take in a capsule, or massage into area of concern.

Broken Bones & Osteoporosis—Apply diluted with helichrysum, cypress, and wintergreen. Take in a capsule.

Constricted Breathing, Congestion, Cold, Flu, Fever, & Sore Throat, Cough—Apply to chest, bottoms of feet, along spine. Diffuse, and/or inhale from cupped hands.

Candida & Urinary Infections—Take in a capsule. Apply to lower abdomen.

 **PROPERTIES**

Analgesic, Antifungal, Anti-inflammatory, Detoxifier, Energizing, Expectorant, Refreshing, Antiseptic

MAIN CONSTITUENTS

Bornyl acetate, Camphene, δ-3-Carene, α-pinene

 SAFETY

Dilution recommended.

Spanish Sage

Salvia lavandulaefolia

 TOP USES

Alzheimer's Dementia, Cognition & Mental Performance—Inhale from cupped. Apply to back of neck, along spine, and under nose.

Word or Memory Recall, Alertness, Lack of Focus & Concentration—Inhale from cupped hands. Apply to back of neck, along spine, and under nose. Take in water.

Oxidative Stress, Cellular Toxicity & Low Glutathione—Take in water. Apply on bottoms of feet and over liver area. Dilute as needed.

Dermatitis & Eczema, Hair Loss—Apply to areas of concern. Add to shamoo or conditioner.

 PROPERTIES

Analgesic, Anti-inflammatory, Antioxidant, Antispasmodic, Mucolytic, Neuroportective, Warming

SAFETY

Avoid during pregnancy, breastfeeding, with asthmatics, or with low seizure threshold.

Sourced— Russia

Sourced— Spain

Spearmint

Mentha spicata

 TOP USES

Indigestion, Nausea & Colic, Constipation or Diarrhea—Apply over abdomen. Dilute as needed. Take in a capsule.

Bronchitis & Respiratory Issues—Apply to chest and back, or diffuse.

Overheated, Heatstroke, Fever—Apply to back of neck, on spine, and/or bottoms of feet.

Cystitis, Incontinence, Kidney Stones—Take in a capsule or glass of water. Apply on back over kidney areas.

Bad Breath & Sore Gums—Swish and swallow in water.

Slow Metabolism/Fat Burning, Appetite Imbalances—Take in a capsule or glass of water.

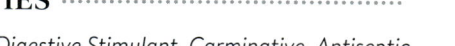 ⭐ **PROPERTIES**

Anti-inflammatory, Digestive Stimulant, Carminative, Antiseptic

 **MAIN CONSTITUENTS**

 SAFETY

Carvone, Limonene

N/A

Spikenard

Nardostachys jatamansi

 TOP USES

Aging & Irritated Skin—Add to facial cleanser or moisturizer.

Insomnia, Stress, Muscle Tension & Spasms—Diffuse, and apply to bottoms of feet and/or area of concern.

Candida & Vaginal Thrush—Apply to affected area diluted.

PMS & Menstrual Issues, Infertility—Apply to lower abdomen, back of neck, and pulse points.

Brain Issues, Convulsions & Seizures—Apply to back of neck or affected area.

Detoxing, Diuretic & Cellulite—Apply to affected area or bottoms of feet.

⭐ **PROPERTIES**

Anti-inflammatory, Antispasmodic, Sedative, Antibacterial, Antifungal, Deodorant, Laxative, Tonic

MAIN CONSTITUENTS

⚠ **SAFETY**

Jatamansone, Gurjunene

Not safe for internal use.

Sourced— India

Sourced— Nepal

Steady™

....

Children's Grounding Blend

TOP USES

Uncooperative & Obstinate, Out of Control—Apply to chest, forehead, and/or bottoms of feet.

Overstimulated & Overwhelmed—Apply under nose, to back of neck, and forehead.

Disconnected from Reality Ungrounded or Unstable—Apply under nose, and/or to bottoms of feet.

Focus Issues & Mood Swings—Apply under nose, over heart, and/or to forehead.

Restless & Wound Up—Apply under nose, to back of neck, along spine, and/or bottoms of feet.

Anger & Frustration, Tantrums—Apply under nose, to back of neck, along spine, over heart, and/or bottoms of feet.

 ★ **MAIN INGREDIENTS**

Amyris, Balsam Fir, Coriander, Magnolia

⚠ **SAFETY**

Not safe for internal use.

Stronger™

....

Children's Protective Blend

TOP USES

Bacteria & Viruses, Airborne Pathogens—Apply to areas of concern, bottoms of feet, under nose, and/or across forehead.

Flu, Weak Immunity, Poor Recovery—Apply under nose, over heart, along spine, and/or bottoms of feet.

Cuts & Scrapes—Apply to areas of concern.

Emotional Distress & Poor Boundaries—Inhale deeply from cupped hands. Apply to bottoms of feet and over heart.

Staph, Strep Throat & Cough—Apply to throat/neck, chest, along spine, and/or bottoms of feet.

Cold Sores, Warts & Infected Wounds—Apply to areas of concern.

★ **MAIN INGREDIENTS**

Cedarwood, Frankincense, Holiday Joy, Litsea, On Guard®, Rose

⚠ **SAFETY**

Not safe for internal use.

Supermint™
....
Mentha Blend

Tamer™
....
Children's Digestive Blend

 TOP USES

Nausea, Indigestion, Bloating, Gas, Heartburn, Gastritis, IBS—Take in a capsule or water, and/or apply over upper abdomen. Diluted as needed.

Mental Strain, Lack of Focus or Alertness, Overwhelm, Memory—Diffuse, and apply to back of neck. Combine with rosemary.

Cravings & Appetite Issues—Take 1 drop on tongue before meals. Inhale or apply under nose.

Headaches & Migraines, Overheated—Diffuse, and apply to temples and/or back of neck.

Respiratory Issues, Cough, Cold & Flu, Sinus Congestion—Apply to chest and back and diffuse.

 ⭐ **MAIN INGREDIENTS** ....

Peppermint, Japanese Mint, Spearmint, Bergamot Mint

⚠ **SAFETY** ....

N/A

🖌 **TOP USES**

Motion, Travel & Morning Sickness—Apply to upper and lower abdomen and/or to bottoms of feet.

Bloating, Gas, Nausea & Upset Stomach—Apply to upper or lower abdomen and/or to bottoms of feet.

Bronchitis, Asthma, Cough, Chest Cold—Apply to chest and back.

Constipation, Diarrhea, Irritable Bowel Syndrome, Crohn's Disease—Apply to upper and lower abdomen and/or to bottoms of feet.

Fever & Chills, Cold/Flu, Body Aches—Apply to chest, back, forehead, areas of discomfort, and/or bottoms of feet.

⭐ **MAIN INGREDIENTS** ....

Spearmint, Japanese Peppermint, Ginger, Black Pepper, Parsley

⚠ **SAFETY** ....

Not safe for internal use.

Tangerine
Citrus reticulata

 TOP USES

Antioxidant, Immune Boost & Cell Protection—Take in water or in a capsule.

Sadness & Irritability, Impulsiveness—Diffuse, or inhale from cupped hands. Apply under nose and over heart.

Arthritis & Muscle Pain, Tension—Massage onto area of concern.

Sleep Issues & Anxiety, Nervousness—Diffuse, or inhale from cupped hands. Apply under nose, and/or take in water.

Digestive & Intestinal Disorders, Parasites, Liver & Gallbladder Issues—Take in water or a capsule, and apply to upper or lower abdomen.

 PROPERTIES

Energizing, Sedative, Uplifting, Antioxidant, Cytophylactic, Detoxifier, Mucolytic, Stomachic

 MAIN CONSTITUENTS

Limonene

SAFETY

Avoid exposure to sunlight or UV rays for up to 12 hours after application.

 ***Sourced*— Brazil**

Tea Tree
Melaleuca alternifolia

 TOP USES

Cuts & Wounds & Associated Pain—Apply to affected area.

Bacteria, Viruses, Diarrhea, Food Poisoning, Ulcer—Take in a capsule, or apply to abdomen.

Cankers & Cold Sores, Herpes, Warts—Apply on affected area to treat or prevent from emerging.

Athlete's Foot & Candida Issues, Ringworm, Vaginal Thrush—Take in a capsule. Apply diluted to affected area.

Sore Throat & Tonsillitis, Mumps—Take in a capsule, or gargle with warm water.

Ear Infections—Apply behind and around ear.

 PROPERTIES

Antiseptic, Antibacterial, Antifungal, Anti-parasitic, Antiviral, Analgesic, Decongestant

 MAIN CONSTITUENTS

Terpinen-4-ol, γ-terpinene, α-terpinene

SAFETY

Tea tree remains on the FDA's GRAS list.

***Sourced*— Australia**

TerraShield®
Repellent Blend

Thinker™
Children's Focus Blend

 TOP USES

Insect Repellent—Apply to exposed areas of skin and clothing before going outdoors. Diffuse, and spray on outdoor surfaces.

Poor Emotional Boundaries, Easily Bugged or Bothered—Diffuse, or apply to strengthen one's resolve and maintain healthy emotional boundaries.

Cellular Health & Antioxidant—Apply to pulse points and bottoms of feet to promote healthy cell function.

Skin Complaints—Apply diluted with lavender to troubled skin.

Wood Polish— Mix 4 drops with fractionated coconut oil to polish and preserve wood.

 TOP USES

ADD / ADHD, Hyperactivity—Apply under nose, to forehead, along spine, back of neck, and/or bottoms of feet.

Over- & Underactive Brain Activity—Apply under nose, to forehead, along spine, back of neck, and/or bottoms of feet.

Lack of Mental Clarity, Focus & Concentration—Apply under nose, to forehead, along spine, back of neck, and/or bottoms of feet.

Overwhelmed & Apathetic, Checked Out, Afternoon Slump— Apply under nose, to forehead, along spine, back of neck, and/or bottoms of feet.

⭐ **MAIN INGREDIENTS**

Citronella, Lemongrass, Thyme, Cedarwood, Geranium, Peppermint

⭐ **MAIN INGREDIENTS**

Vetiver, Peppermint, Clementine, Rosemary

 ⚠ **SAFETY**

Not safe for internal use.

 ⚠ **SAFETY**

Not safe for internal use. Avoid sunlight or UV rays to applied area for up to 12 hours.

Thyme
Thymus vulgaris

 TOP USES

Cold, Flu, & Viruses, Sore Throat, Bacterial Infections—Take in a capsule. Apply to bottoms of feet.

Asthma, Croup & Pneumonia, Whooping Cough, Laryngitis, Tonsillitis, Pleurisy—Dilute and massage onto chest. Inhale from cupped hands. Take in a capsule.

Candida & Parasites, Fungal Infections, Eczema, Psoriasis—Take in a capsule, or inhale. Apply highly diluted to affected area.

Infertility, Low Progesterone, Breast, Ovary & Prostate Issues, Irregular Menstruation—Apply to reflex points on feet, and take in a capsule.

⭐ **PROPERTIES** ·····························

Analgesic, Mucolytic, Stimulant, Antioxidant, Anti-rheumatic, Antiviral, Expectorant

 **MAIN CONSTITUENTS**

⚠ **SAFETY**

Thymol, Paracymene

Caution with use with epileptics, during pregnancy and high blood pressure.

 *Sourced*— Kenya

Tulsi
Ocimum Sanctum

 TOP USES

Mental & Adrenal Fatigue, Poor Memory & Cognition, Repeated Tendency Toward Errors & Slow Reaction Time—Diffuse, or inhale from cupped hands. Apply diluted under nose and/or pulse points.

Dandruff & Scalp Issues, Hair Loss—Apply to scalp or add to shampoo or conditioner.

Imbalanced Blood Sugar & Diabetes Related Issues, Poor Circulation, High Cholesterol—Apply to bottoms of feet and over pancrea and/or liver areas.

Headaches, Stress-Induced Muscle Tension & Inflammation—Diffuse. Apply to forehead and/or areas of concern. Dilute as needed.

⭐ **PROPERTIES** ·····························

Relaxant, Antibacterial, Antiviral, Antifungal, Anti-inflammatory, Analgesic, Disinfectant

 MAIN CONSTITUENTS

⚠ **SAFETY**

Eugenol, 1,8-cineole (eucalyptol), Methyl chavicol

Not safe for internal use.

 Sourced— India

Turmeric
Curcuma longa

 TOP USES

Joint Pain & Swelling, Arthritis, Gout, Rheumatism— Apply to areas of concern. Take in a capsule.

Cancer & Tumors, Autoimmmune Disorders— Take in a capsule. Apply to affected areas.

Cooking— Add to dishes for a savory flavor.

Fungal, Bacterial or Viral Infections— Take in a capsule, and apply to affected areas.

Alzheimer, Stroke, Poor Blood Supply— Take in a capsule. Inhale from cupped hands. Apply to forehead, bottoms of feet, and/or along spine.

Intestinal Worms & Parasites— Take in a capsule.

 **PROPERTIES** ·

Anti-inflammatory, Anticarcinogenic, Detoxifier, Antibacterial, Antioxidant, Antimutagenic, Anticarcinoma, Anti-tumoral, Decongestant, Antiviral

MAIN CONSTITUENTS

ar-turmerone, Turmerone

 SAFETY

It does not have the same skin-coloring and fabric staining properties as powdered forms.

Vanilla
Vanilla planifolia

 TOP USES

Euphoric, Warming, Invigorating & Perfume— Combine with favorite citrus, flower, spice, and/or tree oils. Diffuse, or inhale. Add to fractionated coconut oil and apply under nose, to back of neck, and/or on wrists or bottoms of feet as a personal scent to enhance mood and/or delight senses.

Relaxation & Tranquility, Comfort— Combine with favorite calming oil. Diffuse. Apply diluted to pulse points, back of neck, along the spine, and/or bottoms of feet.

Restless & Sleep Issues— Diffuse, and apply under nose and to bottoms of feet.

 PROPERTIES ·

Calming, Relaxant

MAIN CONSTITUENTS

Vanillin

 SAFETY

Dilution recommended. Possible skin sensitivity.

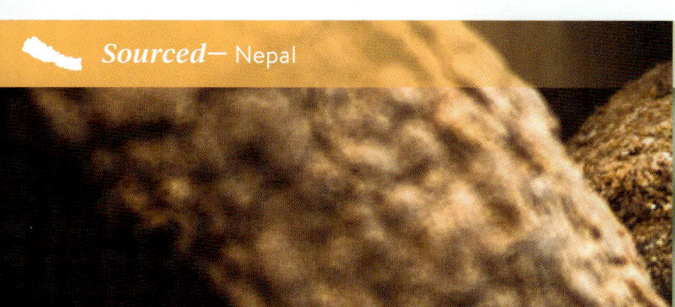

Vetiver
Vetiveria zizanioides

 TOP USES

ADD, ADHD, Focus & Concentration—Apply to back of neck, along spine, and/or under nose. Combine with lavender.

Learning Difficulties & Poor Retention—Apply to back of neck and/or under nose. Diffuse during learning times with lavender.

Insomnia & Irritability—Apply to bottoms of feet or back of neck.

Nerve Issues & Debility, Numbness—Apply to affected area.

PTSD, Depression & Anxiety, Shock, Fear, Trauma—Apply to back of neck, forehead, and pulse points. Diffuse with lavender.

 **PROPERTIES**

Stimulant, Tonic, Sedative, Antiseptic, Immunostimulant, Vermifuge, Antispasmodic, Rubefacient

MAIN CONSTITUENTS

Isovalenceno, Khusimol

SAFETY

N/A

Whisper®
Women's Perfume Blend

 TOP USES

Perfume—Apply to wrists and base of neck.

Lack of Sex Drive or Sexual Interest—Apply to wrists, neck, and/or chest.

Lack of Self-Confidence or Creativity—Inhale from cupped hands, and/or apply to forehead and over heart.

Hot Flashes—Apply to base of neck and/or lower abdomen.

Lack of Self-Expression or Presence—Inhale from cupped hands. Apply under nose, on wrists, neck, and pulse points.

Anger & Irritability—Inhale from cupped hands, and/or apply to pulse points.

Imbalanced Hormones—Apply to pulse points, back of neck, and bottoms of feet.

 MAIN INGREDIENTS

Patchouli, Bergamot, Sandalwood, Rose, Vanilla Bean, Rose, Jasmine, Cinnamon, Vetiver, Labdanum, Cocoa Bean, Ylang Ylang

SAFETY

Not safe for internal use. Avoid exposure to sunlight or UV rays for up to 12 hours after application.

Sourced— Haiti

White Fir
Abies Alba

 TOP USES

Sinusitis & Asthma—Apply to bridge of nose and chest, or diffuse to ease breathing.

Muscle & Joint Pain—Massage diluted on affected areas.

Muscle Fatigue & Regeneration—Apply diluted to areas of concern.

Bursitis & Rheumatism—Apply to affected areas.

Airborne Pathogens—Diffuse to fight germs.

Circulation Issues & Bruising—Massage into affected areas.

Stress & Foggy Mind—Diffuse with frankincense for increased focus and clarity.

Bronchitis & Congestion—Apply to chest or bridge of nose.

 PROPERTIES

Analgesic, Antiarthritic, Antiseptic, Stimulant, Antioxidant

 MAIN CONSTITUENTS

Limonene, β-pinene, Bornyl acetate

⚠ **SAFETY**

Not safe for internal use.

Wild Orange
Citrus sinensis

 TOP USES

Depression, Fear, Isolation, Irritability—Apply under nose, across forehead, or pulse points. Diffuse, or inhale from cupped hands.

Lack of Energy, Creativity & Productivity or Concentration—Take in a capsule. Apply under nose, or diffuse.

Cancer & Tissue or Cellular Regeneration—Take in a capsule, and/or apply to affected areas.

Heartburn & Sluggish Bowels, Diarrhea, Colic, Jaundice—Take in a capsule with ginger, or apply diluted to abdomen.

 PROPERTIES

Energizing, Sedative, Anti-carcinoma, Carminative, Antiseptic, Antidepressant, Immunostimulant

 **MAIN CONSTITUENTS**

Limonene

⚠ **SAFETY**

Avoid exposure to sunlight or UV rays for up to 12 hours after application.

Sourced— Austria

Sourced— Brazil

Wintergreen

Gaultheria fragrantissima

 TOP USES

Arthritis, Gout & Rheumatism—Dilute, and apply to affected areas.

Poor Circulation & Cold Extremities, High Blood Pressure—Dilute, and apply to affected areas.

Dandruff—Add to shampoo, and apply to scalp.

Muscle Pain, Cramps & Lack of Tone—Dilute, and apply to area of concern.

Bone or Nerve Pain, Sciatica—Apply diluted to affected area.

Broken Bones, Spurs, Cartilage Injury & Bruising Osteoporosis—Dilute, and apply to affected area.

 **PROPERTIES**

Anti-inflammatory, Analgesic, Anti-rheumatic

 MAIN CONSTITUENTS

Methyl salicylate

SAFETY

Not safe for internal use. Dilution recommended. Possible skin sensitivity.

 Sourced— Nepal

Yarrow|Pom

Achillea millefolium

 TOP USES

Bleeding, Hemorrhaging, Internal Wounds & Scarring—Take in a capsule or in water.

Varicose Veins & Hemorrhoids, Sagging, Dry or Aging Skin, Poor Collagen Production—Apply to affected area. Add a hot compress to take deeper.

Irregular or Absent Menstruation & Early Menopause—Apply to abdomen, drop in a sitz bath, and/or take in a capsule.

Depression, Anxiety & Fatigue—Inhale from cupped hands, apply under nose, and/or bottoms of feet.

 PROPERTIES

Antihemorrhagic, Anti-rheumatic, Antiviral, Emmenagogue, Regenerative

 MAIN CONSTITUENTS

Punicic acid, β-caryophyllene, Chamazulene

SAFETY

Dilution recommended. Possible skin sensitivity. May stain surfaces, fabric, and skin.

 Sourced— Bulgaria

Ylang Ylang
....
Cananga odorata

 TOP USES

Low Libido, Impotence, Infertility, Hormone Imbalance, Low Testosterone—Apply to lower abdomen, pulse points, and/or take in a capsule.

Adrenal or Mental Fatigue, Apathy or Loss of Will—Diffuse, or inhale from cupped hands. Apply over heart. Take in a capsule.

Irregular Heartbeat & Palpitations—Apply to bottoms of feet and over the heart. Inhale from cupped hands. Take in a capsule.

Distress, Grief, Heartbreak, Crying, Fear, Shock, Trauma—Diffuse, or inhale from cupped hands. Apply over heart, and/or back of neck. Take in a capsule.

⭐ **PROPERTIES** ....

Hypotensive, Aphrodisiac, Antispasmodic, Sedative

 MAIN CONSTITUENTS

Germacrene D, β-Caryophyllene, Farnesene

⚠ **SAFETY**

N/A

Zendocrine®
....
Detoxification Blend

 TOP USES

Kidney, Gallbladder & Liver Toxicity & Issues—Take in a capsule, or apply diluted over organ area and/or reflex points on feet.

Heavy Metal Detoxification—Take in a capsule. Apply on bottoms of feet.

Constipation & Urinary Tract Infection—Take in a capsule, and/or apply diluted over abdomen.

Weight Loss & Detoxification—Take in a capsule.

Colitis & Jaundice—Take in a capsule, and/or apply diluted to abdomen or bottoms of feet.

Endocrine & Hormone Imbalance—Take in a capsule, or apply diluted to abdomen or bottoms of feet.

⭐ **MAIN INGREDIENTS** ....

Tangerine, Rosemary, Geranium, Juniper Berry, Rosemary, Cilantro

⚠ **SAFETY** ....

Avoid exposure to sunlight or UV rays for up to 12 hours after application.

Sourced— Madagascar

OIL	BY OUTCOME	BY CHEMISTRY
Abōde™ (Distilled Lime, Cassia, Litsea, Lemon Eucalyptus, Tea Tree, Arborvitae, Eucalyptus, Cilantro, Lavandin, Lemon Myrtle)	Air-X™, Arborvitae, Cassia, Cilantro, Eucalyptus, Lemon Eucalyptus, Lemon Myrtle, Lime, Niaouli, Purify, Tea Tree	Purify
Adaptiv™ (Wild Orange, Lavender, Copaiba, Spearmint, Magnolia, Rosemary, Neroli, Sweet Gum)	Cedarwood, Copaiba, Magnolia, Neroli, Rosemary, Wild Orange	Copaiba, Jasmine, Lavender, Neroli, Serenity®, Wild Orange
Air™ (Litsea, Tangerine, Grapefruit, Frankincense, Cardamom)	Abōde™, Breathe®, DDR Prime®, HD Clear®, Lemongrass, Litsea, Melissa	Cardamom, Litsea
Align (Bergamot, Coriander, Marjoram, Peppermint, Jasmine, Rose)	Arborvitae, Black Spruce, Copaiba, Northern Escape	Basil, Coriander, Marjoram
Amavi® (Buddha Wood, Balsam Fir, Black Pepper, Hinoki, Patchouli)	Balance®, Black Spruce, Hinoki	Black Pepper, Patchouli
Anchor (Lavender, Cedarwood, Frankincense, Cinnamon Bark, Sandalwood, Black Pepper, Patchouli)	Arborvitae, Balance®, Black Spruce, Cedarwood, Frankincense, Guaiacwood, Patchouli, Sandalwood	Cedarwood, Frankincense, Sandalwood, Patchouli
Arborvitae	Abōde™, Align, Anchor, Cedarwood, Clary Sage, Jasmine, Petitgrain, Roman Chamomile	Clary Sage, Jasmine, Petitgrain, Roman Chamomile
Arise (Grapefruit, Lemon, Osmanthus, Melissa, Siberian Fir)	Beautiful, Citrus Bloom™, Elevation, Hinoki, Melissa	Beautiful, Melissa
AromaTouch® (Cypress, Peppermint, Marjoram, Basil, Grapefruit, Lavender)	Basil, Coriander, Cypress, Marjoram	Basil, Cypress, Grapefruit, Marjoram
Balance® (Spruce, Ho Wood, Frankincense, Blue Tansy, Blue Chamomile, Osmanthus)	Amavi®, Anchor, Black Spruce, Frankincense, Steady™	Black Spruce, Blue Tansy, Frankincense

OIL	BY OUTCOME	BY CHEMISTRY
Balsam Fir	Balance®, Black Pepper, Black Spruce, Cypress, Douglas Fir, Frankincense, Pink Pepper, Steady™	Black Pepper, Cypress, Douglas Fir, Frankincense, Pink Pepper
Basil	AromaTouch®, Coriander, Fennel, Marjoram, Rosemary, Tulsi	Coriander, Rosemary
Beautiful (Lime, Osmanthus, Bergamot, Frankincense)	Arise, Beautiful Body Mist, Citrus Bloom™, Elevation, Magnolia	Beautiful, Magnolia
Bergamot	Citrus Bliss®, Hope®, Magnolia, Neroli, Petitgrain, Pink Pepper, Whisper®	Magnolia, Neroli, Petitgrain
Bergamot Mint	Clary Sage, Island Mint®, Lavender, Petitgrain, Spearmint, Supermint™	Clary Sage, Lavender, Petitgrain
Birch	Deep Blue®, PastTense®, Wintergreen	Deep Blue®, Wintergreen
Black Pepper	Balsam Fir, Copaiba, Hinoki, Juniper Berry, Yarrow|Pom, Ylang Ylang	Balsam Fir, Copaiba, Juniper Berry, Yarrow|Pom, Ylang Ylang
Black Spruce	Align, Amavi®, Anchor, Balance®, Forgive®, Hinoki, Jasmine, Lavender, Northern Escape, Petitgrain, Siberian Fir	Lavender, Petitgrain, Siberian Fir
Blue Tansy	Deep Blue®, Juniper Berry, Roman Chamomile, Rosemary, Tulsi, Yarrow|Pom	Deep Blue®, Juniper Berry, Rosemary, Yarrow|Pom
Brave™ (Wild Orange, Amyris, Osmanthus, Cinnamon)	Harvest Spice, Holiday Joy, Passion®, Wild Orange	Cinnamon, Holiday Joy, Passion®, Wild Orange

OIL	BY OUTCOME	BY CHEMISTRY
Breathe® (Laurel Leaf, Eucalyptus, Peppermint, Tea Tree, Lemon, Cardamom, Ravintsara, Ravensara)	Air-X™, Eucalyptus, Laurel Leaf, Peppermint, Ravintsara, Spanish Sage	Air-X™, Eucalyptus, Laurel, Peppermint, Ravintsara
Calmer™ (Lavender, Cananga, Buddha Wood, Roman Chamomile)	Console®, Lavender, Roman Chamomille, Serenity®, Ylang Ylang	DigestZen®, Serenity®, Tamer™
Cardamom	Celery Seed, Coriander, DigestZen®, Dill, Eucalyptus, Passion®	Breathe®, Celery Seed, Coriander, DigestZen®, Eucalyptus, Laurel Leaf
Cassia	Abōde™, Cinnamon	Cinnamon, Laurel Leaf, Lemon Mrytle, Summer Savory
Cedarwood	Adaptiv™, Anchor, Arborvitae, Copaiba, Frankincense, Guaiacwood, Holiday Peace, Hygge™, Sandalwood, Serenity®, Spikenard, Stronger™, TerraShield®	Copaiba, Ginger, Frankincense, Spikenard
Celery Seed	Cardamom, Dill, Green Mandarin	Cardamom, Cumin, Dill, Green Mandarin
Cheer® (Wild Orange, Star Anise, Ginger, Bergamot, Ylang Ylang, Frankincense, Lemongrass, Tonka Bean, Vanilla)	Elevation, Harvest Spice, Holiday Joy, Motivate®, Vanilla, Wild Orange	Elevation, Harvest Spice, Holiday Joy, On Guard®
Cilantro	Abōde™, Citronella, Coriander, Lemon Eucalyptus, Marjoram, Melissa	Citronella, Coriander, Lemon Eucalyptus, Melissa
Cinnamon	Cassia, Clove, MetaPWR®, On Guard®, Passion®, Tulsi	Cassia, Clove, MetaPWR®, On Guard®, Passion
Citronella	Cilantro, Laurel Leaf, Lemon Eucalyptus, Rose, TerraShield®	Geranium, Laurel Leaf, Lemon Eucalyptus, Rose

OIL	BY OUTCOME	BY CHEMISTRY
Citrus Bliss® (Wild Orange, Lemon, Grapefruit, Red Mandarin, Green Mandarin, Litsea, Tonka Bean, Vanilla)	Citrus Bloom™, Grapefruit, Lemon, Red Mandarin, Tangerine, Vanilla, Wild Orange	Citrus Bloom™
Citrus Bloom™ (Wild Orange, Grapefruit, Lavender, Roman Chamomile, Magnolia)	Arise, Beautiful, Citrus Bliss®, Elevation, Magnolia	Citrus Bliss®
Clary Sage	Bergamot Mint, ClaryCalm®, Davana, Jasmine, Lavender, Magnolia, Petitgrain, Roman Chamomile	Arborvitae, Bergamot Mint, Clary Calm®, Jasmine, Lavender, Petitgrain, Roman Chamomile
Clementine	Grapefruit, Green Mandarin, Red Mandarin, Tangerine, Wild Orange	Grapefruit, Green Mandarin, Red Mandarin, Tangerine, Wild Orange
Clove	Cinnamon, DDR Prime®, On Guard®, Oregano, Thyme, Tulsi	Cinnamon, On Guard®, Oregano, Thyme, Tulsi
Console® (Frankincense, Patchouli, Ylang Ylang, Labdanum, Amyris, Sandalwood, Rose, Osmanthus)	Calmer™, Deep Blue®, Frankincense, Geranium, Helichrysum, Myrrh, Patchouli, Rose, Ylang Ylang	Frankincense, InTune®, Patchouli, Rose, Sandalwood
Copaiba	Adaptiv™, Align, Black Pepper, Cedarwood, Deep Blue®, Deep Blue® Stick, Rescuer™, Tulsi, Ylang Ylang	Black Pepper, Cedarwood, Deep Blue®, Rescuer™, Tulsi
Coriander	AromaTouch®, Basil, Cardamom, Cilantro, DigestZen®, Magnolia	Basil, Cardamom, Cilantro, DigestZen®, Lavender, Magnolia
Cumin	Celery Seed, DigestZen®, Dill, Summer Savory	Celery Seed, DigestZen®
Cypress	AromaTouch®, Douglas Fir, Hinoki, Juniper Berry, Neroli, Northern Escape, Siberian Fir, Spanish Sage	AromaTouch®, Balsam Fir, Douglas Fir, Hinoki, Neroli, Siberian Fir

OIL	BY OUTCOME	BY CHEMISTRY
Davana	Clary Sage, Frankincense, Geranium, Jasmine, Neroli, Rose	Extremely Unique
DDR Prime® (Frankincense, Wild Orange, Litsea, Thyme, Clove, Summer Savory, Niaouli, Lemongrass)	Air-X™, Clove, Frankincense, Lemongrass, Pink Pepper, Thyme, Tulsi, Wild Orange	Frankincense, HD Clear®, Pink Pepper, Wild Orange
Deep Blue® (Wintergreen, Camphor, Peppermint, Ylang Ylang, Helichrysum, Blue Tansy, Blue Chamomile, Osmanthus)	Blue Tansy, Copaiba, Helichrysum, PastTense®, Peppermint, Rescuer™, Spanish Sage, Wintergreen	Blue Tansy, Copaiba, Rescuer™
DigestZen® (Peppermint, Coriander, Ginger, Caraway, Cardamom, Fennel, Anise)	Cardamom, Coriander, Fennel, Ginger, Peppermint, Supermint™, Tamer™	Cardamom, Coriander, Cumin, Dill, Ginger, Peppermint, Tamer™
Dill	Cardamom, Celery Seed, DigestZen®, Fennel, Peppermint, Spearmint	Cardamom, Celery Seed, Cumin, DigestZen®, Peppermint, Spearmint
Douglas Fir	Cypress, Frankincense, Northern Escape, Pink Pepper, Siberian Fir, Yarrow|Pom	Balsam Fir, Cypress, Frankincense, Hinoki, Yarrow|Pom
Elevation (Lavandin, Tangerine, Lavender, Amyris Bark, Clary Sage, Hawaiian Sandalwood, Ylang Ylang, Ho Wood, Osmanthus, Lemon Myrtle, Melissa)	Arise, Beautiful, Cheer®, Citrus Bloom™, Melissa	Cheer®
Eucalyptus	Abōde™, Breathe®, Cardamom, Laurel Leaf, Ravintsara, Rosemary	Breathe®, Cardamom, Laurel Leaf, Niaouli, Ravintsara, Rosemary
Fennel	Basil, Cardamom, DigestZen®	DigestZen®
Forgive® (Spruce, Bergamot, Juniper Berry, Myrrh, Arborvitae, Nootka Tree, Thyme Leaf, Citronella)	Arborvitae, Black Spruce, Holiday Peace, Northern Escape, Thyme	Holiday Peace, Northern Escape, Zendocrine®

OIL	BY OUTCOME	BY CHEMISTRY
Frankincense	Anchor, Balance®, DDR Prime®, Douglas Fir, Ginger, Immortelle, InTune®, Myrrh, Pink Pepper, Siberian Fir, Spanish Sage, Spikenard, Stronger™, Turmeric	Balsam Fir, Balance®, DDR Prime®, Douglas Fir, Hinoki, Immortelle, Pink Pepper
Geranium	ClaryCalm®, Console®, Davana, HD Clear®, Helichrysum, Lavender, Neroli, Rose, Zendrocrine®	Citronella, Lavender, Neroli, Palmarosa, Roman Chamomile, Rose, Zendocrine®
Ginger	Cedarwood, DigestZen®, Frankincense, MetaPWR®, Tamer™, Turmeric	Cedarwood, DigestZen®, Fennel, MetaPWR®
Grapefruit	Citrus Bliss®, Green Mandarin, Tangerine, Wild Orange	Clementine, Green Mandarin, Red Mandarin, Tangerine, Wild Orange
Green Mandarin	Celery Seed, Grapefruit, Tangerine, Wild Orange	Celery Seed, Clementine, Grapefruit, Kumquat, Lemon, Red Mandarin, Tangerine, Wild Orange
Guaiacwood	Anchor, Cedarwood, Hawaiian Sandalwood, InTune®, Sandalwood, Spikenard, Vetiver	Hawaiian Sandalwood, Sandalwood, Vetiver
Harvest Spice (Cinnamon Bark, Clove, Eucalyptus, Cedarwood, Cassia, Nutmeg)	Brave™, Cheer®, Holiday Joy, On Guard®, Passion®, Tulsi	Cheer®
HD Clear® (Black Cumin Seed, Ho Wood, Tea Tree, Litsea, Eucalptyus, Geranium)	Abōde™, Air-X™, DDR Prime®, Forgive®, Geranium, Litsea, Tea Tree	DDR Prime®
Helichrysum	Deep Blue®, Geranium, Immortelle, Ravintsara, Yarrow|Pom	Deep Blue®, Immortelle, Ravintsara, Yarrow|Pom
Hinoki	Amavi®, Black Pepper, Black Spruce, Cypress, Douglas Fir, Frankincense, Juniper Berry, Northern Escape, Siberian Fir	Amavi®, Black Pepper, Black Spruce, Cypress, Douglas Fir, Frankincense, Juniper Berry, Northern Escape, Siberian Fir

OIL	BY OUTCOME	BY CHEMISTRY
Holiday Joy (Wild orange, Clove, Cassia, Siberian fir, Frankincense, Styrax, Ginger Co2, Balsam fir, Cistus)	Brave™, Cheer®, Harvest Spice, On Guard®, Passion®, Tulsi	Brave™, Cheer®, Harvest Spice, On Guard®, Passion®, Tulsi
Holiday Peace (Siberian Fir, Grapefruit, Douglas Fir, Himalayan Fir, Frankincense, Vetiver)	Cedarwood, Northern Escape, Siberian Fir	Cedarwood, Northern Escape, Siberian Fir
Hope® (Bergamot, Ylang Ylang, Frankincense, Vanilla Bean Absolute)	Bergamot, Motivate®, Vanilla, Ylang Ylang	Bergamot, Motivate®, Vanilla, Ylang Ylang
Hygge™ (Wild Orange, Cedarwood, Amyris, Frankincense, Myrrh, Cistus, Vetiver, Tonka Bean)	Anchor, Cedarwood, Frankincense, Harvest Spice, Holiday Joy, InTune®, Peace®, Steady™	Holiday Joy
Hyssop	Manuka, Peppermint, Spearmint, Turmeric	Manuka, Peppermint, Spearmint, Turmeric
Immortelle (Frankincense, Hawaiian Sandalwood, Lavender, Myrrh, Helichrysum, Rose)	Frankincense, Helichrysum, Lavender, Myrrh, Rose, Sandalwood, Yarrow|Pom	Frankincense, Rose, Sandalwood
InTune® (Amyris, Patchouli, Frankincense, Lime, Ylang Ylang, Hawaiian Sandalwood, Roman Chamomile)	Frankincense, Guaiacwood, Hawaiian Sandalwood, Patchouli, Peace®, Serenity®, Thinker™, Vetiver	Patchouli, Sandalwood, Steady™
Island Mint® (Lime, Distilled Lemon, Peppermint, Spruce)	Bergamot Mint, Peppermint, Spearmint, Supermint™, Tamer™	Unique
Jasmine	Arborvitae, Clary Sage, Davana, Magnolia, Neroli, Passion®, Petitgrain, Roman Chamomile, Rose, Whisper®, Ylang Ylang	Clary Sage, Petitgrain, Roman Chamomile
Juniper Berry	Black Pepper, Blue Tansy, Celery Seed, Coriander, Cypress, Rosemary, Yarrow|Pom, Zendrocrine®	Black Pepper, Blue Tansy, Hinoki, Yarrow|Pom

OIL	BY OUTCOME	BY CHEMISTRY
Kumquat	Grapefruit, Green Mandarin, Tangerine, Wild Orange	Green Mandarin, Red Mandarin
Laurel Leaf	Breathe®, Cardamom, Eucalyptus, Ravintsara, Rosemary	Cardamom, Eucalyptus, Niaouli, Ravintsara, Rosemary
Lavender	Adaptiv™, Anchor, Bergamot Mint, Black Pepper, Black Spruce, Calmer™, Clary Sage, Geranium, Immortelle, Petitgrain, Serenity®	Black Spruce, Clary Sage, Geranium, Petitgrain
Lemon	Citrus Bliss®, Green Mandarin, Lime, Purify	Lime, Green Mandarin, Red Mandarin
Lemon Eucalyptus	Abōde™, Cilantro, Citronella, TerraShield®	Cassia, Citronella, Lemon Myrtle
Lemon Myrtle	Air-X™, Abōde™, Cassia, DDR Prime®, Lemon Eucalyptus, Litsea, Melissa	Cassia, Lemon Eucalyptus, Litsea
Lemongrass	Abōde™, Air-X™, DDR Prime®, Litsea, Melissa, TerraShield®	Air-X™, Lemon Myrtle, Litsea, Melissa
Lime	Abōde™, Black Pepper, Lemon, Purify	Lemon
Litsea	Abōde™, Air-X™, Lemongrass, Lemon, Melissa, Stronger™	Lemongrass, Lemon Myrtle, Melissa
Magnolia	Beautiful, Bergamot, Citrus Bloom™, Clary Sage, Coriander, Jasmine, Neroli, Petitgrain, Rose, Steady™, Ylang Ylang	Beautiful, Coriander, Rose

OIL	BY OUTCOME	BY CHEMISTRY
Manuka	Patchouli, Spikenard, Ylang Ylang	Hyssop, Patchouli, Spikenard, Ylang Ylang
Marjoram	AromaTouch®, Basil, Cilantro, PastTense®, Tea Tree	AromaTouch®, Basil, Cilantro, Peppermint, Tea Tree
Melissa	Air-X™, Arise, Black Pepper, Cilantro, Elevation, Lemongrass, Litsea, On Guard™+ Softgels	Black Pepper, Cilantro, Citronella, Litsea, Lemongrass, Lemon Myrtle
MetaPWR® (Grapefruit, Lemon, Peppermint, Ginger, Cinnamon)	Cinnamon, Ginger, Grapefruit, Lemon, Peppermint, Supermint™	Cinnamon, Ginger, Grapefruit
Midnight Forest (Siberian Fir, Cypress, Juniper Berry, Black Spruce, Wild Orange, Frankincense, Pimento Leaf, Pimento Fruit, Cistus, Caraway, Labdanum)	Black Spruce, Cypress, Holiday Peace, Northern Escape, Siberian Fir	Black Spruce, Cypress, Holiday Peace, Northern Escape, Siberian Fir
Motivate® (Peppermint, Wild Orange, Clementine, Lemon, Rosemary, Coriander, Basil, Spearmint, Tonka Bean, Cardamom, Melissa, Vanilla)	AromaTouch®, Cheer®, Clementine, Hope®, Peppermint, Supermint™	Unique
Myrrh	Frankincense, Immortelle, InTune®, Patchouli, Sandalwood, Spikenard, Turmeric, Vetiver	Unique
Neroli	Adaptiv™, Bergamot, Cypress, Geranium, Jasmine, Magnolia, Petitgrain	Cypress, Geranium, Petitgrain
Niaouli	Breathe®, Eucalyptus, Laurel Leaf, Ravintsara	Eucalyptus, Laurel Leaf, Ravintsara
Nootka	Arborvitae, Cedarwood, Northern Escape	Cedarwood

OIL	BY OUTCOME	BY CHEMISTRY
Northern Escape	Align, Black Spruce, Cypress, Douglas Fir, Forgive®, Holiday Peace, Siberian Fir, Tulsi	Holiday Peace
On Guard® (Wild Orange, Clove, Cinnamon, Cinnamon, Eucalyptus, Rosemary)	Cheer®, Cinnamon, Clove, Harvest Spice, Holiday Joy, Passion®, Stronger™, Tulsi	Cinnamon, Clove, DDR Prime®, Passion®, Stronger™
Oregano	Clove, On Guard™+ Softgels, Thyme	Clove, Thyme
Osmanthus	Beautiful, Magnolia	Magnolia
Palmarosa	Citronella, Coriander, Geranium, Roman Chamomile	Citronella, Coriander, Geranium, Roman Chamomile
Passion® (Ginger, Jasmine, Sandalwood, Ylang Ylang, Wild Orange, Magnolia, Lemon, Cardamom, Bergamot, Damiana, Tonka Bean, Vanilla, Cinnamon Bark)	Cardamom, Cinnamon, Ginger, Harvest Spice, Holiday Joy, Jasmine, On Guard®	On Guard®
PastTense® (Wintergreen, Lavender, Peppermint, Frankincense, Cilantro, Marjoram, Roman Chamomile, Basil, Rosemary)	AromaTouch®, Basil, Deep Blue®, Marjoram, Motivate®, Peppermint, Wintergreen	AromaTouch®
Patchouli	Anchor, Console®, InTune®, Myrrh, Sandalwood, Spikenard, Vetiver, Whisper®	InTune®, Manuka, Sandalwood, Spikenard, Vetiver
Peace® (Vetiver, Lavender, Ylang Ylang, Frankincense, Clary Sage, Marjoram, Labdanum Absolute, Spearmint)	Anchor, Hygge™, InTune®, Lavender, Serenity®, Thinker™, Vetiver, Ylang Ylang	Lavender, Serenity®, Vetiver
Peppermint	Breathe®, Deep Blue®, DigestZen®, Island Mint®, Motivate®, PastTense®, Spearmint, Supermint™, Tamer™, Thinker™	Basil, Deep Blue®, DigestZen®, Dill, Hyssop, Spearmint

OIL	BY OUTCOME	BY CHEMISTRY
Petitgrain	Arborvitae, Bergamot Mint, Black Spruce, Clary Sage, Jasmine, Lavender, Magnolia, Neroli, Roman Chamomile	Arborvitae, Bergamot Mint, Black Spruce, Clary Sage, Jasmine, Lavender
Pink Pepper	DDR Prime®, Douglas Fir, Frankincense	Balsam Fir, Douglas Fir, Frankincense
Purify (Lemon, Siberian Fir, Citronella, Lime, Tea Tree, Cilantro)	Abōde™, Cilantro, Citronella, Lemon, Lime, Siberian Fir, Tea Tree	Abōde™
Ravintsara	Breathe®, Eucalyptus, Helichrysum, Laurel Leaf	Eucalyptus, Helichrysum, Laurel Leaf, Niaouli
Red Mandarin	Grapefruit, Green Mandarin, Lemon, Tangerine, Wild Orange	Lemon
Rescuer™ (Copaiba, Lavender, Spearmint, Zanthoxylum)	Copaiba, Deep Blue®, Deep Blue® Stick, Lavender, Spearmint	Copaiba, Deep Blue®
Roman Chamomile	Arborvitae, Blue Tansy, Calmer™, ClaryCalm®, Clary Sage, Jasmine, Lavender, Palmarosa, Petitgrain, Serenity®	Arborvitae, Clary Sage, Jasmine, Palmarosa, Geranium
Rose	Citronella, Console®, Davana, Geranium, Immortelle, Jasmine, Magnolia, Stronger™, Whisper®, Ylang Ylang	Citronella, Geranium, Immortelle, Magnolia
Rosemary	Basil, Blue Tansy, Eucalyptus, Juniper Berry, Laurel Leaf, Thinker™	Blue Tansy, Eucalyptus, Laurel Leaf
Sandalwood	Anchor, Cedarwood, Guaiacwood, Immortelle, InTune®, Myrrh, Patchouli, Spikenard, Vetiver	Patchouli, Vetiver

OIL	BY OUTCOME	BY CHEMISTRY
Serenity® (Lavender, Cedarwood, Coriander, Ylang Ylang, Marjoram, Roman Chamomile, Vetiver, Sandalwood, Tonka Bean, Vanilla)	Calmer™, Cedarwood, ClaryCalm®, Frankincense, Lavender, InTune®, Peace®, Ylang Ylang	Cedarwood, Lavender, Peace®
Siberian Fir	Black Spruce, Cypress, Douglas Fir, Frankincense, Hinoki, Holiday Peace, Northern Escape, Purify	Black Spruce, Cypress
Spanish Sage	Breathe®, Cypress, Deep Blue®, Frankincense, Rosemary	Rosemary
Spearmint	Bergamot Mint, Island Mint®, Peppermint, Rescuer™, Supermint™, Tamer™, Turmeric	Dill, Hyssop, Peppermint, Turmeric
Spikenard	Cedarwood, Guaiacwood, Myrrh, Patchouli, Ylang Ylang	Cedarwood, Patchouli, Ylang Ylang
Steady™ (Amyris, Balsam Fir, Coriander, Magnolia)	Balance®, Hygge™, InTune®, Magnolia	InTune®
Stronger™	Cedarwood, Frankincense, Holiday Joy, Litsea, On Guard®, Rose	On Guard®
Summer Savory	DDR Prime®, Melissa	Cumin, Melissa
Supermint™	Bergamot Mint, Motivate®, Peppermint, Spearmint, Tamer™	Bergamot Mint, Peppermint, Spearmint, Tamer™
Tamer™ (Spearmint, Japanese Peppermint, Ginger, Black Pepper, Parsley)	DigestZen®, Ginger, Island Mint®, Peppermint, Spearmint, Supermint™	DigestZen®

OIL	BY OUTCOME	BY CHEMISTRY
Tangerine	Citrus Bliss®, Grapefruit, Green Mandarin, Wild Orange	Clementine, Grapefruit, Green Mandarin, Kumquat, Red Mandarin, Wild Orange
Tea Tree	Abōde™, HD Clear®, Marjoram	Marjoram, Neroli
TerraShield® (Citronella, Lemongrass, Thyme, Cedarwood, Geranium, Peppermint, Sesame Seed Oil)	Abōde™, Arborvitae, Citronella, Lemon Eucalyptus, Lemongrass, Thyme	Arborvitae, Citronella, Lemongrass
Thinker™ (Vetiver, Peppermint, Clementine, Rosemary)	InTune®, Peace®, Peppermint, Rosemary, Vetiver	Vetiver
Thyme	Clove, DDR Prime®, Forgive®, Oregano, TerraShield®, Tulsi	Clove, Oregano
Tulsi	Basil, Blue Tansy, Clove, Copaiba, Coriander, Fennel	Blue Tansy, Clove, Copaiba, Ylang Ylang
Turmeric	Ginger, Myrrh, Spearmint	Ginger, Myrrh, Spearmint
Vanilla	Cheer®, Citrus Bliss®, Hope®, Whisper®	Unique
Vetiver	Guaiacwood, InTune®, Myrrh, Patchouli, Peace®, Sandalwood, Thinker™, Whisper®	Patchouli, Sandalwood
White Fir	Arborvitae, Douglas Fir, Grapefruit, Neroli, Northern Escape, Pink Pepper, Siberian Fir	Siberian Fir, Black Pepper

OIL	BY OUTCOME	BY CHEMISTRY
Whisper® (Patchouli, Bergamot, Sandalwood, Vanilla Bean Absolute, Rose, Jasmine, Cinnamon Bark, Vetiver, Labdanum, Cocoa Seed, Ylang Ylang)	Bergamot, Jasmine, Neroli, Patchouli, Rose, Sandalwood, Vanilla, Vetiver, Ylang Ylang	Patchouli, Rose, Sandalwood
Wild Orange	Adaptiv™, Cheer®, Citrus Bliss®, DDR Prime®, Grapefruit, Green Mandarin, Tangerine	DDR Prime®, Clementine, Grapefruit, Green Mandarin, Red Mandarin, Tangerine
Wintergreen	AromaTouch®, Birch, Deep Blue®, PastTense®	Birch, Deep Blue®
Yarrow|Pom	Black Pepper, Blue Tansy, Douglas Fir, Helichrysum, Immortelle, Juniper, Ylang Ylang	Black Pepper, Blue Tansy, Douglas Fir, Juniper Berry, Ylang Ylang
Ylang Ylang	Black Pepper, Calmer™, ClaryCalm®, Console®, Copaiba, Hope®, Jasmine, Magnolia, Peace®, Rose, Tulsi, Whisper®, Yarrow|Pom	Black Pepper, Yarrow|Pom
Zendocrine® (Tangerine, Rosemary, Geranium, Juniper Berry, Cilantro)	Cilantro, Forgive®, Geranium, Juniper Berry, Rosemary, Tangerine	Forgive®, Geranium

SUPPLEMENTS

A2Z Chewable™

Children's

TOP USES

Low energy and fatigue, compromised digestion and immunity, brain fog, oxidative cell damage, malnutrition, and poor health.

★ MAIN INGREDIENTS

- Vitamins A, C, D3, E, K and full B-complex
- Mineral blend of calcium, copper, iron, iodine, magnesium, manganese, potassium, and zinc
- Superfood blend of pineapple, pomegranate extract, lemon bioflavonoids, spirulina, sunflower oil, rice bran, beet greens, broccoli, brown rice, carrot, mango, cranberry, rose hips, acerola cherry extract, and spinach
- Cellular vitality complex of tomato extract, turmeric extract, boswellia serrata extract, grape seed extract, and marigold flower extract

⚠ SAFETY

No GMOs, gluten, wheat, dairy, soy, or nut products. Pregnant or lactating women should consult a physician or healthcare provider before use.

Adaptiv™

Calming Blend Capsules

TOP USES

Manage stress, boost mood, balance mind and body, promote positive attitude, improve state of mind, invite resiliency, agility, and mental well-being.

★ MAIN INGREDIENTS

- Lavender oil
- Coriander oil
- Wild orange oil
- Fennel oil
- Sceletium root extract
- GABA
- Ahiflower seeds

⚠ SAFETY

Keep out of reach of children. If pregnant, nursing, or under a doctor's care, consult physician. Do not use if safety seal is broken or missing. Store in cool, dry place.

Alpha CRS® +
Cellular Vitality Complex

 TOP USES

Pain and inflammation, arthritis, osteoarthritis, fibromyalgia, foggy brain, cirrhosis, jaundice, cellular repair, fatigue, mood, and cancer prevention.

⭐ **MAIN INGREDIENTS**

- Boswellia serrata gum resin
- Scutellaria root (baicalin)
- Milk thistle (silymarin)
- Polygonum cuspidatum (resveratrol)
- Green tea leaf (EGCG)
- Pomegranate fruit extract
- Pineapple (bromelain)
- Turmeric extract (curcumin)
- Grape seed extract
- Sesame seed extract
- Pine bark extract (pycnogenol)
- Gingko Biloba leaf
- Acetyl-L-Carnitine
- Alpha-Lipoic acid
- Coenzyme Q10
- Quercetin

⚠ **SAFETY**

For men, women, and teens. Pregnant or lactating women should consult a physician or healthcare provider before use.

*Included in LLV pack and vegan LLV pack

Bone Nutrient
Complex

 TOP USES

Weak or fragile bones, osteopenia and osteoporosisprone individuals, bone fractures, growing individuals, and anyone needing more bone density.

⭐ **MAIN INGREDIENTS**

- Vitamins C, D2, and D3
- Biotin
- Mineral blend of calcium, magnesium, zinc, copper, manganese, and boron

⚠ **SAFETY**

Safe for use by women, teens, and men. Pregnant or lactating women should consult a physician or healthcare provider before use. GMO and gluten-free.

Breathe®

Respiratory Drops

Copaiba

Softgels

 TOP USES

Congestion, head cold, sore throat, bronchitis, asthma, allergies, cough, sinusitis, bad breath, and motion sickness.

 TOP USES

Cardiovascular, immune, and digestive system support, powerful antioxidant; addresses lungs, respiratory, and mood concerns.

 MAIN INGREDIENTS ································

- Cardamom oil
- Peppermint oil
- Eucalyptus oil
- Lemon oil
- Thyme oil
- Melissa oil

 MAIN INGREDIENTS ································

- Copaiba essential oil: promotes a healthy immune function and response, while supporting cellular health and function.

⚠ **SAFETY** ···

Be aware with small children that are prone to choking.

⚠ **SAFETY** ···

Keep out of reach of small children. If pregnant or lactating, women should consult a physician or healthcare provider before use.

DDR Prime®
Cellular Complex Softgels

 TOP USES

Damaged or mutated cellular diseases, oxidative stress, autoimmune diseases, and anything that requires cellular regeneration and healthy cellular function.

⭐ **MAIN INGREDIENTS** ·

- Frankincense oil
- Wild orange oil
- Lemongrass oil
- Thyme oil
- Summer savory oil
- Clove oil
- Niaouli oil
- Litsea oil

 ⚠ **SAFETY** ·

Not for small children. If pregnant or lactating, women should consult a physician or health care provider before use.

Deep Blue
Polyphenol Complex®

 TOP USES

Joint pain, inflammation, arthritis, rheumatoid arthritis, fibromyalgia, sore muscles, Alzheimer's disease, and cancer prevention.

⭐ **MAIN INGREDIENTS** ·

- Frankincense (boswellia serrata) gum resin extract
- Curcumin
- Ginger root extract
- Green tea leaf extract (caffeine-free)
- Pomegranate fruit extract
- Grape seed extract
- Resveratrol
- Stomach comfort blend of peppermint, ginger, and caraway seed

 ⚠ **SAFETY** ·

Not for use for children. If pregnant or lactating, women should consult a physician or healthcare provider before use. Gluten-free.

DigestTab®
·············
Chewable Tablets

 TOP USES

Upset stomach, poor digestive health, belching and bloating, heartburn, and acid indigestion/reflux.

⭐ **MAIN INGREDIENTS** ·································

- Anise oil
- Peppermint oil
- Ginger oil
- Caraway oil
- Coriander oil
- Tarragon oil
- Fennel oil

⚠ **SAFETY** ·····································

Keep out of reach of children. Not intended to be used with other acid reducers. If taking a prescription drug, consult a physician or healthcare provider before use. Vegan friendly. GMO and gluten-free.

DigestZen®
·············
Digestive Blend Softgels

 TOP USES

Upset stomach, constipation, diarrhea, IBS, vomiting, heartburn, and acid indigestion/reflux.

⭐ **MAIN INGREDIENTS** ·································

- Ginger oil
- Peppermint oil
- Tarragon oil
- Fennel oil
- Caraway oil
- Coriander oil
- Anise oil

⚠ **SAFETY** ·····································

Can be taken with food. Useful for all ages that can swallow capsules. Keep out of reach of small children.

DigestZen Terrayme®
Digestive Enzyme Complex

 TOP USES

Poor nutrition, heartburn or indigestion, slow metabolism, upset stomach, bloating, and flatulence.

⭐ **MAIN INGREDIENTS**

- Protease
- Papain
- Amylase
- Lipase
- Lactase
- Alpha galactosidase
- Cellulase
- Sucrase
- Anti-gluten enzyme blend
- Glucoamylase
- Betaine HCL
- Stomach comfort blend: peppermint, ginger, and caraway

⚠ **SAFETY**

Can be taken by all ages that can swallow capsules. If pregnant or lactating, women should consult a physician or healthcare provider before use.

Fiber
Dietary Supplement

 TOP USES

Weight management, metabolic issues, cardiovascular concerns, unhealthy lifestyle, and Vitamin C source.

⭐ **MAIN INGREDIENTS**

- Prebiotic blend (fructooligosaccharide)
- Fiber blend
- Flaxseed powder
- Lemon oil

⚠ **SAFETY**

Keep out of reach of small children. If pregnant or lactating, consult a physician or healthcare provider before use. Keep in a cool, dry place. GMO and gluten-free.

Ginger
Digestive Drops

 **TOP USES**

Upset stomach, indigestion, nausea, morning and motion sickness.

⭐ **MAIN INGREDIENTS** ·······················

- Ginger oil
- Lemon oil
- Organic cane sugar
- Organic brown rice syrup

 SAFETY ·······················

Be aware with small children that are prone to choking. For children under 5 years, consult a physician before use.

Greens
Dietary Supplement

TOP USES

Weight management, metabolic issues, poor nutrition; gluten-free and vegan alternatives, and source of dietary fiber.

⭐ **MAIN INGREDIENTS** ·······················

- Green blend (kale, spinach, broccoli, dandelion leaf, parsley, alfalfa, barley grass)
- Superfood blend (moringa leaf, noni fruit, acai berry)
- Fruit blend (pineapple, mango, guava, acerola cherry)
- Essential oil blend (lemon and ginger essential oils, ginger root extract)
- Monkfruit

 SAFETY ·······················

Keep out of reach of small children. If pregnant or lactating, women should consult a physician or healthcare provider before use. Vegan friendly. Keep in a cool, dry place. GMO and gluten-free.

GX Assist®
GI Cleansing Formula Softgels

 TOP USES

For overgrowth of candida albicans and other negative pathogens, autoimmune diseases, compromised digestive system, brain fog, illness, and infections.

⭐ **MAIN INGREDIENTS**

- Oregano oil
- Tea Tree oil
- Lemon oil
- Lemongrass oil
- Peppermint oil
- Thyme oil
- Caprylic acid

⚠ **SAFETY**

Keep out of reach of small children. If pregnant or lactating, women should consult a physician or healthcare provider before use.

IQ Mega
Omega 3 Supplement

 TOP USES

Brain fog, ADD/ADHD, cardiovascular disease, dry skin, joint pain and arthritis, weak muscles, and compromised immune system.

⭐ **MAIN INGREDIENTS**

- Fish oil (from cod, saithe, and haddock)
- DHA
- EPA
- Wild orange oil

⚠ **SAFETY**

Keep out of reach of small children, keep refrigerated after opening.

MetaPWR™
Advantage

 TOP USES

Reverse effects of metabolic aging, promote healthy metabolism, reduce cravings, normalize blood glucose levels, improve insulin response, increase cellular levels of NAD+ and NADH, support improved cognitive function, promote skin density.

 MAIN INGREDIENTS

- CPTG® MetaPWR essential oil blend
- Infused Marine Collagen Tripeptides
- NMN (Nicotinamide Mononucleotide)
- Liposomal vitamin C
- Sea buckthorn fruit extract
- Grape trans-Resveratrol
- Red Orange extract
- Sodium hyaluronate
- Rose Love Apple fruit extract
- Phytoceramides bran/germ extract
- NADH (Nicotinamide Adenine Dinucleotide)
- Biotin (B7)

 SAFETY

Keep out of reach of small children. If pregnant, nursing, or under a doctor's care, consult physician or healthcare provider. Store in cool, dry place.

MetaPWR®
Assist

 TOP USES

Support metabolic health and function, help normalize blood glucose levels, slow the glycemic response, promote healthy insulin activity, sensitivity, and response, activate AMPK, and stimulate healthy adipose cell reduction.

MAIN INGREDIENTS

- Mulberry leaf extract
- Berberine hydrochloride
- MetaPWR Assist® Blend (cinnamon bark powder + MetaPWR™ essential oil blend)
- Macro-minerals

SAFETY

Keep out of reach of children. If pregnant, nursing, or under a doctor's care, consult physician or healthcare provider. Store in a cool, dry place.

MetaPWR™
Metabolic Blend Softgels

 ## TOP USES

Slow metabolism, overweight or obese individuals, lack of energy (fatigue), diabetes, toxic liver, and compromised endocrine system.

⭐ ## MAIN INGREDIENTS

- Grapefruit oil
- Lemon oil
- Peppermint oil
- Ginger oil
- Cinnamon bark oil

 ⚠️ ## SAFETY

Not for children. Keep out of reach of small children. If pregnant or lactating, women should consult a physician or healthcare provider before use.

Mito2Max®
Energy & Stamina Complex

 ## TOP USES

Body fatigue and tiredness, adrenal fatigue, hormonal imbalance, libido, physical stress, anxiety, and poor circulation.

⭐ ## MAIN INGREDIENTS

- Acetyl-l-carnitine HCL
- Alpha-lipoic acid
- Coenzyme Q10
- Lychee fruit and Green Tea Leaf Polyphenol extracts
- Quercetin dihydrate
- Cordyceps mycelium
- Ginseng (panax quinquefolius) root extract
- Ashwagandha (withania somnifera) root extract

 ⚠️ ## SAFETY

Not for children. Keep out of reach of small children. If pregnant or lactating, women should consult a physician or healthcare provider before use. GMO and gluten-free.

On Guard™+
Protective Blend Softgels

 TOP USES

Protect the immune system from pathogens.

⭐ **MAIN INGREDIENTS** ⋯⋯⋯⋯⋯⋯

- Wild orange oil
- Clove oil
- Black pepper oil
- Cinnamon bark oil
- Eucalyptus oil
- Oregano oil
- Rosemary oil
- Melissa oil

⚠ **SAFETY** ⋯⋯⋯⋯⋯⋯⋯⋯⋯⋯

Not for children. Keep out of reach of small children. If pregnant or lactating, women should consult a physician or healthcare provider before use.

On Guard®
Protective Blend Tablets

 TOP USES

Compromised immune function, as well as high seasonal and environmental threats.

⭐ **MAIN INGREDIENTS** ⋯⋯⋯⋯⋯⋯

- Wild orange peel
- Clove bud
- Cinnamon leaf/bark
- Eucalyptus leaf
- Rosemary flower/leaf
- Vitamin C
- Vitamin D
- Zinc
- Beta glucan

⚠ **SAFETY** ⋯⋯⋯⋯⋯⋯⋯⋯⋯⋯

Keep out of reach of small children. If pregnant or lactating, women should consult a physician or healthcare provider before use. Keep in a cool, dry place. Vegan friendly, sugar-free, non-GMO, and gluten-free.

On Guard®

....

*Protective Blend
Throat Drops*

 TOP USES

Sore or dry throat, cough, cold and flu, illness, laryngitis, preventative care, and compromised immunity.

⭐ **MAIN INGREDIENTS** ....

- Wild orange oil
- Clove
- Cinnamon bark
- Eucalyptus
- Rosemary
- Myrrh
- Organic cane juice
- Organic brown rice syrup

 SAFETY ....

Be aware with small children that are prone to choking.

PB Assist®

....

*Probiotic Defense
Formula*

 TOP USES

Flatulence, constipation or diarrhea, malabsorption, irritable bowel, compromised immune system, leaky gut, allergies, autoimmune diseases, anxiety and depression, mental disorders, and infections.

⭐ **MAIN INGREDIENTS** ....

- L. acidophilus, L. salivarius, L. casei
- B. lactis, B. bifidum, B. longum
- FOS (fructooligosaccharides) prebiotic

 SAFETY ....

If pregnant or lactating, women should consult a physician or healthcare provider before use. Keep in a cool, dry place. GMO and gluten-free.

PB Assist Jr.®
Probiotic Defense Formula

 TOP USES

Flatulence, constipation or diarrhea, malabsorption, irritable bowel, compromised immune system, leaky gut, allergies, autoimmune diseases, anxiety and depression, mental disorders, and infections.

⭐ **MAIN INGREDIENTS** ·····························

• Probiotics: L. acidophilus, L. salivarius, L. plantarum (LP01, LP02), B. breve, B. lactic strains

• FOS prebiotic

⚠ **SAFETY** ·····························

For all ages. Can be consumed with or without food. NOTE: Do not mix with hot water. Non-GMO and gluten-free.

Peppermint
Softgels

 TOP USES

Ease and relax gastrointestinal muscles, while calming stomach and intestinal tract; helpful to an irritable bowel or spastic colon with conditions such as IBS, Crohn's Disease, and colitis.

⭐ **MAIN INGREDIENTS** ·····························

• Peppermint: with a high menthol content, gastrointestinal applications include appetite reduction, relief of gas, bloating, and stomach upset, soothing digestion and heartburn.

Note: Other internal use benefits can include helping ease respiratory congestion, improve alertness, stimulate brain, decrease breast milk supply, overcome loss of sense of smell.

⚠ **SAFETY** ·····························

Keep out of reach of children. If pregnant, nursing, or under a doctor's care, consult physician. Store in cool, dry place.

Phytoestrogen
Complex

 TOP USES

Menopause, perimenopause, andropause, estrogen dominance and deficiency, hormonal imbalances, endometriosis, uterine fibroids, fibrocystic breasts, prostate inflammation, gynecomastia, painful menstruation, night sweats, hot flashes, and mood swings (PMS).

⭐ **MAIN INGREDIENTS**

• Genistein (soy extract): an isoflavone antioxidant that promotes healthy breast and uterine tissue and brings balance to hormones in both men and women. Also shown to help prevent prostate cancer in men and ovarian and breast cancer in women.

• Flax seed extract (lignans): decreases estrogen metabolites for further hormone balance and protection of the sex organ tissues and cells.

• Pomegranate extract: powerful antioxidant shown to help the reduction of free radical damage to the cells.

⚠ **SAFETY**

Not for children. Keep out of reach of small children. Okay for men and women. If pregnant or lactating, women should consult a physician or healthcare provider before use.

Protein
Whey Dietary Supplement

 TOP USES

Weight management, poor nutrition, GMO, soy, and gluten free alternatives, weak immune system, amino acid imbalance, high protein/low carb diets, and unhealthy lifestyle.

⭐ **MAIN INGREDIENTS**

• Whey protein

• Monk fruit extract

• Flaxseed powder

• Flavors: chocolate and vanilla

⚠ **SAFETY**

Keep out of reach of small children. If pregnant or lactating, women should consult a physician or health care provider before use. Keep in a cool, dry place. Soy, GMO, and gluten-free.

Protein
....
Plant Dietary Supplement

Serenity®
....
Restful Complex Softgels

 TOP USES

Weight management, poor nutrition, GMO, soy, and gluten free alternatives, weak immune system, amino acid imbalance, high protein/low carb diets, and unhealthy lifestyle.

 TOP USES

Insomnia, inability to fall asleep or wake up easily, groggy feelings upon rising in morning, lack of adequate sleep, negative impact due to lack of sleep: decreased ability to lose weight, learn, or control emotions.

⭐ **MAIN INGREDIENTS** ....

• Pea protein

• Protein blend

• Monk fruit extract

• Quinoa grain powder

⭐ **MAIN INGREDIENTS** ....

• Lavender oil

• L-Theanine [non-protein amino acid found in green tea (camellia sinensis)]

• Lemon balm oil

• Passionflower oil

• German chamomile oil

 SAFETY ....

Keep out of reach of small children. If pregnant or lactating, women should consult a physician or healthcare provider before use. Keep in a cool, dry place. Vegan friendly. Dairy, soy, GMO, and gluten-free.

 SAFETY ....

Keep out of reach of children. If pregnant, nursing, or under a doctor's care, consult a physician.

TriEase®
Seasonal Blend Softgels

 TOP USES

Seasonal allergies, hay fever, congestion, head colds, headaches, bronchitis, asthma, and sinusitis.

⭐ **MAIN INGREDIENTS** ··········

- Lemon oil
- Lavender oil
- Peppermint oil

 ⚠ **SAFETY** ··········

Be aware with small children that are prone to choking.

Turmeric
Dual Capsules

 TOP USES

Cancer, tumors, leukemia, cellular and immune health, autoimmune conditions, joint pain and swelling, arthritis, gout, rheumatism, neurological diseases, fungal; bacterial, viral infections; cognitive dysfunction, stroke, poor circulation

⭐ **MAIN INGREDIENTS** ··········

- Turmeric oil: increases bioavailability of curcuminoids for better potency and absorption, supports healthy nervous, glucose, immune response; helps prevent cancer cells from forming and multiplying.

- Turmeric extract: anti-inflammatory, anticancer compounds, help fight foreign invaders, heart disease, cancer, metabolic syndrome, Alzheimer's, and degenerative conditions.

 ⚠ **SAFETY** ··········

Keep out of reach of children. If pregnant, nursing, or under a doctor's care, consult physician. Store in cool, dry place.

vEO Mega®
Vegan Omega Complex

 TOP USES

Compromised immune system, brain fog, arthritis, joint pain, poor mobility, cardiovascular disease, dry skin, and skin issues.

⭐ **MAIN INGREDIENTS** ....

- Flax Seed oil
- Algae oil (DHA)
- Inca Inchi seed oil
- Borage oil
- Cranberry oil
- Pomegranate oil
- Pumpkin oil
- Grape oil

- Natural Vitamin E
- Astaxanthin
- Lutein

 ⚠ **SAFETY** ....

Keep out of reach of children. If pregnant, nursing, or under a doctor's care, consult physician. Vegan friendly. GMO, and gluten-free.

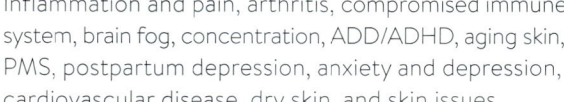

xEO Mega®
Omega Complex

TOP USES

Inflammation and pain, arthritis, compromised immune system, brain fog, concentration, ADD/ADHD, aging skin, PMS, postpartum depression, anxiety and depression, cardiovascular disease, dry skin, and skin issues.

⭐ **MAIN INGREDIENTS** ....

- Fish oil (from anchovy, sardine, mackerel, and calamari) concentrate
- Echium plantagineum seed oil
- Pomegranate oil
- Vitamin A (as Alpha and Beta carotene),
- Vitamin D3 (as natural Cholecalciferol)

- Vitamin E
- Astaxanthin
- Lutein
- Zeaxanthin
- Essential oil blend of caraway, clove, cumin, frankincense, German chamomile, ginger, peppermint, thyme, and wild orange

 ⚠ **SAFETY** ....

Can be taken by all ages that can swallow capsules. If pregnant or lactating, consult a physician or healthcare provider before use.

VMz® Microplex
Food Nutrient Complex

 TOP USES

Overall health, low energy and fatigue, compromised digestion and immunity, oxidative cell damage, malnutrition, poor health, and imbalanced nutrition.

⭐ **MAIN INGREDIENTS**

- Water soluble vitamins, B-complex, and C
- Fat soluble vitamins A, E and K
- Vitamin D3
- Macro-minerals
- Polyphenol blend
- Whole Foods blend
- Stomach comfort blend of ginger, peppermint, and caraway

⚠ **SAFETY**

Can be taken by all ages that can swallow capsules. Wheat used in the fermentation process. However, no gluten detected in the final product.

*Included in LLV pack

VMz® Microplex
Food Nutrient Complex Vegan

 TOP USES

Overall health, low energy and fatigue, compromised digestion and immunity, oxidative cell damage, malnutrition, poor health, and imbalanced nutrition. GMO-free and vegan alternatives.

⭐ **MAIN INGREDIENTS**

- Water soluble vitamins, B-complex and C
- Fat soluble vitamins A, E, and K
- Vitamin D3
- Macro-minerals
- Polyphenol blend
- Whole Foods blend
- Stomach comfort blend of ginger, peppermint, and caraway

⚠ **SAFETY**

Not for children. Keep out of reach of small children. If pregnant or lactating, women should consult a physician or healthcare provider before use. Vegan friendly. GMO and gluten-free.

*Included in vegan LLV pack

Yarrow|Pom
Cellular Beauty Capsules

TOP USES

Cellular, skin, immune and nervous system support; metabolic health, improve skin firmness, reduce skin imperfections, illuminate and brighten complexion, and calm mind and body.

⭐ **MAIN INGREDIENTS** ·········

- Yarrow|pom
- Pomegranate
- Celery seed
- Frankincense
- Palmarosa
- Turmeric
- Melissa
- Grape seed extract

- Zinc citrate
- Vitamin C
- Melon extract

⚠️ **SAFETY** ·········

Keep out of reach of children. If pregnant, nursing, or under a doctor's care, consult physician. Store in cool, dry place.

Zendocrine®
Detoxification Complex

TOP USES

Toxic liver, jaundice, cirrhosis, bloating, toxic gallbladder, pancreatitis, kidney damage, respiratory issues, colon issues, and constipation.

⭐ **MAIN INGREDIENTS** ·········

- Barberry leaf, milk thistle seed, burdock root, clove bud, dandelion root, garlic fruit, and red clover leaf
- Turkish rhubarb stem, burdock root, clove bud, dandelion root
- Psyllium seed husk, turkish rhubarb stem, acacia gum bark, and marshmallow root

- Osha root, safflower petals
- Kelp, milk thistle seed, burdock root, clove bud, and garlic fruit
- Enzyme assimilation system of amylase and cellulase their natural mineral cofactor magnesium and manganese

⚠️ **SAFETY** ·········

Not for children. Keep out of reach of small children. If pregnant or lactating, women should consult a physician or healthcare provider before use.

Zendocrine®

*Detoxification Blend
Softgels*

 TOP USES

Toxic liver, jaundice, cirrhosis, bloating, toxic gallbladder, pancreatitis, kidney damage, and hormonal imbalances.

 MAIN INGREDIENTS

- Tangerine
- Rosemary
- Geranium
- Juniper berry
- Cilantro

⚠ **SAFETY**

Not for children. Keep out of reach of small children. If pregnant or lactating, women should consult a physician or healthcare provider before use.

EAT RIGHT / PROPER NUTRITION *Chapter* 4

PROACTIVE MEDICAL CARE

SELF CARE

REDUCE TOXIC LOAD/
HEALTHY HOME

REST & MANAGE STRESS

MOVEMENT & METABOLISM

EAT RIGHT/PROPER NUTRITION

Healthcare

Lifestyle

"When diet is wrong, medicine is of no use. When diet is correct, medicine is of no need." – Ayurvedic proverb

EAT RIGHT/PROPER NUTRITION

Eating right is the foundation for lifelong health and vitality. Your body needs essential nutrients, vitamins, and minerals in order to function properly. Combined with physical exercise, your diet can help you to reach and maintain a healthy weight, reduce your risk of chronic diseases, and positively impact the other components of healthy lifestyle behaviors. Goals for eating right include the following:

Proper Nutrition and Clean Eating

Avoiding Overeating

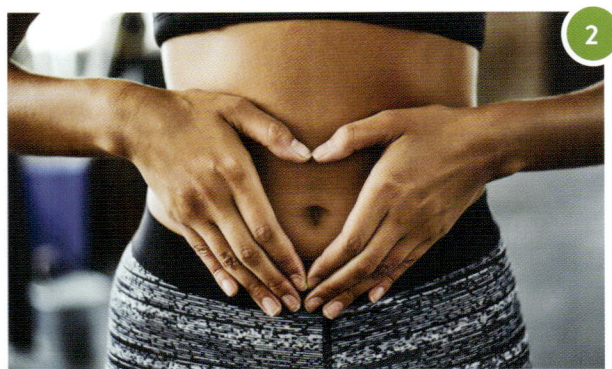

Healthy Digestion

Weight Management

PROPER NUTRITION

For your body to function at its peak, you need essential macronutrients, vitamins, and minerals. A clean diet that minimizes processed foods and focuses on whole foods should also be complemented by the right nutritional supplements. See tips for eating right on page 374, and see below for solutions to support proper nutrition and clean eating.

SOLUTIONS TO HELP

GREENS

A blend of powdered fruits, grasses, and greens along with lemon peel and ginger root to enhance the nutrition of people with busy and stressful lifestyle habits.

MICROPLEX VMZ®

Whole food micronutrient supplement with balanced amounts of vitamins, minerals, trace elements, phytonutrients, and antioxidants. Supports a healthy diet and lifestyle.

XEOMEGA®

A blend of marine-and land-based Omega-3 essential fatty acids in a unique assimilation capsule with essential oils and fat-soluble vitamins.

ALPHA CRS® +

Packed with antioxidants, natural anti-inflammatories, and energy cofactors to support cellular longevity, healthy cell function, and metabolism.

A2Z CHEWABLES

Multivitamin, mineral, and botanical chewable for children and adults that have difficulty swallowing.

IQ MEGA®

Omega-3 liquid supplement with Wild Orange essential oil to give it a fresh orange flavor. Provides 1300 mg of Omega-3 fatty acids per serving.

PROTEIN (CHOCOLATE, VANILLA, & VEGAN)

A convenient and delicious weight-management shake mix that provides low-fat, low-calorie, high-protein, and high-fiber nutrients.

HEALTHY DIGESTION

Maintaining digestive health is crucial to the body's overall well-being. All other health functions can be compromised if you are not properly digesting, absorbing, and eliminating your food. Improving digestive function is one of the most important steps you can take in improving your health. Drink plenty of water; eat wholesome foods, as well as raw fruits and vegetables; and use the following products to supplement your nutrition and improve your health.

SOLUTIONS TO HELP

DIGESTZEN TERRAZYME®

A blend of several active whole-food enzymes and mineral cofactors that help the breakdown of proteins, fats, complex carbohydrates, sugars, and fiber, giving the body better digestion and allowing nutrients to be readily available for absorption and utilization. Also supports a healthy cellular metabolism.

PB ASSIST® + /PB ASSIST® JR

Available as a probiotic capsule or powdered probiotic supplement, this product includes six different strains of good bacteria and prebiotic fiber for maximum delivery and cultivation of healthy gut flora.

GX ASSIST®

A blend of essential oils that support a healthy gastrointestinal tract by decreasing the overgrowth of pathogens in the gut, thereby increasing gut integrity and creating a healthy environment for new, good bacteria to thrive.

ALPHA CRS® +

Packed with antioxidants, natural anti-inflammatories, and energy cofactors to support cellular longevity, healthy cell function, and metabolism.

A2Z CHEWABLES

Multivitamin, mineral, and botanical chewable for children and adults that have difficulty swallowing.

IQ MEGA®

Omega-3 liquid supplement with Wild Orange essential oil to give it a fresh orange flavor. Provides 1300 mg of Omega-3 fatty acids per serving.

PROTEIN (CHOCOLATE, VANILLA, & VEGAN)

A convenient and delicious weight-management shake mix that provides low-fat, low-calorie, high-protein, high-fiber nutrients.

OVEREATING

Eat Right/Proper Nutrition

Your body uses some of the calories you consume for energy. The rest are stored as fat. Overeating can lead to obesity, increase your risk for cancer, and other chronic problems. It also takes a toll on your digestive system and can even impact your sleep. See tips to avoid overeating on page 368. Solutions that can help you avoid overeating include the following products.

SOLUTIONS TO HELP

DIGESTZEN® BLEND

A blend of essential oils that helps relieve gas, bloating, nausea, indigestion, and heartburn.

DIGESTZEN® SOFTGELS

A synergistic blend of essential oils that helps ease digestion and increase digestive health. This softgel helps relieve gas, bloating, nausea, indigestion, and heartburn.

DIGESTTAB®

A calcium carbonate tablet infused with DigestZen® Digestive Blend that delivers the benefits of digestion-supportive essential oils as well as the acid-neutralizing benefits of calcium carbonate.

PEPPERMINT

The high menthol content of this oil helps alleviate an upset stomach and relaxes smooth muscles, making it a great antispasmodic. This helps relieve gas, bloating, indigestion, and abdominal pain.

PEPPERMINT SOFTGELS

This enteric-coated capsule ensures that peppermint passes through the stomach undissolved for delivery to the large intestine, where it is most effective.

368 | ESSENTIALLIFE.COM

WEIGHT MANAGEMENT

People struggling with obesity are at increased risk for many serious diseases and health conditions. Although obesity receives a lot of focus from the medical world, there are also negative effects from being underweight. Given that extremes in eating patterns tend to disorder the body, it's important to learn how to maintain proper weight through proper nutrition, appropriate levels of exercise, and wholesome lifestyle habits. Solutions that can support healthy weight levels include the following products.

SOLUTIONS TO HELP

GREENS

This blend of powdered fruits, grasses, and greens along with lemon peel and ginger root enhances the nutrition of people with busy and stressful lifestyle habits. Helpful for weight management, compromised digestion, and immunity.

PROTEIN (CHOCOLATE, VANILLA, & VEGAN)

A convenient and delicious weight-management shake mix that provides low-fat, low-calorie, high-protein, and high-fiber nutrients. A lean alternative for individuals trying to lose fat or maintain a lean body composition through calorie reduction and exercise.

METAPWR™

A blend of essential oils that helps reduce cravings, balance blood sugar, and enhance metabolism. This blend promotes a positive mood, cleanses the body, aids digestion, curbs appetite, provides a stimulating and positive effect on the endocrine system, and assists with weight loss.

METAPWR™ SOFTGELS

A blend of essential oils in convenient softgels that help reduce cravings, balance blood sugar, and enhance metabolism. This blend promotes a positive mood, cleanses the body, aids digestion, curbs appetite, assists with weight loss, and provides a stimulating and positive effect on the endocrine system.

TURMERIC DUAL CAPSULES

A unique dual-chamber capsule with an inner layer of botanical extract and outer layer of essential oils, intended to promote better absorption in a convenient delivery system. Turmeric can provide anti-inflammatory support to joint pain and swelling, help improve muscle recovery, improve exercise performance, aid in neuro-plasticity, help you stay more alert and focused, reduce weight gain, and help with fat loss.

MITO2MAX®

A blend of adaptogenic herbs and extracts with energy co-factors that increase overall energy and decrease stress from physical activity and daily life.

PEPPERMINT

One drop on tongue to help prevent sugar cravings.

THE SIX ESSENTIAL NUTRIENTS

———

It is important to consume essential nutrients when it comes to eating right. Essential nutrients must come from an outside source because your body cannot make them on its own or in an adequate amount. If you want your body to function properly, you must consume these nutrients daily. The six essential nutrients are proteins, carbohydrates, fats, vitamins, minerals, and water. Let's take a closer look at each essential nutrient.

Proteins

- *Increase* satiety and the thermic effect of eating
- *Support* muscle growth and repair
- *Support* tissue development and red blood cell production

- *Aim* to get 3 to 5 palm-sized portions a day (*circumference and thickness of palm*)

Carbohydrates

- *Provide* the main source of energy for the body
- *Consist* of and are best consumed through high fiber, low glycemic fruits and vegetables

- *Aim* to get 5 to 7 servings a day (*each serving, the size of a clenched fist*)

Fats

- *Provide* hormone support
- *Improve* brain function
- *Boost* the immune system.
- *Suppress* excess inflammation
- *Serve* as key absorbers of fat-soluble vitamins (*A, D, E, K*)

- *Aim* to get 5 to 7 servings a day (*each serving, the size of your thumb*)

Minerals

- **Build** strong teeth and bones
- **Transmit** proper nerve function
- **Help** maintain proper fluid balance
- **Make** hormones
- **Activate** enzymes

- **Serving size** varies per person. Eat a variety of whole foods, fruits, and veggies to get a diverse amount of vitamins

Water

- **Helps** cells, tissues, and organs function properly
- **Flushes** waste
- **Lubricates** joints
- **Helps** break down vitamins, minerals, and nutrients

- **Aim to drink** half your body weight per day in ounces, up to a maximum 90 ounces, and an equivalent amount of water for each caffeinated drink you consume

Vitamins

- **Free** the energy found in food
- **Keep** tissues healthy
- **Knit** wounds together
- **Act** as antioxidants
- **Promote** healthy growth and reproduction

- **Serving size** varies per person; eat a variety of whole foods, fruits, and veggies to get a diverse amount of vitamins

Proteins:

Proteins are the major structural component of cells and are responsible for building and repairing tissue in the body. The building blocks of proteins are amino acids, nine of which are essential because the body can't make them. Approximately 35% of your calories should come from lean protein sources such as grass-fed beef, free-range chicken, wild-caught seafood, plant protein, peas, nuts, seeds, dairy, beans, or eggs. Limit your amount of deli meats like sausage, processed lunched meats, hot dogs, etc.—which are high in sodium and nitrates.

Carbohydrates:

Carbohydrates are the brain's primary source of energy. Approximately 40% of your calories should come from healthy carbohydrate sources, such as ripe fruits, leafy greens, a variety of colored vegetables, root vegetables, non-inflammatory whole grains such as brown rice, and healthy sugars (e.g., honey, maple syrup, and coconut sugar).

Fats:

Fats provide essential nutrients, such as omega-3 fatty acids, and increase the absorption of fat-soluble vitamins A, D, E, and K. Fats also help with proper growth and development, maintaining your body temperature, and providing a cushion for your major organs. Approximately 25% of your calories should come from healthy fat sources, such as coconut oil, grass-fed butter, ghee, olives, avocado, fish oil, nuts, seeds, and dairy.

Vitamins:

Your body needs 13 essential vitamins: A, B (riboflavin, thiamine, niacin, pantothenic acid, biotin, B6, B12, and folate), C, D, E, and K. Most people can get all their vitamins from the foods they eat, but if you are a vegetarian or vegan, it is critical to supplement with B-12. Vitamins are either water-soluble or fat-soluble.

Water-soluble vitamins:

- cannot be stored in your body
- do not stay in your body for long
- are excreted in the urine
- need to be replaced more often than fat-soluble ones

Fat-soluble vitamins:

- are easier for your body to store than water-soluble ones
- are stored in the fatty tissues and the liver
- include vitamins A, D, E, and K
- can stay in the body as reserves for days or sometimes months
- are absorbed through the intestinal tract with the help of fats

Minerals:

Our bodies do not manufacture minerals, so we have to get them from our diet. Minerals come from rocks, soil, and water. They are absorbed by plants as they grow and by animals when they consume a plant. Minerals help our body grow, develop, and stay healthy. They contribute to building strong bones, transmitting proper nerve function, helping maintain a normal heartbeat, making hormones, and activating enzymes.

Minerals break down into two groups: major minerals and trace minerals. Major minerals—stored in large amounts in the body—include calcium, chloride, magnesium, phosphorus, potassium, and sodium. Trace minerals—which we do not need in large quantities—include iron, iodine, cobalt, copper, chromium, manganese, selenium, zinc, and molybdenum.

Water:

All your cells, tissues, and organs need water to function correctly. Aim to consume water each day, up to a maximum of 90 ounces. For example, if you weigh 160 pounds, try to drink 80 ounces of water per day. Also, drink an equivalent amount of water for each caffeinated beverage you consume.

WHAT DOES WATER DO FOR YOUR BODY?

1. Regulates body temperature

2. Provides a cushion for the brain, spinal cord, and other sensitive tissues

3. Helps your bowels perform properly

4. Flushes the waste out of your body

5. Helps your body maintain blood pressure

6. Helps prevent kidney stones and kidney damage

7. Helps your body break down vitamins, minerals, and nutrients.

8. Lubricates your joints, keeping them healthy

9. Keeps the mouth clean

10. Keeps skin plump and healthy

11. Rehydrates your body after exercise

12. Helps prevent or treat headaches

13. Keeps your energy levels up

14. Helps relieve constipation

15. Helps with weight loss

TIPS FOR EATING RIGHT

• *Eat a variety of grass-fed proteins,* wild caught seafood, fatty fish, farm-raised poultry, ripe fruits, berries, leafy greens, root vegetables, healthy fats, nuts, seeds, dark chocolate, green tea, and non-inflammatory grains (like brown rice).

• *Drink half your body weight* in ounces of water.

• *Eat the rainbow* when it comes to fruits and vegetables.

• *Aim for your calories to be 35% lean protein,* 40% carbohydrates, and 25% fats.

• *Eat foods that are an ingredient on a label* rather than foods that have an ingredient label.

• *Include three drops of citrus oils* in your water as you drink throughout the day, such as Lemon, Lime, Tangerine, Wild Orange, Bergamot, or Grapefruit.

• *Avoid inflammatory foods* such as white bread, cookies, cakes, pastries, donuts, fried food, fast food, commercial dairy, excess caffeine, soda and other sweetened beverages, artificial sweeteners, margarine, shortening, processed meats, deli meats, prepackaged foods, and processed cheese.

• *Avoid common stressors that affect your digestive system:* excess emotional stress, physical stress, hormone imbalances, poor diet, food intolerances, chronic inflammation, and insulin imbalances.

• *Add Lifelong Vitality supplements,* TerraZyme®, PB Assist®, and a drop of Lemon or another citrus essential oil to your water. Add a scoop of Protein or Greens to a smoothie for breakfast or enjoy as a snack throughout the day.

TIPS TO AVOID OVEREATING

 *Clear your cupboards, fridge, or freezer of unhealthy foods.*

 *Avoid distractions when you eat, such as watching TV or using electronic devices.*

 *Eat healthful portion sizes.*

 *Eat slowly.*

 *Eat sensibly throughout the day.*

 *Drink water before and after meals.*

 *Fill up on fresh fruits and vegetables.*

 *Reduce stress.*

BRAIN

Omega Fats, Butter, Curry, Broccoli, Cauliflower, Pecans, Chickpeas, Blueberries, Coconut Oil, Olive Oil, Avocado, Crab, Celery, Fish Oil, Whole Milk, Grass-fed Beef, Walnuts, Macadamia Nuts, Eggs

LIVER AND GALLBLADDER

Ripe Fruits, Carrots, Celery, Fennel, Millet, Apples, Strawberries, Broccoli, Lime, Cabbage, Plum, Eggplant, Beets, Scallions, Grapefruit, Quinoa, Cucumber, Romaine, Turmeric, Green Tea, Garlic, Lemon, Olive Oil, Leeks, Avocado, Dandelion Greens, Green Beans, Spinach, Walnuts, Bok Choy

HEART

Endive, Red Wine, Fish Oil, Watercress, Arugula, Dark Chocolate, Red Beans, Cherries, Kale, Blueberries, Tomatoes, Beets, Salmon, Sweet Potato, Raspberries, Flaxseed, Omega Oils, Seafood, Brocooli Rabe, Lentils, Coconut Oil, Red Grapes, Bitter Melon, Watermelon, Carrots, Red Pepper, Pomegranates, Sardines, Figs, Strawberries

LUNGS

Almonds, Omega Oils, Ocean Fish, Ginger, Grapefruit, Asparagus, Peaches, Chickpeas, White Beans, Cauliflower, Horseradish, Raw Honey, Flaxseed, Eggs, Onions, Garlic, Berries, Carrots, Nuts, Pears, Spinach, Beets, Fennel, Scallions, Celery, Sesame Seeds, Cabbage

STOMACH AND SPLEEN

Papaya, Grapefuit, Sweet Potato, Carrots, Rice, Fennel, Cardamom, Ginger, Apples, Cranberries, Onions, Tea, Squash, Greens, Fermented Foods, Oranges, Barley, Eggs, Peanuts, Radish, Taro Root, Oatmeal, Garlic, Pumpkin, Ripe Fruits, Bone Broth, Cantaloupe, Leeks

KIDNEY AND BLADDER

Cherries, Walnuts, Seafood, Onions, Watermelon, Black Beans, Goji Berries, Cinnamon, Nut Oils, Garlic, Bone Marrow, Seaweed, Olive Oil, Cranberries, Cashews, Sesame Seed, Cauliflower, Pine Nuts, Kidney Beans

SMALL INTESTINE

Salmon, Sweet Potato, Raspberries, Omega Oils, Lentils, Seafood, Endive, Flounder, Watermelon, Watercress, Tomatoes, Walnuts, Red Beans, Arugula, Bell Peppers, Squash, Pomegranates, Kale, Red Wine, Figs, Beets, Tuna, Dark Chocolate, Coconut Oil, Cherries, Flaxseed, Sardines, Broccoli, Rabe, Blueberries, Fermented Foods, Red Grapes, Bitter Melon, Carrots, Strawberries, Bone Broth

LARGE INTESTINE

Digestive Enzymes, Omega Oils, Ripe Fruits, Almonds, Chickpeas, White Beans, Ginger, Horseradish, Raw Honey, Peaches, Eggs, Garlic, Cauliflower, Carrots, Raw Nuts, Fermented Foods, Spinach, Flaxseed, Berries, Water, Apple Cider Vinegar, Pre/Probiotics, Leafy Greens, Beets, Asparagus, Scallions, Bone Broth, Pears, Fennel, Collagen, Protein, Cabbage, Sesame Seeds, Onions, Fish, Celery

PANCREAS

Blueberries, Cherries, Broccoli, Spinach, Leafy Greens, Digestive Enzymes, Berries, Tomatoes, Sweet Potato, Reishi Mushrooms, Greek Yogurt, Red Grapes, Grass-fed Beef, Free-range Poultry, Garlic

OVARY, UTERUS, PROSTATE, AND TESTES

Omega Oils, Leafy Greens, Flaxseeds, Bananas, Ripe Fruit, Vitamin D, Walnuts, Cashews, Seafood, Antioxidants, Vitamins A, C, E, Selenium, Soybeans, Prunes, Chia Seeds, Free-range Poultry, Pumpkin Seeds, B Vitamins, Citrus Fruits, Almonds, Maca Root

THYROID

Ripe Fruits, Squash, Atlantic Dulse, Sweet Potato, Spirulina, Coconut Oil, Barley Grass, Broccoli, Cilantro, Cucumbers, Turmeric, Leafy Greens, Ginger, Greek Yogurt, Artichokes, Bone Broth, Asparagus, Collagen, Brown Rice, Brussels Sprouts, Omega Oils, Nut Butters, Avocado, Ghee, Olive Oil, Cooked Greens, Grass-fed Beef, Selenium, Chia Seeds, Free-range Poultry, Brazil Nuts, Root Vegetables, Pumpkin Seeds, Hemp Seeds, Lemon Lime, Celery Juice, Bamboo Shoots, Seaweed, Spinach, Walnuts

ADRENAL GLANDS

Omega Oils, Avocado, Olive Oil, Grass-fed Beef, Free-range Poultry, Root Vegetables, Squash, Sweet Potato, Berries, Whole Eggs, Coconut Oil, Butter, Cucumbers, Leafy Greens, Cooked Greens, Ghee, Greek Yogurt, Bone Broth, Collagen, Protein, Pea Protein, Almonds, Brown Rice, Quinoa, Nut Butters, Chia Seeds, Maca Root, Pumpkin Seeds, Fatty Fish, Broccoli, Brussels Spouts, Chaga Mushrooms, Vitamin C

EAT THE RAINBOW

A straightforward way to incorporate a variety of nutrients into your daily diet is to focus on eating the rainbow. Not only does eating a variety of colors look good on your plate, but different colors of food provide you with different types of vitamins and minerals. If we ensure that we eat a variety of colors, we can be confident that we are providing our body with the diversity it needs to function optimally.

Color Foods	Positives
RED	Helps fight cancer; reduces the risk of diabetes; reduces the risk of heart disease and stroke; lowers risk of macular degeneration; fight off colds, flus, and allergies; improves the quality of your skin
ORANGE	Improves immune system function; promotes eye health and protects vision; protects the skin against the sun; reduces the risk of heart disease; promotes healthy joints; decreases the risk of various cancers
YELLOW	Improves digestion; improves immune system function; promotes eye health; protects vision; protects the skin against the sun; reduces the risk of heart disease; promotes healthy joints; decreases the risk of various cancers

High In	Examples
antioxidants (such as vitamin A (*beta-carotene*), vitamin C, manganese, fiber, quercetin, lycopene, and ellagic acid)	red apples, red bell peppers, rhubarb, tart cherries, tomatoes, raspberries, strawberries, apples, watermelon, grapes, red onions, pomegranate, beets, cranberries
vitamin C, lutein, zeaxanthin, vitamin A, carotenoids, hesperidin, fiber, vitamin B6	oranges, sweet potatoes, mangoes, papayas, pumpkin, nectarines, squashes, carrots, cantaloupe, orange peppers, peaches
vitamin C, potassium, vitamin B6, manganese, vitamin A, fiber, magnesium, carotenoids, hesperidin	lemons, grapefruit, yellow squash, corn, yellow peppers, golden beets, pineapple, bananas

Color Foods	Positives
 **GREEN**	Detoxifies the body; provides digestive enzymes; aids tissue healing; reduces the risk of certain cancers, boosts the immune system; provide antioxidants for the eyes and skin, restores energy; increases vitality
 **BLUE**	Boosts memory; reduces the risk of Alzheimer's disease, promotes longevity; fights inflammation; slows the aging process; protects cells against oxidative stress
 **PURPLE**	Boosts memory; reduces the risk of Alzheimer's disease, promotes longevity; fights inflammation; slows the aging process; protects cells against oxidative stress; protects blood vessels from breakage; prevents the destruction of collagen
 **TAN/ WHITE**	Keeps bones strong; lowers the risk of cardiovascular disease, reduces inflammation; helps to balance hormones; increases HDL; has an antibacterial effect against Candida; helps lower cholesterol

High In	Examples
lutein, isothiocyanates, chlorophyll, zeaxanthin, vitamin K, folate	kale, spinach, collard greens, broccoli, swiss chard, arugula, brussels sprouts, lettuce, green apples, green beans, green grapes, kiwi, avocado, asparagus, peas, zucchinis
anthocyanins, resveratrol	blueberries, blue potatoes, blue carrots
vitamin A, flavonoids, anthocyanins, resveratrol	purple grapes, purple cabbage, eggplant, plums, figs, prunes, blackberries, concord grapes, currants, radicchio, purple potatoes, purple carrots
sulforaphane, vitamin C, vitamin K, folate, fiber, allicin, fiber, potassium, magnesium, quercetin.	bananas, cauliflower, onions, rutabagas; garlic, potatoes, leeks, turnips; corn, parsnips, mushrooms, radish, jicama

MOVEMENT & METABOLISM *Chapter* 5

PROACTIVE MEDICAL CARE

SELF CARE

REDUCE TOXIC LOAD/
HEALTHY HOME

REST & MANAGE STRESS

MOVEMENT & METABOLISM

EAT RIGHT/PROPER NUTRITION

Healthcare

Lifestyle

"Exercise is more than just physical—it's therapeutic."
—Anonymous

MOVEMENT & METABOLISM

Regular exercise can make a huge impact on your physical, mental, and emotional health. It can extend your lifespan and increase your quality of life. See page 392 for twelve health benefits of exercise. For most healthy adults, get at least 150 minutes of moderate aerobic activity or 75 minutes of vigorous aerobic activity a week. Do strength training exercises for all major muscle groups at least two times a week. A healthy and active lifestyle includes the following goals.

Improved Energy and Vitality

Maintaining Bone & Joint Health

Recovery from Exercise & Related Injuries

Weight Management

IMPROVED ENERGY & VITALITY

Feeling tired or lacking energy on a regular basis is extremely common when stressors are high and life balance is off. In most cases, it is caused by simple lifestyle factors. Too many refined carbohydrates, lack of exercise, low-quality sleep, inadequate nutrition and hydration, and high stress levels could be contributing to a lack of energy. As you make lifestyle changes to improve your energy, use the following solutions for support.

SOLUTIONS TO HELP

MITO2MAX®

A blend of adaptogenic herbs and extracts with energy co-factors that increases overall energy, enhances mitochondrial function and decreases stress from physical activity and daily life. Enhances stamina and efficient use of oxygen. Supports metabolic adaptation for all types of activities from working at your desk to mountain climbing.

GREENS

A blend of powdered fruits, grasses, greens, lemon peel, and ginger root to enhance the nutrition of people with busy and stressful lifestyle habits.

MICROPLEX VMZ®

Whole food micronutrient supplement with balanced amounts of vitamins, minerals, trace elements, phytonutrients, and antioxidants. Supports a healthy diet and lifestyle.

XEOMEGA®

A blend of marine-and land-based Omega-3 essential fatty acids in a unique assimilation capsule with essential oils and fat-soluble vitamins.

ALPHA CRS®+

Packed with antioxidants, natural anti-inflammatories, and energy co-factors to support cellular longevity, healthy cell function, and metabolism.

A2Z CHEWABLES

Multivitamin, mineral, and botanical chewable for children and adults who have difficulty swallowing.

IQ MEGA®

Omega-3 liquid supplement with Wild Orange essential oil to give it a fresh orange flavor. Provides 1300 mg of Omega-3 fatty acids per serving.

PROTEIN (CHOCOLATE, VANILLA, & VEGAN)

A convenient and delicious weight-management shake mix that provides low-fat, low-calorie, high-protein, and high-fiber nutrients.

RECOVERY

Proper recovery is important after exercise so your body can repair, rebuild, and strengthen. It can also help you maintain a better balance between home, work, and exercise goals. Higher levels of exercise or athletic activity can also expose you to possible sports or exercise-related injuries. Proper rest and medical care helps you heal but also helps you return to your chosen activity both physically and mentally stronger. Support your body in recovery efforts with the following solutions.

SOLUTIONS TO HELP

DEEP BLUE® RUB / DEEP BLUE® BLEND / DEEP BLUE® STICK

Naturally reduces pain and inflammation in soft tissues and is an effective substitute for topical ointments and creams.

DEEP BLUE POLYPHENOL COMPLEX®

Oral supplement clinically proven to help with soreness and discomfort from physical activities and daily life.

AROMATOUCH®

Encourages muscle tissue healing, relaxes/soothes muscles, and enhances blood flow.

FRANKINCENSE

Alleviates inflammation. Provides support for back pain, sciatica, cellular health, and mood.

WINTERGREEN

When mixed with coconut oil, this oil provides pain relief when rubbed into sore and achy muscles post-workout.

TURMERIC DUAL CAPSULES

Provides anti-inflammatory support to joint pain and swelling. Helps improve exercise performance and muscle recovery. Aids in neuroplasticity. Helps with focus and alertness, reducing weight gain, and losing fat.

COPAIBA

Helps alleviate inflammation.

LEMONGRASS

Supports soft tissues such as muscles, fascia, tendons, and ligaments.

MARJORAM

Supports muscle spasms, sprains, stiff joints, aches, and pains.

CYPRESS

Helps remove excess fluid in the body.

MAINTAINING BONE & JOINT HEALTH

Healthy bones and joints are essential to a healthy body as you grow, and as you grow older. A number of factors can impact bone health, including levels of calcium in the diet, physical activity, hormone levels, age, and gender. Joint health is equally important and can be affected by increasing age, injury, or carrying too much body weight. In addition to proper nutrition and appropriate exercise, the following can support your bone and joint health.

SOLUTIONS TO HELP

BONE NUTRIENT COMPLEX

This blend contains whole food–created vitamins, minerals, and other cofactors necessary for bone integrity, strength, and overall health. This complex is bioavailable so that the body's cells will recognize and utilize the compounds for bone formation.

COPAIBA

Supports healthy osteoblast (bone building) function.

BLACK PEPPER

Supports healthy inflammatory response along with healthy osteoblastic activity.

PHYTOESTROGEN COMPLEX

Provides support for healthy bones by maintaining a balanced ratio of estrogen metabolites which, if imbalanced, can have a negative effect on bone health.

MICROPLEX VMZ®

Whole food micronutrient supplement with balanced amounts of vitamins, minerals, trace elements, phytonutrients, and antioxidants. Supports a healthy diet and lifestyle.

XEOMEGA®

A blend of marine-and land-based Omega-3 essential fatty acids in a unique assimilation capsule with essential oils and fat-soluble vitamins.

ALPHA CRS® +

Packed with antioxidants, natural anti-inflammatories, and energy cofactors to support cellular longevity, healthy cell function, and metabolism.

IQ MEGA®

Omega-3 liquid supplement with Wild Orange essential oil to give it a fresh orange flavor. Provides 1300 mg of Omega-3 fatty acids per serving.

WEIGHT MANAGEMENT

When it comes to losing weight, the more physical activity you do, the more calories you will burn. While exercise alone will not lead to a significant amount of weight loss, regular physical activity is wonderful at keeping off the weight once you've lost it. A regular exercise program can increase your metabolism, which means that burn more calories throughout the day—even while you are sleeping. It can also help you achieve and maintain a lean body mass. A lean body mass is important as you age because it helps protect you from diabetes and insulin resistance. It also helps you recover from illness and disease faster than someone who is overweight or obese. In addition to exercise, the following can support your weight management goals.

SOLUTIONS TO HELP

METAPWR™ SOFTGELS

A blend of essential oils in convenient softgels that help reduce cravings, balance blood sugar, and enhance metabolism. This blend promotes a positive mood, cleanses the body, aids digestion, curbs appetite, assist with weight loss, and provides a stimulating and positive effect on the endocrine system.

PEPPERMINT

Add one drop onto your tongue to reduce sugar cravings.

GRAPEFRUIT

Helps curb cravings, support healthy blood sugar levels, enhance metabolism, and offer detoxifying benefits. Using grapefruit oil helps to activate enzymes in the body that work to breakdown body fat.

LEMON

Breathing in Lemon essential oil improves the neurological activity that promotes the breakdown of body fat.

GINGER

Stimulates weight loss through lipolysis (the way your body lets go of fat in your cells) and helps your body produce more epinephrine.

CINNAMON

Helps reduce obesity by stopping your body from producing more fat cells. Assists in appropriate metabolizing of sugars.

MICROPLEX VMZ®

Whole food micronutrient supplement with balanced amounts of vitamins, minerals, trace elements, phytonutrients, and antioxidants. Supports a healthy diet and lifestyle.

PROTEIN (CHOCOLATE, VANILLA, & VEGAN)

A convenient and delicious weight-management shake mix that provides low-fat, low-calorie, high-protein, and high-fiber nutrients.

12 HEALTH BENEFITS OF EXERCISE *Movement & Metabolism*

1 ***Reduces the risk of cardiovascular disease.*** Regular aerobic exercise strengthens your heart and improves your circulation. It has been shown to raise the oxygen levels in your body, which can decrease the risk of high cholesterol, high blood pressure, and heart attacks.

2 ***Decreases your risk for obesity.*** Some studies show that inactivity is a major factor in weight gain and obesity. In addition to eating right, regular exercise can play a major role in controlling your weight and maintaining muscle mass, which increases your overall metabolism.

3 ***Builds a strong body.*** Regular exercise helps your body build strong bones. Incorporating strength-training exercises regularly can also maintain your muscle mass and keep your body strong.

4 ***Helps prevent type 2 diabetes.*** Exercise can lower your blood sugar and helps your body better manage insulin. If you already have type 2 diabetes or metabolic syndrome, exercise can still help you to better manage these conditions.

5 ***Helps keep your brain sharp.*** Exercise stimulates chemicals that improve the structure and function of your brain, helping with judgment skills, learning, and thinking as you age.

6 ***Promotes a better night's sleep.*** Exercise can help you fall asleep more quickly and drastically improve the quality and longevity of your sleep.

7 ***Reduces your risk of accidents or falls.*** Doing balance and strength-training exercises (in addition to moderate aerobic activity) can reduce the risk of accidents and falls in older adults.

8 ***Promotes a better mental and emotional outlook.*** Regular exercise can improve your mood and increase your mental and emotional well-being. During exercise, your body releases certain feel-good chemicals (endorphins) that relax you, improve your mood, and reduce your perception of pain. Exercise can also provide a good distraction for those who are in a cycle of negative thoughts that feed depression.

9 ***Increases your energy levels.*** Engaging in a regular exercise program can increase your overall energy levels, even for those suffering from persistent fatigue and chronic illnesses.

10 ***Reduces chronic pain.*** While it may sound like the opposite is true, regular exercise can actually reduce feelings of chronic pain and improve quality of life for those who suffer from chronic pain. Regular physical activity can also raise pain tolerance and decrease pain perception.

11 ***Increases your self-confidence and body image.*** Sticking to your exercise plan and eating right can give you a serious confidence boost— not to mention the benefits you'll gain from your new overall appearance after completing a month or two of tough strength-training or HIIT workouts.

12 ***Increases your creativity.*** Studies show that regular aerobic exercise can boost creativity for up to two hours. This is the result of the increased blood flow to the brain and body during a great sweat session. Being outdoors also increases creativity, so consider jogging through the woods or hitting the bike trail the next time you need a creative boost.

THE FOUR TYPES OF EXERCISE

Movement & Metabolism

Most people tend to focus on one type of physical activity and think they are doing enough. Still, research has shown that it is essential to get four different types of exercise: aerobic, anaerobic, balance and flexibility, and strength training. Each type of exercise has unique benefits, and doing just one type of exercise can improve your ability to do the other types. Incorporating various exercises into your weekly routine will improve your fitness, allow you to more easily perform daily activities, and reduce your risk of getting injured.

Aerobic

Balance & Flexibility

Anaerobic

Strength Training

1 AEROBIC:

Aerobic means "with oxygen." Aerobic exercise includes any type of cardiovascular conditioning. During aerobic activity, your breathing and heart rate will elevate. Carbon dioxide is expelled from your body as you increase your activity and breathe more heavily. When you do aerobic exercise, your body uses glycogen and fat for fuel.

Benefits:

Aerobic exercise makes your body more efficient at delivering oxygen to the rest of the body, helping heart health and lung function. It also burns fat, improves mood, reduces the risk of diabetes, and improves your entire cardiovascular system.

Examples:

- Running
- Jogging
- Walking
- Swimming
- Biking
- Dancing
- Aerobic fitness classes
- Ballroom dancing
- Low-impact aerobics
- Water aerobics
- Hiking
- Cross-country skiing
- Kickboxing
- Elliptical trainer
- Speed-walking
- Stair-climbing

TIPS

- Aerobic activity can be done at a low, moderate, or high intensity.
- Aim for 150 minutes per week of moderate intensity activity.

2 ANAEROBIC:

Anaerobic means "without oxygen." In general, anaerobic exercise is more challenging than aerobic exercise but is done for shorter periods. When you exercise anaerobically, your body uses glycogen as fuel. Once all the glycogen depletes, your body may hit a wall and tire out. During this exercise your body builds up lactic acid, which causes discomfort and fatigue the longer you exercise. This is why high-intensity training is done in short bursts.

Benefits:

As we age, we lose muscle mass and anaerobic exercise helps us to build the muscles back up. This exercise also helps build strong bones, lower blood sugar, improve balance, reduce pain and stress in your lower back and joints, build endurance, and increase your fitness levels. Anaerobic exercise is also helpful for weight loss because when your body has more muscle, it burns calories more efficiently.

Examples:

- HIIT (*high-intensity interval training*)
- Sprinting
- Weight lifting
- Jumping rope
- Short-burst exercises
- Plyometrics

3   BALANCE & FLEXIBITY

Balance

During balance exercises, your body and mind work together to perform an intricate series of checks and balances: your inner ear senses the motion of your head, your eyes and vision keep you aware of the environment around you, and your somatosensory system relays information to your brain on what is going on underneath your feet. To maintain balance, you need to plan carefully your movements, coordinate your reaction time, and monitor your attention to keep yourself from stumbling or falling. Balance is a complex system, and a sharp mind not only helps you to think but also to stay on your feet.

Benefits:

Balance exercises are essential to incorporate into your weekly routine because they help prevent falls and accidents. They strengthen your ligaments and tendons, helping your body maintain healthy joints. They also strengthen your core, allowing you to control your body's positioning and maintain an upright posture—which is vital for stability as you age.

Balance exercises also help keep your brain sharp regarding to proprioception or the body's sense of its position in the spaces around it. Examples include having a sense of where you are in the dark without losing your balance, or closing your eyes and touching your nose. This sense of bodily awareness can carry over to everyday activities outside your home or gym.

Examples:

- Wobble-board exercises
- Standing on one leg while brushing your teeth—one minute while brushing the top teeth and one minute while brushing the bottom teeth
- Tossing a ball to a partner while balancing on one leg
- Tai Chi
- Balancing on one foot and then the other for a period of time
- Balancing on one foot and then the other with arms outstretched to the side
- Balancing on one foot and then the other with arms overhead
- Getting up from a chair without using your hands or arms
- Doing a heel-to-toe walk. As you walk, put the heel of one foot just in front of the toes of your other foot. Your heel and toes should touch or almost touch
- Squat with outer thigh lift
- One-legged standing abdominal crunch, then tucking your arms under the raised leg
- Plank with alternating outstretched arms
- Lower-body strength-training exercises

TIPS

- When starting balancing exercises for the first time, hold one or both arms out to the side.
- When balancing on one foot, make sure to have a table or chair nearby to hold if you feel unsteady.
- When standing on one foot, start with a short amount of time and work yourself up to a minute.

Flexibility:

Stiff joints, tight muscles, and limited range of motion can affect your everyday life as well as impact recreational activities. Every action your body does requires your joints to work together. Think about scratching your back, bending over to tie your shoes, or climbing a ladder—do you notice any limited range of motion when you do these activities? Having a healthy range of motion in all the major joints in your body is vital to moving your body, lifting objects, and completing daily activities. Flexibility allows your joints to move through this full range of motion.

Benefits:

Maintaining flexibility increases athletic performance, prevents injury, decreases soreness, and allows for a quicker comeback post-injury. Improved flexibility will help you with even the most basic everyday tasks. When you improve flexibility in your lower body, you will notice a difference when you bend over to tie your shoes, paint your toenails, or put on socks. When you increase flexibility in your upper body, you will notice a difference when you look over your shoulder, reach high into a cabinet, or move your outstretched arm to grab something out of reach. Flexibility exercises also keep you limber as you age.

Examples:

- Shoulder rolls
- Cat stretches
- Standing hamstring stretch
- Glute or buttock stretch
- Seated spinal twist
- Shoulder stretches
- Abdominal stretches
- Tricep stretch
- Quadriceps *(front of leg)* stretch
- Calf stretch
- Side reach and stretch
- Lay on your back and bringing your legs to your chest, both together and one at a time
- Neck rolls
- Butterfly stretch

TIPS

- Do at least 10 minutes of activity before you stretch—do not stretch a cold muscle.
- Stretch after aerobic and anaerobic activities.
- Do not stretch so far that you feel pain—you should feel a gentle stretch. Hold it for 30 seconds without bouncing. Wait 10 seconds and repeat 4 times.
- Refrain from holding your breath; breathe normally when you hold a stretch.

4 STRENGTH TRAINING

Strength training:

Strength-training exercise is considered anaerobic exercise. When you do strength-training exercises, you create micro-tears in your muscles that begin to break your muscles down. As your body repairs the muscle fibers, it grows and builds stronger muscles. This process allows you to lift heavier weights and increases your overall strength. During strength-training exercises, your heart rate and blood flow also increase, delivering oxygen-rich blood to your brain and muscles.

Benefits:

Strong muscles make everyday activities easier, such as carrying groceries, climbing stairs, getting up from a chair, and taking care of chores around the house. Strength training can also ensure that you stay strong and independent as you age by helping with your balance, preventing accidents and falls, and improving joint health.

Examples:

- Lifting weights

Squat	Upright row
Deadlift	Rows
Bench Press	Tricep kickbacks
Overhead press	Pull-down exercises
Bicep curls	Front and side raises
Shoulder press	

- Circuit training
- Push-ups
- Resistance bands
- Isolation Training

- Kettlebell training
- CrossFit
- Bootcamp workouts
- Plyometrics or jumping exercises
- Strength-training interval workout

TIPS

- The best strength-training exercises that you can do are the ones that you will commit to. If you don't have the motivation to work out at home, consider joining a gym or a fitness class. If you don't have time to go to the gym, try an app that helps you exercise in the morning or evening.

- When starting a strength-training program, work all of your major muscle groups at least twice a week, but avoid working out the same muscle group for two days in a row.

- To prevent injuries, start with lighter weights in the beginning—a weight you can lift or push eight times. Once it becomes easy to lift, you can increase the weight by 2 to 10 percent. Increase the weight again when you no longer feel challenged.

- Use proper form and safety with smooth, steady movements—do not jerk or thrust weights.

- Avoid "locking" your elbow or knee joints in a straight position.

- If you are not familiar with an exercise, ask for help or look it up online. Injuries happen when you are not familiar with equipment and when you are not using proper form.

- Breathe out as you lift or push, and breathe in as you relax and return to starting position—do not hold your breath. Once you have this habit down, it will become second nature.

Endurance:

Endurance activities are considered aerobic exercise. Depending on the type of endurance exercise you are doing, your body only has enough energy for a few minutes of exercise—and then your body has to manufacture its own energy 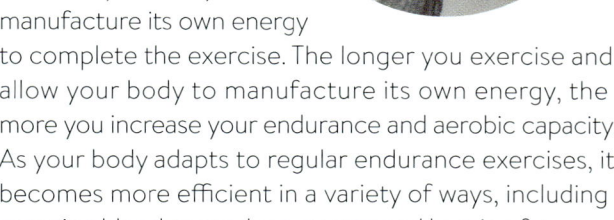 to complete the exercise. The longer you exercise and allow your body to manufacture its own energy, the more you increase your endurance and aerobic capacity. As your body adapts to regular endurance exercises, it becomes more efficient in a variety of ways, including pumping blood to produce oxygen and burning fat.

Benefits:

Endurance exercise improves your cardiovascular system and helps you perform daily activities more easily. This type of exercise can also prevent or delay many diseases that are common as we age: heart disease, cancer, diabetes, and osteoporosis.

Examples of endurance exercise:

- Brisk walking
- Biking
- Swimming
- Climbing stairs
- Dancing

- Yard work
- Playing sports such as tennis, basketball, or racquetball
- Rollerblading

TIPS

- Strive to spend 150 minutes a week doing an activity that makes you breathe hard.

- Listen to your body and rest when you need to. Endurance activity should not cause chest pain, dizziness, or extreme shortness of breath.

- Stay hydrated by drinking plenty of water when doing any activity that makes you sweat.

- Warm up before you begin and cool down when you finish by doing light activity such as easy walking or light jogging.

- If you are exercising outdoors, pay attention to your surroundings. If you are wearing earbuds or headphones, make sure you can also hear any people or traffic around you.

- Use a helmet when riding a bike or pads when rollerblading or ice skating.

- Dress in layers during inclement weather to stay comfortable.

IMPORTANCE OF JOINT FLEXIBILITY *Movement & Metabolism*

It's essential to keep your joints healthy as you age. Flexibility—the range of motion available in a joint—indicates of joint health. Just because a person is flexible in one joint does not mean they are flexible in all their joints. Good flexibility improves your posture and the ergonomics of your body, and gaining a certain degree of flexibility in all your major joints is critical for everyday and athletic activities.

Lack of flexibility can lead to a breakdown in body tissue, inflammation, and, eventually, injury. We know that flexible muscles perform better than tight ones, and we must stretch to create flexible muscles. If you do not stretch, it becomes a matter of when—not if—you get injured. Doing balance and flexibility exercises and stretches for each of the following body parts will help you increase your flexibility. Make sure to incorporate them into your weekly routine.

BACK

KNEE-TO-CHEST STRETCHES

Do this stretch about 10-15 times, repeating one or two times per day (or as needed for tight back muscles).

1. Lie on your back with your knees bent and your feet flat on the floor.

2. Slowly raise one bent knee up enough to grasp your lower leg with both hands. Interlace your fingers just under the knee.

3. Gently pull your bent knee toward your chest, using your hands.

4. While you are pulling your knee toward your chest, try to relax your back, legs, and pelvis as much as you can.

5. Hold for 10 seconds.

6. Return your leg to the floor.

7. Repeat on the other side.

BIRD DOG POSE

You will need an exercise mat or a soft surface and enough space to extend both an arm and leg at the same time. Do five reps on both sides (10 reps total). As this gets easier, work up to three sets of 10 repetitions. To vary the exercise, you can do five reps on one side, then switch to the other side. Make sure your movements are slow and controlled.

1. Kneel on your mat with your knees hip-width apart and hands placed firmly on the ground, shoulder-width apart. Keep your abdominal muscles engaged by contracting them tight, like you are squeezing water out of a sponge.

2. Slowly bring your right hand and left leg off the floor while balancing on the other hand and leg. Keep your weight centered.

3. When you feel steady, bring your right hand all the way out in front of you, pointing straight forward, and extend your left leg straight out behind you. Your right hand and left leg should form a straight line. Keep your hips squared to the ground. If your lower back is sagging, raise your leg only as high as possible while keeping your back straight.

4. Hold for a few seconds and then repeat on the opposite side.

SHOULDERS

SHOULDER ROWS

This exercise is great for your upper back and thoracic muscles, which stabilize the shoulder joint. You should use hand weights that you feel comfortable performing 15 repetitions with.

1. Pick up your hand weights and stand with your feet shoulder-width apart, with knees slightly bent.

2. Bend forward at the waist and keep your back straight.

3. Row both arms back, pinching your shoulder blades together, and pause.

4. Return to the starting position.

5. Do three sets of 15 repetitions.

SHOULDER ROTATION WITH DUMBBELLS

This exercise warms up your shoulders for overhead and throwing motions.

1. Stand with your feet shoulder-width apart while holding a light dumbbell in your right hand.

2. Raise your right arm, so your elbow is at shoulder height. The palm of your hand should face the ground.

3. Rotate your shoulder to bring your arm and dumbbell up to 90 degrees, raising your hand towards the ceiling.

4. Slowly return to the starting position.

5. Do three sets of 15 repetitions on each side.

ELBOWS

1. Hold a 2- or 3-pound dumbbell (*or use a canned good as substitute*) in your hand.

2. Bend the affected elbow at a right angle.

3. Extend your hand out with your palm facing up.

4. Twist your wrist around, so that your palm is now facing down.

5. Hold the position for a few seconds.

6. Do three sets of 10 repetitions.

WRINGING OUT THE WATER

1. Roll up a hand towel and place your hands on either end.

2. Keep your shoulders relaxed.

3. Twist the towel by moving your hands in opposite directions as if wringing out water.

4. Repeat 10 times.

5. Reverse direction and repeat 10 times.

WRISTS

CLENCHED FIST CURLS

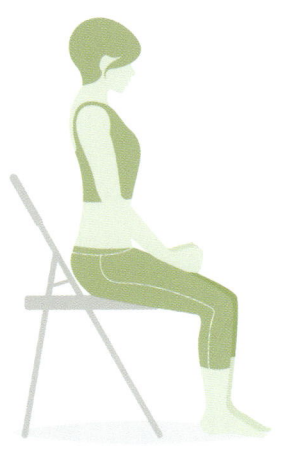

You can do this exercise with or without hand weights.

1. Sit down and place your hands on your thighs, palms up.

2. Close your hands into fists or grasp a light hand weight. Do not grab too tight.

3. With your arms still resting on your legs, raise your wrists toward the ceiling and face your body— bending the wrists.

4. Lower back to the starting position and open your fingers.

5. Repeat 15 times.

PRAYING HANDS STRETCH

This exercise warms up your shoulders for overhead and throwing motions.

1. While standing or sitting, place your palms together in a praying position.

2. Touch your elbows together and place your hands in front of your face.

3. Your arms should be touching each other from the tips of your fingers to your elbows.

4. Keeping your palms pressed together, slowly spread your elbows apart and lower your hands to your waist. Stop when you reach your belly button or when you feel the stretch.

5. Hold the stretch for 30 seconds, then repeat.

HIPS

HIP FLEXOR STRETCH

1. Get into a lunge position on a mat or rug. To do this, place your left knee on the floor and bend your right leg 90 degrees, placing the right foot flat on the floor.

2. Place your hands on your hips or out to the side for balance.

3. Move your pelvis and torso forward until you feel a stretch in your left hip flexor.

4. Hold for 1 minute, going further into the stretch as you become looser.

5. Repeat three times.

6. Switch legs and stretch the opposite side.

PIGEON POSE

1. Get on your hands and knees on a mat or rug.

2. Bring your right knee forward, placing it on the inside of your right wrist with your ankle near your left hip.

3. Straighten your left leg behind you and let your upper body fold over your right leg.

4. Hold the stretch for up to 1 minute.

5. Repeat on the other side.

KNEES

STANDING QUADRICEP STRETCH

1. Stand with your feet shoulder-width apart and raise your left arm out in front of you.

2. Keeping your knees as close together as you can, bend your left knee.

3. Grab your left ankle and bring your left foot back behind you.

4. Pull your left leg up and back, moving your pelvis toward the front and not allowing your thighs to separate too much.

5. Keep your head and body in alignment.

6. Hold for 30 seconds.

7. Repeat two times per leg.

8. Repeat on the opposite side.

INNER THIGH STRETCH

1. Stand upright, with legs opened wide.

2. Lunge to one side. You should feel a deep stretch in your inner thighs.

3. Hold for 30 seconds.

4. Repeat on the opposite leg.

5. Repeat on each leg three times.

ANKLES

1. Sit on the floor or stand with your hand on a table or chair.

2. If you are seated on the floor, place a rolled towel under your ankle.

3. Trace the alphabet letters with your big toe in the air, allowing your ankle to move with the letters.

4. Make sure you only use your ankle and not your leg.

5. Repeat on the opposite ankle.

STANDING HEEL DROPS

1. Stand on the step of a staircase.

2. Keep your weight on the balls of your feet and hang your ankles off the step.

3. Use a banister or railing for support.

4. Raise up on your toes and then slowly lower your feet, with your heels dropping below the step.

5. Do three sets of 15 repetitions.

REST & MANAGE STRESS *Chapter* **6**

PROACTIVE MEDICAL CARE

SELF CARE

Healthcare

REDUCE TOXIC LOAD/
HEALTHY HOME

Lifestyle

REST & MANAGE STRESS

MOVEMENT & METABOLISM

EAT RIGHT/PROPER NUTRITION

"The greatest weapon against stress is our ability to choose one thought over another" —Williams James

REST & MANAGE STRESS

Proper sleep is a vital, often neglected, component of health. Sleep allows for our minds to process and our bodies to be restored and strengthened. Achieving proper sleep goes hand-in-hand with managing stress, as all types of stress can harm sleep quality, and sleep deprivation can also fuel increased stress levels and anxiety. Besides affecting proper sleep, the inability to manage stress and negative emotions is increasingly becoming a factor in most health conditions. Despite this, proper sleep and the management of stress are possibly the most underrated and ignored factors of overall health and well-being. To the right are the goals for rest and managing stress.

For more information on stress management, see Emotions Made Simple, written by the same authors of Essential Oils Made Simple.

Proper Amount & Quality of Sleep

Managing Stress

Improving Emotional Health

PROPER AMOUNT & QUALITY OF SLEEP

The amount and quality of your sleep influence nearly every aspect of your health. Lack of sleep can affect hormone levels, mood, weight, and immune function (see How Much Sleep Do We Need on page 413). Poor sleep deprives the body of the time needed to repair, strengthen, and restore itself. Our body performs many vital functions during sleep, like muscle growth, protein synthesis, and tissue repair. Lack of sleep can also cause issues with the brain's ability to learn and problem-solve. The brain needs time to process the day's events recharge, and refocus. Ensuring you get the proper amount of deep, restful sleep a tremendously and positively impact on your overall health and mental well-being. See tips for getting enough sleep and improving your sleep quality on page 416. Incorporate the following solutions into your daily and night-time routine to support healthy sleep habits.

SOLUTIONS TO HELP

SERENITY®/SERENITY® SOFTGELS

Calms the mind and emotions. Can be used for sleep issues.

LAVENDER

Soothes emotions and helps with sleep, stress, anxiety, and habitual teeth-grinding.

VETIVER

Helpful for PTSD, depression, anxiety, ADHD (inattentive and/or hyperactive/impulsive), focus, concentration, poor memory retention, insomnia, and irritability.

CALMER™

Relaxing, unwinding, and pacifying.

PETITGRAIN

Helps with feelings of fear, anxiety, anger, shock, hysteria, loneliness, and insomnia.

SANDALWOOD

Helpful for insomnia and restlessness; calms, grounds, and relaxes.

SPIKENARD

Helpful for anxiety, depression, emotional blocks, insomnia, stress, and tension.

ROMAN CHAMOMILE

Helpful for anger, irritability, agitation, insomnia, overexcitement, stress, and shock.

HOW MUCH SLEEP DO WE NEED?

- Adults need 7 to 9 hours of quality sleep each night.
- Teens need 8 to 10 hours of sleep each night.
- School-aged children need 9 to 12 hours of sleep each night.
- Preschoolers need to sleep between 10 and 13 hours a day (including naps).
- Toddlers need to sleep between 11 and 14 hours a day (including naps).
- Babies need to sleep between 12 and 16 hours a day (including naps).

MANAGING STRESS

As a society, we often embrace a "go, go, go" mentality. We are accustomed to living a fast-paced lifestyle and being rewarded for the long, hard hours of work we put in. We may even feel that taking time to hit the "pause" button or recharge mentally is lazy or indulgent, which can lead to feelings of guilt and selfishness. This type of thinking will eventually take a toll on our overall physical, mental, and emotional health. Optimal health and well-being requires a serious commitment to stress reduction and management. See ways to manage stress on page 417. Below you will find natural solutions to help you manage stress.

SOLUTIONS TO HELP

ADAPTIV™

This blend provides stress-relief, energizes, uplifts, and soothes anxious feelings.

LAVENDER

Soothes emotions and helps with sleep, stress, anxiety, and habitual teeth-grinding.

ROMAN CHAMOMILE

Helpful for anger, irritability, agitation, insomnia, overexcitement, stress, and shock.

VETIVER

Helpful for PTSD, depression, anxiety, ADHD (inattentive and/or hyperactive/impulsive), focus, concentration, poor memory retention, insomnia, and irritability.

BERGAMOT

Helps with anxiety, addictions, managing stress, low self-esteem, and emotional balance.

NEROLI

Helps with chronic stress, nervousness, hysteria, panic, grief, shock, overthinking, feeling overwhelmed, confusion, and increasing feelings of intimacy.

BASIL

Supports adrenal glands.

CEDARWOOD

Helps calm anxiety and improve low GABA, an important neurotransmitter that boosts sleep and increases relaxation.

GREEN MANDARIN

Helpful for children and adults with depression, agitation, nervousness, inner child work, situational anxiety, mental fatigue, or emotional balance.

IMPROVING EMOTIONAL HEALTH

A critical aspect of managing stress is managing your emotions. Stress responses often include negative emotions, which can linger after physical stressors have passed. These emotions can include depression, anxiety, anger, and distress. Ignored, they can cause problems with your physical and emotional health. They are a signal that something in your life is or isn't working. Instead, choose to understand and deal with negative emotions. Essential oils are an excellent resource for supporting emotional health. In addition, the solutions below can support your efforts to manage your emotional health.

SOLUTIONS TO HELP

PEACE®

Helps to release fear and worry and brings a sense of safety and security to heal. Helps with nervousness and irritability.

CHEER®

Helps with hysteria and anxiety. Can be used to support depression and discouragement.

PASSION®

Can help with low libido and sexual performance. Clears up mental fog and memory issues. Assists with apathy, depression, and energy issues.

CONSOLE®

Helps promote feelings of comfort and hope and reduce unsettled feelings during times of loss.

MOTIVATE®

Helps support mental fatigue, exhaustion, confusion, and feeling overwhelmed.

FORGIVE®

Can help support ulcers and liver issues. Supports anxiety and aids in forgiveness.

YLANG YLANG

Helpful for adrenal fatigue, loss of will, apathy, low libido, anger, frustration, stress, and fear.

CITRUS BLISS®/COPAIBA

Helps with stress, anxiety, depression, sleep issues, and supporting emotions.

HYGGE™

This blend supports comfort, relaxation and quieting. It invites rest and reflection while enjoying good times with good people.

THE IMPORTANCE OF SLEEP

Did you know we spend nearly one-third of our life asleep?
Leading experts recommend that adults get seven to nine hours of quality sleep per night. We now know sleep deficiency has a negative effect on lifestyle behaviors as well as a direct link to dysfunction of nearly every system in the body.

Lack of sleep can affect hormone levels, mood, weight, and immune function. It can also cause issues with our brain's ability to learn and problem-solve. Aside from these negative effects, sleep deficiency also deprives our body of time to heal. During sleep, our body performs many restorative functions. In addition to restoring the brain's energy, muscle growth, protein synthesis, and tissue repair also occur. Sleep is both physically and mentally healing, allowing our bodies to recuperate from the day as well as recharge and refocus. Here are some ways you can make sure you get enough sleep and improve your sleep quality:

• *Avoid excess caffeine,* alcohol, stimulants, and nicotine.

• *Develop a sleep routine* that works best for you.

• *Avoid excessive screen use, especially before bed.*
Not all light is created equal, and blue light has been shown to have a significant impact on your circadian-rhythm, or body clock. Blue light can cause a disruption in sleep patterns which can greatly affect every aspect of your health.

• *Do an Epsom salt bath or foot soak.* Epsom salt is a natural exfoliant that can help tremendously with sleep and lowering blood pressure as well as reduce stress.

2 cups of Epsom salts per tub of warm water, or 1/4th cup of Epsom salts for a foot soak.

Bathe for about 12–20 minutes before bedtime, because the detoxification aspect of using Epsom salts can make you tired.

If desired, add your favorite relaxing essential oils to the bath or foot soak.

• *Have a cup of tea.* The simple act of sipping a hot cup of tea has demonstrable effects on brain waves, leading to relaxation and drowsiness.

• *Read.* Reading has been shown to reduce heart rate, create sleep readiness, and reduce stress.

• *Practice Tai Chi or yoga.* Both of these practices have been shown to promote restful sleep. Tai Chi is often described as "meditation in motion."

WAYS TO MANAGE STRESS

- *Sleep more*.

- *Exercise outdoors.* Sunshine exposure naturally increases serotonin, which positively impacts your mood. Exercise releases endorphins, which also boosts your mood and can assist in reducing pain.

- *Promote positive thoughts and emotions.* As humans, sometimes tend to prioritize bad over good. When we acknowledge the good in our lives, we can help to "rewire" our brain. Having a consistent negative attitude can create chronic stress and negatively affect the immune system.

- *Dry brushing.* This practice of exfoliating and unclogging pores causes an energy boost by increasing circulation. It can have multiple benefits and costs pennies.

   Find a natural-bristle shower brush with a long handle.

   Brush your skin in long strokes toward your heart, going over each area two or three times. Brush in a clockwise motion over your belly.

   Do this about 2–3 times per week before showering.

- *Use a sauna.* Sauna use stimulates the release of endorphins, which naturally suppresses the production and release of cortisol, a stress hormone.

- *Meditate.* Meditation leads to a deep state of relaxation that research has shown to be more effective than six hours of sleep. Certain kinds of meditation can help alleviate stress, fear, and anxiety.

- *Get a massage*.

- *Sit in a sunny window.* Feeling sunshine on your skin promotes peace and happiness.

- *Get acupuncture,* reflexology, or a foot massage.

- *Attend a dance class*.

- *Listen to soothing music*.

- *Write.* You can do a free write, writing whatever comes to mind, or write about what you'd like your life to look and feel like.

- *Journal.*

- *Talk with a friend*.

- *Keep a stress diary*.

- *Say "no"* to activities or social invites you do not want to attend.

- *Set boundaries* with your time and energy.

- *Allow yourself* down time to rejuvenate.

- *Make time* for things that you love and enjoy.

- *Eat a healthy diet*.

- *Incorporate deep breathing exercises* into your routine.

Emotions are strong feelings that arise from our moods, circumstances, or relationships. Our emotions are based on how we interpret an event, not necessarily what truly happened. When we feel excitement, happiness, peace, or pleasure, we refer to these as positive emotions. Feeling good feels good. On the flip side, when anxiety, rejection, anger, or worry occur, we refer to these as negative emotions, which can be tougher to navigate.

Learning how to manage our emotions can take practice. One of the most important concepts to recognize is we are the ones who interpret and assign meaning to an event or circumstance. How one person interprets an event can be entirely different from how another person interprets that very same event. We see the world through our own lens. The good thing about that is that once we understand this concept, we get to choose how we interpret an event and assign meaning to it. At this point in the process, this is where essential oils shine. Our sense of smell is greatly affected by the essential oil's chemical makeup. When we inhale the scent of an essential oil, there is an impact on our limbic system, the place in our brain where our emotions and memories process.

The next time you are met with a wave of emotions, try these tips to navigate them.

For more information on managing emotions, see Emotions Made Simple, written by the same authors of Essential Oils Made Simple.

1 *Ask yourself the following questions.*

- What am I feeling right now? Name the emotion.
- What happened that made me feel this way? Describe the event and why you feel the way you do.
- Could this situation have a different explanation that may make sense? Consider if the person is sick, stressed out, or dealing with something that is out of their control.
- What would I like to do about these feelings? Text back how I really feel, yell, scream, or punch something?
- Is there a better way for me to deal with these emotions right now? Most likely, YES.
- How would I like to feel right now?
- What can I do, think, or say that would help me feel this way?
- Find an essential oil for support and do something that makes you feel that better feeling emotion.
- Keep these questions in a mood journal to track patterns and triggers.

2 *Take time to breathe.* Pick a mood-enhancing essential oil like Bergamot, Adaptiv, or Lavender. Place one drop of oil in your palms. Cup your palms over your face and inhale deeply and slowly, holding your breath for a count of three. Let it out slowly. Once you have uncovered distorted thoughts and replaced them with more accurate or helpful ones, consider a mantra like "I am relaxed" or "I am at peace." Do this several times until you find yourself more relaxed.

3 *Get to know your triggers.* Understand when it's important to express your feelings and when to keep them to yourself.

4 *Take a time out.* Try to distract yourself from your emotion temporarily by distancing yourself from it. Watch a funny movie, take a walk or play with your children. Healthy distractions are temporary, so be sure to come back to your emotions when you are in a better place to deal with them.

5 *Give meditation a try.* Meditate to increase your awareness of your feelings and to help you manage stress regularly.

6 *Seek professional help.* If you continue to have a difficult time dealing with emotions, seek professional help from a Certified Life or Wellness Coach or therapist.

REDUCE TOXIC LOAD/ HEALTHY HOME *Chapter* **7**

PROACTIVE MEDICAL CARE

SELF CARE

REDUCE TOXIC LOAD/ HEALTHY HOME

REST & MANAGE STRESS

MOVEMENT & METABOLISM

EAT RIGHT/PROPER NUTRITION

Healthcare

Lifestyle

"The route back to health is to retrace your steps through sickness to understand the toxins you were exposed to."
—Steven Magee

REDUCE TOXIC LOAD

"Toxic Load" refers to the accumulation of toxins and chemicals in our bodies. These toxins come from a variety of sources, including the environment, the food we eat, the water we drink, and the personal care and household products we use. The lungs, the digestive tract, and the skin are the three most vulnerable pathways for toxins and chemicals to enter our bodies. This toxic accumulation can have a massive impact on your health. Your toxic load influences your hormones, weight, skin appearance, and digestion, and it has a dramatic effect on systemic inflammation—a major contributing factor to chronic disease. Look to the right for goals around reducing your toxic load.

Reducing exposure to toxins in & on your body

Reducing exposure to toxins in your environment

Cleansing & detoxing your body

REDUCING EXPOSURE TO TOXINS IN & ON YOUR BODY

The lungs, digestive tract, and skin are the most vulnerable pathways for toxins to enter our bodies. Therefore, we need to be mindful about the quality of the air we breathe, the food we eat, and the products we use on our skin. See pages 424–425 for ways to purify the air around you. Additional solutions that can support you in reducing the toxins in and on your body include the following.

SOLUTIONS TO HELP

YARROWIPOM ACTIVE BOTANICAL NUTRITIVE DUO, YARROW/POM CELLULAR BEAUTY COMPLEX, YARROW / POM BODY RENEWING SERUM

Promotes a healthy metabolism and immune response. Reduces the appearance of blemishes and promotes young and healthy skin. Soothes tension.

VERÁGE® SKINCARE KIT

Nourishes and hydrates skin and helps reduces visible signs of aging.

ZENDOCRINE® BLEND/SOFTGELS

Cleanses the body of toxins and free radicals that slow down crucial body systems.

LEMON

Helps detox the body and gives lymphatic support.

GERANIUM

Provides purifying effects against unhealthy substances and supports the liver, gallbladder, pancreas, and kidney.

OTHER SKIN & HAIR PRODUCTS

Essential Skin Care Facial Cleanser, Tightening Serum, Hydrating Cream, Pore Reducing Toner, Anti-Aging Moisturizer, Invigorating Scrub, Reveal Facial System, Brightening Gel, Anti-Aging Eye Cream

Refreshing body wash, Protecting Shampoo, Smoothing Conditioner, Root to Tip Serum, Healthy Hold Glaze

Baby Hair & Body Wash Hydrating Body Mist, hand lotion

Citrus Bliss and Serenity Bath Bar, Lip Balm

REDUCING EXPOSURE TO TOXINS IN YOUR ENVIRONMENT

Toxins in the environment come from many sources. Radiation, chemicals in the air, environmental threats, and even your cell phone contribute to toxic load. While some things may be out of your control, your immediate environment is an ideal place to focus on in terms of its impact on your health. See pages 424–425 for ways to purify the air around you. Use the following products to provide a cleaner environment.

SOLUTIONS TO HELP

ON GUARD® PRODUCTS

A blend of several essential oils that protect the immune system from foreign invaders or pathogens. On Guard® Foaming Hand Wash, On Guard® Hand Sanitizer, On Guard® Cleaner Concentrate, and On Guard® Laundry Detergent, On Guard® Blend, On Guard® Chewable Tablet.

PURIFY

An exclusive combination of essential oils that purify and eradicate odors in a natural, safe way. Contains essential oils known for their powerful cleaning properties that purify the air and protect against environmental threats.

LEMON

Helps detox the body and gives lymphatic support.

WILD ORANGE

Assists detox and regeneration.

GERANIUM

Provides purifying effects against unhealthy substances and supports the liver, gallbladder, pancreas, and kidney.

ABŌDE™ LINE OF PRODUCTS: MULTI-PURPOSE SURFACE CLEANER CONCENTRATE/LIQUID DISH SOAP/DISHWASHER PODS/LAUNDRY PODS/FOAMING HAND WASH AND LOTION INFUSED WITH CITRUS BLOOM™ BLEND

Refreshing, cleansing and purifying, the new Abōde™ line of products supports green cleaning. Natural, non-toxic and effective, you're getting the finest quality ingredients from Mother Nature without the toxic load.

DIFFUSER IDEAS TO CLEANSE THE AIR AROUND YOU

2 drops Purify
3 drops Lemon
2 drops Grapefruit
3 drops Tea Tree

....

3 drops On Guard®
3 drops Wild Orange
2 drops Purify

....

3 drops Siberian Fir
3 drops Eucalyptus
2 drops Purify

....

3 drops Pink Pepper
2 drops Purify
2 drops Lemon

....

2 drops Lavender
2 drops Lemon
2 drops Geranium

....

3 drops Eucalyptus
2 drops Lavender

....

3 drops Clove
2 drops Cinnamon
2 drops Thyme

4 drops Tea Tree
3 drops Lemon

....

4 drops On Guard®
3 drops Grapefruit
2 drops Cinnamon

....

2 drops On Guard®
2 drops Citrus Bliss®
1 drop Black Pepper

....

4 drops On Guard®
4 drops Serenity®

....

3 drops Peppermint
3 drops Wild Orange
2 drops Lavender

....

3 drops On Guard®
4 drops Citrus Bliss®
2 drops Peppermint

....

3 drops Balance®
3 drops Wild Orange
1 drop Patchouli

GO ORGANIC

Conventional produce is generally grown and raised using industrial herbicides, unsafe fertilizers, and dangerous pesticides. A recent study by the Environmental Working Group (EWG) found that even after being thoroughly washed and peeled, 70% of non-organic fresh produce in the United States is routinely sprayed with a noxious legal cocktail containing pesticide residues. These pesticide residues build up in your tissues and fat cells, increasing your body's cumulative toxic load. Eating organic eases this toxic load and its burden on your body's detoxification systems.

For many Americans, choosing an all-organic diet isn't financially feasible. Thankfully, some resources can help you prioritize when to choose organic produce so that you don't break your budget. The EWG has developed two annual shopper guides for consumers—the Dirty Dozen and Clean Fifteen compares the pesticide contamination of 47 popular conventional fruits and vegetables. The Dirty Dozen is a list of produce with the most pesticide contamination. The Clean Fifteen is a list of produce with the least pesticide residue.

Strawberries

Spinach

Kale

Nectarines

Apples

Grapes

Peaches

Cherries

Pears

Tomatoes

Celery

Potatoes

CLEAN FIFTEEN

Avocados

Sweet Corn

Pineapples

Onions

Papayas

Frozen Sweet Peas

Eggplant

Asparagus

Cauliflower

Cantaloupe

Broccoli

Mushrooms

Cabbage

Honeydew Melon

Kiwi

LOCALLY SOURCED

Another cost-effective way to eat organic is to buy produce from local farms. Supporting your local farmers also provides better nutrition to you and your family. As soon as a fruit or vegetable is harvested, it starts to lose nutritional value over time. The more distance a fruit or veggie travels, the more its nutrient content diminishes—and fruits and vegetables grown locally do not have to travel far, providing you with better nutrients.

When you do end up with non-organic produce, you can use the following recipes to clean your produce and reduce the risk of pesticide exposure.

VEGGIE WASH

Partially fill your kitchen sink with water. Add 10-15 drops of Lemon essential oil and 1 cup of vinegar. Soak your produce for 15 minutes, pat dry, and enjoy!

VEGGIE WASH

Add 2 cups of water, ½ cup distilled white vinegar, and 10 drops of lemon essential oil to a spray bottle. Shake before each use and spray your produce liberally to clean it.

Regardless of whether you choose conventionally or organically grown produce, experts agree that the health benefits of a diet rich in fruit and vegetables outweighs the risks of possible pesticide exposure.

USE GREEN BEAUTY PRODUCTS

Beauty and personal care products are a staple for most people, but chemicals contained in conventional beauty products can impact your health and longevity. Many of these products are applied directly to the skin—an organ that's extremely vulnerable to toxic exposure—where ingredients can be absorbed directly into the bloodstream. Some contaminants in beauty products have been causally linked to serious problems, such as cancer and reproductive issues. Unfortunately, the Food and Drug Administration (FDA) has sharply limited authority when it comes to regulating chemicals and contaminants associated with daily use of personal care products. Using green beauty products ensures that your body isn't regularly exposed to harmful toxins as part of your daily routine.

AVOID SYNTHETIC FRAGRANCES

Synthetic fragrances are possibly one of the most harmful invading offenders in daily life. You can find synthetic fragrances in countless household items, such as garbage bags, room sprays, laundry soap, and fabric softener. These fragrances contain hundreds of synthetic chemicals, and inhalation of these chemicals can harm your most susceptible tissue, such as your throat, mouth, and nose.

So, how do you avoid harmful fragrances? Here are a few helpful tips.

- *Make* Your Own Products

  Make your own cleaning products, air fresheners, and deodorant using pure essential oils—it's easier than you think! (See "Clean with Green Products" in this chapter for recipes).

- *Read* Labels

  Avoid products that list ingredients such as fragrance, parfum/parfume, linalool, limonene, DEHP, DBP, DEP, aldehydes, and phthalates. These words could mean the product includes over 3,000 different ingredients not required by law to be declared. Even products that are labeled "unscented" could still have a masking fragrance meant to cover up an underlying base formula. Instead, look for products containing essential oils.

- *Choose* Candles Carefully

  Only buy candles made with all-natural ingredients like soy wax or beeswax, and be sure they are made with a lead-free wick. You still need to check the label to make sure the candle doesn't contain fragrance or parfum, since even all- natural candle companies cut corners by using synthetic fragrance.

- *Ditch* the Perfume

  Using an essential oil blend in place of perfume will not only make you smell better but give you added health benefits.

- *Avoid* Hidden Chemicals in Clothes

  Clothing is often made with thousands of synthetic chemicals and can prevent your skin from properly discharging toxins. Be sure to choose natural materials like organic cotton, linen, silk, hemp, and wool. These fabrics allow your body to regulate its temperature and to breathe. Try to choose second-hand clothing when possible. You can rest easy knowing the garment has been washed several times prior to landing on your body.

CLEANSING & DETOXING YOUR BODY

Exposure to toxins is unavoidable. Encouragingly, the human body has built-in detoxification systems to remove the chronic buildup of toxins. Because the steady increase of modern synthetic substances into most lifestyles compromises our body's detoxification systems, they need targeted support. See pages 434-437 for a 30-day cleansing protocol to help your body clean out toxins. The following natural solutions will support the cleansing process.

SOLUTIONS TO HELP

CLEANSE & RESTORE KIT

Filled with the essentials to promote lifelong health.

ZENDOCRINE® COMPLEX

Supports healthy, cleansing filtering.

ZENDOCRINE® SOFTGELS

Cleanses the body of toxins and free radicals.

ZENDOCRINE® DETOX BLEND

Supports the healthy function of the liver, kidneys, colon, lungs, and skin.

DIGESTZEN TERRAZYME®

Supports better digestion and absorption of nutrients. Supports a healthy cellular metabolism.

GX ASSIST®

Provides immediate detoxification. Purifies and cleanses the digestive system. Supports overall digestive health and microbial balance.

PB ASSIST®

Encourages healthy microflora growth.

DDR PRIME® SOFTGELS

Promotes a healthy response to free radicals while supporting healthy cellular function.

DDR® PRIME

Protects the body against oxidative stress to cellular DNA.

LEMON

Helps detox the body and gives lymphatic support.

CILANTRO

Helps with heavy metal detoxification and supports liver and kidneys.

CITRONELLA

Helps with the side effects of detoxing, digestive upsets, and intestinal inflammation.

JUNIPER BERRY

Supports detoxification.

OREGANO

Helpful for intestinal worms and parasites.

MICROPLEX VMZ®

Whole food micronutrient supplement.

XEO MEGA®

Promotes heart and circulatory health, supports healthy joint function, provides cellular protection for each cell in the body, and supports immune system function.

ALPHA CRS®+

Supports mental clarity and brain function. Reduces the inflammatory response in the body. Protects cell membranes and other connective tissues from free radical damage.

30-DAY CLEANSING PROTOCOL

Reduce Toxic Load

BENEFITS

- *Increased energy*
- *Better sleep*
- *Reduced digestive issues*
- *Clearer skin*
- *Weight loss*
- *Less inflammation*
- *Better digestion*
- *Improved mood*

Just like we "spring clean" our home each year, it's important for our health and vitality to do the same with our body. Body cleanses have an important function and can be an excellent choice for anyone who wants to remove toxins and accumulated waste. Body cleanses can help you if you suffer from bloating, lack of energy, mood swings, constipation, or dull skin. Cleansing a few times every year can also help increase the amount of oxygen, nutrients, and quality of blood supplied to your organs. As toxins are removed, cellulite and fat deposits are often reduced as well.

There are many different cleanses available, so it can be hard to find a trusted, science-based cleanse. The best cleanses are clinically studied, safe, natural, and effective, and focus on the following three areas:

- *Eliminating waste*
- *Eliminating bad bacteria* from the gut
- *Restoring the necessary bacteria* for a healthy gut

Be aware that side effects may (and often do) emerge as a result of body cleansing; however, they will pass.

Side effects could include headaches, nausea, dizziness, diarrhea (a normal part of the cleansing process), fatigue, and gassiness. Starting the cleansing process gradually may help to mitigate some of these side effects. Keep in mind that it likely took many years (or even your entire lifetime) to accumulate this toxic buildup, so it is completely normal to have the cleansing process take time. This cleanse can be done once or twice per year or seasonally if you experience chronic health challenges. This 30-day cleansing protocol will help you flush your organs, cleanse your gut and restore your gut microbiome.

30-DAY CLEANSE & RESTORE PROTOCOL

FOUNDATION

LIFELONG VITALITY

*Blend of essential nutrients and powerful metabolic factors for optimal health, energy, and longevity.**

Take xEO Mega®, Microplex VMz®, and Alpha CRS+® per day with food based on your needs. Continue daily after the cleanse completion.

4 CAPSULES EACH PER DAY WITH MEALS

Reduce the amount or discontinue if GI upset occurs. Take all supplements with food.

ENDOCRINE

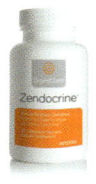

ZENDOCRINE COMPLEX®

*Botanical blend to support liver, kidneys, colon, lungs, and, skin.**

Take Zendocrine Complex® both AM and PM with meals for the 30 days.

1-2 CAPSULES WITH AM & PM MEALS

Reduce the amount or discontinue if GI upset occurs. Take with food.

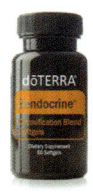

ZENDOCRINE®

*Botanical blend to support the body's natural ability to rid itself of unwanted substances.**

Take a Zendocrine® capsule with AM and PM meals for 10 days. Continue daily after the cleanse completion.

1-2 CAPSULES WITH AM & PM MEALS

Reduce the amount or discontinue if GI upset occurs. Take with food.

GASTROINTESTINAL

TERRAZYME®

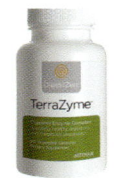

Blend of digestive enzymes to aid in the digestion of food and absorption of nutrients.*

Take Terrazyme® on empty stomach in the morning and night or at meal times, for a total of 5 capsules per day for 30 days. Continue daily after the cleanse completion.

1-3 CAPSULES PER MEAL OR TWICE DAILY ON AN EMPTY STOMACH *Reduce the amount or discontinue if GI upset occurs.*

GX ASSIST®

Combination of essential oils and caprylic acid to help cleanse and support the digestive system.*

Take GX Assist® for 10 days

Optional as needed: 1 softgel with each meal, rather than just AM and PM meals.

1 CAPSULE WITH AM & PM MEALS, DAYS 11-20
Reduce the amount or discontinue if GI upset occurs. Take with food.

PB ASSIST®+

6 billion CFUs of 6 different strains of probiotics.*

Take PB Assist®+ for 10 days. After the cleanse, consume 1 capsule per day.

1 CAPSULE PER MEAL, DAYS 21-31
Reduce the amount or discontinue if GI upset occurs. Take with food.

CELLULAR

DDR PRIME®

Essential oil blend to support cellular health, function and renewal.*

Take DDR Prime® with AM and PM meals for 10 days. Continue daily after the cleanse completion.

2 CAPSULES TOTAL PER DAY WITH AM & PM MEALS
Reduce the amount or discontinue if GI upset occurs. Take all supplements with food.

LEMON OIL & WATER

Naturally cleanses the body and aids in digestion.*

Take 1 to 2 drops of Lemon in 8 oz. of water. Continue daily after the cleanse completion.

1-2 DROPS 5 TIMES PER DAY

JUICE CLEANSE

A juice cleanse helps unleash your body's natural healing power by flooding your system with antioxidants and powerful nutrients. Juicing is beneficial for those with skin conditions, autoimmune diseases, elevated cholesterol, high blood pressure, and inflammatory conditions such as arthritis.

During a juice cleanse, you drink only water and juice from fruits and vegetables and do not consume any solid food. A juice cleanse typically lasts one to three days. About five days before the cleanse, you should increase your intake of fluids and fresh fruits and vegetables and gradually eliminate dairy products, caffeine, alcohol, meat, wheat, and nicotine. This protocol will help your body prepare for the cleanse and reduce withdrawal symptoms, such as headaches and cravings. Once you have completed the cleanse, gradually reintroduce your typical food intake over the course of several days.

What juice should you use for a juice cleanse? Most people buy juice cleansing kits online and are shipped fresh juice to last the duration of their cleanse. Many of these are cold-pressed and retain nutrients, and some are raw. You can also use shelf-stable juice cleanse powder as a more affordable option. Another option is to make your own juices—and the following recipes can help get you started.

JUICE CLEANSE RECIPES

A typical juice cleanse recommends drinking six juices a day, alternating the colors. For this juice cleanse, simply rotate the listed recipes. Each recipe makes about three juices. If there are leftovers, store them in the refrigerator to use for the next day of your juice cleanse.

HARVEST MOON BLISS

INGREDIENTS:

3 small beets

2-3 apples

8 oz. blackberries

1 drop Ginger essential oil or **1 piece** of fresh ginger

Add ingredients to a blender. If needed, add water until juice reaches desired consistency.

GREEN GOODNESS

INGREDIENTS:

1 bunch celery

4-5 kale leaves

1 small handful of parsley leaves

1 green apple

1 lime and/or **1 drop** of Lime essential oil

1 drop of Celery Seed essential oil

1 lemon and/or **1 drop** of Lemon essential oil

1 inch of fresh ginger and/or 1 drop of Ginger essential oil

1 Tablespoon organic coconut oil

Add ingredients to a blender. If needed, add water until juice reaches desired consistency.

SPICY DANDY BERRY BLISS

INGREDIENTS:

2 cups strawberries

1 teaspoon dandelion leaf powder

1 cup raspberries

1 drop of Wild Orange essential oil

Optional: 1 small seed from a jalapeño or chili pepper (or more, depending on your heat preference) and/or 1 teaspoon maple syrup or liquid stevia.

Add ingredients to a blender. If needed, add water until juice reaches desired consistency.

JUST ANOTHER DAY IN PARADISE

INGREDIENTS:

1 medium ripe papaya, peeled, seeded, and sliced

1 small pineapple, peeled, cored, and sliced

1 piece peeled fresh ginger or **1 drop** Ginger essential oil

1 medium kiwi, peeled

½ cup fresh young coconut water

Add papaya, pineapple, ginger, and kiwi to a blender. If needed, add water until juice reaches desired consistency. Stir in coconut water.

WHITE WARRIOR

INGREDIENTS:

½ cup raw cashews

1 Tablespoon honey

1 Tablespoon cinnamon

Add ingredients to a blender. If needed, add water until juice reaches desired consistency.

HEAVY METAL CLEANSES

Having small amounts of some heavy metals, such as iron and zinc, is essential for a healthy body. However, your body can also be exposed to toxic levels of heavy metals through various means, such as pesticide residue on produce, soil erosion, mining, and smoking tobacco. Heavy metal toxicity can affect the function of organs such as the lungs, liver, and brain, as well as affect blood composition and energy levels. Long-term exposure can lead to severe, irreparable degenerative conditions such as Alzheimer's disease and Parkinson's disease.

You can cleanse your body from heavy metals through a process called chelation. During chelation, certain substances—often found foods and medications—bind to heavy metals in your body and transport them out. Before you attempt to cleanse your body of heavy metals, you should have a baseline knowledge of your body's heavy metal buildup. Contact your medical practitioner or healthcare provider to measure heavy metal levels.

To begin a heavy metal cleanse, gradually introduce the plants listed below into your diet. These plants will help reduce your heavy metal toxicity. Depending on your toxicity levels, it can take time to cleanse your body—sometimes a month and other times up to a year. If you have difficulty consuming the following plants, try to find products containing these foods instead.

Spirulina. This edible alga can draw heavy metals from the liver, brain, and central nervous system.

Barley Grass Extract Powder. Barley is a grass that can draw heavy metals out of your reproductive system, spleen, pancreas, intestinal tracts, and thyroid.

Atlantic Red Seaweed. This alga removes mercury and binds to copper, nickel, cadmium, aluminum, lead, and mercury.

Milk Thistle. This herb supports the liver by enhancing toxins and liver regeneration. It can also heal the liver when jaundice is present.

Wild Blueberries. Wild blueberries are extremely effective for pulling heavy metals out of the brain and repairing and healing locations in the body where metals have resided. Because of their effect on the brain, it is the most powerful food for reversing Alzheimer's disease.

Dandelion. Dandelion detoxifies the brain, liver, and spleen and helps purify your body when exposed to toxins, heavy metals, and radiation.

Burdock root. This root helps reduce adhesions in the liver, improving scar tissue when liver exhaustion is present.

If you wish to attempt advanced heavy metal cleansing, make sure you have your doctor's approval before starting.

NATURALLY CLEANSING FOODS

THE FOLLOWING FOODS NATURALLY SUPPORT YOUR BODY'S DETOXIFICATION PATHWAYS:

Lemons	Ginger	Beetroot	Artichokes
Watercress	Pomegranate	Fennel	Blueberries
Apples	Cranberries	Grapefruit	Pineapple
Broccoli	Cabbage	Cauliflower	Brussel Sprouts
Turmeric	Almonds	Avocados	Water

Leafy greens and green juices
(Arugula, Kale, Kelp, Wheatgrass, Spinach, Parsley, Mustard greens, Dandelion greens)

SELF CARE *Chapter* **8**

Level	Category
PROACTIVE MEDICAL CARE	Healthcare
SELF CARE	Healthcare
REDUCE TOXIC LOAD/ HEALTHY HOME	Lifestyle
REST & MANAGE STRESS	Lifestyle
MOVEMENT & METABOLISM	
EAT RIGHT/PROPER NUTRITION	

"Your health is what you make of it. Everything you do and think either adds to the vitality, energy and spirit you possess or takes away from it." —Ann Wigmore

INFORMED SELF-CARE

As we move towards taking more responsibility for your own health, it's important to understand what you can do on your own and when you need to seek medical care. Many of your family's day-to-day wellness needs can be addressed from the comfort of your own home by using essential oils and other natural solutions. However, be wise and exercise caution when faced with serious injury or life-threatening situations. When unsure regarding the potential seriousness of your injury or condition, seek medical care.

STEP 1

A great place to begin your own informed self-care is by following the Foundational Protocol found on page 447. This protocol can serve as a blueprint for daily habits to promote eating right, proper exercise, achieving rest, managing stress, and reducing your toxic load in general.

STEP 2

For more targeted self-care solutions to address specific ailments and conditions, refer to the Ailments and Protocols chapter of this book. You can quickly find solutions for many of your health challenges. The protocols included in this book cover the most commonly experienced ailments.

STEP 3

If your particular condition is not included, in addition to following the Foundational Protocol, refer to pages 448-470. These pages highlight different systems of the body and indicate what essential oils and natural solutions to use to support those systems. Follow the recommendations to support those body systems that are most affected by your ailment or condition.

FOUNDATIONAL PROTOCOL

Adults: 1 drop of Frankincense and Copaiba under tongue morning and evening

Adults: Lifelong Vitality supplements twice a day, 2-3 TerraZyme® with meals, 1 PB Assist® daily

Adults: 1-2 drops of Lemon, Grapefruit, or other citrus oil in water each day

Children age 4 and older:
A2z Chewables™: 2 tablets daily with meals, 1 PB Assist® Jr, IQ Mega®: 1 teaspoon daily

Adults and children: Choose an emotional oil (Passion®, Motivate®, Cheer®, Peace®, Console® or Forgive®) or a mood oil (Balance®, Serenity®, Elevation™ or Citrus Bliss®) and mix 1 drop with 5 drops of fractionated coconut oil in your palm. Apply it topically to the bottoms of feet, wrists, and down back of neck.

Diffuse 1-2 drops aromatically (diffuser, diffuser necklace, bracelet, or cotton ball). The kids kit is also an option (Brave™, Calmer™, Thinker™, Steady™, Stronger™, Tamer™, Rescuer™).

Adults: Massage a dime-sized amount of Deep Blue® rub over the impacted muscles or joints after exercise if needed.

Children: Use a ½ dime size amount.

Adults: Take 1 On Guard® softgel in the evening or diffuse 5 drops of On Guard®.

Adults: Take 1-2 Serenity® Softgels at bedtime.

Adults and Children: Diffuse 5 drops of Lavender or Serenity® (or favorite oil for relaxation) in the evening and put 1 drop on the bottoms of feet before bed.

Adopted from Dr. Hill and Daily Essentials Kit

The heart and circulatory system make up the cardiovascular system. The heart works as a pump that pushes blood (carrying oxygen and nutrients) to the organs, tissues, and cells of the body through a complex network of arteries, arterioles, and capillaries. Blood carrying cellular waste is returned to the heart through venules and veins. It is also responsible for keeping the body's temperature in a safe range. The oxygen and nutrient-rich blood that bring life and health to all the cells and tissues of the body, also transport essential oils. When applied topically, essential oils are absorbed through the skin. They move through the circulatory system within thirty seconds and are able to permeate cells and tissues throughout the body for targeted support within fourteen to twenty minutes.

PRODUCTS / OILS

LifeLong Vitality Supplements, Frankincense, Cinnamon, Ylang Ylang, Cypress, Thyme, Basil, Lavender, Marjoram, AromaTouch®, Black Pepper, or Peppermint

✚ SYSTEM SELF-CHECK

Invest in a blood pressure cuff. Home monitoring of your blood pressure and heart rate is a great way to watch for high blood pressure and hypertension. Take your readings twice per week and write down your numbers. Normal blood pressure numbers are less than 120/80. Hight blood pressure (hypertension stage 1) is 130-139 on the top and 80-89 on the bottom. High blood pressure (hypertension type 2) is 140 or higher on the top and 90 or higher on the bottom. If you numbers are over 180 on the top OR 120 or higher on the bottom, notify your doctor right away. Your pulse rate should be between 60 and 100 bpm. Keep track of your readings in a journal so you can show your doctor at your next visit.

✚ HOW TO IMPROVE / MAINTAIN

Eat a healthy diet with proper amounts of proteins, carbohydrates, healthy fats, vitamins, minerals and drink plenty of water. Eat a variety of fresh fruits and vegetables, lean meats, fatty fish and whole grains. Avoid inflammatory foods, trans fats, fried foods, and commercially baked goods. Maintain a healthy weight and exercise a minimum of 30 minutes per day. Include strength training, balancing exercises, joint flexibility exercises, and endurance training throughout the week. Don't drink excess alcohol or smoke. Rest and manage stress with a variety of lifestyle activities and essential oils. Get plenty of sleep and stay as active as you can throughout the day.

✚ WARNING/PROACTIVE MEDICAL CARE

If you have ongoing feelings of being sluggish or winded, have a rapid heart rate, pain that moves down your arm, or a rapid or irregular pulse, call your doctor. If you experience any severe or persistent episodes of the following symptoms, seek medical attention right away: tightness in your chest; sudden chest pain or pressure; feeling like a belt is being tightened around your chest; pain that spreads from the center of the chest to your arms; shoulders; neck or jaw; excessive sweating; nausea, vomiting, dizziness; shortness of breath; a fullness; indigestion or choking feeling; rapid or irregular heartbeat; extreme weakness or anxiety.

DIGESTIVE

The digestive system is a series of hollow, connected organs (mouth, esophagus, stomach, small/large intestines, and rectum) along a thirty-foot pathway responsible for chewing food, digesting and absorbing nutrients and expelling waste. Accessory organs, such as the teeth, tongue, salivary glands, pancreas, liver, and gallbladder, are also part of the digestive system. The digestive tract also works closely with the immune system to protect the body from pathogens and foreign invaders. When digestive system problems are present, natural remedies offer ample opportunity for balance and restoration. Start with good nutrition, clear the primary pathways of elimination so waste and toxins can be eliminated, use essential oils specifically targeted to help remove harmful bacteria, take a good prebiotic to encourage growth of good bacteria, and ingest a probiotic to repopulate the gut with live strains of helpful bacteria.

PRODUCTS / OILS

LifeLong Vitality Supplements, TerraZyme®, PB Assist®, GX Assist®, DigestTabs®, DigestZen® softgels, Peppermint Softgels, Celery Seed, Fennel, Peppermint, Spearmint, Lemon or Ginger, DigestZen® or Tamer™ blend, emotional kit oils as needed for stress related to the digestive system

➕ SYSTEM SELF-CHECK

Monitor any symptoms of gas, bloating, constipation, diarrhea or abdominal pains in a journal so you can see if there is a pattern. If you have symptoms on a regular basis, look at your diet to see what you are eating or drinking and note how fast you eat and how much you chew your food. Bring this list with you for your annual checkup and report any abnormalities to your health care provider.

➕ WARNING/PROACTIVE MEDICAL CARE

If you have ongoing, severe, or persistent feelings of fatigue, moodiness, weight gain or loss, blood sugar spikes, hair loss, swelling in your feet, problems focusing, or a low libido, call your doctor for a visit. If you have excessive thirst or hunger, fatigue, frequent urination or vision changes, call your doctor right away. If you have persistent feelings of depression, weight gain, constipation, feel anxious or tired, cold intolerance, dry hair, hair loss, or missed periods, make an appointment with your doctor. If you have difficulty sleeping, heat intolerance, rapid heart rate, unexplained weight loss, tremors, heart palpitations, or irritability, make an appointment with your doctor. If you have chronic or persistent erectile dysfunction, infertility, loss of libido, missed or frequent menstrual cycles, or unexplained milk production, call your doctor for an appointment.

➕ HOW TO IMPROVE / MAINTAIN

Eat a healthy diet with a variety of lean proteins, fatty fish, Omega-3 fatty acids, whole grain carbohydrates, and colorful fruits and vegetables. Avoid trans fats, fried food, and processed foods. Pay attention to portion sizes, how quickly you eat and how much you chew your food. You should eat smaller portions, put your utensils down between bites, and chew your food 20-30 times before swallowing. Drink half your body weight in ounces of water. Avoid soda or carbonated beverages because they can produce gas and bloating. Avoid excess alcohol consumption. Get to know the foods that upset your digestive tract and avoid them. Get to know the events and circumstances that trigger digestive issues (like travel, hormones, etc.) and prepare in advance for them. Rest and manage your stress levels if they affect your digestive system. Reduce your toxic load by eating organic as much as possible. Make sure to use proper hygiene. Carry around products that support your digestive health to prepare for any emergencies: essential oils for digestion, wet wipes, extra clothes and underwear, plastic bags for soiled items, and disposable garments (if needed).

ENDOCRINE

The endocrine system consists of glands in the body that produce and secrete hormones directly into the circulatory system. The endocrine system is responsible for bodily functions and processes, such as cell growth, tissue function, sleep, reproductive functions, metabolism, and more. Endocrine disorders are common and include such conditions as obesity, thyroid malfunction, and diabetes. Endocrine disorders typically occur when hormone levels are too high or too low. Essential oils also use the circulatory system and are able to profoundly benefit cells they encounter throughout the body as they circulate. There are also specific oils that have been shown to be incredibly supportive of certain gland/organ functions.

PRODUCTS / OILS

LifeLong Vitality Supplements, Mito2Max®, DDR Prime® Softgels, ClaryCalm®, Zendocrine® oil or softgels, On Guard® product line, MetaPWR™, Rosemary, Lemongrass, Tulsi, and Frankincense to support your hypothalamus, thalamus, pituitary, pineal, parathyroid, thyroid, pancreas and adrenal health

✚ SYSTEM SELF-CHECK

Keep a journal if you experience any of these symptoms at least once or twice a week: fatigue, moodiness, unexplained weight gain or loss, blood sugar spikes, hair loss, swelling in your feet, problems focusing, low libido, excessive thirst or hunger, fatigue, frequent urination, depression, weight gain, constipation, anxiousness, fatigue, cold intolerance, dry hair, hair loss, missed periods, difficulty sleeping, heat intolerance, rapid heart rate, unexplained weight loss, tremors, heart palpitations or irritability, missed or frequent menstrual cycles, or unexplained milk production. Write down the day, date, and time of these symptoms and how long they last. If the symptoms are severe or persistent, make an appointment with your doctor and bring this journal with you.

✚ HOW TO IMPROVE / MAINTAIN

Eat a healthy diet with a variety of lean proteins, plant based proteins, nuts, seeds, fatty fish, Omega-3 fatty acids, whole grain carbohydrates, and colorful fruits and vegetables, especially berries. Avoid trans fats, fried food, and processed/packaged foods. Avoid excess alcohol, sugar, and caffeine. Exercise a minimum of 30 minutes per day, making sure to add in yoga, cardio, strength, balance, and joint flexibility exercises. Resting and managing your stress is important to your endocrine system. Getting 7-9 hours a night of sleep and developing a good sleep routine is important as well. Reduce your toxic load by choosing organic fruits and vegetables whenever possible and eliminate toxic household and personal hygiene items, as these can contain endocrine disruptors and wreak havoc on your hormones.

✚ WARNING/PROACTIVE MEDICAL CARE

If you have ongoing, severe or persistent feelings of fatigue, moodiness, weight gain or loss, blood sugar spikes, hair loss, swelling in your feet, problems focusing, or a low libido, call your doctor for a visit. If you have excessive thirst or hunger, fatigue, frequent urination, or vision changes, call your doctor right away. If you have persistent feelings of depression, weight gain, constipation, feel anxious or tired, cold intolerance, dry hair, hair loss, or missed periods, make an appointment with your doctor. If you have difficulty sleeping, heat intolerance, rapid heart rate, unexplained weight loss, tremors, heart palpitations, or irritability, make an appointment with your doctor. If you have chronic or persistent erectile dysfunction, infertility, loss of libido, missed or frequent menstrual cycles, or unexplained milk production, call your doctor for an appointment.

The immune and lymphatic system work closely together to protect the body from harmful pathogens and disease. A healthy immune response consists of the body's ability to properly identify a pathogen and engage in a series of responses designed to prevent pathogens from entering targeted cells. Natural essential oils help the immune system bring itself into balance because they are lipophilic (soluble in fat) and thus are able to penetrate the cell membrane. For threats that exist outside the cell, essential oils can assist in warding off such risks. Oregano essential oil, for example, also has hydrophilic properties that allow it to effectively target threats that exist outside the cell.

PRODUCTS / OILS

LifeLong Vitality Supplements; GX Assist®; PB Assist®; TerraZyme®; TriEase®; On Guard® Chewable Tablets, On Guard® toothpaste, mouthwash, cleaner concentrate, hand wash, softgels, and essential oil blend, Zendocrine®; Purify; Lemon; Lime; Wild Orange; Tangerine; Grapefruit; Turmeric Dual capsules, DDR Prime®; Thyme; Celery Seed; Tea Tree

✚ SYSTEM SELF-CHECK

Keep a journal if you experience any of the following symptoms on a regular basis (more than once or twice a week): you have a cold, swollen glands—write down if they are painful or not, low grade fever, runny nose, constant fatigue, get sick often, frequent diarrhea, constipation, wounds are slow to heal, persistent cough, skin infections, anxious feelings that won't go away, swelling (in the feet, legs, or ankles) burning or pressure when urinating, ongoing joint pain, or trouble concentrating.

✚ WARNING/PROACTIVE MEDICAL CARE

If you have been using natural solutions and continue to experience any of these symptoms on an ongoing or persistent basis, seek medical care: continuous cold symptoms, swollen glands, low grade fever, runny nose, constant fatigue, get sick often, frequent diarrhea, constipation, wounds are slow to heal, persistent cough, skin infections, anxious feelings that won't go away, swelling (in the feet, legs, or ankles) burning or pressure when urinating, ongoing joint pain, or trouble concentrating.

✚ HOW TO IMPROVE / MAINTAIN

Eat a healthy diet with a variety of proteins, carbohydrates, healthy fats, vitamins, minerals. 85-90% of your diet should consist of fresh fruits and vegetables, lean meats, fatty fish, and whole grains. Switching up the types of food in each category is important for your gut health, which is the backbone of the immune system. Drink half your body weight in ounces of water and add citrus oils such as lemon, lime, wild orange, grapefruit, tangerine and bergamot to support your lymphatic health. No more than 10% of your diet should contain inflammatory foods, trans fats, fried foods, and commercially baked goods. Maintain a healthy weight and exercise a minimum of 30 minutes per day. Include strength training, balancing exercises, joint flexibility exercises, and endurance training throughout the week. Don't drink excess alcohol or smoke. Rest and manage stress with a variety of lifestyle activities and essential oils. Get plenty of sleep and stay as active as you can throughout the day. Reduce your toxic load by choosing organic fruits and vegetables whenever possible and eliminate toxic household and personal hygiene items, as these can contain endocrine disruptors and wreak havoc on immune system and gut health, causing your lymphatic system to work overtime.

MUSCULAR

The muscular system consists of 650 muscles in three main categories: skeletal, smooth, and cardiac. It is controlled by the nervous system *via* two pathways: somatic and autonomic. The muscular system is constantly in motion as it supports body functions. Essential oils have a unique ability to affect muscles and connective tissue and support muscle function on a cellular level. Once oils are applied, users often experience near instant relief. Minor issues and injuries are easily managed with either topical or internal application. For more serious muscle and tendon issues, professional medical care is appropriate. Traditional Western treatment methods can be enhanced and supported with essential oil and nutritional supplement solutions.

PRODUCTS / OILS

Deep Blue®, Deep Blue® Stick with Copaiba, Deep Blue Polyphenol®, Turmeric Dual Capsules, AromaTouch®, Lemongrass, Blue Tansy, Copaiba, Frankincense, Marjoram, Wintergreen, DDR Prime®, PastTense®, Cypress

➕ SYSTEM SELF-CHECK

Keep a journal of any muscles aches and pains that you feel. Write down the day, date, time, how often you experience discomfort, and how long it lasts. Identify the pain level on a scale of 1-10 (with 10 indicating extreme pain). Note if you have any other symptoms. Notice, for example, any swelling, bruising, or tenderness in affected areas. Describe the type of pain you feel: does it burn or tingle; is it sharp or dull, etc.?

➕ HOW TO IMPROVE / MAINTAIN

Eat a nutrient rich diet with a variety of proteins, carbohydrates, healthy fats, vitamins, minerals. Include fresh fruits and vegetables, lean meats, fatty fish, nuts, seeds, and whole grains. Drink half your body weight in ounces of water and an additional glass of water for every cup of caffeine you consume. Avoid inflammatory foods, trans fats, fried foods, and commercially baked goods. Maintain a healthy weight and exercise a minimum of 30 - 45 minutes per day. Include a variety of exercise types to maintain healthy muscles: stretching, yoga, strength training, balancing exercises, joint flexibility exercises, and aerobic exercise throughout the week. Don't drink excess alcohol or smoke. Rest and manage stress with a variety of lifestyle activities and essential oils. Get plenty of sleep and stay as active as you can throughout the day. Get massages often and do foam rolling to remove trigger points.

➕ WARNING/PROACTIVE MEDICAL CARE

If you have been using natural solutions and continue to experience any of these symptoms on an ongoing or persistent basis, seek medical care: ongoing pain in a muscle or joint; stiff or swollen joints; swelling or joints that are hot to the touch; redness around a joint; dull aches and pains; muscle weakness; tingling or numbness in your arms, legs, hands or feet; decreased range of motion that interfere with your daily activities.

The nervous system is a complex system of nerves and specialized cells that allow the body to transmit and receive messages. It serves as the body's primary control and communications center, responsible for transmitting and receiving messages between every other system in the body. Nerve cells are responsible for gathering sensory information and transmitting them to the brain and spinal cord. It is passed along nerve fibers by electrical impulses and chemicals known as neurotransmitters. Essential oils can facilitate the complex messaging that occurs throughout the nervous system. They help with homeostasis, circulation, and brain function as the brain interprets and sends out data. They help the neurons transmitting and receiving messages be more efficient due to their regenerative and soothing properties. They address root causes of ailments connected to the nervous system, helping improve symptoms as the body has support in helping itself.

PRODUCTS / OILS

Frankincense, DDR Prime®, Bergamot, Adaptiv™, Copaiba, xEO Mega®, Rosemary, Lavender, Black Pepper, Peppermint, Vetiver, Cedarwood, Lemon, Helichrysum, Basil, Cilantro, Turmeric Dual Capsules, Turmeric, Marjoram, Spearmint, Hygge™, Madagascar Vanilla

WARNING/PROACTIVE MEDICAL CARE

If you experience any of the following symptoms, please contact your health care provider immediately: persistent or sudden onset of a headache; headache that changes or is different; numbness; tingling; weakness; or inability to move a part or all of one side of the body (paralysis); impaired mental ability; memory loss; muscle rigidity; weakness or loss of muscle strength; loss of sight or double vision; back pain radiating to the toes; feet or other parts of the body; muscle wasting; slurred speech, tremors, and seizures; lack of coordination; confusion; or new language impairment (expression or comprehension).

⊕ SYSTEM SELF-CHECK

Keep a journal and write down if you experience any of the following symptoms. Write down the day, date, time and describe symptoms and length of symptoms. If you experience them on a regular basis, make an appointment with your doctor and bring the paperwork with you. Symptoms: a change in your ability to concentrate; blurred or double vision when reading; problems with hand dexterity; writing, holding objects or experiencing a short attention span; numbness or tingling in the upper or lower extremities, poor retention of daily tasks; decrease in memory function or recall; difficulty going up and down stairs, frequent tripping, tremors in the hands or feet; decrease in coordination, loss of balance; loss of smell or taste, frequent dizziness; or loss of muscular strength.

⊕ HOW TO IMPROVE / MAINTAIN

Dark chocolate is rich in the amino acid tryptophan which acts as a neurotransmitter, a substance that transfers a signal from one nerve ending to another. Eat bananas, oranges, prunes, and pomegranates for potassium, as well as milk, eggs, and leafy greens for calcium. These two minerals regulate the electrical impulses generated and transmitted by the nerves. If nerves are left to fire off impulses unchecked, a person may suffer from epilepsy or other nerve disease. Bananas, oranges, pomegranates, and prunes, which are good sources of potassium, while milk, leafy greens, and eggs are rich sources of calcium. Vitamins B-1, 2 ,and 6 help the nerves to send impulses from the brain to the body. B vitamins support the protective coating of the nerves called the myelin sheath. Worn out myelin sheaths are associated with illnesses like Alzheimer's, so it is important for a person to keep up their intake of B-12 found in beef, poultry, eggs, and seafood. Folate, found in spinach, pomegranates, and beets is a B vitamin that protects the nerves from chemicals that can cause damage. Eat healthy fats as they are good for the brain. Fish, avocados, green leafy vegetables and sea vegetables are good choices. Get your spine adjusted by a chiropractor. When your spine is not in appropriate alignment, the messages that are carried through the spine are interrupted and delivered slower. Drink half your body weight in ounces of water. No more than 10% of your diet should contain inflammatory foods, trans fats, fried foods, and commercially baked goods. Maintain a healthy weight and exercise a minimum of 30 minutes per day. Obesity is linked to degenerative arthritis, diabetes and diabetic neuropathy. Include strength training, balancing exercises, joint flexibility exercises, and endurance training throughout the week. Don't drink excess alcohol or smoke. Get plenty of sleep and stay as active as you can throughout the day. Stimulate your brain with activities like writing by hand or playing mind games like chess or Sudoku. Avoid exposure to toxic chemicals, chronic stress, and activities involving repetitive motion. The nervous system handles the stress response, which, if overworked, can eventually lead to diseases ranging from high blood pressure to diabetes.

The principal function of the renal/urinary system is to maintain the volume and composition of body fluids within normal limits. This includes ridding the body of waste products that accumulate as a result of cellular metabolism. Most individuals are in a constant state of dehydration, which takes its toll on overall health, but particular kidney health. In addition to adequate water intake, there are some essential oils that are effective in supporting kidney health and helping the body to rid itself of urinary tract infection discomfort and other infections. While it is of utmost importance to utilize the services of medical professionals in the case of a prolonged or serious condition, essential oils can serve as a powerful first line of defense.

PRODUCTS / OILS

Lemongrass, Celery Seed, Zendocrine®, Zendocrine® softgels, Turmeric Dual capsules, Cypress, Juniper Berry, Rosemary, Lemon, Black Pepper, Clove, Myrrh, Cilantro, On Guard® softgels, Oregano, Tea Tree, Clary Sage, Lavender, Ylang Ylang

WARNING/PROACTIVE MEDICAL CARE

If you have an ongoing, severe or a persistent urge to urinate, a continual burning sensation when urinating, urine that appears red, bright pink or cola-colored, a sign of blood in the urine or unusual vaginal discharge, seek medical care promptly. If you experience sudden or rapidly intensifying back pain between the shoulder blades and pain in right shoulder; sudden onset of upper back and side (flank) pain; high fever; shaking and chills; nausea; vomiting or swelling around the extremities, contact your doctor right away.

✚ SYSTEM SELF-CHECK

Monitor any symptoms such as a strong, persistent urge to urinate, a burning sensation when urinating, passing frequent, small amounts of urine, urine that appears cloudy or that appears red, bright pink, or cola-colored, a sign of blood in the urine, strong-smelling urine, pelvic pain (in women, especially in the center of the pelvis and around the area of the pubic bone), burning with urination, discharge, swelling or edema in the tissue directly under skin, increased abdominal size or shiny skin, sudden or rapidly intensifying pain in upper right portion of the abdomen, back pain between the shoulder blades and pain in right shoulder (could indicate gallstones), upper back and side (flank) pain, high fever, shaking, and chills, nausea, vomiting (kidneys-acute pyelonephritis) high blood pressure, puffy eyes, and swelling around the extremities.

✚ HOW TO IMPROVE / MAINTAIN

Drink half your body weight in ounces of water. Eat a healthy diet with a variety of lean proteins, fatty fish, Omega-3 fatty acids, whole grain carbohydrates, and colorful fruits and vegetables; avoid trans fats; fried food, and processed foods. Eat a lot of berries including cranberries, raspberries, and blueberries. Eating garlic and cultured dairy products such as kefir and yogurt can improve gut health and immune function. Eat foods with fiber, such as whole-grain breads, apples, bananas, and legumes (dried beans, lentils, etc.). Oranges, lemons, strawberries, and green leafy vegetables are packed with vitamin C which makes urine more acidic. This helps prevent bacteria from growing in the system. Consider drinking coconut water, as it is a natural diuretic. Avoid soda or carbonated beverages because they can produce gas and bloating. Avoid excess alcohol consumption. Reduce your toxic load by eating organic as much as possible and make sure to use proper hygiene. Avoid constipation, keep a healthy weight, exercise regularly (physical exercise can help prevent bladder problems, as well as constipation), do pelvic floor muscle exercises. Pelvic floor exercises, also known as Kegel exercises, help hold urine in the bladder. Daily exercises can strengthen these muscles, which can help keep urine from leaking when you sneeze, cough, lift, laugh, or have a sudden urge to urinate. Use the bathroom often and when needed. Try to urinate at least every 3 to 4 hours. Holding urine in your bladder for too long can weaken your bladder muscles and make a bladder infection more likely. Take enough time to fully empty the bladder when urinating. Be in a relaxed position while urinating. Relaxing the muscles around the bladder will make it easier to empty the bladder. For women, hovering over the toilet seat may make it hard to relax, so it is best to sit on the toilet seat if conditions allow. Wipe from front to back after using the toilet. Both women and men should urinate shortly after sex to flush away bacteria that may have entered the urethra during sex. Wear cotton underwear and loose-fitting clothes.

The male reproductive system consists of a number of sex organs that play a role in the reproductive process of reproduction. These organs are located on the outside of the body and within the pelvis. Part of maintaining health and well-being includes adjusting to fluctuating hormone levels and other physical and emotional changes that take place as men mature. Since men are independent by nature, empowering themselves with knowledge and practical application of natural remedies can help them reduce health risks while managing mood and helping the body maintain better reproductive health.

 PRODUCTS / OILS

Sandalwood, Patchouli, Ylang Ylang, Jasmine, Rose, Roman Chamomile, Thyme, Cinnamon, Basil, Lavender, Ginger, Clove, Black Spruce, Spikenard

✚ WARNING/PROACTIVE MEDICAL CARE

If you have been using natural solutions and continue to experience any of these symptoms on an ongoing or persistent basis, seek medical care: dribbling urine; pain or burning during urination; frequent urination, blood in the semen or urine; frequent pain or stiffness in the lower back, hips, pelvic or rectal area, or the upper thighs; urinary incontinence (the inability to urinate); painful ejaculation; pain or swelling in the testicles; altered sexual desire; issues with ejaculation and sperm health or small firm testicles.

✚ SYSTEM SELF-CHECK

Testicular exam: The best time to examine your testicles is during or after a bath or shower, when the skin of the scrotum is relaxed. Hold your penis out of the way and examine each testicle separately. Hold your testicle between your thumbs and fingers with both hands and roll it gently between your fingers. Look and feel for any hard lumps or nodules (smooth rounded masses) or any change in the size, shape, or consistency of your testicles. Keep in mind that it's normal for one testicle to be slightly larger than the other, and for one to hang lower than the other. You should also be aware that each normal testicle has a small, coiled tube called the epididymis that can feel like a small bump on the upper or middle outer side of the testis. Normal testicles also contain blood vessels, supporting tissues, and tubes that carry sperm. Some men may confuse these with abnormal lumps at first. If you have any concerns, ask your doctor. Regularly screen for STDs, and practice good hygiene by washing your genitals regularly to prevent the accumulation of dirt and germs in your genitalia that can potentially cause infection. Quit smoking as smoking clogs the small arteries that feed blood into the penis, making it difficult to attain an erection during sexual intercourse.

✚ HOW TO IMPROVE / MAINTAIN

Exercise regularly, drink a lot of water to flush out the kidneys. Eat oysters, shellfish, lean beef, lean pork, or legumes which are full of zinc to help protect against cellular damage that leads to prostate cancer. Zinc also helps with sexual functioning of the male reproductive system, including increased sperm counts. Eat bananas, orange juice, milk, tomato products, or beans to get potassium into your diet. Fatty fish rich in Omega-3 such as salmon, sardines, tuna, mackerel, herring should be eaten a few times a week. These are high in Vitamin D as well. Flaxseeds, walnuts, soy, canola oil, and fortified products such as eggs are good sources of Omega-3. Broccoli, cabbage, bok choy, cauliflower, or Brussels sprouts. Eat Brazil nuts, whole grains, berries, such as blackberries, blueberries, strawberries, raspberries; and cranberries or cherries; red-orange vegetables, such as red bell peppers, carrots, pumpkin, or sweet potatoes; and dark, leafy greens.

The female reproductive system is made up of internal and external sex organs that function in reproduction. The female reproductive system is immature at birth and develops to maturity when a woman hits puberty. Women face a range of health challenges when it comes to reproductive health, including fertility, weight gain, fatigue, and hormone issues. Physical and emotional stress can be a cause and symptom of these and many other issues. Hormones like estrogen and progesterone are vital to reproductive health and fertility, but they also play a role in the balance of a woman's emotional and physical health. Nutrition and hydration are important keys in this supporting this system. Daily supplements that include whole food nutrients, omega oils, a phytoestrogen complex, and bone support will help regulate hormones properly. Also, mood enhancing oils can help with depression and other emotional challenges.

🝖 PRODUCTS / OILS

Phytoestrogen Essential Complex, Bone Nutrient Essential Complex, Whisper®, Thyme, Ylang Ylang, Jasmine, Sandalwood, Rosemary, Clary Calm, Clary Sage, Geranium, Roman Chamomile, Basil, Rose, Bergamot, Serenity® Softgels, Serenity®, Peppermint, Cypress, Adaptiv™, Vetiver

✚ SYSTEM SELF-CHECK / HOW TO IMPROVE / MAINTAIN

Journal your menstrual cycle each month, keeping track of things such as mood, breakthrough bleeding, intensity, cramping, bloating, and clots. An ovulation kit is a great tool, as well. Keep track of how you are feeling each day and certain stressors that may trigger you. *Mammogram Recommendations:* women between 40 and 44 have the option to start screening with a mammogram every year. Women 45 to 54 should get mammograms every year. Women 55 and older can switch to a mammogram every other year, or they can choose to continue yearly mammograms. Screening should continue as long as a woman is in good health and is expected to live at least 10 more years. *Clinical Exams/Self-Exams:* research has not shown a clear benefit of regular physical breast exams done by a health professional or by women themselves especially among average-risk women at any age. However, for those at high-risk due to family history, it is not a bad idea to perform a self-exam or get a clinical breast exam. Most often when breast cancer is detected because of symptoms like a lump, this is found during normal activities like bathing and dressing. Women should be familiar with how their breasts normally look and feel and should report any changes to a health care provider right away. Some women might still be more comfortable doing regular self-exams as a way to keep track of how their breasts look and feel. Before menopause, the best time to do the exam is two weeks after the start of your monthly period. After menopause, choose a day and examine on that day each month.

✚ WARNING/PROACTIVE MEDICAL CARE

Should you experience any of the following symptoms, contact your health care provider immediately: heavy or painful periods or bleeding between periods; feeling "full" in the lower abdomen or pelvic area; pain during sex; lower back pain; reproductive problems, such as infertility, multiple miscarriages, or early labor; abdominal or pelvic mild discomfort; frequent urination; a feeling of urgency to urinate; intense pain in the bladder or pelvic region; severe lower abdominal pain that intensifies as the urinary bladder fills or empties; acne, oily skin, or dandruff; baldness or thinning hair; excess hair growth on the face, chest, stomach, thumbs, or toes; patches of thickened brown or black skin; nipple discharge; unusual breast tenderness; breast or nipple skin changes; or lump or thickening in or near the breast or underarm area.

HOW TO PERFORM A BREAST SELF-EXAM *Reproductive Female*

1 VISUAL INSPECTION

Position yourself in front of the mirror with hands-on-hips. Pay attention to skin changes and nipple changes. Some skin changes to look for are redness, swelling, and puckering. Nipple changes to look for are indentation, scaling, and discharge. Then follow these same steps, but with your hands over your head, instead of on your hips. Check again for any change in appearance or contour.

2 PALPATION

Position yourself in an upright and reclining position. Upon touch, the breast should feel soft and smooth, like an extra firm pillow. Remember to check underarm and upper chest areas. Using the soft pad of your 3 middle fingers, move them in a circular motion starting at the outer edge and work your way towards the nipple. If you notice changes or discover a lump or knot like a small hard pebble, notify your doctor. How to improve or support the female reproductive system: aim for 30 – 45 minutes of movement at least four days a week. Exercise is one of the best ways to prevent heart disease, the leading cause of death for American women. Walking, swimming, dancing, jogging, HIIT training, yoga, and CrossFit® are great examples of exercises to do. Be sure to combine exercise with strength training to build muscle and help maintain stronger bones. This is especially important in postmenopausal women. Eat a balanced, colorful diet with low-inflammatory foods. Avoid packaged or processed foods, unhealthy fats and excess sugar or salt. Aim for fresh fish, fiber-rich foods, such as leafy greens and beans, nuts, seeds, olive oil, and whole grains. Shop the perimeter of the store where you will find fresh foods. Do not drink alcohol in excess or use tobacco products. Work on managing stress effectively.

RESPIRATORY

Respiration is the process of inhaling, warming, filtering, controlling the humidity of and exhaling air. Lungs exchange oxygen for carbon dioxide and the heart pumps oxygenated blood to the rest of the body. In general, respiratory illness can have a debilitating effect on one's overall health. Essential oils can be used to soothe irritated airways and help keep them clear. Many people mistake respiratory illness for other health problems, particularly when they experience and overall feeling of fatigue and malaise. Loss of appetite, indigestion, severe weight loss, and headaches are quite common to respiratory diseases. Medical attention is absolutely necessary for any respiratory ailment that is severe or persistent. Milder conditions can be resolved with the support of natural and simple home remedies.

PRODUCTS / OILS

Breathe®, Eucalyptus, Peppermint, Cardamom, Douglas Fir, On Guard®, Lemon, Breathe Respiratory Drops, Frankincense, Basil, Oregano, Ginger, Cinnamon, Ylang Ylang, Thyme

✚ WARNING/PROACTIVE MEDICAL CARE

If you have been using natural solutions and continue to experience any of these symptoms on an ongoing or persistent basis, seek medical care: chronic cough lasting a month or longer, labored or difficult breathing, a bluish tinge to your fingers and lips, swelling or a full feeling in your throat and lips, inability to talk due to difficulty breathing a rapid increase any symptoms, chronic mucus production, wheezing, coughing up blood, chronic chest pain lasting a month or longer (especially if it is worse when you take a deep breath in or cough, and shortness of breath). Any time your shortness of breath is accompanied by severe symptoms such as confusion, chest or jaw pain, or pain down your arm, call 911 right away.

✚ SYSTEM SELF-CHECK

Stair test and journal symptoms of lung issues. If you are having mild difficulty breathing, an occasional cough or a hard time taking a deep breath in occasionally, journal these symptoms to ensure they do not get worse. Try doing an at-home stair climbing test. If you can walk very fast up three floors of stairs without stopping, or fast up four floors without stopping, you have good functional capacity. If not, it is a good indication that you need more exercise. Try to do those four floors in under a minute.

The 6-Minute Walk Test is a sub-maximal exercise test used to assess aerobic capacity and endurance. The 6-minute walk test measures the distance someone can walk quickly on a flat, hard surface in 6 minutes. The test reflects the person's ability to perform daily physical activities.

✚ HOW TO IMPROVE / MAINTAIN

Avoid tobacco use or cigarette smoking. Cigarette smoke can narrow the air passages and make breathing more difficult. It causes chronic inflammation, or swelling in the lungs, which can lead to chronic bronchitis. Avoid exposure to indoor pollutants, and minimize exposure to outdoor air pollution. Avoid secondhand smoke, chemicals in the home or at work, avoid exercising outdoors on bad air days. Engage in diaphragmatic breathing, which allows for a deeper inhale. This will separate the organs in the abdomen from the lungs. This allows for a deeper inhale. Try counting your breaths by increasing the length of your inhalations and exhalations. Start by counting how long a natural breath takes. If it takes to the count of five to inhale, it should take to the count of five to exhale. You will want them to be of equal length. Once you have established your average breath count, add one more count to each inhale and exhale until you can comfortably extend the length of time it takes to fill and empty your lungs. Be aware of your posture. Sit tall in a stable chair, lifting the chest and open the front of your body as you breathe deeply. This gives your lungs more physical room to do their job. Hydrate. This helps keep the mucosal linings in the lungs thin increasing the efficiency of the lungs. Engage in moderately intense activities such as jogging, biking, or brisk walking. Laugh. Laughter is not only good for increasing feel-good-chemicals in the body, yet it also clears out your lungs by forcing stale air out, allowing fresh air to enter more areas of the lungs increasing lung capacity.

Eat apples, citrus fruits, apricots (high in Vitamin A, which supports respiratory tract linings and may reduce risk of lung infections), broccoli (high in antioxidants), chicken, turkey, walnuts, kidney beans, pinto beans, black beans, berries (such as acai and blueberry are two of the top recommended berries along with cranberries, grapes, and strawberries).

SKELETAL

The body's skeletal structure comprises the framework upon which all other organs and tissues depend for proper placement and coordination. Bones are not inert material; they are alive and need blood and oxygen to metabolize nutrients and produce waste. They respond to external stresses by changing shape to accommodate new mechanical demands. When there is a skeletal injury, the use of essential oils can accelerate the healing process and recovery time. For example, in the case of a broken bone, essential oils has been demonstrated to be useful in relieving and resolving inflammatory conditions and supporting injury recovery. Additionally, they have been shown to support the healing of any connective tissue damage as well.

PRODUCTS / OILS

Ginger, Turmeric Dual Capsules, Helichrysum,Siberian Fir, Black Pepper, Frankincense, Rosemary, Thyme (these last two are effective inhibitors of bone resorption and have numerous benefits on bone formation and against inflammation), Clary Sage, AromaTouch®, Wintergreen, DDR Prime®, Cypress, PastTense®, Copaiba, Bone Nutrient Essential Complex, Peppermint, Lifelong Vitality, Deep Blue® Stick with Copaiba

 ## WARNING/PROACTIVE MEDICAL CARE

Seek medical attention right away if you have sudden onset of back pain, caused by a fractured or collapsed vertebra, loss of height over time, a stooped posture, or a bone that breaks much more easily than expected. You may want to consult a doctor if you went through early menopause or took corticosteroids for several months at a time, or if either of your parents had hip fractures. Contact your doctor if symptoms such as sudden fatigue or unintended rapid weight loss especially if accompanied by bone pain that comes and goes, becomes worse at night, or is not helped by over the counter pain medications.

SYSTEM SELF-CHECK:

Keep a journal of any aches and pains that you feel. Write down the day, date, time, how often you experience it, and how long it lasts. Write down a pain level on a scale of 1-10—with 1 being hardly and pain and 10 being extreme pain.

HOW TO IMPROVE / MAINTAIN

Consume dark leafy greens such as bok choy, Chinese cabbage, kale, collard greens, and turnip greens provide calcium and vitamin K. Sweet potatoes provide magnesium and potassium. If you are low on magnesium, it may affect Vitamin D balance, and potassium neutralizes acid in your body that can leach calcium out of bones. Figs are an excellent source of calcium and other nutrients like potassium and magnesium. Eat salmon and other types of fatty fish contain vitamin D, which helps your body use calcium, and Omega-3 fatty acids, which may also aid bones. Almond butter is an easy way to boost your calcium intake. Consume "plant milks," such as almond, coconut, and soybean. Vegetarian proteins contain calcium so tofu is a great choice. Prunes help improve bone density by slowing down the breakdown of bone in your body. Molasses contains a lot of calcium, as well. Eat a nutrient rich diet with a variety of proteins, carbohydrates, healthy fats, vitamins, minerals. Include fresh fruits and vegetables high in Vitamin C to help stimulate production of bone forming cells. Greens and yellows have been shown to help with bone mineralization lean meats, fatty fish, nuts, seeds and whole grains. Drink half your body weight in ounces of water and an additional glass of water for every cup of caffeine you consume. Avoid inflammatory foods, trans fats, fried foods, and commercially baked goods. Maintain a healthy weight and exercise a minimum of 30-45 minutes per day. Include a variety of exercise types to maintain healthy muscles: stretching, yoga, balancing exercises, joint flexibility exercises, and aerobic exercise throughout the week. Add Vitamin D to your diet to help absorb calcium. Most adults need 1,000 to 2,000 IU of vitamin D daily. Strength training is especially important for those who suffer from lower extremity joint deficiencies such as knee or hip arthritis, which are conditions that may limit your ability to perform weight-bearing exercise. Resistance training or bone loading exercises help activate the osteoblasts (bone building cells) and favor bone deposition. These should be limited if you have been diagnosed with osteopenia or osteoporosis. Do not drink excess alcohol or smoke. Loss of bone mineral density is associated with tobacco use and excessive alcohol consumption. Rest and manage stress with a variety of lifestyle activities and essential oils.

PROACTIVE MEDICAL CARE *Chapter* **9**

```
PROACTIVE MEDICAL CARE

SELF CARE

REDUCE TOXIC LOAD/
HEALTHY HOME

REST & MANAGE STRESS

MOVEMENT & METABOLISM

EAT RIGHT/PROPER NUTRITION
```

Healthcare

Lifestyle

"Physicians and patients need to work together to pursue care that improves health, avoids harm and eliminates wasteful practices." —Dr. Amir Qaseem

PROACTIVE MEDICAL CARE

Each of us has a responsibility to take ownership of our health. In addition to our own choices concerning lifestyle behaviors, a relationship with a trusted and qualified medical professional is one of the foundational pillars of lifelong health. The goal is to be proactive instead of reactive about necessary medical care.

You have a myriad of options when considering your healthcare needs and priorities. It is important to make sure that your care provider's philosophy lines up with your own. Nowadays, there are more medical professionals who are open to using natural solutions than there were in the past. In choosing your care team, realize that you have options that can include a medical doctor, an emotional or physical wellness practitioner, a naturopath, a chiropractor, a Board-Certified Life and Wellness Coach, etc. In any event, make sure that any practitioners you engage are coordinating with each other, and that you proactively respond to their recommendations for care. You are ultimately responsible for your own health care decisions.

Consider using these tips when selecting a primary care physician. They provide organic ways you can talk with your potential provider about integrating essential oils and other natural solutions into your care plan, while also learning about their approach to wellness.

1 *Be open with your doctor about your philosophy.* When choosing a healthcare professional, it is important they're open-minded enough for you to share your perspective on using natural solutions for proactive care or a first line of defense. This conversation will give you an idea if this is a doctor that you wish to work with or not. If they are not open to having a conversation with you about your choices, then thank them and choose a physician that is.

2 *Provide them with information.* If your doctor is open to learning more about the natural solutions you are using, provide them with both written information and links to additional research. PubMed has tens of thousands of scientific research on using essential oils, and this is a good place to start. Gather any pertinent research articles and highlight important details in those studies. Emphasize studies conducted at other research hospitals, or hospitals in general, who are benefiting from using essential oils. This helps to establish credibility and speaks to them in a language they understand.

3 *Ask around and do some research on your own.* Talk to your friends, family, and co-workers to find out which doctors in your area are reputable. Collect information about their specialties or areas of interest.

4 *Look for a doctor who spends time getting to know you as an individual.* Choose a doctor who gets to know you as a "whole" person, not just a disease or illness, who doesn't make you feel rushed.

5 *Choose a doctor that listens.* This is one of the most important attributes of a care provider. Someone who truly listen to their client's story (in a non-judgmental way) helps to establish trust, and ultimately, a partnership. You should be comfortable opening up to them about any and all health concerns.

6 *Trust your intuition.* Be sure to trust your gut and ask a lot of questions. If answers to your questions are satisfactory, and you feel comfortable as a result, they're likely a good fit.

INDEX